MUSLIM POPULATION BY POLITICAL AREAS

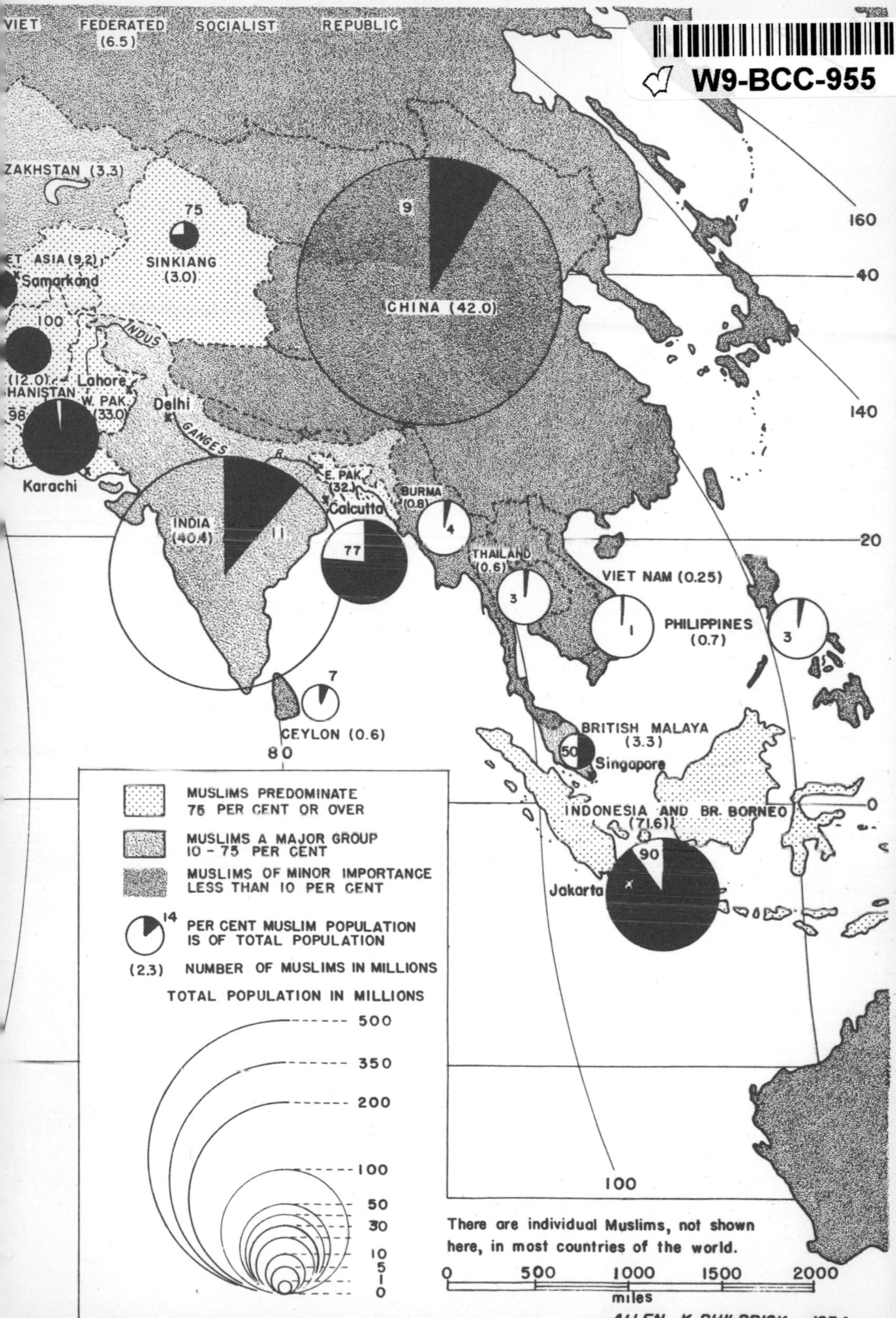
VIET FEDERATED SOCIALIST REPUBLIC
(6.5)
ZAKHSTAN (3.3)
75
SINKIANG
(3.0)
ET. ASIA (9.2)
Samarkand
100
INDUS
(12.0)
HANISTAN
Lahore
W. PAK.
(33.0)
98
Delhi
Karachi
GANGES
9
CHINA (42.0)
INDIA
(40.4)
11
E. PAK.
(32.1)
Calcutta
77
BURMA
(0.8)
4
THAILAND
(0.6)
3
VIET NAM (0.25)
1
PHILIPPINES
(0.7)
3
7
CEYLON (0.6)
BRITISH MALAYA
(3.3)
50
Singapore
INDONESIA AND BR. BORNEO
(71.6)
90
Jakarta
160
40
140
20
0
80
100
MUSLIMS PREDOMINATE
75 PER CENT OR OVER
MUSLIMS A MAJOR GROUP
10 - 75 PER CENT
MUSLIMS OF MINOR IMPORTANCE
LESS THAN 10 PER CENT
14
PER CENT MUSLIM POPULATION
IS OF TOTAL POPULATION
(2.3) NUMBER OF MUSLIMS IN MILLIONS
TOTAL POPULATION IN MILLIONS
500
350
200
100
50
30
10
5
1
0
There are individual Muslims, not shown
here, in most countries of the world.
0 500 1000 1500 2000
miles
ALLEN K. PHILBRICK 1954.

Unity and Variety in Muslim Civilization

Comparative Studies of
Cultures and Civilizations

Edited by
ROBERT REDFIELD *and* MILTON SINGER

Studies in Chinese Thought
ARTHUR F. WRIGHT, *Editor*

**Studies in Islamic Cultural History*
G. E. VON GRUNEBAUM, *Editor*

Language in Culture
HARRY HOIJER, *Editor*

The Little Community
ROBERT REDFIELD

**Islam: Essays in the Nature and Growth of a Cultural Tradition*
G. E. VON GRUNEBAUM

Village India
McKIM MARRIOTT, *Editor*

Unity and Variety in Muslim Civilization
G. E. VON GRUNEBAUM, *Editor*

* Available only as a Memoir of the American Anthropological Association. All other volumes, whether or not originally distributed as memoirs, published by and now available only from the bookseller and The University of Chicago Press.

UNITY AND VARIETY IN MUSLIM CIVILIZATION

Edited by

GUSTAVE E. VON GRUNEBAUM

With Papers by

ARMAND ABEL

J. N. D. ANDERSON

ROBERT BRUNSCHVIG

CLAUDE CAHEN

WERNER CASKEL

G. W. J. DREWES

JACQUES DUCHESNE-GUILLEMIN

RICHARD ETTINGHAUSEN

FRANCESCO GABRIELI

G. E. VON GRUNEBAUM

ROGER LE TOURNEAU

BERNARD LEWIS

FRITZ MEIER

VLADIMIR MINORSKY

JOSEPH SCHACHT

BERTOLD SPULER

THE UNIVERSITY OF CHICAGO PRESS

Library of Congress Catalog Number: 55-11191

THE UNIVERSITY OF CHICAGO PRESS, CHICAGO 37
Cambridge University Press, London, N.W. 1, England
The University of Toronto Press, Toronto 5, Canada

 Published 1955. Composed and printed by THE UNIVERSITY OF CHICAGO PRESS, *Chicago, Illinois, U.S.A.*

FOREWORD

Unity and Variety in Muslim Civilization is the seventh in the series of "Comparative Studies of Cultures and Civilizations," and the third to deal with Islâm. The previous two volumes in this field dealt with the historical processes of evolution of Muslim civilization from the nuclear Arab culture and with that civilization's cultural expressions. This book adds a new dimension: How is Muslim civilization related to the local cultures over which it came to predominate? The results of these studies show how the unity of Muslim civilization, which is of a complex and emergent kind, is a compound of the official "great tradition" and of the local and national traditions of the different countries to which it traveled. Turkish Islâm differs from Indonesian, and both from that of the Arab heartlands.

The highlights of these results are summarized by Professor Duchesne-Guillemin, who was Secretary of the Conference, in his introductory review, written from notes taken at the time. It is a good guide to the reader.

We are grateful to Professor von Grunebaum for organizing the Conference and to his distinguished colleagues who participated in it. The question posed to them is not one usually treated by specialists. It is a tribute to their flexibility, deep knowledge, and resourcefulness that they came together to consider so successfully a problem of which they would ordinarily treat only a small part.

We also wish to thank Miss Anna Pikelis and Dr. Marshall Hodgson for their help in seeing the manuscript of this volume through the press.

The support of the Ford Foundation, a grant from which made possible the original Conference at Spa and now the publication of the results, is gratefully acknowledged.

ROBERT REDFIELD
MILTON SINGER

PREFACE

Early in 1953 Professors Robert Redfield and Milton Singer, with whom I had been associated in intercultural studies, asked me to organize a Conference on Unity and Variety in Muslim Civilization. The Conference was held in Liége and Spa (Belgium) from September 21 to September 25, 1953; it was cosponsored by the University of Chicago and the University of Liége. Professor J. Duchesne-Guillemin assumed the secretaryship of the Conference and took charge of local arrangements.

The problem which was set for the Conference may be formulated as that of the relation between Islamic civilization and the local cultures of the areas which in the course of time have become more or less Islamized. Islamic civilization was to be considered as it has developed through amalgamation of certain traditions from the original core of the message of the Arabic Prophet. The underlying assumption of the existence of a Muslim identification had, of course, to come under scrutiny as well.

It seemed expedient to open the Conference with a statement of the problem and its implications and then to follow it through in some detail in several fields to which Islamic civilization has made characteristic contributions, such as law or art. Consideration of structure was then to give way to that of specific areas. While the structural analyses were to be based mainly on historical materials, the analyses of the several areas were to concentrate on the present and the more recent past; the study of Islâm in Spain and Iran provided an apt transition.

With these objectives in mind, the following scholars attended under my chairmanship: Professor A. Abel (Free University of Brussels), Professor R. Brunschvig (University of Bordeaux), Professor C. Cahen (University of Strasbourg), Professor W. Caskel (University of Cologne), Professor J. Duchesne-Guillemin (University of Liége), Professor G. W. J. Drewes (Rijks-University at Leiden), Professor F. Gabrieli (University of Rome), Professor R. Le Tourneau (University of Algiers), Professor B. Lewis (University of London), Professor F. Meier (University of Basel), Professor V. Minorsky (Cambridge University), Professor J. Schacht (Oxford University; now at Leiden), Dr. R. Sellheim (Goethe-University,

Frankfurt am Main), Professor B. Spuler (University of Hamburg), and Professor G. Stadtmüller (University of Munich). Professor E. Cerulli, at the time Italian ambassador to Iran, who had undertaken to discuss Islâm in Ethiopia, was at the last moment prevented by political developments from leaving Teheran.

While there was no intention to try for completeness in the discussion of the Muslim countries, it was with regret that we found ourselves unable to include a study on Islâm in India and Pakistan. The contemporary Arab world is given especial attention in the papers by Professors Caskel and Le Tourneau.

The proceedings of the Conference began, on September 21, with the opening in the Library of the University of Liége of an exhibit of books and documents illustrating the activities of Victor Chauvin, the great Islamist of the University of Liége (d. 1913), for which the Conference is indebted to Mme J. Gobeaux-Thonet, the Chief Librarian, who presented to the gathering a paper on "Un manuscrit latin inédit du *Tacuinum sanitatis* d'Ibn Buṭlân (Bibliothèque de l'Université de Liége, MS 1041)."

The University of Liége honored the Conference with a dinner reception at which the Rector, Professor F. Campus, welcomed the members. After a sight-seeing tour of Liége by night, the members went on to Spa, where the actual sessions took place at the Hotel Britannique. On the evening of the twenty-second, the city of Spa held a reception in honor of the Conference, which was followed by a recital of folk dances, *Danses et chansons de chez nous*, by Mme Fanny Thibout and her group. On the evening of the twenty-fourth, the Parrenin Quartet, of Paris, presented a program of music by Schumann, Debussy, and Beethoven.

The present volume unites in some cases under modified titles the papers presented to the Conference and a résumé of the discussions. The papers by Professor J. N. D. Anderson (London) and by Dr. R. Ettinghausen (Washington) were prepared for but not actually read at the Conference, since both scholars found themselves unable to attend. Professor Abel's discussion of Islâm in Spain was prepared in its present form after the conclusion of the Conference. Professor Brunschvig's "Perspectives" was published in the original French in *Studia Islamica* (I, No. 1 [1953], 5–21) and is here reissued in translation by permission of the publisher, V. Larose (Paris). Professor Duchesne-Guillemin's "How Does Islâm Stand?" was first published under the title "Où en est l'Islam?" in *Synthèses*

(Brussels), April, 1954, and has been made part of this volume in a somewhat changed form with permission of the editor of *Synthèses*, M. Maurice Lambilliotte.

The translation of the French and German papers has been in the hands of Mrs. Helen Singer (Brunschvig, Gabrieli), Mrs. G. E. von Grunebaum (Caskel, Meier), and Dr. M. G. S. Hodgson, of the University of Chicago. Dr. A. Hottinger, of Basel, at present a Fellow at the University of Chicago, took responsibility for preparing the English summary of the discussions on the basis of notes that were taken at Spa under the supervision of Professor Duchesne-Guillemin, with the assistance of Dr. Sellheim, by Mlle Thérèse Dupont (Tournai) and Drs. Paule Mertens and A. Nivelle of the University of Liége. The map was prepared by Professor A. K. Philbrick, University of Chicago, in consultation with Dr. Hodgson, who also prepared the Index. To all of our collaborators the Conference is deeply indebted.

Especial thanks are due to Professor Duchesne-Guillemin for his part in organizing and administering the Conference and to Mme Marcelle Duchesne-Guillemin for her part in selecting the artistic programs and in maintaining an atmosphere of effortless warmth. The mayor of Spa, Dr. Jean Barzin, and M. François Leyh, the proprietor of the Hôtel Britannique, by their efficient co-operation, have placed the Conference under a great obligation.

I wish to conclude by repeating here the thanks which I expressed at the Conference to the scholars who contributed to the proceedings and by registering my gratitude to Professor Redfield and to the Ford Foundation for the support lent us in organizing the Conference and in publishing its results as a volume of the series on "Comparative Studies of Cultures and Civilizations."

G. E. von Grunebaum

TABLE OF CONTENTS

PART I. INTRODUCTORY REVIEW

PART II. ISLAM AS RELIGION AND AS CIVILIZATION

PART III. MODES OF EXPRESSION OF THE CULTURAL TRADITION

PART IV. REGIONAL EVOLUTIONS

PART V. THE CHALLENGE

APPENDIX

INDEX

PART I

INTRODUCTORY REVIEW

HOW DOES ISLAM STAND?

JACQUES DUCHESNE-GUILLEMIN

THE disorder and poverty which rage in the Middle East, and which are a constant threat to peace, seem incapable of being remedied except by a greater solidarity among Islamic countries and by a general modernization of those countries. But though modernization is a tangible fact, only the pace of which might require control and acceleration, Muslim solidarity is only a fleeting, variable, uncertain supposition. The most modern—and the most stable—Islamic state is also the least Muslim. For Turkey, if it has not expressly repudiated Islâm, has nonetheless broken, in a systematic secularization, with the traditions of the Muslim past.

We are led then, if we are at all concerned with the defense of Suez, the relations between Israel and her neighbors, Moroccan autonomy, the independence of Persia or of Pakistan, and the resistance of all these regions to external and internal Communist danger, to wonder what in our day can still be involved in the fact of being Muslim, which is potentially the basis of a confederation of which the Arab League is only the dream.

Islâm, a religion which set out to conquer the world, has twice constituted an empire which, if not world-wide, at least united under a single political authority the whole or the great majority of the peoples won to the word of Mohammed. The first of these empires, that of Hârûn al-Rashîd, was contemporary with that of Charlemagne. Lacking deep cohesiveness, it lost any but a nominal existence well before the sack of Baghdad by the Mongols in 1258 formally put an end to it. As to the second great Muslim empire, that of the Ottomans, its gradual dismantlement and its dissolution in 1918 as a consequence of the first World War have left the political vacuum in the east which has yet, after thirty-five years, to be filled.

Although, then, Islâm is not an empire except at certain moments in its history, neither is it a group of peoples of the same language or of the same race. For Arabic, although in principle the only language of religious instruction and practice, does not have even this role in several parts of the immense domain which reaches from China to Barbary, including Indonesia (speaking Malay), Pakistan (where Urdu is spoken), Persia, Turkey, etc. (not to speak of the Muslims of the U.S.S.R.); as to the role played among all these by the Arab race (formerly the initiator of conquest and the wielder of power), it is today negligible.*

Can Islâm, then, be said to be only a religious fact? Yet it is not at all organized like a church and, since the dissolution of the caliphate in 1924, no longer has anything resembling a hierarchy—to say nothing of its being broken up into a large number of often quite distinct sects.

Are we to say that the reality of Islâm is purely subjective—that it is defined strictly by the feeling of belonging to it? This would be evading the problem, which is to know to what degree belonging to Islâm involves an actual solidarity, a will to mutual aid, a community of customs, of interests, of aspirations. In other words, does there exist an Islamic civilization strong enough to survive?

For a century and a half all the Islamic countries have undergone, more or less, a European influence, have more or less willingly been following Europe's lead. Whence a series of upheavals, a permanent state of crisis in which Islâm is in danger of foundering. Turkey and Egypt, in the nineteenth century, and Persia, in the twentieth, have adopted national institutions and more or less genuine forms of democratic government. About 1900, woman, as in Europe, set about emancipating herself; polygamy is tending to disappear. Lay education took root, historical criticism tackled the divine revelation, while the vast scientific and material culture from the West was invading men's minds and threatening the traditional, theological culture with atrophy. The industrial revolution made its appearance: in Egypt in the introduction of cotton, a little everywhere in the building of railroads, irrigation dams, etc.

In the age of the airplane, of gasoline, and of electricity, this modernization is speeding up, but sporadically and without a clear vision of its social consequences, as a result of which we see, for example, cities such as Casablanca being added to what is age old. Another new factor: the U.S.S.R., pole of attraction for the Islamic

* [The end papers offer a map showing the density as well as the proportion of Muslims in various parts of the world. As satisfactory statistics are often not available, such a map is only approximate—in China, hardly even that. For population, the 1952 estimates reported by the United Nations were used chiefly (*Statistical Yearbook, 1953*). To estimate the Muslim percentages, the following were consulted: H. W. Hazard, *Atlas of Islamic History* (Princeton, 1951); *The Statesman's Yearbook* for 1953; V. Monteil, "Essai sur l'Islam en U.R.S.S.," *Revue des études islamiques*, XX (1952), 5–144; the *Indian and Pakistan Yearbook, 1951;* and Dr. Edwin S. Munger, of the University of Chicago, who kindly put his knowledge of African matters at our service.—Ed.]

countries, to which it gives the example at once of a rapid modernization and of a social overturn. In the face of such a rival, can Europe still be satisfied to export capital and ideas haphazardly to Islamic countries?

CONFERENCE OF SCHOLARS

It has begun to be realized among us that the social problems of the Near East merit a serious study. This is attested by two scientific conferences which have taken place within the year quite independently of one another. In each of them Belgium, a country without political connections with Islâm and thus impartial, had an important place.

We want to speak of the conference reported in the present volume, which brought together European Islamists. It was designed to draw their attention to the general and present-day problems posed by the civilization with which they all are concerned, but of which each ordinarily investigates only one sector. This meeting was due to the initiative of Mr. von Grunebaum, acting in the name of the Department of Anthropology of the University of Chicago, who had chosen the participants—fifteen scholars of the principal countries of Europe—and outlined for them an unambiguous program designed to cover the various aspects of a single question: "Unity and Variety in Muslim Civilization." The present volume presents the elements of a synthesis such as we hardly possess on any other civilization. The following modest summary of it depends on notes taken continuously during these days of study and does not claim to bring out more than a few salient points.

"GREAT" AND "LITTLE" TRADITIONS

Using a concept defined by American anthropology, Mr. von Grunebaum envisages the history of Islâm as that of the mutual reactions of a "great" and of "little" traditions. The unity of customs and of conceptions which the religious ideal demanded was never able to realize itself entirely; always it was necessary to compromise with local civilizations, often clearly superior to that of primitive Arabia. The present crisis, resulting from the contact with Europe, is by no means the first which Islâm has had to face. From the eighth century it had to open itself up to the Hellenic civilization. Mr. von Grunebaum, who has especially studied the intellectual and aesthetic currents of medieval Islâm, notes that Islâm adopted the logical framework of Greek thought as well as certain forms of expression and a mass of material accumulated by Greek science, but without entering into its spirit, without taking over its impulse, and only, in the end, to reject Hellenism categorically after three or four centuries of mediocre assimilation. (Today the situation is not exactly the same: Islâm is faced not only with a different civilization but also with a superior power; to hold its own against the West, it must adopt its arms, its secrets, its spirit.)

To what is it due that the West outdistanced the Islamic countries? As Mr. von Grunebaum said during a meeting which he had already organized in 1952 at Mainz, Europe reinvigorated itself with Platonism and the spirit of free inquiry, while the Arabs fossilized themselves in a rigid Aristotelianism; Europe discovered nonclerical sources of a prodigious abundance, while the Arabs could rediscover in their past only the desert. Undertaking to trace more particularly the role of the "great tradition," the speaker pointed out how the intellectual conceptions of the Muslim are dominated by a religious attitude: that which makes man the *slave of God.* Further, a change took place in Muslim piety about the year 1000. Up till then based on fear, it rested from then on upon confidence. Now, a very similar development took place concomitantly in Byzantine piety. The change was due in both cases, according to Mr. von Grunebaum, to analogous political circumstances, which caused tottering powers to seek the support of the masses of the people, athirst for a tangible piety. The local "little traditions" likewise imposed everywhere something of the cult of saints—which the "great tradition" condemned in principle—multiplied the holy places (for example in Palestine, and this shortly after the conquest), etc. The "great tradition" was never completely unified; not to mention the sects, in open conflict with the Sunna, the teaching of the Koran was not carried out in the same way all through the Muslim domain.

Mr. Minorsky reproached Mr. von Grunebaum with still giving religion too much credit in human conduct, with returning to a religious definition of Islâm—rather the way Bossuet saw the history of Europe in terms of Christianity. According to Mr. Minorsky, it is not religious faith, though it may look so, which causes the individuals and peoples of Islâm to act. It does not shape their life; it is often only an instrument in the hands of governments, classes, factions. Islâm is a *mirror,* in which these particular interests look at themselves and justify themselves. "A theological mirror, at any rate," Mr. von Grunebaum said, and the only one the Muslim has with which to interpret his situation. A middle position was then set forth by Messrs. Spuler and Brunschvig: religious theory is sometimes the mirror of action and sometimes its lever.

In his paper Mr. Meier, a specialist in Persian mysticism and acquainted with the disciples of Jung, treated of principles and method. He believes that the search for historical relationships causes us to fail to recognize the unique and, at the same time, universal in the facts of religion. But he is wrong, according to Mr. von Grunebaum, to neglect the sociological aspect of these facts, which situates them in a historical sequence. M. Abel cited well-established cases of influence: of Muslim mysticism upon St. John of the Cross (cf. the works of M. Asín Palacios) or, in the reverse direction, of the cult of Jesus upon the quasi-divinization of Mohammed. M. Cahen noted that influences are rarely easy to prove and that, in any case, one borrows what one can. The important point is not to look for relationships but to establish comparisons. In fact, Islamic history is a century behind European history, since we are still disputing in it for or against relationships or, as just now, about the role played in the course of events by what the Marxists call the "ideological superstructure."

THE SPECIFICITY OF ISLÂM

M. Brunschvig resolutely posed the question: Is there a Muslim civilization? It would not be characterized either by belief or by observances but by the more or less numerous influences of the religion upon a multitude of activities. There would be degrees, then, of belonging to this civilization. The Berbers, for instance, in spite of their Muslim faith, reject the Islamic law. Law cannot serve any more than language as absolute criterion; the same is true of morality, and there is nothing, even theology, which is not heterogeneous in its origins. Theology only gradually became a unifying factor. (Yet sometimes it helps to preserve a pre-Muslim practice.) The limits of sects, of languages, etc., do not coincide; a survey of these differentiating factors will be made.

In the discussion that followed, M. Abel divided the history of Islâm into three phases. The first is that of the conquest and assimilation; the second, which begins at the end of the eleventh century, is a phase of reaction, with elimination of lay motifs, whence a rigidity which became total from the fourteenth century on; the third phase begins at the end of the eighteenth century in the contact with Europe, which produces a return of lay motifs, whence breakdown of the equilibrium. Against the impermeability of Islâm (maintained by Messrs. Stadtmüller and Spuler), Mr. Minorsky cited the example of Turkey, a lost province. To which Mr. von Grunebaum answered that the Turks—to judge them by those who took part in a conference recently held at Princeton—consider themselves Muslims. That alone matters, as Mr. Spuler had said; to which Mr. Lewis answered with a question: Are the followers of the Agha Khan, for example, really anything but Hindus under a light Muslim veneer?

LAW, LETTERS, POLITICS, ART

The Conference then took up certain particular—and essential—aspects of the Islamic civilization: law, literature, politics, and art.

Mr. Schacht recalled that the Muslim law does not have a Muslim (and still less a Koranic) basis. It is Roman, Byzantine, Persian, etc., law assimilated—never perfectly—to a "revealed" system of moral requirements. It is an integration presented by the Muslim legists as a deduction starting from what is given in revelation; for every Muslim law is dictated by religion, and must be so. This gives rise to a malaise, a permanent tension in the countries which, like Egypt in the nineteenth century or Pakistan today, have sought or seek to adopt democratic forms without abandoning Islâm. During the phase of conquest and assimilation (the first phase, according to M. Abel), the foreign elements were brought in by the upper classes, which converted to Islâm on account of social interests (or at least had their children brought up in it) and naturally retained their Hellenic culture and their experience of local law.

The basis of Islamic literature is also not Muslim. Mr. Gabrieli showed that the principal literary movements of Islâm have their source in "little traditions," either pre-Muslim Arabic or "humanistic" of Hellenic origin, the latter provoking a real renewal in the time of the Abbasids but soon degenerating into a new classicism, tainted with preciousness, which weighed upon the whole literature and ossified it; or else in Persia the national tradition with which the epic was nourished and which leaves very little place to Islâm; finally, Ṣûfî mysticism, the principal subject matter of Persian poetry, is perhaps Christian and Gnostic in origin, rather than Iranian, but certainly not Muslim.

[Islamic art, dealt with by Mr. Ettinghausen, shows throughout its marked diversity a readily recognized common character, resulting from three processes of integration. Not only art objects, but artists, their patrons, and whole ethnic groups moved readily throughout the Islamic world—freely or under various sorts of compulsion. Second, partly because of the political patronage of art, everywhere the older traditions vied with the sense of a new Islamic standard; older symbols were taken over in Muslim garb, and even figural representation found a large place. The artist often won an honored, even religious position in the face of orthodox condemnation. Finally, art from lower social levels entered the more elevated tradition. Thus the art of Islâm became a symbol of its universality.]

M. Cahen, who is not only an Islamist but also a professor of European history, noted parallel developments, concomitances. Originally there was an essential difference to which Mr. Stadtmüller had already alluded: because in Islâm there was no state previous to the coming of the religion (as had been the case for Christianity), there were not two separate powers. A theocracy, the Muslim form of government had had a predecessor only among the Hebrews. It was a form of government which in practice ceased to be possible at the death of Mohammed. The political unity on a religious basis which the Abbasids wanted did not last long; it had never been very deep. Quite soon, at Baghdad as well as in the provinces, power passed to the army—a militarization and fragmentation which coincided with our feudalism. More especially, it was a foreign military element which gained the upper hand, in the east as well as in the extreme west: in Persia the Turks, in whom alone persisted a zeal for the holy war, fought in the name of orthodoxy (the Sunna); in Spain the Almoravid Berbers organized the fight against the Christian reconquest. From now on we have no longer a Muslim state but Muslim states—bankruptcy of the doctrine. In short, politically the difference is not between Christians and Muslims, it is between medieval state and modern state. How, indeed, was the modern state born? When Europe rediscovered and restored the separation between church and state, which Islâm could not do, having never known it.

Mr. Spuler pointed out a consequence of the confusion between "church" and "state": every political secession inevitably took the form of a religious secession (a sect), from which followed in practice a breach in the unity of the state. Further, the growing power of the *ʿulamâʾ* (theologians) was due to the absence of a civil power which might counterbalance it.

M. Brunschvig, in connection with Messrs. Cahen's and Schacht's papers, pointed out that the Abbasid jurists did not write in a vacuum; no doubt they were weaving theory, just like Western legists, but this theory was called forth by reality, so that the different schools can produce, for example, almost identical treatises on public law.

REGIONAL TABLEAUS

We pass now to the examination of certain provinces of the Muslim world: Iran, North Africa, Spain, Indonesia, Turkey.

From a panorama of the religious and political dissensions of medieval Iran, Mr. Minorsky drew several conclusions. It is going too far to reduce the life of the Muslim states to the single influence of the law of Islâm. Persia had—and kept—a strong pre-Islamic culture and underwent many extra-Islamic influences. The epic, which is outside religion like miniature painting, counterbalances the quietism of the Ṣûfîs; and there was clearly in Persia a "religious party" which used religion for purposes of government. The foreign conquests burdened the poor classes economically; the opposition turned more and more heterodox and popular; a religion cluttered up with miracles, with living incarnations of divinity, and breathing an aroma of martyrdom and revolt, such as is Shîᶜism, was suitable to an oft-conquered people long subjected to foreign rule.

M. Brunschvig, to illustrate the connection which was brought about from the seventeenth century on (Safavids) between Shîᶜism and the state interests, pointed out the great sanctuaries, so typical of Persia, toward which the sovereigns diverted the faithful at the expense of the pilgrimages to Iraq. With regard to the discrepancy between literature, which ceased to be outstanding after the fourteenth century, and painting and architecture, which survived it for more than two hundred years, can be cited the Western parallel of the *quattrocento* (cf. J. Huizinga, *The Waning of the Middle Ages*). The rigid forms of literature had strangled all expression, in Persia, whereas the Safavid policy of encouraging the sanctuaries developed architecture.

North Africa, which was dealt with by M. Le Tourneau, was always distinguished by its lack of creative originality. The elites there are divided into conservatives, reformists, and modernists. The conservatives are the *ᶜulamâᵓ*, the marabouts and heads of brotherhoods, and their students; although they now accept women students and have made a place for the teaching of a few new subjects, their spirit remains scholastic. The reformists want a return to primitive purity and direct relations between Allâh and man: an intellectual, urban, bourgeois movement which seems to be doomed by the general tendency toward progress. The modernists, pupils from the modern schools, no longer feel at ease in Islâm and are tempted by secularism; nevertheless, they do not separate religion and politics, and they have hardly posed the problem of Islâm and the modern world.

As to the religion of the masses in North Africa, it can be defined in two words: rigorism in ignorance. Veneration for the sultan and for whatever he touches, for the saints dead or living; magic, sorcery, nature cults; ascendancy of the marabouts and brotherhoods—so many local traits with nothing authentically Muslim about them. Finally, the tepidity or the indifference of the intellectuals or the workers under the European ascendancy do not arouse any reaction among the faithful; these hope only for a return to the past, without thinking of preparing for the future.

M. Abel showed that the conquest of Spain, a country fundamentally divided and already not fully submissive to its Visigothic masters, was more superficial than elsewhere because Spain was farther away from Arabia and because an alien element—the Berbers—was already mingled with the invaders. The conquerors never *adopted* the converts, nor did the latter give up their old Romance tongue for Arabic. Accordingly Islâm never grew deep roots in Spain, especially since the Umayyads of Cordova were not touched by the sort of renewal which was the work of the Abbasids of Baghdad. In the armed conflicts which were almost constantly tearing the country apart, religion counted for less than race and blood. "And Islâm finally lost in Spain a match which it had never begun to win."

Mr. Drewes described the situation of Indonesia, a country converted late, at a time when Islâm had crystallized. Islâm penetrated into Indonesian society through the lower classes and has replaced only in part local custom (*ʿâda*). Modified by its passage through Persia and India, the Muslim propaganda in Indonesia emphasizes thought more than action; the ground was prepared in this direction by the previous religious teachings, those of Shivaism and of Mahayana Buddhism, and—among the people—by the primitive sense of the unity of life. Nevertheless, at the present time a movement which is having much success among the middle classes, the Muḥammadiyya, following the example of the Protestant missions, insists on the rational character of Islâm and devotes itself to works: schools, orphanages, hospitals, etc.

Mr. Lewis, of London, analyzed the formation of the Turkish nation in its three sources: Anatolian, Turkish, and Muslim. The Ottomans, almost always at war with Christendom, identified their cause with that of Islâm and were the first to try really to enforce the Muslim law. Islâm, there as elsewhere, included foreign or assimilated elements: such were the dervish orders, whirling and others, the origin of which was perhaps Buddhist, Manichean, or shamanist, but certainly not Muslim. But the principal characteristic of Ottoman Islâm was that it involved a hierarchy. Thus it was where clericalism had gone farthest that secularization was most violent. In contrast to all the other regions of Islâm, Turkey was able to assimilate, with all their consequences, two notions which seem to define the West: that of *process* and that of *organic structure*. The realism of the Turks, which has, notably, caused them to join the Atlantic Pact, comes to them, according to Mr. Lewis, from their long tradition of independence.

Today, when we are witnessing a certain renewal of faith, the problem arises anew of reconciling this faith with modernization.

WHERE IS ISLÂM GOING?

Two studies of modern Islâm served to conclude the work of the Conference. Mr. Caskel noted especially that the modernization of society, which started about 1860 in Turkey and in Egypt, came about more slowly in French Africa and in India because the Muslims there had European masters, to whom they refused to believe themselves basically inferior. In general, Europeanization came from above, the women of the upper classes imitating the European women and being, in their turn, imitated by the other classes. The economy of the Islamic countries is shackled by an age-old distrust which prevents any productive investment. Against European culture, and especially against the Universal Histories of a rationalist or positivist spirit, or the like, Islâm is absolutely defenseless. It can be wondered if belief in the afterlife is not in the course of disappearing in the cultivated classes, as is the case in Protestantism. The only positive element in the Islâm of the Near East is represented by the Muslim Brotherhood, a recently created movement—its founder was assassinated in 1949—which tries to translate the faith into acts: founding mosques, schools, workshops, and co-operatives.

Nothing of the like exists up till now in French Africa—of which M. Le Tourneau, who has lived there for seventeen years, drew a picture from life—which applies by and large to the whole of the Muslim world. Two opposing tendencies come to light in the Muslim of today: on the one hand, an attachment to the traditional values, with the desire to see reborn the effective institutions of the old Islâm; on the other hand, the need to escape from an inferiority complex with regard to Europe, and the wish to use for this purpose the tools, even the methods, conceptions, etc., of the European civilization. (All adopt our idea of the "nation"; all, our need for action.) The conflict between the two tendencies shows itself especially in the interminable debate about the constitution to be given Pakistan and in the periodic debates which threaten the very existence of the Arab League.

In North Africa, Arabic culture and Western culture can be seen developing parallel. The number of students in the mosques of Morocco has tripled in thirty years; the traditional university of Tunis (Zeituna) numbers 15,000 of them—a development made easier by the press, by the Cairo radio, and by the modern convenience of the Pilgrimage. French culture is making progress even in Morocco, where the number of students has increased from 35,000 in 1945 to more than 100,000 at present.

From the social point of view, we are witnessing the birth of a new proletariat due to a demographic pressure and to the development of European industry: a mass of uprooted people which is not yet aware of itself as a working class. Further, a change is taking place in family ways. The advanced Moroccans are more and more monogamous; the practice of European-type engagements is spreading; the young couples live by themselves and no longer in the patriarchal "large family," and this, in order to live in a Western way. In proletarian circles the development is different, moving in the direction of an abuse of their liberty (with regard to the vanished norms of Islâm) on the part of the men as well as of the women. The countryside remains absolutely conservative.

From the political point of view, finally, the population includes a great mass of indifferents, conservative through inertia but susceptible to bursts of sentiment which arouse them, as witness the riot of Constantine. Among the more aware of them can be seen the same tendencies as in religion: conservatism (which has just triumphed in Morocco); reaction (in Algeria, centering on the reformist *ʿulamâʾ*; in Tunisia, the Old Dastûr Party); progressive modernism (the party of Ferhat Abbas in Algeria, the Istiqlâl, the New Dastûr). For Algeria must be added the proletarians of Messali Haji, a formation analogous to that of the Muslim Brotherhood, the class-consciousness of which is quite marked; Morocco will sooner or later have its equivalent; in Tunisia the Union Générale des Travailleurs Tunisiens, which might have served as nucleus for a party at once Muslim and proletarian, is closely tied to the New Dastûr. Finally the Communist, Socialist, Radical, Mouvement Républicain Populaire parties, and the like, number a few adherents.

All these groups except for the conservatives are in principle hostile to France, or to the presence of France. For a time, in Morocco, for example, confidence between natives and French seemed quite well established. Then the Muslims discovered a divergence between their deep aspirations and those which were being brought them from outside; they doubted the disinterestedness of France; they realized that it was time to press on at full speed. The resentment is pretty general; as to the means of obtaining independence, the few positive plans proposed at this time are vague and contradictory.

In tropical Africa, a region dealt with by Mr. Anderson, Islâm extends from northern Nigeria to the Zambezi, but it is mixed there, in variable proportions, with the indigenous customs. The infiltration of Islâm, which is the work of merchants or of "holy men," proceeds from the simple acquisition of charms, of prayers, of rites—the contamination being made possible by a certain similarity between Allâh and the supreme god of most of the Negroes, between the jinn and the spirits of animism, between the rites of circumcision and the like practiced on both sides—to formal adherence, to the conversion either of individuals or of tribes. In this last case, of which the Somalis are an example, the Muslim law is in force in almost all circumstances of life and is gaining ground.

In places the mixture is inextricable, just as in the case of Arabic and Bantu in the Swahili language. There is often a conflict among several legal systems, but this is resolved more easily than would seem possible, thanks to the good sense of the African, who is no formalist but always looks for a compromise, a practical solution.

Some progress is to be found in the spirit of Muslim instruction, which for the most part is still limited to the purely mechanical Koranic apprenticeship, and in the intellectual relations between Negro Africa and Arabia or Morocco.

The Muslim law, however mixed with indigenous elements, constitutes a unifying factor. Negro paganism being essentially parochial, Islâm was bound to come to the fore in a time of more frequent communication and multiplied contacts. Wherever it preceded Christianity and the Europeans, it retains its integrative role. Elsewhere it remains a rival of Christianity, being easier to adopt. Islâm has raised the Negro's level of civilization; nevertheless, it has owed a good part of its success to the fact that, like Negro custom, it allows polygamy, circumcision, and slavery.

PART II

ISLAM AS RELIGION AND AS CIVILIZATION

THE PROBLEM: UNITY IN DIVERSITY

G. E. VON GRUNEBAUM

I

Any study of the Islamic world as a whole will sooner or later come up against the problem of the relation between Muslim civilization and the local cultures of the areas which in the course of time have become technically Islamized. The problem of the relation between coexisting layers of a "universal" and a "provincial" civilization is by no means peculiar to the Islamic world; it is, in fact, typical of all areas culturally identified with a civilization of a supernational or "universal" outreach. The supernational civilization is characteristically but not necessarily associated with, and in its leading aspirations largely developed from, a religious message claiming universal validity, and it is in its beginnings championed by a distinct ethnic element. Hellenistic culture is perhaps the outstanding exception to the paramountcy of the religious identification in a universal civilization—the civilization of the Christian West, the most striking exception to ethnic sponsorship of the beginnings of a cultural movement. The civilization of Islâm, however, conforms to this tentative typology, having grown from the original core of the message of the Arabic Prophet through amalgamation of certain cultural traditions to which it became exposed through the political successes of the Prophet's Arab adherents.

The realization of this relational problem presupposes not only the existence of a Muslim identification but also the separability, in the analysis of outlook and attitudes of a given area at a given time, of elements to which an Islamic origin may be ascribed from others whose presence cannot be connected with Islâm. This assumption will sometimes be readily substantiated by the historical situation as such, which may be dominated by a clearly felt and openly discussed conflict between two cultural heritages; resolution is attempted within the framework of the universal culture whose essential tenets and values are, consciously at least, not to be compromised. At other times the conflict will not be acute, but the self-consciousness of the people themselves will have registered the heterogeneity of the ideas and of the mores to which they profess their allegiance; in actual life, however, adherence to one or the other of the insufficiently integrated traditions will depend on social stratification or on some other segmentation regulated by custom, owing to which certain activities will be governed by what is felt to be the Islamic norm while others will be conducted in accordance with the local tradition, which may be considered an awkward but unavoidable deviation from the universal ideal. It would be erroneous to suppose that it is always the upper strata of society who live out and promote the universal norm; in the Islamic area it has been, as often as not, the local elite who struggled to maintain the local cultural tradition or at least as much of it as could be upheld without eliminating its bearers from influencing the political structure and the political fate of the universal civilization. Again it is the local elite who may forsake sooner, or to a greater extent, the universal religious civilization toward which the lower orders of the local society continue to cherish a strong attachment. Present developments under Western impact in many Muslim countries will illustrate this observation.

In an encounter of disparate civilizations a subjective criterion as well as a series of objective criteria may be found in order to establish which of the two must be considered leading, that is to say, to which of them the essential cachet of the local integration is primarily due. The subjective criterion, which may on occasion conflict with the objective, analytically obtained evidence, is best described as the self-identification of the members of the particular culture community. The cohesion of the culturally Muslim-dominated area is in a large measure due to the firm conviction held by the most outlying groups that they form a part of a larger and religiously defined entity. For this unreflecting identification the problem does not arise which in its simplest form may be stated in terms of this question: What does, say, a North African Muslim have in common with a Muslim from Java? It is taken for granted that all Muslims, whatever their "national" background, are at one in their essential beliefs and practices. That even those elementary beliefs, when scrutinized, would reveal implications and associations not altogether identical is as little suspected as are the actually rather significant variations in social and legal practice. And even were the awareness of existing differences keener than it is and has been for centuries, a community's consciousness of belonging with like-minded communities would hardly be affected. As a matter of fact, the identification in large measure creates, as it were, the affinities on which it is presumably based.

For the purpose of ascertaining at least some unequivocal objective criteria enabling us to determine the leading element(s) among coexisting and interpenetrating civilizations one may perhaps describe culture, with more than one grain of salt, "as a 'closed' system of questions and answers concerning the universe and man's behavior in it which has been accepted as authoritative by a human society. A scale of values decides the relative position and importance of the individual 'questions and answers.' "[1] In the event of a conflict or even the mere coexistence of two such systems, the resultant civilization by which people actually live will be organized according to certain fundamental value judgments in which the aspirations of one of the participating cultures will be more deeply represented and by which these aspirations will be better promoted than those of the other(s).

In addition to changing the basic values of the pre-Islamic cultural system of a conquered and converted region, the new religion in its cultural unfolding will, to put it in the abstract, (*a*) introduce, or admit as legitimate, new questions, for which appropriate answers will be offered; and (*b*) suggest new answers to old questions, or legitimize answers that seem disrupting or otherwise inacceptable within the competing tradition.

From this point of view the self-identification as a Muslim of a "nationalistic" Persian of the Samanid period would appear perfectly legitimate, inasmuch as he would continue to accept the Islamic axioms of monistic theism and prophetism as well as the value judgment which dedicates the life of man to the service of God. It is only within this intellectual-emotional framework that he strives after the political independence of his people and the revival of the cultural glories of the Iranian past. Under the surface of the Muslim identification no end of changes may occur, but they will hardly ever affect the identification as such.

We can perhaps generalize in societal terms with regard to the structure of such a supernational civilization by viewing it, not as one closely knit organism, but rather as a vast number of groups which may almost be described as self-sufficient. Islâm superimposes "a common veneer of general religious culture" but does not cause those groups "to lose the peculiar shade of mystical-magical feeling of their own particular life."[2] The medieval Muslim himself articulated a certain awareness of this cultural dichotomy at a fairly early time, although, as might have been expected, within an entirely different frame of reference. Thus, for example, differences in body build and intelligence are accounted for on climatic grounds by the Muᶜtazilite, al-Naẓẓâm (d. 845).[3] His disciple, al-Jâḥiẓ (d. 869), adduces climatic considerations to explain why Zoroaster threatened his followers with eternal cold rather than with eternal fire. He goes on to argue that, since this threat would be effective only among the inhabitants of the mountainous region where Zoroaster actually began to preach his religion, this very doctrine would prove the local limitations of his mission and his message. In contrast to the merely provincial validity of Zoroastrianism, the Koranic hell-fire, whose terror is not based on local apprehensions—considering that the Arabs were exposed to both heat and cold—gives evidence of the universal character of Mohammed's mission and message (an interpretation which, incidentally, Jâḥiẓ finds it useful to corroborate from Revelation itself).[4] What matters in our context is, of course, not the conclusiveness of the argument but the desire to establish on whatever grounds the universal validity of Islâm, within whose fold other religious and cultural systems can be observed to exist whose inherent imperfection could be described precisely in terms of the limited validity of the truths on which they are predicated.

The cultural area united by the *Gemeingefühl* of the followers of the Prophet has always harbored a multitude of local civilizations of greater or lesser completeness and of varying independence with regard to the dominant strain of Islamic civilization; and it cannot be said that this situation has changed significantly in our own day. Not only the Moroccan Berber, the Moro in Mindanao, the Hausa, but recently converted to Mohammedanism, but even the Turk of Central Asia or the Punjabi, whose allegiance to Islâm is inherited from twenty or thirty generations of devout believers, will cling faithfully and often consciously to patterns of social organization and behavior, sets of beliefs and "superstitions" that are compatible with the specifically Islamic patterns not through any kinship or natural affinity but merely in terms of the actual symbiosis. The coexistence obtains *de facto* but hardly *de jure*—as the local spokesmen of the universal tradition, the *faqîh* and the more educated *ḥâjj*, never tire of explaining to their moderately attentive fellows. Although in theory the acceptance of Islâm would seem to imply the acceptance of a complete way of life designed to unify the faithful wherever they be by methodically unifying the rhythm of their existence, in fact a latitudinarian interpretation of the nature of an Islamic society has prevailed. The Muslim coming from the heartlands of the faith may be amazed, shocked, or moved to contempt at what he sees in the outlying provinces,[5] but he will not, in general, be inclined to contest the provincial claim to orthodoxy as long as he is satisfied of the community's determination to identify itself with the *umma Muḥammadiyya.*

The essential changes which full Islamization will bring about may be inferred from the changes imposed on the pagan Arabs by the acceptance of the Prophet's message. In terms of our heuristic definition of culture, the cultural transformation imposed or induced by Islâm may perhaps be described as primarily due to the introduction of three new valuations: (1) Islâm sets for life an otherworldly goal. Life in this world is no longer an end in itself but rather a means to secure eternal felicity. Accordingly, the aims of heathen ambition, such as wealth, power, fame, remain acceptable aspirations only inasmuch as they are integrated in the organizational structure of the new life. (2) By making the individual responsible for his fate in the next world, the new faith completed, or at least advanced significantly, the process of legal and moral individuation. Besides, it made every moment of the believer's life supremely relevant; for the effort to gain salvation must never be relaxed. (3) By accentuating the indispensability of the community to the fulfilment of some of the basic obligations of the individual Muslim, Islâm stressed the necessity of political organization. Where the pagan Arab had thought in terms of clans and tribes, the Muslim was led to think in terms of the political community coextensive with the area of the faith—and therefore ultimately destined to dominate the world. Mankind no longer divided into members of different tribes—it split into believers and unbelievers, and this cleavage was to continue beyond the grave.

The introduction of these revaluations entailed at least three new fundamental "questions": how to live correctly, how to think correctly, and how to organize correctly.

Paganism had left everyday life exempt, on the whole, from religious supervision. It was only through Islâm that the problem arose as to which one of the two or more possible ways of performing this or that erstwhile irrelevant routine action was more pleasing, or possibly the only one acceptable, in the eyes of the Lord. Similarly, the pagan's conclusions on transcendental problems had not affected his metaphysical standing. With Islâm correctness of belief became essential, and belief involved areas of thought never touched by the pagan. Islâm widened the horizon of the Arab in that it unlocked the doors of theology and metaphysics and introduced him to a new anthropology as well. The limited success of pre-Islamic attempts at state formation was due, in part at least, to the lack of any ideological purpose the proposed state was to embody or realize. The Muslim commonwealth, by contrast, was to implement the precepts of the faith, to make possible and to guarantee their punctual performance; its organization and policy had ideally to be justified by religious considerations.

But Islâm not only raised questions. It also indicated novel solutions for recognized problems: it revised prevailing ideas concerning the correct education of the individual by substituting new ideal types for the human models of the pagan era; it revised the relative rating of human activities. Warfare as such is no longer deemed valuable. The fighter for the faith ranks high, but his indispensability does not bestow leadership on him. Islâm turns from the aimlessness of the Bedouin to the discipline of the townsman. The ground is laid for the later precedence of the pen over the sword, the scholar over the soldier, the merchant over the peasant. The religious specialist becomes an accepted type. Only under Islâm does the introvert find a place in society; only in Islâm is the thinker felt to be closer to God than the doer.

So the achievement of Islâm in transforming the ancestral Arab culture may be presented as the introducing of four fundamental changes: (*a*) a widening and refinement of human sensibilities; (*b*) an extension of the intellectual world and of the means of its mastery by man; (*c*) the creation of a morally justified and at the same time effective political organization of a locally unprecedented structure; and (*d*) the delineation of a new "standard" type of life, that is, a new human ideal, and a detailed pattern for its realization in a model biography extending from conception to beyond the day of judgment.[6]

The analysis of the mental world of yesterday's Arab Bedouin reveals how much of the cultural momentum of Islâm has been lost again over the centuries in favor of a revival of pre-Islamic cultural attitudes, in spite of the fact that the Islamic identification has remained unquestioned. It is only on a more sophisticated level of introspection (and possibly under the impact of Western categories of cultural interpretation) that the differentiation within the spiritual heritage between a national and a religious strand could be made explicit, as was attempted, to quote only one example, by the Turkish writer Ziya Gök Alp (d. 1924).[7]

II

The civilization which the conquering Arabs brought out of the Peninsula was itself the result of a first integration of local cultural elements with elements derived from the Jewish, the Christian, and, through their mediation, the Hellenistic traditions, with the message of Islâm serving at the same time as an additional constituent and as the crystallizing catalyst. This first Islamic integration imposed itself on a sizable proportion of the subject populations while it was undergoing a keen struggle with the autochthonous cultures. As a result of this *Auseinandersetzung* the philosophical and scientific potential of Islâm was actualized and restated in terms acceptable to the representatives of the older traditions with which the new religious civilization had to deal. Persian administrative and political thinking, Hellenistic techniques of philosophizing and of secular science, Indian mathematics and medicine were mastered effortlessly. The linguistic Arabization of the borrowings contributed to their assimilation—the foreign viewpoint when expounded in an Islamized setting and in an Islamized terminology would be experienced as genuinely Islamic; on the other hand, the progressive expliciting of the primitive data of the faith and of their cultural implications would enlarge the basis of intercivilization receptivity. The flowering of the Abbasid Empire between A.D. 760 and 840 thus came to represent a second integration of Islamic civilization, in which room had been made for "local" traditions which were in part admitted in a bookish fashion but which mostly forced themselves into the new synthesis through the realities of an actual symbiosis.

This second integration was that classical Islamic civilization which competed with Byzantine civilization, which had to withstand the rise of Iranian nationalism in the ninth and tenth centuries, and which, most important of all, found itself exposed to the criticism of a competing attempt at integrating Islamic and local elements undertaken by the radical Shîʿa and at times propagated by the political power of the Fatimids. With the help of the Seljuq Turks and the unwitting assistance of the Christian Crusaders, the threat of the Bâṭinite integration was eliminated, and the emergent Sunnite orthodoxy consolidated Islâm in a third ecumenical integration which was, by and large, completed by the middle of the twelfth century, and has so far remained the universally accepted self-definition of the Islamic world.

In this third integration, which is only now slowly yielding under regionally disparate reactions to the West, the piety of the popular strata was more securely anchored than it had been before the equipollence of local traditions was assured by an elastic application of the *consensus doctorum* as the verifying authority; a keener sense was shown of what elements of Hellenism are compatible with the Muslim aspiration, and an inclusive feeling about membership in the community which, notwithstanding the awareness of local variations, came to be experienced as increasingly unified in doctrine and lore, made possible the rise of a body spiritual whose hold over the faithful was well-nigh independent of the political realities of the day.

The stability which, in the consciousness of the believers, Islâm as constituted in this third integration had reached in providing a balance between the claims of the universal and of the local tradition neutralized the disruptive effects of the supplanting of the multinational empire of the early Abbasid caliphs by an increasing number of rival local, and in certain cases clearly national, states. It also counteracted the disintegration potential of the local renaissances to which in the later Middle Ages Islâm owed most of its significant cultural acquisitions. A limited cultural pluralism within, and under the protection of, the ideal unity of Islâm—such was the solution provided by the third integration to the inescapable conflict of cultural traditions. Theology and the law, on the one hand, and the forms of conceptualization, argument, and presentation, on the other, provided the most potent means of communicating a sense of cohesion to the overextended and disorganized domain.

The medieval Muslim was himself keenly alive to the regional variations of his civilization, which he was inclined to account for in terms of national differences. Political tensions were apt to create a feeling of national distinctness accompanied by dislike or even hate of one's fellow-Muslims. In Spain, during and after the last reigns of the Umayyad dynasty (deposed in 1031), the "natural aversion," *al-nafâra al-ṭabîᶜiyya*, between the Muslim Berbers from Morocco and the Andalusian Muslims was almost taken for granted.[8] The "solidarity," *ᶜaṣabiyya*, of the Berbers and the opposing "solidarity" of the Andalusians were important political factors. The antagonism between the Baghdâdîs and the Turks in the ninth and tenth centuries, to offer but one more example, was hardly less intense. And both in Spain and in Iraq the dislike of the more highly civilized "native" population for the culturally less Islamized group is experienced and voiced in terms of ethnic or "national" hostility.

By the ninth century the interest in national characteristics had developed a generally applied technique of ethnographic description (used as much by geographers as by littérateurs) whose literary descent from Greek ethnographic technique, while obvious, still needs to be traced through the several phases of its transmission. The various nations inside and out of Islâm were classified as "civilized" or "barbarous,"[9] their contributions to the sciences were inventoried, and their psychological peculiarities listed in a few striking phrases which were presumably well taken before the presentation was frozen into a number of clichés. But as a result of this semiscientific concern, the average Muslim carried in his mind a reasonably definite concept of what his "foreign" coreligionists were like as compared with himself.

Ibn Ghâlib (eleventh century) describes the Andalusian Muslims as Arabs by genealogy and feeling for independence, by the loftiness of their thoughts, the eloquence of their language, and their inability to suffer oppression; as Hindus in respect to their extreme love for the sciences; as Baghdâdîs because of their polished ways, the refinement of their manners, and the subtlety of their minds; as Greeks for their excellence in agriculture.[10] Only rarely does the analysis transcend the limitations of the ethnographic notebook, as when al-Jâḥiẓ, possibly for propagandistic reasons, devotes a lengthy essay to a study of the Turks in which he offers a certain number of comprehensive characterizations.

> The Turks know not how to flatter or coax, they know not how to practice hypocrisy or back-biting, pretense or slander, dishonesty or haughtiness on their acquaintance, or mischief on those that associate with them. They are strangers to heresy, *bidaᶜ*, and not spoiled by [intellectual] caprice, *ahwâ*ᵓ; and they do not make property lawful by quibbles. Their fault which makes them most unpopular is their love of land and love of moving freely up and down the country and propensity for raiding and preoccupation with plunder, and the intensity of their attachment to it, besides their custom of dwelling on the experienced joy of successive victory, on the delight and frequency of their plunder, and their exploits in such deserts, and their return again and again to the same prairies; and the fact that the excellence of their prowess does not become dulled from long continued idleness, and that their courage is not exhausted by the course of time . . . love of the homeland, *maḥabbat al-waṭan*, is common to all nations and prevails over all mankind. But it is peculiarly strong among the Turks, and counts for more among them owing to their mutual similarity and homogeneity of idiosyncrasy.[11]

In general, the characterization remains confined to the aphoristic quip or at any rate to concise and usually undocumented observations that are as often as not elicited by nationalistic rivalries within Islâm.[12]

Awareness extended beyond the distinctive traits to such (extra-religious) elements as would reflect and perpetuate the regional peculiarities within Islâm. Thus Ibn Khaldûn (d. 1406) observes that throughout the Islamic domain the children are taught the Koran. The Holy Book provides the basis of instruction. However, "the methods of instructing the children in the Koran differ in accordance with the attitudes, *malakât,* which are to result from this instruction."[13] The Moroccan children are strictly confined to the study of the Koran; they are instructed in the spelling of the text, certain variant readings, and the like, but neither *ḥadîth* nor jurisprudence, nor again Arabic grammar and poetry, are taken up during elementary education. In Spain, on the other hand, reading and writing are taught first. Since the Koran is the foundation of all instruction and the source of religion and all the sciences, the Spaniards will take it as the basis of their teaching. They will not, however, make it the sole object of their instruction. On the contrary, the Spanish teachers will at an early stage introduce their pupils to poetry and make them memorize the rules of Arabic grammar; a great deal of attention is also given to calligraphy. In Ifrîqiya (Tunisia) instruction in the *ḥadîth* and the principles of the religious sciences is added to instruction in the Koran, with some considerable emphasis reserved for calligraphy. Ibn Khaldûn observes[14] that the educational program of Tunis is close to that of al-Andalus, owing to the influence of eastern Spanish *émigré* scholars who had settled in Tunis because of the Christian advance southward. In the Muslim east the Koran is taken as the point of departure, but instruction in various sciences is not neglected; calligraphy, however, does not form part of general education but has to be acquired as a special skill from a separate master. Ibn Khaldûn indorses the proposal which the judge Abû Bakr b. al-ᶜArabî (d. 1148) directed to the eastern Muslims to the effect that the "Orientals" should adopt the Spanish system and begin the curriculum with the study of the Arabic language and poetry. Next, there should be given a cursus in arithmetic, and only then should the study of the Koran be undertaken, which would be greatly facilitated by the preliminary training the pupil would have received. From the Koran instruction should proceed to the *uṣûl al-dîn,* "the Principles of Theology," and the *uṣûl al-fiqh,* "the Principles of Jurisprudence," and finally reach the sciences of Tradition.[15]

The different civilizational outlook of the Muslim elites in Spain, Morocco, and Tunis (and to some extent of the east) is clearly grasped in its molding effect on prevailing ideas of education. But at the same time it is obvious that Ibn Khaldûn, in accordance with the Islamic erudites of all times, views the different systems of instruction but as relatively insignificant variants of one and the same universally accepted education which mirrors the ideal unity of the *dâr al-Islâm*. This idea of unity was not to be impaired by nationalistic pride, as it had developed with particular strength and aggressiveness on both sides of the Arabic heartlands—in Persia as well as in Spain.[16] Almost to the present time the overriding concern of the Islamic elites (and perhaps even of most of the Muslim populations in the Near East and North Africa) has been for the integrity of the *dâr al-Islâm* as a whole rather than for the integrity of any particular component state.

The beautiful and moving passage with which Ibn al-Athîr (d. 1234) introduces, *sub anno* 617/1220, his account of the first Mongol invasion of Muslim lands is informed by an intense feeling for the oneness of all the faithful, and it betrays an intense sensitivity to any event affecting Islâm in any part of the world. The misery of the Persian Muslims is experienced as a calamity that has befallen all mankind but more particularly all Muslims.[17] A comparable feeling of oneness transcending regional differentiation, but this time founded specifically on the realization of the unity of Islâm as a civilization rather than solely as a religion or a sociopolitical community, was on several occasions voiced by al-Bêrûnî (d. 1048). At the beginning of his book on India, Bêrûnî sets forth the difficulties he has had to contend with in its preparation. "The barriers which separate Muslims and Hindus rest on different causes." It is always the cultural unit of Islâm which is confronted with the cultural unit of Hindu India. Neither the oneness nor the identifiability in civilizational terms of Islâm is ever questioned. Bêrûnî goes on to point out some of the essential differences: ". . . they totally differ from us in religion, as we believe in nothing in which they believe, and vice versa . . . in all manners and usages they differ from us to such a degree as to frighten their children with us, with our dress, and our ways and customs, and as to declare us the devil's breed, and our doings the very opposite of all that is good and proper." Bêrûnî adds that among the Muslims as among all nations a similar disparagement of foreigners can be found.[18] Here, again, it is the world of Islâm, not any particular country or tradition, with which the individual feels identified.

III

Conflict, coexistence, and interaction of the Islamic and the local culture patterns can be experienced and described in different ways depending on which aspect of the phenomenon is felt or perceived most vividly.

1. The patterns may be maintained in the relation of the great to the little tradition.[19] This is to say that one of the two patterns is recognized as the more advanced; it is assumed to make authority; it is almost exclusively represented in the writings as well as the public actions of the elite; social prestige is dependent on its adoption. In the *dâr al-Islâm* the Islamic pattern is in general in the position of the great tradition. In contrast, the little tradition is the catchment of the popular undercurrent; its effectiveness is still felt by the intelligentsia, but "officially" it will be denied or deprecated. Where the hypotheses of the great tradition are considered beliefs, the hypotheses of the little tradition will be considered superstitions. In fact, the social position of a person may depend on which of the two traditions he determines to live by.

The actual accommodation of the two traditions in such areas of the life of the community as are judged important may be effected through various methods of adjustment.

a) The great tradition admits the little tradition as the religion of the ignorant.[20]

b) The great tradition develops a "latitudinarian" attitude toward the practice of the little tradition. This approach can be exemplified by the custom prevailing, e.g., in Turkey and in Syria which permits Muslims to resort to the invocation of Christian saints and vice versa. Such devotion to the saints of a religion not one's own will not arouse any suspicion that the individual concerned intends to leave his native religious community.[21]

c) An integration of the two traditions may be tried:

(1) A Christian saint may, for example, be identified with a Muslim saint; or he may be considered to have been a crypto-Muslim.[22]

(2) The local cult tradition will be tied in with, and accounted for, in terms of the "genuine" great tradition. The Prophet himself set the precedent for this procedure by giving an Islamic meaning to the heathen pilgrimage rites which he welded into the Muslim *ḥajj* to Mecca, ʿArafa, and Minà. By the same token, the Islamic pilgrimages to the Temple area in Jerusalem or to the tombs of the patriarchs in Hebron are but the Islamization of practices familiar from Old and New Testament times.[23] The practices were sanctioned by the local clergy when their ineradicability had been evidenced over a sufficiently long period. Great care is given in such cases to establishing the legitimacy of the practice in terms of the great tradition,

whose more self-conscious or more learned representatives are apt to preserve a certain uneasiness about the admissibility of the successful intruder. The extreme attention bestowed by the mystical orders on the *silsila* which is to provide the great tradition's authorization for their practices, which are more than a little affected by folkways, is a case in point.

(3) The little tradition may be taken into the great tradition by means of an appropriate theological or philosophical explanation. In Islâm one of the most characteristic examples of this tendency is the justification within the framework of orthodoxy of the cult of the saints. The saint is interpreted as the possessor of Gnostic knowledge; he is closer to God than are his fellow-Muslims, and his miracles are accounted for by the grace of Allâh, who uses His elect as an instrument in furthering His mysterious ends and, according to some, even as His agent in the actual government of the universe. Koranic evidence is found to prove the existence of familiars of the Lord, and the theosophy of Ibn al-ᶜArabî (d. 1240) reconciles the saint of the little tradition with the prophet of the great tradition by arguing that "all prophets are also saints but that the saintly aspect of each prophet is higher than the prophetic aspect." Besides, all prophets and saints are but "manifestations of the Spirit or Reality of Mohammed."[24]

2. The relationships of the two cultural strains may be interpreted as that of sunna, the legitimate tradition of the Prophet, and *bidᶜa*, unauthorized innovation. Local custom appears to the guardians of the universal culture as an illicit deviation of a kind allegedly envisaged by Mohammed himself. It is then their duty to combat such customs or at least to confine the practices to the local circles already dedicated to them. The *faqih* from the Maghrib who is brought face to face with the mores of his Egyptian or Syrian coreligionists is apt to feel outraged by their unwarrantable "innovations," which will appear to him as relaxations and corruptions of the strictness of the sunna.[25]

3. Canon law and customary law, canon law and executive law, may coexist as an expression of divergent approaches to the social realization of the ideal Muslim community. The legal system sidestepping the *sharîᶜa* may owe its origin to administrative exigencies; it may reflect the superimposition of an alien though Islamized ruling class on the generality of local Muslims; or it may openly constitute a systematization of regional usage with only the slightest admixture of the legal system of Islâm.

4. Cultural divergencies may crystallize in sectarian develop-

ments. The success of the Khârijites among the Berbers, like that of the Shîᶜite extremists in the mountainous areas of Syria and southeastern Asia Minor, is to a large extent due to the sectarian movement catching up, as it were, religious and cultural motifs that had been important to the local people before Islâm and which the (sometimes but nominally) Muslim sect was able to reintegrate.

5. Variations of local sentiment will support the proliferation of experiential and organizational variants within a movement sanctioned by the universal orthodoxy. The history of the legal rites, and even more so that of the mystical *ṭarîqas* with their emphasis on different aspects of the supreme experience of the *tauḥîd* or on different social-technical means to attain to it, can to a considerable extent be accounted for through an investigation of their relations to local cultural traditions.

6. The precepts of the universal and of the local traditions may knowingly be contrasted as norm and practice. In this situation the several areas of social life will be unevenly resistant to the Islamic pattern which in theory has been accepted as the pervasive norm; the perseverance of the social strata will differ when it comes to maintaining the traditional against the inroads of the "true" order of things; the society of women may continue an attachment that has been abandoned by the men in their extradomestic relations, and the like. The passage is well known in which Ibn Baṭṭûṭa (d. 1377) describes his failure, when a judge in the Maldive Islands, to induce the local women to adopt a manner of dress consonant with the Muslim custom. It would seem from his account that, with all his zeal in carrying out the prescriptions of the canon law, he did not even attempt to uproot the peculiar type of temporary marriage which was then widely practiced in those islands. At the same time, he emphasizes the piety of the inhabitants and their attachment to Islâm.[26]

The traditions will, on occasion, conflict not so much on the fundamental religious level as on a cultural level more narrowly defined. The bilingual culture of modern Egypt and of certain Berber areas, on the one hand, and that of the Iranian elite from the ninth through the eleventh centuries, on the other, is not the result of opposing religious attitudes toward an interpretation of the universal faith of Islâm but rather of an unwillingness to sacrifice a cultural aspiration which, while not rooted in the prophetic norm, is yet valued as an adequate means of collective self-expression. It would seem that the submergence or survival of a local culture that has been overrun by another culture of geographically (and spiritually) wider outreach depends in large measure on the continued identification with the ancestral tradition of the local ruling classes who buttress their self-respect and justify their self-perpetuation by upholding the tradition within which alone their position is truly meaningful. More or less fictional attempts to integrate this tradition in the historical mythology of the conquerors are often pragmatically successful, although they may not find credence among the authoritative guardians of the Islamic tradition. The Islamization of the Persian *dihqân* and, on a lower cultural level, that of the Berber chieftain, who both on the whole maintained their social role, are cases in point. The evolution of a vernacular tradition in Egypt is of course to be explained in a different manner.

IV

The universal culture of Islâm disposes of several means to further the adjustment to the local cultures. Of those, the most characteristically Islamic is the *ijmâᶜ*. The *consensus omnium*, narrowed down to a *consensus prudentium*, is authorized to rule on the legitimacy of any individual belief or practice which the community may have adopted. Its verifying verdict includes its object among the normative elements of the Muslim tradition.[27] There is no appeal against the *ijmâᶜ* except to a later *ijmâᶜ*. It has often been shown how significant elements of local and popular piety were allowed to enter the orthodox norm. A typical progress leads from appraisal of a phenomenon as *bidᶜa (sayyiʾa)* to that as *bidᶜa ḥasana* and thence to fissureless integration in the teachings of the doctors of the faith. The existence of a merely local *ijmâᶜ* is recognized. But while the *ijmâᶜ* of the *Ḥaramain* (Mecca and Medina) may count for more than that of an outlying area, and while attempts may be made to bring the local *ijmâᶜ* in line with that of more holy or more advanced places, yet even the local *ijmâᶜ* will serve to ward off from the native Muslims the suspicion of heresy; it will serve also to prevent the cleavage between universal norm and traditional practice from rendering an "Islamic" life impossible.

Genealogical theories or fictions, the sacred language, literature in the *Hochsprache* (principally Arabic, but in certain regions Persian), and, in general, the content of education as dispensed by all but the most modernist (which may imply, nationalistic) institutions, effectively assist in the adjustment of the conflicting cultural traditions. In Islâm, as elsewhere, historiography plays a special part in shaping the identification of a community. The specifically Muslim elaboration of the concept of unilinear history, leading from creation to resurrection, provides a firm if elastic frame in which the fate of the individual Muslim nations can be rendered meaningful through their function in originating and spreading ultimate truth. This is not to suggest that local traditions have failed to influence local historiography. On the contrary, every type of historical writing shows in some way the peculiar outlook of its country of origin. The Arab-Muslim biography is rich in personal facts and colorful anecdote, while its Persian-Muslim counterpart is less concerned with the personal elements but more generous in offering the reader quotations from the works of the biographee. The little tradition, too, develops a historiography representative of its aspirations. The *ᶜAntar Novel* goes back as far as the eighth century A.D.[28] Local histories need not but often will represent a local cultural outlook. Yet, seen in its entirety, historiography has proved itself an exceptionally powerful instrument of universalization.

A common style of argumentation and formulation, most clearly visible in the peculiar cachet of the *ḥadîth*[29] and the unmistakable atmosphere which its use conveys to practically all literary manifestations of the Islamic tradition, effectively promotes the impression of cultural uniformity. The local tradition, which has to assert itself through formal means recognizably borrowed from its competitor, is by this very fact put at a disadvantage. The formal unity of Muslim theological and scientific writing has done almost as much to make possible its international distribution as the international acceptance of the Arabic language.

But the factor which is in the last analysis most influential in adjusting the relations of the civilization of Islâm and the traditional civilizations of the Muslim lands is the voluntary and deliberate identification of the individual believer. He may actually lead his life by ethnically or nationally inherited practices, but at the same time he recognizes his behavior as a forgivable shortcoming for which he is able to adduce numbers of reasons; besides, and this is the decisive point, his day-by-day behavior appears irrelevant to him when he views himself and his society in relation to his Creator and to the rest of mankind. For in this universal context his insignificant person appears among the followers of the Prophet, and it is from this association that he derives his dignity in this, and his invulnerability in the next, world.

NOTES

1. The writer, in *Conflict of Power in Modern Culture: Proceedings of the Seventh Conference on Science, Philosophy, and Religion*, ed. Lyman Bryson, Louis Finkelstein, and R. M. MacIver (New York, 1948), p. 218.

2. A. D. A. de Kat Angelino, *Colonial Policy* (The Hague, 1931), I, 67–68; quoted by H. A. R. Gibb and H. Bowen, *Islamic Society and the West*, I, i (London, New York, Toronto, 1950), 211, n. 6.

3. Cf. Jâḥiẓ, *Kitâb al-ḥayawân* (2d ed.; Cairo, 1356–64/1938–45), V, 35–36 (=1st ed. [Cairo, 1907], V, 12–13).

4. *Ibid.*, V, 66–71 (=1st ed., V, 24–25). The same Jâḥiẓ quotes the Muᶜtazilite, Thumâma b. Ashras (d. 828), for use of the grain-snatching cocks of Marw as proof that the avarice of its human inhabitants is due to the influence of their land and its water: *Kitâb al-bukhalâ*ᵓ, ed. G. Van Vloten (Leiden, 1900), p. 19 (ed. A. al-ᶜAwâmirî and ᶜAlî Jârim [Cairo, 1338/1939], I, 46; ed. Ṭ. al-Ḥâjirî [Cairo, 1948], p. 14; trans. C. Pellat [Beirut and Paris, 1951], p. 26). The geographer, Ibn al-Faqîh (*fl.* after A.D. 902), insists that inspection reveals the untruth of Thumâma's statement concerning the behavior of the cocks of Marw: *Mukhtaṣar kitâb al-buldân*, ed. M. J. de Goeje (Leiden, 1885), pp. 316–17. In this connection the passage in Yâqût (d. 1229), *Muᶜjam al-buldân*, ed. F. Wüstenfeld (Leipzig and St. Petersburg, 1866–73), III, 630[ult]–31[7], may be referred to in which the author co-ordinates the excellencies of the Iraqis with the virtues of the climate of Iraq.

5. Cf., as one example for many, the shock which the Moroccan traveler, Ibn Baṭṭûṭa, receives when he sees the visitors to the public bath in the Egyptian township of Munyat Ibn Khaṣîb refreshing themselves in complete nakedness; cf. *Riḥla*, ed. trans. C. Defrémery and B. R. Sanguinetti (Paris, 1853–58), I, 100.

6. Cf. the writer's paper, "Transformation of Culture as Illustrated by the Rise of Islam" in *Conflict of Power in Modern Culture*, pp. 219–24.

7. Cf., e.g., in the poetical volume *Qyzyl Elma* (Istanbul, 1330) the poem "ᶜUthmân Ghâzî qurultay-da" with its characteristic line: *Türklük-le Islamlaq qardash olajaq* (p. 101; trans. E. Pritsch, *Festschrift F. Giese*, ed. G. Jäschke [Berlin, 1941], p. 122: "Zum Türkentum wird der Islam sich gesellen"), and also in "ᶜAsker duᶜâ-sy" (p. 88) the verse: *ana-myz waṭan, baba-myz millet.* For Ziya Gök Alp's ideology, see U. Heyd, *Foundations of Turkish Nationalism* (London, 1950), esp. pp. 84 ff. For the attitude, cf. also Saᶜîd Ḥalîm Pasha's (d. 1921) *Islamlashmaq*, ed. A. Fischer (Leipzig, 1928).

8. Cf. H. Pérès, *La Poésie andalouse en arabe classique au XIe siècle* (Paris, 1937), p. 9; cf. also p. 13. Yâqût, *op. cit.*, I, 541[19]–42[4] and 542[18]–43[8], quotes a number of unfavorable judgments on the Berbers.

9. Cf., e.g., Ṣâᶜid al-Andalusî (d. 1070), *Kitâb ṭabaqât al-umam*, ed. L. Cheikho (Beirut, 1912), pp. 7–8 (trans. R. Blachère [Paris, 1935], p. 35), who bases his classification of the nations on their active interest in the sciences, *ᶜulûm*. On the political level, too, three to six Great Kings are set apart from the other kings of the world. This division follows a literary tradition which has been traced back to the China of A.D. 240–50; it occurs in Arabic literature for the first time in A.D. 851; cf. G. Ferrand, *Bulletin of the School of Oriental and African Studies*, VI (1930–32), 329–39. The same technique of ethnographic description is to be met with in the *Letter of Tansar*, where the author vaunts the Persian nation as uniting the *suwârî* of the Turks and the *zîrakî* of the Hind with the *khûbkârî* and the *ṣinâᶜat* of the Rûm. In

addition, all the sciences of the world have fallen to the Persians' lot: *wa-ᶜilm-hâ-yi jumla rû-yi zamîn ba-mâ rûzî gardânîd* (ed. trans. J. Darmesteter, *Journal asiatique*, 9th series, Vol. 3 [1894], 241–44, esp. 242 and 243[2]; 546–49, esp. 547).

In *Ḥayawân*, VI, 14–15 (=1st ed., VI, 5–6), Jâḥiẓ lists the principal problems which an anthropology would have to take up: the distinction between male and female, the different life-expectancies of people, *aᶜmâr*, their different sizes and intellectual abilities, *maqâdîr al-ᶜuqûl*, the different valuations of their crafts, *tafâḍul al-ṣinâᶜât* (and the arguments brought forward in establishing their rating), and the position of man above the jinn but below the angels.

10. Abridged from Pérès' translation, *op. cit.*, pp. 18–19; for a similar pattern of description, cf. *ibid.*, p. 116, Bakrî's characterization of al-Andalus.

11. Ed. G. Van Vloten in *Tria opuscula* (Leiden, 1903), pp. 39–41 (=Cairo, 1324/1906, pp. 38–39); trans. C. T. Harley Walker, *Journal of the Royal Asiatic Society*, 1915, pp. 678–79; cf. also the somewhat idealized portrayal of the Arab, pp. 683–84 (Leiden, pp. 44–45; Cairo, pp. 42–43).

12. Cf., e.g., the interesting remarks on Greeks, Indians, Arabs, etc., of Tauḥîdî (d. 1023), *Kitâb al-imtâᶜ wa'l-muᵓânasa*, ed. A. Amîn and A. al-Zain (Cairo, 1939–44), I, 212–13.

13. *Prolegomena*, ed. Quatremère (Paris, 1858), III, 260.

14. *Ibid.*, III, 262. In 1540–41 Nicolas Clenard observes grammar to form part of elementary education in Fez; the concentration on the Koran as the starting point and basis of all instruction is as intense as it was in Ibn Khaldûn's time; and Tunis is still ahead of Fez in the cultivation of learning outside of the sciences of the Koran and grammar; besides, the study of grammar does not seem to have been effective with many of the Fâsîs of Clenard's day; cf. R. Le Tourneau, "Un humaniste à Fès au XVIe siècle," *Revue de la Méditerranée*, Nos. 54 and 55 (1953), pp. 19–20 of reprint.

15. *Prolegomena*, III, 263–64.

16. For nationalism in Spain, cf. Pérès, *op. cit.*, pp. 52–53, 54. S. Pines, "La 'Philosophie orientale' d'Avicenne et sa polémique contre les bagdadiens," *Archives d'histoire doctrinale et littéraire du moyen âge*, XIX (1952), 32–34, describes the "nationalism" of eastern Iran in the tenth and eleventh centuries. The Spaniard Ibn Jubair (d. 1217), *Travels* (2d ed. by W. Wright and M. J. de Goeje [Leiden and London, 1907], pp. 78–79; trans. R. J. C. Broadhurst [London, 1952], pp. 73–74), insists that only the Maghrib has the true Islâm; Ibn Baṭṭûṭa, *op. cit.*, IV, 334–37, vaunts the Maghrib above Egypt and Syria on various grounds. Ibn Khallikân (d. 1282) quotes Thaᶜâlibî (d. 1038) for the statement that Ibn Darrâj al-Andalusî (d. 1030) "was for the country of Andalus, that which al-Mutanabbî (d. 965) was for Syria, a poet of the highest order, and equally elegant in what he said and wrote" (*Wafayât al-aᶜyân*, trans. W. MacGuckin de Slane [Paris, 1843–71], I, 120). Long before these authors, Yaᶜqûbî (d. 897), *Kitâb al-buldân*, ed. M. J. de Goeje (Leiden, 1891), pp. 236–37 (trans. G. Wiet, *Yaᶜḳûbî, Les pays* [Cairo, 1937], pp. 7–8), had characterized the several regions of the caliphal empire such as Syria, Ifrîqiya, and Egypt, and compared them to their disadvantage with Iraq, making his bias for Mesopotamia rather obvious; five hundred years later, Qalqashandî (d. 1418), *Ṣubḥ al-aᶜshà* (Cairo, 1913–19), III, 286, thought it worth his while to rebut Yaᶜqûbî's verdict (cf. Wiet, *op. cit.*, p. 8, n. 1). In Egypt a distinctly national, not to say nationalistic, feeling antedates the Muslim conquest; *ca.* A.D. 492 Horapollon refers to his country as

"our fatherland, *patris*," and the use of *patrios* in the sense of "national" as opposed to "Greek-imported" is frequent throughout the fifth century. In a derogatory sense Anastasios Sinaita (writing *ca.* A.D. 622) speaks of *hoi aigyptiazontes ton noun*, "intellects of an Egyptian type"; cf. J. Maspéro, *Histoire des patriarches d'Alexandrie* (Paris, 1923), p. 24; G. Bardy, *La Question des langues dans l'église ancienne*, I (Paris, 1948), 52. The conflict between possible religious and ethnic alignments comes out well in the account given by Yâqût, *op. cit.*, III, 534–35, of the princeling, *ra'îs*, of Ṭuraithîth (in Khurâsân, not far from Nîshâpûr) who *ca.* A.D. 1136 tries to ally himself to the Turks against the Ismâ'îlîs but finds himself compelled, owing to the aggressiveness of his *soi-disant* friends, to reverse his loyalties; he does so quite successfully but with a bit of a bad conscience.

17. *Kâmil*, ed. C. J. Tornberg (Leiden, 1851–76), XII, 233–35; trans. F. Gabrieli, *Storia della letteratura araba* (Milan, 1951), pp. 232–34. Cf. also Yâqût, *op. cit.*, IV, 859^{4-5}, qualifying the conquest of Nîshâpûr by the Mongols in 1221 as "an unparalleled calamity for Islâm."

18. Ed. E. Sachau, *Alberuni's India* (London, 1887), pp. 9–10; trans. by the same (London, 1888), I, 17–20; cf. also the passage in Bêrûnî's *Kitâb al-ṣaidana*, trans. M. Meyerhof in *Islamic Culture*, XI (1937), 27, in which Bêrûnî aligns Muslim civilization with Greek, contrasting it again with that of India. Contrast with Bêrûnî the naïve statement of Jâḥiẓ, *Ḥayawân*, VII, 29 (1st ed., VII, 12): "The Hind are agreed with the Arabs in every respect except for the circumcision of men and women."

19. To use R. Redfield's terminology; cf., e.g., "The Natural History of the Folk Society," *Social Forces*, XXXI (1952/53), 224–28, esp. the last paragraph of the paper.

20. Cf., e.g., Jabartî (d. 1822), *Merveilles biographiques et historiques* (Cairo, 1888–96), VI, 92. The contrast between the popular and the learned tradition comes out well in Yâqût's presentation of the legend of Bait Lihyâ, *op. cit.*, I, 780^{4-9}.

21. For sanctuaries shared by Muslim and Christian devotion, cf., e.g., J. Sauvaget, *Matériaux pour servir à l'histoire de la ville d'Alep* (Beirut, 1933–50), I, 84 and n. 3. The ambiguous attitude of the Muslim populace toward objects of Christian worship comes out well when Saladin sends a cross to Baghdad: the relic is first despised but ends by being held in reverence; cf. R. Levy, *A Baghdad Chronicle* (Cambridge, 1929), pp. 237–38.

22. Cf., e.g., F. W. Hasluck, *Christianity and Islam under the Sultans* (Oxford, 1929), pp. 58–59.

A Biblical figure may become the goal of a pilgrimage even though he plays no part in the specifically Muslim ideas of prophetic history. Thus the Damascenes are fond of visiting the exact spot where Abel was killed on Mount Qâsiyûn; cf. Ibn Baṭṭûṭa, *op. cit.*, I, 231–33.

23. Cf. C. D. Matthews, *Palestine—Mohammedan Holy Land* (New Haven, 1949), p. xxiv.

24. A. J. Arberry, *Sufism: An Account of the Mystics of Islam* (London, 1950), p. 101. In this context the angelology and demonology of the theologians may be compared with popular ideas on the subject of jinn, *malâ'ika*, and the like. Jâḥiẓ, *Ḥayawân*, VI, 158–281 (with digressions; 1st ed., VI, 48–90), devotes what amounts to a monograph to the demonological notions of the Arabs; his material may be conveniently contrasted with, say, Ghazzâlî's ideas as presented by A. J. Wensinck,

La Pensée de Ghazzâlî (Paris, 1940), pp. 168–75. In general, it may be said that the consolidation of orthodoxy which took place in the eleventh and twelfth centuries was brought about to some extent by the admission (or readmission) of beliefs appertaining to the little tradition into the great tradition, where, to the outside observer, they sometimes cut a peculiar figure. Cf., e.g., the rules recorded by Ghazzâlî on the proper behavior in the lavatory, where behind every regulation there lurks a "superstitious" motivation—*Bidâyat al-hidâya* (Cairo, 1358/1934), pp. 6–7; trans. W. M. Watt, *The Faith and Practice of al-Ghazâlî* (London, 1953), pp. 92–93; or the admonitions tendered by Zarnûjî (*fl.* 1203) to the student, *Taᶜlîm al-mutaᶜallim,* trans. this writer and T. M. Abel (New York, 1947), pp. 67–69, where the opinions of the vulgar are provided with the rationale of (debased) science. Consider also the acceptance by Ghazzâlî of the efficacy, in speeding a difficult delivery, of magic squares placed under the feet of a woman in labor—*al-Munqidh min al-ḍalâl* (Damascus, 1939), pp. 157–58; trans. Watt, *op. cit.*, pp. 79–80. In this connection the reading of Bukhârî's (d. 870) *Ṣaḥîḥ* as a measure to fortify Islâm and to ward off a present danger should be mentioned. It was widely practiced in the Ottoman Empire; thus in Rajab, 1202/April–May, 1788, the Sultan ordered the shaikhs of al-Azhar to read Bukhârî as a protection against an impending public calamity; again on 20 Dhû 'l-ḥijja, 1220/12 March, 1806, the shaikhs unite to read Bukhârî, with a view to staving off the dangers of an attack by the English (Jabartî, *op. cit.*, V, 27–28, and VIII, 51). In 1228/1813, Bukhârî is read to keep the plague away. Jabartî observes at this point: "People gathered at al-Azhar [for those readings] during three days; then proceedings were stopped because of laziness" (*ibid.*, IX, 9). The reading was again ordered when victory against the Wahhâbîs was in doubt during September/October, 1817 (*ibid.*, pp. 250–51). Cf. further the last three instances recorded by Jabartî for March, 1818 (*ibid.*, pp. 266–67), September, 1818 (*ibid.*, p. 270), and January, 1821 (*ibid.*, p. 329). Muḥammad Rashîd Riḍà (d. 1935), *Tafsîr al-Manâr* (Cairo, 1927–34), IV, 119, and XII, 246, still finds it necessary to ridicule the official readings of Bukhârî; cf., further, J. Jomier, *Le Commentaire coranique du Manâr* (Paris, 1954), p. 257.

25. Cf., e.g., Ibn al-Ḥâjj (d. 1336), *al-Mudkhal* (Cairo, 1348/1929); and ᶜAlî b. Maimûn al-Maghribî (d. 917/1511–12), whose work was analyzed by I. Goldziher, *Zeitschrift der deutschen morgenländischen Gesellschaft,* XXVIII (1874), 293–330. It is worthy of note that already Ibn Ḥauqal, *Bibliotheca Geographorum Arabicorum,* II, ed. M. J. de Goeje (Leiden, 1873), p. 70 (2d ed. by J. H. Kramers [Leiden, 1938–39], pp. 98–99), in A.D. 977 speaks of the moral and religious superiority of the Islamic west over the Islamic east. His contemporary, al-Muqaddasî, writing in A.D. 985, *Descriptio Imperii Moslemici,* ed. M. J. de Goeje (Leiden, 1906), p. 440[21–22], remarks on regional differences in funerary customs. For conflicting reactions to what in the eyes of an author from a different region will appear as deviations from accepted or canonical practice, compare Ibn Baṭṭûṭa's adverse reaction to the mourning ceremonies which he observes in Îdhaj (Khûzistân), *op. cit.*, II, 35–36, with his approval of the manner in which the people of Damascus celebrate the Day of ᶜArafât, *ibid.*, I, 243–44.

26. *Riḥla,* IV, 114, 123, and 151–52.

27. The invocation of the name of Allâh will often suffice to convince the conscience of the believer that his practices are in keeping with Islamic precept. It is by this device that the use of magic is legitimized in many parts of the Muslim world.

By the same means the Kazak-Kirghiz, whose Islâm is, however, far from recent, justify the continuation of shamanism; cf. M. Éliade, *Le Chamanisme et les techniques archaïques de l'extase* (Paris, 1951), pp. 200–201. R. O. Winstedt's *Shaman, Saiva, and Sufi* (London, New York, Toronto, 1925) contains a great number of illuminating examples of the naturalization on diverse levels of Islamic ideas in the mental world of the Muslims of the Malay Peninsula. The several possibilities of amalgamation or adjustment of two (or more) cultural strands are clearly instanced in Winstedt's material, which was collected primarily to illustrate the evolution of Malay magic. Of special interest are cases of (sunken) learned tradition, as, for instance, the following passage from the *Garden of Kings* (written in A.D. 1638 by an Indian missionary of Islâm in Acheen, Sumatra): "Jan, the father of all jinn, was originally an angel, called firstly Aristotle but later ᶜAzazil" (p. 33). Cf. also the Islamized invocation of a Malay shaman, *ibid.*, pp. 62–63.

28. Cf. F. Rosenthal, *A History of Muslim Historiography* (Leiden, 1952), pp. 164–70, where under the heading "The Historical Novel" a great deal of pertinent material has been assembled.

29. On the mode of presentation typical of the *ḥadîth*, cf. this writer, "Islam and Hellenism," *Scientia*, XLIV (1950), 24, n. 2 (French ed., p. 14, n. 6). Reprinted, with modification, in G. E. von Grunebaum, *Islam: Essays on the Nature and Growth of a Cultural Tradition* ("American Anthropological Association Memoirs," No. 81 [1955]).

METHODS OF APPROACH

FRITZ MEIER

I SHOULD like to emphasize a point of view which is well known but, it seems to me, frequently not sufficiently appreciated. What I hope to do by stressing this perspective is to get up a certain impetus which will set in motion our discussion.

Before the present scholarly epoch there was, as you know, a time when the literary heritage of past generations was read, not as history, but rather for enjoyment. Homer was read in a mood similar to that in which we read novels today. And the philosophers were read with the unconcealed intention either to measure oneself against them or to quarry stones from them for one's own philosophy. Reading was done for combat or for edification.

Only in more recent times did attention turn to source connections, and everywhere it was asked: Whence does the author take this and that? To which chain of development does the author belong? Or: What is the origin of the constituent elements in his intellectual achievement? Again, it is only in more recent times that our judgment of the intellectually significant personalities of the past has been made to depend on a historical analysis of this kind. By adopting this approach, the study of civilization limits itself to one level of research, namely, to the inquiry into origins. True, this approach allows a fairly free rein to the drive to the "Mothers," but at the same time it has led to a separation of knowledge into fields of history and science.[1] As a consequence of the historical approach the haste with which one book is exchanged for another has increased, and it has become the general habit to read at books only from one point of view, namely, the point of view of one's own problem. All this is well known. It shows strikingly in the indexes without which a book nowadays is unusable and in the great book collections without which scholarship—to be precise, historical scholarship—seems unthinkable.

It would be a mistake, and it certainly is not my intention, to lament this development, by which we all live and which has produced and is sure to go on producing such great achievements. Also the clinging to the word, the insistence on the documentary proof, the faith in the transmitted testimonies, which go hand in hand with this development, have opened up many a path and have prevented many a false step. No one can afford to deprecate with impunity research into the sources and philological method for as much as one moment. But general considerations as well as experiences repeated a thousand fold do show that a historizing science, when cultivated one-sidedly, forever inquiring into sources and schools, forever trying to reconstruct phenomena inductively from the word, not only has a destructive educational effect but does in the end, even as far as mere knowledge is concerned, find itself holding nothing but knots and wires in its hands; it often breeds unviable phantoms and frequently reaches quite patently mistaken results. Besides, the question, "Who gets what from whom?" can be continued *ad infinitum*, and recognized "aliases," like "neo-Platonic," "Ptolemaic," "Greek," "Arabic," etc., can again be dissolved and replaced by the names of their substrates. The tracing-back of cultural phenomena to peoples or countries like "Iran," etc., is quite often like fighting one's own shadow, since the concepts "Iranian" or "Semitic" are far too imprecise. How many elements of the so-called "Iranian" culture are not actually "Semitic"! So not a little of what one would at first blush describe as "Iranian" could in the end turn out to be "Semitic," with all due honor to its having at some point been borrowed directly from Iran—if such a transfer has been proved! In order to avoid here from the outset the sowing of seeds of error, it is absolutely necessary to study the matter first, or at least simultaneously, apart from all proper names—yes, perhaps even to leave all reports aside and to consider the specific phenomenon directly—in short, to strive for a knowledge of facts rather than of words. By this method two gains are made.

First, the understanding of the phenomena improves the understanding of the literature. It is a platitude that at bottom only a zoölogist is able to write a history of zoölogy. I have been told that C. H. Becker (d. 1933) said, after resigning from the Prussian Ministry of Education, that *now* he would like to write on history. M. Henry Corbin confided to me that he refuses to write on anything and everything Iranian; he feels familiar only with *la spiritualité iranienne* into which he, as a philosopher with existentialist interests, has penetrated.

Moreover, the sources will be understood at a more profound level, for, if one previously has had a concrete experience, the unspoken too will be understood, and one can interpret what is said from what was left unsaid. Since the factual background and the wider contexts are known, many contradictions contained in the wording can be separated out from the subject matter and resolved. It is well known that the clinging to the word has been most calamitous for the theologians, about whom the Buddhist legend of the blind men and the elephant, or at least its Muslim adaptation (in Tauḥîdî, Ghazzâlî, Sanâ᾿î, Maulânâ-i Rûmî, and ᶜAzîz-i Nasafî), has been told.[2] But the same goes for us philologists. We sometimes believe we discover a contradiction in facts in a change of concepts, when the intention of the authors has been only to throw light on one and the same thing. Conversely, the same term may be used for different things. Who does not think in this connection of the contradictory sayings of the Ṣûfîs about the extinction of self, the will, the being, which considered in relation to their objects prove perfectly justifiable or even obvious, and in any case completely unsuitable as the dividing line between different schools—although we do not mind admitting that sometimes the history of a word or of a turn of phrase can be interesting and revealing.

When we work on the basis of the facts themselves, the further possibility opens up of discovering faults in the tradition, of filling in gaps in the text or at least of guessing the implied meaning, of correcting mistakes, and otherwise of forming an opinion about the achievement of the author. To take another example from Ṣûfism: from the nature of the phenomenon of mystical education as such it is to be expected that the visions of the novice while he is guided by the master will also play a certain part in Ṣûfism. Yet the clear and unambiguous tradition on this matter begins only with Najm al-Dîn al-Kubrà (d. 1221). His teacher, ᶜAmmâr al-Bidlîsî (d. between 1194 and 1207), has left two tracts, but in neither of these is there any information on this kind of Ṣûfî education. If it were not for the fact that Kubrà happens to drop some remarks, a wordbound philologist might feel justified in construing a divergence of positions between the two men and in denying that the Ṣûfîs before Kubrà led their pupils with the help of their visions. In actual fact, however, Kubrà introduces an innovation merely into literary history. The written tradition is not life itself, and a philologist who does not know the phenomena will ever so often, with all his documentation, misconstruct the reality of history.

In the second place—and here we come one step closer to the theme of our Conference—a knowledge of life and the recognition of a direct relation of man to life will induce consideration of the question of origins from a higher vantage point. It is again a platitude that the African as well as the European, each for himself and ever anew, apprehends his environment and comes to grips with it. No one advances the view that the Greeks borrowed the concept of "heaven" from the Chinese or vice versa. Also, statements like "The brook murmurs," and questions like "Whence does the world come?" can occur in the culture of American Indians and in the culture of Asian peoples without a borrowing being assumed. These statements and questions may then evolve into intricate speculations without there being any need, in principle, necessarily to attribute the occurrence of such complicated statements to influences from a different culture. It is true that diachronic and synchronic connections on the historical level *may* exist; they have been attested a thousand times and often practically force themselves on one, but, if man's actual facing of things is not taken into consideration and everywhere only proofs for borrowings are sought, one is bound to be misled, and especially in the field of religious fantasy. Although the force of a dominant tradition happens to be extraordinarily strong in this particular area,[3] psychology and comparative mythology have shown that under certain conditions such as in dreams, but also in classificatory thought, a modern consciousness, too, may produce concepts that are known to us from the myths of the ancients and of the primitives. That is to say, certain principles of classification are inherent in the human psyche and carry through all ages and all peoples. C. G. Jung calls "archetypes" those ever-recurring main motifs according to which man's imagination has always been forming the world and especially the unknown world of the metaphysical. If we venture to advance beyond, or to retrograde from, the Kantian *Critique of Pure Reason* and admit that in a sense the percepts inhere in the things themselves rather than solely in the apparatus of our apprehension and cognition, we may even speak *stricto sensu* of an internal world which would constitute as real an object of human experience as the external world. On the basis of our anthropological and psychological premises, and also perhaps of a certain *tanabbuʾ* ("prophetic behavior") and *tawâjud* ("imitative ecstasy")—in other words, by driving the shaft of cognition into the depth of the phenomenological rather than into the breadth of the historical level—we unquestionably assure ourselves of the possibility of allowing for the coexistence in different religious cultures of like phenomena that do not possess any historical connection.

For this, examples need hardly be looked for. Apart from the fact that religion is a need of each human soul (even where this is being denied), the different forms of religion and the questions connected with this very differentiation are spread all over the world. Everywhere there exists a religious doctrine side by side with a religious experience: frequently there exists the tension between "church" and "state," mysticism and the law.

To the religious concepts which occur everywhere belong the ideas of the Divine Man, of the maternal goddess, of a triad, a tetrad, etc., of gods. So far it has not been possible to trace the idea of incarnation of the extreme Shîᶜa to Christianity or to Mazdaism. In Christianity, only *one* man is God; and if in some Shîᶜite heresies the imâm is called the "Spirit of God," which is a name given to Christ in Islâm, this only illustrates the well-known statement that such concepts always tend to be joined to already existing traditions, that in most cases they indeed attract, magnet-like, a whole lot of frequently very heterogeneous traditions. Let us only consider Ibn ᶜArabî (d. 1240)!

On closer inspection the divine light incarnated in the imâm of the extreme Shîᶜa has to be distinguished from the Mazdean *khwarnah*, the Tyche. A Persian king is left by the Tyche when he falls into sin. The pontiff-caliph of the Shîᶜites, as the carrier of the divine spark, is unable to commit a sin; as the possessor of this spark, he is right even where according to appearances and the external law he is wrong. The mutual contact of the three religions reduces, upon closer inspection, to the idea of the god-man and to the identification of the divine with the light, that is, to a number of basic gnostic notions which occur now in this, now in that, shape and which, even if some elements may have spread by external transmission, must have been fed on the whole from internal sources.

To say, finally, a few words about Ṣûfism, the phenomena that are traceable to the oneness of human nature do include, after all, certain forms of psychic training, like the constant remembrance of God, or *dhikr*. In different variations it is known in early Christian monasticism (under the name of *mnêmê Theou* or *mnêmê Iêsou*) as well as in India and in the Far East and, in connection with it, the seeking of solitude, frequently in caves. No one will construe a historical connection between the Ṣûfî *khalwa* and the cave of Trophonios, but typologically they do belong together. Indeed, many mystical experiences are archetypal phenomena. I believe Otto Weinreich is mistaken when he assumes that the so-called "formula of reciprocal identity" of the mystics ("I am you and you are I," and the like) originated independently in two countries, Egypt and India: from Egypt he sees one stream go forth into the mysticism of Islâm and another into the mysticism of the Occident; besides, he perceives another stream coming from India into the mysticism of Islâm.[4] I consider this assumption mistaken, for this formula obtrudes itself everywhere on the mystical experience. Even if it were possible to follow an out-of-the-way formulation of this idea on its migrations, it could only have traveled in conjunction with an original mystical experience or a concrete objective fitting its description.

And what holds for God holds for the Devil—experiences involving the Devil can be original, too. In a passage of his *Fawâʾiḥ al-jamâl*, Najm al-Dîn al-Kubrà, in Turkestan, reports on the peculiar effect on man of the Devil's whisperings (*khawâṭir*). Under the impact of the Devil, man finds himself in a state of internal irritation; he is ceaselessly on the alert, and his limbs are as though crushed with stones.[5] Three hundred years later St. Teresa will write in Spain: "If the address has been the Devil's, it does not leave any good, but rather a bad aftermath. . . . Not to speak of the great drought that remains, an unrest springs up in the soul . . . of which one does not know whence it comes. The soul appears to resist, it is perplexed and sad and does not know why. It is annoyed and excited and does not feel any good effect."[6] *Khawâṭir* and *palabras* are hardly to be separated from the *logismoi* of a Joannes Klimakos (sixth century A.D.) even though their experience is ever new; yet there does not seem to exist a bridge between Kubrà and Teresa, and so far I have nowhere discovered a common source. So we shall have to accept the recurrence of a primary experience.

I have suggested the dangers and deviations to which a philology is exposed when it is one-sidedly oriented to history. It is hardly necessary for me to point up expressly the dangers of a research that is one-sidedly oriented to phenomenology and which takes its departure from a phenomenological foreknowledge. In the field of the history of religion it would be only too easy to project one's own psychology into the past. How far would truth be left behind were one to connect as a matter of course the statements of the Koran with the psychology of Mohammed without reflecting that he owed a great many points to the traditions of older religious cultures. Let us also consider that there is no such independent learning as was claimed by Ibn Ṭufail (d. 1185) in his philosophical novel, *Ḥayy b.*

Yaqẓân. Actually people do lend each other support, and so a solid mass of "concretized mind" forms the foundation of each and every intellectual personality.

As it has always done, philology will continue to be the police of all historical science. The art of the true philologist and historian consists in integrating "horizontal," historically oriented research with "vertical," phenomenologically oriented research into a harmonious unity.

DISCUSSION

M. Abel has two remarks concerning details. Mr. Meier is doubtless right to criticize certain theories about "influences" and historical conditioning in cases in which he is able to point to the probability of an independent parallel development. But perhaps he has seen the problem from a limited point of view only. When, e.g., M. Asín Palacios treats the similarities between St. John of the Cross (1542–91) and certain aspects of Islamic mysticism, he not only emphasizes general parallels between the two currents of mysticism but points out at the same time certain particular expressions, certain special conceptions and ways of proceeding, which seem to M. Abel to furnish clear proof of influence.

Mr. von Grunebaum mentioned Ibn ᶜArabî's (1165–1240) effort to reconcile the veneration of "saints" with Muslim religious doctrine. M. Abel has been intrigued for a long time by the development the figure of the Prophet himself has taken in Muslim minds. Mohammed was gradually deified, attracting—in the course of the Muslim-Christian polemics—some of the divine attributes of Christ. M. Abel mentions the mystical Beautiful Names applied to Mohammed and the stories of Christ which are told of Mohammed. One should assert the presence of "influences" only where the circumstances and the spiritual dispositions on both sides suggest them; but they should be admitted where such circumstances and dispositions do exist.

Mr. Stadtmüller, from the point of view of the historian, explains that modern history, though it should never emancipate itself from the methods of "philology," ought to give more interest to phenomenology: the study of actual facts and groups of facts and their inherent principles of evolution. Only both elements together, phenomenology and "philological" study of influences, reflect the point of view of the modern historian. Our present manuals treating the methods of history are generally eighty years behind the actual state of historiography.

Mr. Minorsky, thanking Mr. von Grunebaum for his detailed presentation—he calls it a highly abstract *muqaddima*—thinks it should be taken as a guide for the discussion. Mr. von Grunebaum's pan-Islamic survey of the Muslim countries, which stresses the religious factor and finds a religious impulse for every action, seems to him to resemble an earlier conception of medieval history where everything was explained by Christian motivations. For Mr. Minorsky Islamic religion is a mirror into which every class, every generation, looks to discover itself.

Mr. Lewis judges that Mr. von Grunebaum's paper shows very well how the Muslim identifies himself subjectively with his religion. But are there, for instance, military and political methods recognized as universally Muslim? Mr. Lewis appreciates the classification of tradition into a great tradition and a little tradition; he would like to know more about the conflict between the two.

M. Cahen has two remarks to make about the general methodological questions raised by Mr. Stadtmüller. He thinks Mr. Stadtmüller is right to stress the importance of the study of the independent development of civilizations, for recently scholars have been looking for "influences" everywhere. This direction of research seems of questionable value, so long as there is no tangible evidence (such as literary conformity, which proves a citation) for the suggested "influence." Otherwise the limits between influence and parallel development will be subject to infinite discussion.

Influences, moreover, can never go deeper than the basic disposition and situation of those influenced allow. M. Cahen cites as an example the influence of Greek philosophy upon Islâm and, later, that of Islamic philosophy upon the West. He recalls the booklet of R. Paret (*Der Islam und das griechische Bildungsgut* [Tübingen, 1950]) which comes to the conclusion that in both cases the ones influenced took over what had an immediate interest for them.

M. Cahen warns of the opposite danger, too: it would consist in studying a society as an absolutely isolated and self-sufficient unit. He suggests simple *comparison* instead of the study of "influences." If two societies present a number of common characteristics, we will have to consider whether such common traits are found within the particular field we are concerned with, and we will have to try to find the reasons for similarities and dissimilarities within that field.

M. Cahen, returning to Mr. Minorsky's statement, thinks that Muslim history in general is about a hundred years behind the stage of development of European history. Trying to make up for this time lag, we must above all not confine ourselves to only one aspect of history but try to embrace all the activities of an epoch at once.

M. Abel, taking his departure from a passage of al-Jâḥiẓ (d. 869) mentioned in Mr. von Grunebaum's paper and from the *Risâla fî al-radd ʿalà al-Naṣârà*, suggests that what he calls the "historical essence" of a people may reveal itself in a nation's aptitude or incapacity for certain techniques. He gives the example of architecture, daring and vigorous in the Greek and Roman world, but dependent on foreign techniques and workmen in Muslim countries from Umayyad Spain to the Syria of the Crusaders. Comparison of the medical techniques of the two areas may give a different picture. He thinks, carrying Mr. Minorsky's suggestion further, that by concentrating our interest on such problems we may rid ourselves of the all-theological conception of Muslim life.

Mr. Spuler stresses the importance of the sentiment of unity within Islâm. Inside the Sunnite community it was much stronger than it was among Christian countries. Governments adopting the point of view suggested by the expression *mirʾât al-Islâm* reinforced, at least outwardly, Islamic religion. Religion was not only a mirror for people; rather, because of its dogmatic force, was it a norm which they accepted as a standard of measurement for themselves. Without this normative force of religion, processes such as the mingling of the Persian and Greek elements with the original Islamic factors could not be envisaged. Eventually such melting processes tended to produce new questions and solutions which outgrew the restricted bases of primitive Islâm.

We have to take into consideration, also, the fact that Islâm as a whole has shown a certain common development, independent of the different languages of the empire.

Mr. Lewis adds that he agrees as far as the sentiment of identity is concerned; as regards practical achievements, such as political and military effectiveness, a good deal of what is called "influence" simply means "prisoners of war."

Mr. von Grunebaum agrees to the charge of overabstraction laid against him by Mr. Minorsky, but he still subscribes to "pan-Islamism." He adds that it is unmistakable that in science and in political theory great care was taken not to pursue investigations which could not be reconciled with a religious line of thought. Even in studying scientific phenomena, Muslims are interested in tracing the ways of God. When it comes to explaining himself, a Muslim falls back to a purely religious type of self-interpretation and always withdraws to a line of defense which is religious. Besides, the cleavage which exists in our civilization between the political and the religious spheres does not exist to the same extent at all in the Muslim world.

Recent events do not always reflect what Muslims actually wanted to do. The sentiment of Islâm remains entire despite territorial losses.

As to the conflicts between the great and the little traditions, the guidebooks to the places of pilgrimage are specimens of the desperate attempt made by the spokesmen of the great tradition to offer a justification for the little tradition.

NOTES

1. Church history, too, has its origin in theological controversy.

2. F. Rosenthal, *Islamic Culture*, XIV (1940), 406; Fritz Meier, "Das Problem der Natur im esoterischen Monismus," *Eranos-Jahrbuch*, XIV (1946), 174–80; English translation in *Spirit and Nature: Papers from the Eranos Yearbooks* ("Bollingen Series," Vol. XXX, No. 1 [New York, 1954]), pp. 166–70; cf. also A. Zieseniss, *Zeitschrift der deutschen morgenländischen Gesellschaft*, XCIX (1945–49), 267–73.

3. I should like to point to the observations of Eduard Norden in the introduction to his commentary on the sixth book of the *Aeneid* (*P. Vergilius Maro, Aeneis Buch VI* [Leipzig and Berlin, 1926], p. 7, n. 3): "He who has worked in the field of the history of religion realizes that only too often an apparent *historical* connection turns out to be but an illusion and has to give way to the colorless notion of a mere *analogy* which is to be accounted for by a spontaneous origin. The more comprehensive an investigator's knowledge of peoples that are far removed from ancient civilization the less readily will he operate with the assertion of a historically demonstrable continuity. But this skepticism, too, must keep within limits." Norden goes on to offer two examples of historically demonstrable continuity. Bousset and Reitzenstein have frequently been much less careful in this regard. Gressmann's method, too, has produced some strange bubbles (e.g., what he has to say on the baptism of Jesus in the river Jordan).

4. *Archiv für Religionswissenschaft*, XIX (1916–19), 165 ff.

5. Cf. my edition (in press), §§ 8 and 34.

6. *Vida*, chaps. xxv and xxx.

PERSPECTIVES

ROBERT BRUNSCHVIG

THE progress which Muslim history, understood in the widest sense possible, has made in this century, while certainly remarkable on some points, is, in the last analysis, quite limited. Whole sectors are still dark, although fairly easily accessible documents would permit their being illuminated, if not with an intense light, at least with information suited to ordering solid facts and putting major problems into place. There are whole periods and regions which remain outside the field of systematic exploration and for which the collection and elementary criticism of the sources have yet to be done. But the gap is greatest where research breaks away from the pure history of events to try to get some solid information about the fundamental realities of living. Certain of these enormous lacunae were admitted and deplored by the best of our recently deceased colleagues. "The history of Muslim religion has yet to be written," observed Wensinck.[1] "The history of trade inside the Muslim countries remains completely unwritten," Sauvaget declared.[2] And one of France's most brilliant historians, not himself an Arabist, expressed both his scorn and his skepticism when he said: "We do not know Islâm's social history. Are we ever to know it?"[3]

It would do no good to multiply references, since we have no intention of making an inventory here or of tracing the causes of the ailment. Difficulties peculiar to Islamology, such as the relative youth of the discipline and the small number of its qualified experts, probably justify such backwardness. But that is not the point that interests us here. What we want to emphasize at the beginning of these few pages is the harm that the kind of inadequacies criticized above —and others also—do to Islamology itself as well as to general history. Islamology is—or ought to be—one of the major branches of that history, because of the immense number of human beings it embraces and because of the fundamental nature of the problems which it encounters—or should encounter—at every step. The omissions that we have deplored strikingly limit its part in the network of ever accumulating investigations and information on which a valid knowledge of the evolution of humanity is being tentatively built. Muslim history can retain a restricted kind of usefulness if it improves its position along roads it is presently following; but such an isolation with respect to wider streams of scholarship, besides rightly alienating the majority of non-Orientalist scholars, threatens to desiccate Muslim scholarship and to afflict it in its turn with just that stiffening at the joints which for several centuries has paralyzed the people it studies.

We should like modestly and briefly to present some reflections here, in the hope of bringing some new life into the historical examination of the Muslim world through a consideration of problems of the first order of interest to the general history of "civilizations."

We shall first state the following central question, around which we shall attempt to group our observations: Is it legitimate to speak about "Muslim civilization"? To what degree can this notion be justified and defined?

The faithful of the Islamic religion have from early times constituted a goodly sized body of human beings, which has not stopped growing even in our day, occupying a more and more extensive, almost continuous, territory, roughly oriented in a direction parallel to the equator but noticeably overflowing any fixed geographical zone.[4] Does this population belong, from the very fact of the religious distinctiveness of its members, to some specific "civilization," crossing the barriers of place and time? This is far from a matter of course. In any general classification of historical civilizations—there is no completely satisfactory one today—it seems likely that the large-scale criteria cannot uniformly be of the same nature. The fundamental cultural characteristic can very well have been at one time a material technique, at another a belief. The religious criterion is admissible, at this high taxonomic level and for large populations, if it stands out as a predominant characteristic which differentiates the multitude of believers from the rest of humanity in an extensive area and in all sorts of cultural fields; and that is true only if the religion in the case can be regarded as a determining factor, not only for feelings and for thoughts, but also for the many public and private branches of human activity. Is this true for Islâm?

It is, naturally, not the tentacle-like normative attempts of classical Islâm, that of the severe theoreticians, that should suggest our answer to us but an objective consideration of reality, which everyone knows is often far from a close fit to what the doctors teach. In examining this reality, it is also proper to avoid confusing the truly "Islamic" character of the civilization studied with the depth or sincerity of religious feelings or with a sufficient respect for ritual directives. In spite of the fact that the one is frequently bound up with the other, there is not any necessary concomitance; and if we want to treat cultural history, properly speaking, and not religious history in the narrow sense, when we speak of Muslim civilization, we ought to base our studies essentially not on the quality of belief or the degree of religious observations, as some have a tendency to do,[5] but on the effects this belief exerts in many cultural sectors, from humble material usages all the way to the most complex or most exalted psychocultural manifestations.

At first glance, this condition seems to be satisfied at certain times, in certain countries; for example, in the Middle Ages, in the Arab or Arabized countries. It is true that even in so favorable an instance, which it is tempting a priori to consider as optimum, some closer observations, which may seem to be reservations, must be stated: some non-Muslims, in compact nuclei, participated then in more than one aspect of this "Muslim civilization" and contributed to it; on the other side of the relationship, the Islamized Arab Bedouins were undergoing Islâm's imprint on their mode of existence in only the most limited way. Among the urban population as among the rural, the new religion seems to have had no noticeable effect on the general level of techniques (for their diffusion in detail the case was otherwise), so that the material substructure, which in other cases often has a predominant taxonomic validity, does not bear out our principle of discrimination at all. And yet the Muslim religion's impact is so manifestly powerful, in the case we have just mentioned, on so many elements of human culture—language, arts, literature, ethics, politics, social structure and activities, law—that it would be impossible, taking the situation as a whole, to refuse to recognize an autonomous civilization there which was marked not just by the Islamic *element* but by the Islamic *factor*.

At the other extreme of the Islamic experiment, it is well known that Islâm, among many colored populations, black and yellow, who have officially and sincerely adopted it, exerts only a very weak influence on most aspects of human existence. This constitutes a sometimes transitory cultural condition, which may be only a first stage, rather rapidly followed by deeper and more extensive transformations; but it is one which sometimes also makes its appearance, over the course of the centuries, as a more or less admitted and lasting situation. The expression "Muslim civilization" ought not to be applied to these types of culture which are, so to speak, marginal, except with much reticence and caution. It would probably be wiser to see them as mixed types, still largely attached to African or Far Eastern civilizations clearly distinct from Islâm.

Other less clear-cut cases complicate the problem and may leave the observer puzzled; for example, that of the North African Berbers, of whom many, remaining Berber-speaking, also refused to accept the fundamental legal norms of Muslim personal law in spite of their undeniable Muslim faith. And yet it could not be said that these people differ radically in their way of life and thought from their Arabized kin. The divergences which exist, and which sociologists like to emphasize, do not seem sufficient to place this particular culture in the category of the mixed types. It is probably more correct to include it, just as it is, in the totality of "Muslim civilization," while we are careful to bring out its partially aberrant character. Thus we are led, according to this summary statement of our position, to consider some "degrees" in the idea of "Muslim civilization"—to picture a sort of series of levels, a gradation going from a hard central historicogeographical core toward the more moderated forms, and from these to the peripheral regions subject to frank copartnership of cultures.

Shall we include on one of the levels of our framework, on the edges if not at the heart of Muslim civilization, a country such as contemporary Turkey or, speaking more broadly, for the present or future, any Muslim state that is modernized and Westernized? It would, I think, be premature to decide this. Who can be sure that, despite all the secularizations, all the economic, legal, and social explosions, Islâm will be able in the course of time somehow to recreate its active specificity and to manifest once again its power as a common primordial factor? If this happens, a "Muslim civilization" may be perpetuated or remade in a transformed world. If the case be contrary, the preservation of Islâm as a religious faith, as a moral attitude, would not exclude the passing-away of "Muslim civilization," absorbed as it would be in a possible type of ecumenical civilization the major criterion of which would no longer be religious at all. Islâm would then be resolved into a personal or collective belief which, while deeply affecting feelings and ideas, would no longer have any taxonomic value on the scale of the great cultural categories that would divide mankind.

Let us return to the traditional "Muslim civilization," however, and to the degrees which we thought we were able to uncover there, still with considerable imprecision. It would be an important task for the Islamologist to base this quite provisional and impressionistic classification on definite, rank-ordered criteria, to make subtler gradations in it, to correct it as required, and to let the general study of civilizations, as well as of the very concept "civilization," benefit from the method of research and the results obtained. This hard but exciting undertaking could not be well carried out except through close, objective inquiry free from any aprioristic or prejudicial element. Preparatory work, perhaps rather lengthy, is probably necessary. By this I mean descriptive monographs which go thoroughly into various epochs, countries, and social levels. Although these would sometimes be without obvious major interest in themselves, they would take on direction and a dimension of depth as supporting materials and horizontal analyses providing a base and point of departure for "vertical" soundings. In any case, the discovering and ordering of criteria will not be solidly grounded unless a rather close and detailed inventory is available, both richer in substance and more extensive than are, at present, the data given by our Islamology.

To be sure, analyses and soundings of this type involve cutting up and dissecting the societies studied, a procedure not above criticism; they risk being, at least in part, arbitrary; and, above all, by their very nature they can be accused of disfiguring reality many times over, by dividing it. But is this not the fate of all science, the ineluctable condition of knowledge? It is simply that precautions need to be taken against an excessive or eccentric schematization; in our case they will be severe. It will be remembered as an axiom that no human institution is totally detachable from its "context," which alone clarifies it and permits it to be understood in the proper way. The institution will not be evaluated in its external manifestations only; an effort will be made to penetrate its intimate spirit, to fix its eminently variable tonality hidden under identical gestures and identical names. Care will be taken of the fact that isolated characteristics, strong and expressive though they may be, are not always as decisive as are combinations of characteristics, and these combinations are capable of infinite variety.

Thus the results of the inquiry that is being recommended do not permit guesswork in advance, even by those who think they can see some well-defined lines of cleavage. But it can be foreseen that on more than one score they will undermine some assertions which there is a tendency to regard as postulates today. In such matters the most obvious and attractive thesis is usually far from being the best.

There is good ground for distrusting simplistic theses here. The linguistic argument, for example, which, it is true, is based on an important and easily observed phenomenon, runs a good chance of turning out, upon examination, not to be the major criterion. An illustrious Arabist, whom I deeply respect, writes: "It would only be exaggerating the expression of a correct observation, were one to say that a Muslim people has Muslim institutions just to the extent that the idiom it speaks is close to the language of the Koran."[6] Is this so certain? To mention only a single objection that seems to me to invalidate the proposition, did not the Persians and Turks embody "Muslim civilization" in the course of their history better than did the Arabic-speaking nomads of the desert? Would not giving pre-eminence to the spoken language—which is also to be distinguished carefully from the cultured language, the vocabulary of which is separately diffused—be only a snare and a delusion? The idiomatic aspect has its value, which is certainly large; it is not necessarily to be given complete preference for our purposes here.

Is it more legitimate to envisage, as a working and hence provisional hypothesis, that the degree of a group's "Muslim civilization" varies above all with the degree of application of Muslim law in all the various domains of life, as that law was fixed by the doctors? To take a more precise formula: with the degree of application of the *fiqh?* Perhaps there would be room for initial criticism, from a sociological standpoint, in the reference to an ideal, sometimes artificial construct rather than to concrete, impartially analyzed facts. The *fiqh*, from another standpoint, however totalitarian it may seem, is far from covering the whole field of human activities, at least in a decisive and methodical way. It admits its own limits and shares generously with secular regimentation, with local customs, or with discretionary judgment, being limited, in many legal matters, to loose directives (portions on public law and penal law) or to elementary ethical precepts (portions on business law). In all the fields of life, too, many usages exist which, while traditionally linked with Islâm for centuries in the minds of many Muslims, would find only a doubtful or uneasy support in the *fiqh:* in matters of art, clothing, and eating habits, notably, and including some ritual practices indorsed by the most scrupulous orthodoxy. Lastly, the *fiqh*, which in one sense is so characteristic of classical Islâm, has notwithstanding this no monopoly on transmitting the imperatives of Muslim spirituality into the real world: this spirituality antedates the *fiqh* by at least a century; and during the course of the Middle Ages, before a sort of lasting compromise was worked out, the mystic movement, for example, tended to orient its adepts' behavior into paths very different from the ways of the *fiqh*.

If we should hope to enlarge this narrow base by turning from the letter to the spirit of the prescriptions considered or—better—by appealing to the political or moral theology professed by the Islamic masters, the following qualification would be required: the doctrine is not unified. The *fiqh* itself is, to tell the truth, not one; but, if we restrict ourselves to its fundamental positive rules, divergences between the schools have sociological importance in only a restricted number of cases. When it is, on the contrary, a question of more extensive or higher teachings, which affect dogma or govern a general attitude, differences do appear, and sometimes a split occurs; opposite doctrines stand over against one another; a seemingly unique doctrine bears divergent meanings at various times and places. The historian need not, it seems from all that we know, take sides among sects or tendencies; any of these which invokes the name of Islâm is not, for him, heretical or external to Islâm. Also, he is not engaged in awarding them a common patent of authenticity; he refuses to work for their doctrinal reconciliation, still less to vindicate, from far or near, a militant pan-Islamism. But it is his duty, while noting their respective parts and places in historical evolution, to consider them entitled to equality in so far as they have been inspirational of "Muslim civilization" or of some varied forms of that civilization. This amounts to saying that varied cultural forms do not, we think, necessarily correspond to diverse degrees of "Muslim civilization" but may, with an approximately equal degree of Islamic impregnation, concretize some disparate *modalities* of Islâm.

The consideration of Muslim doctrine as a cultural factor, or, to put it better, its assimilation, on the cultural level, to the "Islâm factor," raises some additional points. This doctrine, rudimentary and unorganized until the end of the first century of the hegira, became, in the course of the second and third centuries, a system that had grown very substantial in various directions and one that was eager to demonstrate coherence within each school or explicit tendency. During this fruitful formative period, Islâm was already—it is undeniable—a powerful factor; but this factor, whatever originality it had in some points and in its texture as a whole, still resulted from multiple components drawing heavily on older civilizations. Islâm thus took its place in a process that assigned it, in many cultural sectors, a role both as cause and as effect: a double aspect which it is often artificial to separate, and one which historical analysis has not come close to elucidating. Moreover, the great period of formation once consummated, the doctrine, now strongly constituted and already sufficiently diversified according to the principal schools, was further affirmed, at the same time ramifying in detail on the primitive trunk. Except in the contemporary period, ulterior developments, whatever interest they may present in themselves, were practically all accessory in relation to the basic elaboration. It follows that, appearing less and less, with the passage of time, as a reflection of the social reality of the moment, the doctrine would better lend itself to examination as a factor at this secondary stage than when it began.

The task would almost always be very difficult, however, if we attached a notion of strict and unadorned causal relation to the term "factor." It would certainly be more profitable and also more legitimate to consider Muslim doctrine as a factor, not only when it happens to introduce a new solution from its own resources or brings about a new solution directly or indirectly, but also each time that, having integrated an interior or foreign solution into its system and colored it in its own way, it contributed to getting it adopted or maintained. How many practices, which have nothing Islamic about them in principle, have been naturalized as Muslim to the point of becoming characteristic of Islâm, thanks to the support of traditional education! It would even no doubt be proper to go outside the limits of traditional Muslim doctrine, as taught by the masters, in order to grant validity and attention to the Muslim collective consciousness wherever it was closely related to Islâm and made some practice or some institution, marginal to official theory, a part of Islâm. The specifically Islamic quality of a cultural element might well, in more than one case, owe nothing to its origin, but simply express the fact that Islâm, by taking it up, put its mark upon it or tended to appropriate it.

Let us now return to where we started when we were maintaining the necessity of fixing adequate taxonomic criteria. Whatever the major criterion may be which we decide definitively to adopt, it would not by itself completely resolve the problem. If it were of a relatively simple nature (language is a model of this), its insufficiency would soon strike us, and auxiliary criteria would be necessary for any rational classification. If it were of an already complex nature (model: the application of the *fiqh*), it would itself need to be diversified, to be subdivided into subcriteria, whether these were equivalent among themselves or arranged in a rank order according to the multiple aspects of human activity that we are led to examine. There must be an expectation of varied associations of characteristics, of overlappings, from one group to the other (as in the same group, at different periods). Just as isoglosses for various linguistic phenomena between related dialects do not perfectly and completely fit each other, it must not be anticipated that the boundaries for the diverse cultural elements will exactly coincide among the provinces of Islâm. One need only think of the triple demarcation which is sometimes made along lines of political order, language, and religion that stubbornly refuse to coincide (and the tracing of lines is itself not always possible)! A notorious example is that of Iraq vis-à-vis Iran, the Arabic language vis-à-vis Persian, Sunnism vis-à-vis Imamian Shîʿism. Associated characteristics, commonly reacting one upon another, contribute by the very variety of their combinations to the cultural differentiation of groups, to their peculiar *tonality*, which itself must find a place in the classificatory criteria.

We are touching here, when we take up the notion of association of characteristics in varied ways, on a methodological problem of the first magnitude: that of "correlations." Nothing could be more fruitful for the general knowledge of civilizations than the study of correlations, not only between this or that detailed trait, but, further and pre-eminently, between great cultural categories which are the principal sectors of human activity. There would be considerable interest in establishing and making precise, for the history of Muslim peoples, many correlations bearing on secular life as well as on religious life: economic life, for example, and its correlations with ethics, law, and social and political structure, would be a research subject which, if successfully handled, could not fail to be revealing. Correlation, to be sure, does not necessarily mean a causal relation;[7] if we define it as a nonaccidental concomitance of variation between two neighboring and related phenomena, it will express their at least partial interdependence, without prejudging the intimate nature of their relationships. Only in favored cases is it susceptible of being resolved into an explicit cause-and-effect relation. A rather serious difficulty awaits us in the demonstration of "nonaccidental," for the historian cannot as a general rule draw up "correlation tables" the way the statisticians do; he is constrained to satisfy himself with less clear indexes. But he must above all take into account that the material he works with is at once so fluid and so complex that the connections he discovers, suggestive as they may be, have nothing immutable or absolute about them.[8] Even Cuvier's old morphological correlations, which passed their test, are not without their limitations.

In this way the research to be undertaken for estimating the degree of "Muslim civilization" in certain fixed groups joins with sociological researches which the whole history of human civilization would be glad to draw upon. As for the Muslim peoples themselves, the comparison of their inner structure, spiritual as well as material, will be, almost certainly, better clarified. It is permissible to hope that a procedure of this kind will isolate the "principal facies" of these peoples' civilization[9] more sharply than we can legitimately do at present, at degrees of "Muslim civilization" which may equally well be close together as far apart. The facies, which may be subtly gradated in space and time, will divide in their turn into cultural types and subtypes. And this precisely stated classification might well bring into question the delimitations between groups and subgroups which considerations that are often superficial have made prevalent to the present day.[10]

All the preceding reflections point in the direction of Islâm's diversity, its plurality. To them would still need to be added an examination of the essential factors of differentiation: geography, pre-Islamic substratum, external influences, and perhaps above all—but this point is likely to remain perpetually clouded—ethnic background; their force has acted either to create or to develop culture along their own lines or to create obstacles and deviations. In the opposite direction, Islâm has acted strongly, whether with a conscious purpose or not, to unify in the same culture as much as possible the populations who have adopted it as a religion: the Pilgrimage to Mecca remains, because of its principle of unity and despite recognized differences in rites, the living symbol of this monistic drive. The attempt at unification has, furthermore, proceeded from different centers in the course of history; it has shown itself sometimes with a slow continuity, sometimes in widely separated, aggressive waves. From the struggle between these two contrary currents, one moving toward differentiation and the other toward homogeneity, there results, in a sometimes unstable equilibrium, the cultural condition of the Muslim peoples—not to be confused with their political situation, despite some obvious correlations. In some excellent comments an eminent specialist,[11] treating Islâm's art, emphasizes its "undeniable unity" at the same time as its diversity; it is only just possible that we have the right to hope that the "common characteristics" of this art and its "family resemblances" will one day, because of appropriate methods of investigation, cease to "vanish when analyzed," as this scholar seems to regret that they do.

As compared with uncertain search for "common characteristics" in this or that cultural element throughout Muslim history, something more useful might be obtained from the study of the great *common cultural problems* in that history. There are indeed such common problems, if not for all Muslim peoples, at least for those who have incontestably shown a high degree of Muslim civilization—and this does not necessarily mean of "civilization," without the adjective, at every moment—since the Middle Ages. The general evolutionary line of their cultural activity, even leaving the Muslim aspect aside, is very similar: the rhythm, especially, of this unfolding is very harmonious, with slight failures of fit (thought, for example, remained original in Spain, in the twelfth century, when it was no longer so in the east). To an archaic period of transformations, whose cadence we do not understand very well for a number of countries, there succeeds a development, with neither excessive haste nor slowness—an evolution which I should like to call "horotelic," borrowing this term from paleontology.[12] Then to the long centuries of stagnation that followed, the term "bradytelic" could be applied, while the accelerated evolution, the revolution that the Muslim world is undergoing under the shock of Western contacts, would obviously be "tachytelic." The description of these phases would profit from being made more precise from many angles, notably with respect to those correlations among the various cultural elements that we said a word about above. And it might be possible to infer from this some over-all views which would contribute to any future theory on the factors and modalities in the evolution of mankind.

There are, to tell the truth, some aspects of "Muslim civilization," especially in the fields of thought and art, the development of which has been admirably investigated, for three-quarters of a century, by first-class Islamists. These last years illustrate the brilliant continuation of their effort on certain points; our knowledge of the beginning and of the first great constructions of legal doctrine was renovated a short time ago, for example, thanks to a masterly work.[13] But since other essential aspects of the civilization are unexploited, these discoveries do not achieve their full effect. The evolutionary table of

Muslim societies, in the periods of initiation and of expansion, shows some considerable gaps which do not facilitate study of the connections. With much greater reason, we are unprovided with data on the subject of the long "bradytelic" period, less attractive in general to scholars. And, yet, how many questions arise about it! The process and the motifs of a civilization's enervation in themselves constitute fundamental historical problems.

Nor could anyone content himself, in matters of cultural history, with the summary notion of enervation or stagnation, and nothing beyond. There is never total immobility but very weak and very slow variation. Islâm is no exception to this rule; it would be well if we could perceive modalities of its application there. When already stiff at the joints, it still experienced some changes and novelties in certain of its aspects: political and military modifications, development of the brotherhoods, artistic evolution, and, to mention a small number of concrete phenomena at random, extension of the use of firearms and coffee and adoption of the use of tea. The power of religious expansion, at least to nonmonotheistic peoples, was in no way broken. Political greatness, a certain flowering of art, the maturity of some remarkable historians, could go along with a manifest incapacity for renewal, for true progress, in the order of techniques, science, literature, or high intellectual spirituality; the Ottoman Empire is Byzantium's worthy heir in this respect. Not that intelligence was asleep; not that the artisan groups themselves, highly conservative as they were, did not try, from time to time, to make something new: Leo Africanus describes how, in the *sûqs* of Cairo at the beginning of the sixteenth century, original masterpieces were prized and rewarded;[14] but there is justice in saying of the Muslim peoples of that time, to borrow a well-expressed formula, that "they turned in a horizontal spiral around their techniques." It was the same for their thinking. It is well known today that "proliferating detail" characterizes civilizations that are moving their feet in one spot but not going beyond themselves.[15]

The explanation for this failure to go beyond oneself, which we call stagnation or stiffening of the joints, in Islamic history, must be studied. In the absence of sure results, which it is risky to anticipate, we might at least aspire to hypotheses of a respectable probability based on many cross-checks. It would no doubt be necessary, while remaining wary of dangerous extrapolations, to confront Muslim facts under this heading with analogous facts in foreign societies. Sorts of tables of the presence or absence of elements would help to eliminate some claims about the cause of stagnation and to put the emphasis on the very probable determinants.[16] Complex determinants these would be, and combined among themselves, I imagine. In this process all those general efforts at the causal explanation of history that are current in our Western world would, with various degrees of acceptance, be passed through the sieve of reality. If the historian distrusts the overly absolute presentation they would get, he must nevertheless in fairness "give them their chance" by establishing the measure of their applicability in his field. Apart from all preconceived notions, there is at least one general phenomenon, the presence or absence of which is always highly meaningful: "borrowing." No cultural history lends itself better to studying this than does that of the Muslim peoples. The negative aspect of the "bradytelic" epoch contrasts with the positive aspect of early times[17] and of the contemporary period.[18] Borrowing is a powerful evolutionary factor, whether it reinforces or dislocates the inner structure of the borrower. Inaptitude for borrowing, by involuntary nonassimilation or by refusal, raises a psychosocial problem of its own, an examination of which leads to the heart of the living forces that govern evolution.

DISCUSSION

The discussion deals first with the problem of the relative dependence of Muslim dogma upon the Koran as compared with that of Christian dogma on the New Testament.

Mr. von Grunebaum recalls that the Koran is poorer in theological motifs than is the New Testament; it lacks, among other things, the concept of original sin.

Mr. Spuler admits that the Christian dogma is more independent of the New Testament than the Muslim dogma of the Koran, but only as far as its formulation, its expressions, are concerned.

Mr. Lewis points out that the Koran is textually and literally the Word of God, and, consequently, in Muslim dogmatics the Koranic formulation has to be preserved.

Mr. Caskel questions the possibility of any comparison, and Mr. Meier recalls the fact that the dogmatists of the Koran had to tackle basically the same problems as those of the New Testament, e.g., the question of the two natures.

M. Abel believes that it is not in the realm of comprehensibility or incomprehensibility of dogmas that we must look for an explanation of the problem of the expansion of Islâm and of its impenetrability by Christian missions. When we go back to the great christological quarrels of Byzantine history, we see that the adherents of the different positions were not individual people who raised philosophical questions but masses who reacted to certain sociological stimuli. A significant case is that of St. Cyril (376–444); he was a popular leader who knew how to give the masses the feeling of their existence, cohesion, and power. The movement of his famous Parabolani implied a popular reaction against a hated aristocracy which had remained pagan and which was liquidated morally and physically by the Christian masses. On the other hand, the Synod of Ephesus (431) marks the opposition of the Egyptian people to the Byzantines.

Considering the problem in this light, we realize that it must have been above all social and political motives, not dogmatic argumentation, which fostered the adherence of the conquered nations to Islâm. If in the time of the conquest, according to a somewhat questionable tradition, the grandfather of St. John of Damascus (d. before 754) came to terms with the invaders, the Christians had certainly not the intention of submitting themselves to the new creed. Later they gradually accepted it, as soon as—from a social, political, and economic point of view—it became in their interest to do so. It is not only in the Balkans that we find Christians who adhere externally to Islâm; a testimony to the same situation has come down to us in the treatise of al-Jâḥiẓ (d. 869) against the Christians (trans. J. Finkel, *Journal of the American Oriental Society*, XLVII [1927], 327), in which the author recalls the formula: "What is in the heart is in the heart." External adherence is quite common; first Christians turn Muslim for social reasons, political and economic advantages; later they enter into the Muslim hierarchy in order to safeguard those same advantages and to amplify them.

As concerns the present defensive position of Islâm in the face of the Christian missions, M. ABEL thinks that there is one thing we should never forget when speaking of Islamic matters: there are at least three different periods in Islâm. There is a time of conquest and assimilation, one of elaboration and settlement, and one of reaction, which may be called one of stagnation as well. It is this period of stagnation we have to consider. It is in that time that the work of al-Ghazzâlî (1059–1111) appeared in a Muslim world which had nearly exhausted all its resources, humanly and materially speaking, and which was conscious of the fact. The reform of al-Ghazzâlî managed to give to Muslim society a sense of conserving its culture, of permanence, which corresponds to the agitation and to the restlessness of the Ismâᶜîlî movement. M. ABEL recalls the work of the same al-Ghazzâlî against the Bâṭinite sect, and the violence of his attacks. Today we see in the movement a symptom of the political and social ills of the epoch, but in the eyes of al-Ghazzâlî it was *the* evil of his times which had to be extirpated. This was done, and very much in the same way all science not related to the "teaching of peace," Islâm, was abolished in favor of "perfect" orthodoxy. Today under the impact of pseudo-scientific modernism the most deplorable disorder reigns in men's minds; in fact, it has reached very much the situation al-Ghazzâlî feared.

There is a second point, adds M. ABEL, which concerns everyone who considers Islâm as a whole; he ought to take into consideration at least a twofold nature in the social organization. Two different social layers are constantly combined in Islâm: on the one hand, the men without outstanding characteristics, peasants or Bedouins, who adhere directly to the great mass movements of Islâm (speaking of them, it would be interesting to trace the social origin of the thinkers of Islâm in the course of history)—M. ABEL is thinking in this respect of the movement of Ibn Ḥanbal (780–855), which shows clearly the characteristics of a movement of dogmatized masses. On the other hand, we find, in contrast to that of the crowds, the Islâm of the urban merchant, curious about everything and consequently easily tempted by new ideas and tendencies. If we keep in mind this internal duality in Islâm, many contradictory problems which appear in Islamic history may be solved.

Mr. VON GRUNEBAUM comes back to the paper of Mr. Stadtmüller (not included in the present volume) and asks him his opinion about the Alawites and the Druzes.

Mr. STADTMÜLLER believes that he can explain the foreign elements in the

Alawite and Druze religions by the fact that paganism remained alive for many centuries in their territories, as is certified by Byzantine sources. Such pagan tendencies may have been picked up by the Druzes and Alawites when they retired before the Arab persecutions into the relatively inaccessible regions of the Lebanon and Anti-Lebanon. In their isolation those tribes must have developed in ways peculiar to themselves.

The tenability of this theory being connected with the date of the definitive Islamization of Syria, a discussion arises over this point among Mr. Spuler, Mr. Stadtmüller, and Mr. Caskel.

Mr. STADTMÜLLER guesses that Islâm became numerically preponderant in Syria only about the year 1000, and he deplores the fact that nothing has been written about the subject.

Mr. VON GRUNEBAUM thinks that the process of Islamization was roughly contemporary with the process of Arabization.

Mr. LEWIS points out that the appearance of the Druzes in Syria seems to be linked with something pre-existing. There certainly were local groups professing similar doctrines before that time, but this does not answer the question. In Persia also there was a sort of substratum, which accounts for later schisms, but is in fact pre-Islamic. Further, Mr. LEWIS recalls that in India Ismâᶜîlism expanded clearly at the expense of the Hindus, not at the expense of orthodox Islâm; in the case of the Druzes this may have been similar.

Mr. MINORSKY, speaking about the losses incurred by Islâm on the periphery, wonders if much of Islâm remains in some places which are considered Islamic. For instance, can we call Turkey Islamic? Yes, in the villages; but the intellectual classes are lost to Islâm.

Mr. VON GRUNEBAUM replies that the position of the Turks has been described by many authors, who say that the Turks have put themselves out of Islâm; but the Turks insist that they are within the pale. Self-identification is what actually counts; to themselves the Turks are still Muslims.

Mr. MINORSKY thinks that everything depends on the person under inquiry. For instance, the ᶜAlî Ilâhîs: many of them like openly to be called Muslims, while actually they do not consider themselves within the pale; not too much importance should be attached to these declarations.

Mr. SPULER, on the contrary, emphasizes that the only objective criterion for deciding a man's religion is his own confession of his faith. From this point of view Islâm has not yet surrendered any people to another religion. After the Spanish *Reconquista* the Muslims preferred to emigrate to North Africa rather than become Christians; and, adds Mr. STADTMÜLLER, in the Balkans the Muslim population has always been a minority, so that it is wrong to speak of a return of those people to Christianity after the expulsion of the Turks. In fact, only a few elements of the population—the heads of families, in order to avoid taxes!—had ever turned Muslim during the Turkish rule.

NOTES

1. Art. *Ṣalât* in *Handwörterbuch des Islam*, ed. A. J. Wensinck and J. H. Kramers (Leiden, 1941), p. 639.
2. J. Sauvaget, *Introduction à l'histoire de l'Orient musulman* (Paris, 1943), p. 187.

3. Fernand Braudel, *La Méditerranée et le monde méditerranéen à l'époque de Philippe II* (Paris, 1949), p. 637.

4. A tentative effort toward general interpretation of Muslim data starting from a consideration of "zonal framework" has just been made by J. Célérier in *Hespéris* (3d–4th Quarters, 1952); it is suggestive on some points, usually too systematic. I do not think it is fully satisfying either to the geographer or to the Islamist.

5. For example, John Spencer Trimingham, whose observations are, otherwise, very instructive, in his *Islam in Ethiopia* (Oxford, 1952), pp. 271–72.

6. M. Gaudefroy-Demombynes, *Les Institutions musulmanes* (3d ed.; Paris, 1946), p. 11.

7. See Robert M. MacIver, *Social Causation* (Boston, 1942), pp. 90 ff.

8. Ruth Benedict, *Patterns of Culture* (French trans.; Paris, 1950), pp. 54–55.

9. On the "principal facies" of the civilization of antiquity, see H. Marrous's, statement of his position in *IXe Congrès International des Sciences Historiques* (Paris, 1950), Vol. I: *Rapports*, pp. 325–40.

10. It does not seem absurd, either, to try to introduce a numerical notation into such a study, which would be accompanied by graphic representation. The rating of characteristics and of their combinations can be given, at least schematically, a numerical form; and it is easy to imagine that a ready scale of coefficients, granted that it is rich and subtly variegated enough, would furnish a useful instrument for "testing," from the point of view that we are interested in, the Muslim historical groupings. This is obviously a very delicate business, because of the fatal gaps and uncertainties in our documentation of the past, and one that might even be illusory or dangerous on this account in certain cases; but it is undoubtedly capable of rendering good service nevertheless, if the scaling remains purposely flexible, and interpretations modest and prudent. Quantification, as everywhere in the social sciences, is admissible as a process of clarification, as an instrument for further, more circumstantial and well-developed investigations, but not as an end in itself.

11. G. Marçais, *L'Art de l'Islam* (Paris, 1946), pp. 5–6, 13.

12. Gaylord Simpson, *Rythme et modalités de l'évolution* (Paris, 1950), chap. iv.

13. J. Schacht, *The Origins of Muhammadan Jurisprudence* (Oxford, 1950). More modest in scope, but moving in the same direction on some points, is my article, "Polémiques médiévales autour du rite de Mâlik," which appeared in *Al-Andalus*, XV (1950), 377–435, the same year.

14. Léon l'Africain, *Description de l'Afrique*, ed. C. Schefer (Paris, 1898), III, 375–76. The burlesque example which is furnished immediately after is symptomatic of a decadent mentality.

15. André Leroi-Gourhan, *Évolution et techniques*, Vol. II: *Milieu et techniques* (Paris, 1945), p. 341. The image of movement in a spiral is borrowed from Henri Bergson.

16. This does not imply any position on the probabilism of historical events, on which see R. Aron, *Introduction à la philosophie de l'histoire* (Paris, 1938), and P. Vendryès, *De la probabilité en histoire* (Paris, 1952).

17. A short and instructive synthesis from the pen of Levi Della Vida, "Dominant Ideas in the Formation of Islamic Culture," will be found in the *Crozer Quarterly*, XXI (1944), 207–16.

18. On the contemporary period, H. A. R. Gibb's penetrating reflections in *Cahiers de l'Orient contemporain* (1st Quarter, 1951) may be read with profit.

PART III

MODES OF EXPRESSION OF THE CULTURAL TRADITION

THE LAW

JOSEPH SCHACHT

THE development of the religious law of Islâm, as recent research has made us understand it, illustrates in a most significant manner the interdependent phenomena of unity and variety in Muslim civilization. This double aspect is, indeed, so typical of what we now know of the history of Mohammedan religious law that in this short survey I can hardly pretend to do more than put before you some of its salient, though perhaps not yet generally known, features that are apt to illustrate the subject of this Conference.[1]

The first stages of the development of Mohammedan religious law are characterized by a far-reaching reception of the most varied elements; its substratum is to a great extent not originally Islamic, let alone Koranic. The essential contribution that Islâm made toward the formation of its sacred law was not material but formal: a fundamental attitude that already exists in the Koran and continues through the whole history of Islamic religious law, that pervades and unites all its parts and has made of it a unique phenomenon *sui generis*. During the first two centuries of Islâm there came to be formed a central core of ideas and institutions which went far beyond the mere contents and even the implications of the Koran but which the Muslims regarded and have continued to regard as specifically Islamic. Foreign elements, which had at first been admitted by a process of almost indiscriminate reception, were rejected in the end because they were felt to be incompatible with this central Islamic core of doctrine. (We argue here in a circle and presume that these elements were incompatible with the central core because they rather than others were rejected by the majority of representative Muslims.) Over those elements of varied provenance that were retained, the central core exerted a strong attracting and assimilating power, permeating them with what was felt to be the true Islamic spirit, until their foreign origin, short of a searching historical analysis, became well-nigh unrecognizable. This assimilating power of the Islamic core over foreign elements anticipates the assimilating power and the spiritual ascendancy of the sacred law of Islâm as a religious ideal over the practice, after the two had irremediably separated. Both phenomena are really stages of one and the same process, and this process, seen from outside, appears as the modification of the positive contents of Mohammedan religious law, whereas, seen from inside, it appears as an expansion, a conquest of new fields by the ever dominant influence that radiates from its core. This process resulted in the creation of an equilibrium between religious ideal and actual practice—an equilibrium delicate in fact but seemingly unshakable in a closed society and (to borrow an expression from M. Brunschvig in his contribution to this Conference) in a stratification with variant shades in each stratum. This equilibrium was destroyed by the impact of Western influences in modern times, and a new period of indiscriminate reception from abroad began. Such is the present situation of Mohammedan religious law in the Islamic countries of the Near East, and an understanding of its nature and history may enable us to envisage possible lines of its future development.

I shall now try to justify these general considerations in detail.

The first important ingredient that went into the making of the subject matter of Mohammedan religious law was the law of family and inheritance, and to a certain extent the procedure, of the pre-Islamic Arabs. This has to some degree to be reconstructed, by subtracting the modifications introduced by the Koran from certain institutions of the religious law of Islâm, the residue of which can then be taken, with certain safeguards, to reflect the pre-Islamic customary law of the Arabs. The dangers inherent in this procedure are obvious. It can, for instance, be safely assumed that the succession of the agnates, the *ᶜaṣaba,* which forms the backbone of the law of inheritance in Islâm and on which the Koran has superimposed a modification by allotting fixed shares to certain named heirs, reflects pre-Islamic conditions. This was naturally taken to apply to the order in which the *ᶜaṣaba* are called upon to inherit in the religious law of Islâm. But M. Brunschvig has discovered a more archaic form of the order of *ᶜaṣaba* in the rules governing the transmission of the right of *walâᵓ*; the underlying principle is expressed by the formula *al-walâᵓ lil-kubr,* or, in M. Brunschvig's explanatory translation: "Le droit de patronat s'exerce par générations successives dans chaque parentèle."[2] M. Brunschvig does not go further than claiming (and this is certainly correct) that this was the rule of inheritance of property among the Arabs at a remote epoch. I should be inclined to go a step further and to say that it was valid (as far as it is possible to generalize) down to the time of Islâm: compared with it, the Islamic system of *ʿaṣaba* shows a concern with material justice which is typical of the activity of the early Islamic specialists in religious law.

Very little, if anything, is known of the pre-Islamic customary law of contracts, but we do know what the practice of the Meccans concerning *ribâ*, or interest, was like. The fact that the principal Koranic passages directed against interest are Medinese and that the Jews are reproached with breaking the prohibition suggests that the Islamic prohibition of *ribâ* owes less to conditions in Mecca than to the Prophet's closer acquaintance with Jewish doctrine and practice in Medina.[3] In any case, early Mohammedan religious law replaced the old Meccan concept of *ribâ* by a much more sweeping, "streamlined," definition; in the details of the doctrine, Jewish influence is undeniable. The commercial law of Mecca must have been a real "law merchant," enforced by the traders themselves, without the sanction of an organized political authority, which hardly existed. The same situation was to repeat itself later in the unofficial commercial law of the Islamic Middle Ages.

Islamic penal law shows the juxtaposition, without fusion, of two elements: the one based on old Arabian ideas—such as the identification of crime and tort and the responsibility of the group for crimes committed by its members—with certain Koranic and Islamic modifications; the other, purely Koranic and Islamic. This was not sufficient to insure the peaceful functioning of a more highly organized society than that of Medina and of the early Umayyads, but the necessary complements which were introduced at relatively early dates (the office of the *muḥtasib*, the criminal jurisdiction of the *shurṭa*, etc.) always had a precarious existence on the outskirts of the official theory of religious law.

Pre-Islamic procedure was characterized by the institution of *rahn*, pledges or securities, which could be either persons or property and had to be given to the arbitrator by the interested parties in order to assure the execution of his decision. Material pledges used also to be given as evidence of contract in the case of time-bargains. The Koran (2:283) took this for granted, but the early specialists rejected it, for religious Islamic and for systematic reasons. The double function of the arbitrator or *ḥakam*, as interpreter of legal custom and as maker of rules, survived in the attributions of the Islamic *qâḍî*.

The aim of Mohammed as a prophet was not to create a new system of law; it was to teach men how to act, what to do and what to avoid, in order to pass the reckoning on the Day of Judgment and to enter Paradise. Had the standards of an altruistic ethic been consistently followed in practice, there would indeed be no room and no need for a legal system in the narrow meaning of the term. Numerous traces of this attitude occur in the Koran, but in effect the Prophet had to resign himself to applying religious and ethical principles to the legal norms and relationships as he found them. This accounts for the religious character of the Koranic "legislation": it stands outside the existing legal system, on which it superimposes moral and not, properly speaking, legal rules. In the second half of his activity, in Medina, the Prophet became the ruler and the lawgiver of a new society on a religious basis, which was meant to, and at once began to, supersede Arabian tribal society. This new society called for a new legal organization, and the seed out of which Islamic legal organization grew can be seen germinating in the Koran. When the Prophet acted as a judge in his community, he continued to function as an arbitrator, or *ḥakam*, whereas the verb *qaḍà*, from which the term *qâḍî* was to be derived, regularly refers in the Koran not to the judgment of a judge but to a sovereign ordinance, either of Allâh or of a prophet. In a single verse (4:65), both verbs occur side by side: "But no, by thy Lord, they will not become [true] believers unless they make thee the arbitrator [*yuḥakkimûka*] of their disputes and do not afterwards feel aversion from what you decide [*qaḍaita*] but submit with submission." This isolated instance is the first indication of the emergence of a new, Islamic, idea of the administration of justice. A somewhat later indication of the same process is provided by the half-legendary person of the so-called "*qâḍî*" Shuraiḥ. The traditional opinion asserts, with some variants of detail, that he was the *qâḍî* of Kûfa over a very long period and died at an incredibly old age. All this is frankly impossible. Shuraiḥ was no more than a *ḥakam* of the old style among the Arab tribes in the neighborhood of Kûfa. His activity coincided with the establishment and spread of Islâm, and his legendary figure reflects the transition from the old to the new form of administration of justice.[4]

All indications point to the first century of the hegira as the most important period in the formation of Mohammedan religious law. After the turbulent interval of the caliphate of Medina, the outlines of what proved to be the essential core of the religious law of Islâm were elaborated under the Umayyads. In this respect, too, the Umayyad period rather than the caliphate of Medina shows itself as the direct continuation and consummation of what Mohammed had created in Medina. The most important single fact in the development of Mohammedan religious law during the first century was the re-emergence of the ancient Arab idea of "sunna," precedent or tradition, in an Islamic garb. The Arabs were, and are, bound by tradition and precedent. Whatever was customary was right and proper; whatever the forefathers had done deserved to be imitated. The Arabs recognized, of course, that a sunna might have been laid down by an individual in the relatively recent past, but then that individual was considered the spokesman and representative of the whole group. The Arab idea of sunna opposed a formidable obstacle to every innovation. Islâm, the greatest innovation that Arabia saw, had to overcome this opposition, and a hard fight it was. But once Islâm had prevailed, even among one single group of Arabs, the old conservatism reasserted itself; what had shortly before been an innovation now became the thing to do, a thing hallowed by precedent and tradition, a sunna. This originally ancient Arab idea of sunna became one of the central concepts of Mohammedan religious law.

Contrary to what might have been expected, but rather in keeping with a recurrent leitmotif in its history, certain norms of earliest Islamic law diverged from the clear and explicit wording of the Koran. One important feature of this kind, which later was to contribute its share in producing the essential tension between theory and practice, is the restriction of legal proof to the oral evidence of witnesses and the denial of validity to written documents. The Koran (2:282) had indorsed the current practice of putting contracts into writing, but John of Damascus, who flourished between A.D. 700 and 750, already mentions the insistence on witnesses as a characteristic custom of the Saracens. This feature probably established itself about the middle of the first century of Islâm.

Hardly much later than the middle of the first century, too, the Umayyads, or rather their governors, took the important step of appointing Islamic judges or *qâḍîs*. The office of the *qâḍî* was created in and for the new Islamic society which came into being, under the new conditions resulting from the Arab conquest, in the urban centers of the Arab kingdom, and for which the arbitration of pre-Islamic Arabia and of the earliest period of Islâm was no longer adequate. The Arab *ḥakam* was supplanted by the Islamic *qâḍî*, and the *qâḍî* was a delegate of the governor. The earliest Islamic *qâḍîs*, officials of the Umayyad administration, by their decisions laid the foundations of what was to become Mohammedan religious law. They gave judgment according to their own discretion or "sound opinion" (*raʾy*), basing themselves on customary practice, which in the nature of things incorporated administrative regulations, and taking the letter and the spirit of the Koranic "legislation" and of other recognized Islamic religious norms into account as much as they thought fit. Though the legal subject matter had as yet not been Islamized to any great extent beyond the stage reached in the Koran, the office of the *qâḍî* itself was an Islamic institution typical of the Umayyad period, in which administrative efficiency and the tendency to Islamize went hand in hand.

I have just alluded to one of two additional important elements that entered the crucible in which the religious law of Islâm was being prepared in the Umayyad period: I mean Umayyad administrative regulations. By a method of reasoning in circles, to which we are only too often reduced when we try to analyze the history and components of early Mohammedan law, we can reconstruct some of these Umayyad administrative regulations from the earliest documents of Mohammedan law itself. In any case, we find them almost exclusively in those fields where other considerations lead us to expect them: in the law of war, in fiscal law, and in the supervision of the administration of penal law.

The remaining element that went into the making of the religious law of Islâm, to which I have just referred, consists of the ideas and customs of the conquered territories. The widespread adoption of legal and administrative institutions of the conquered territories by the Muslims of the first century is, indeed, generally recognized. As examples, I need refer only to the treatment of tolerated religions, to the methods of taxation, to the contract of *emphyteusis*, and, perhaps less generally known, to the institution of *waqf*. The *waqf* is a good example of the composite and qualitatively new character of Islamic religious law as it emerged from the crucible of the Umayyad period: its roots are at one and the same time in the South Arabian endowments of sanctuaries, in the Byzantine foundations in favor of churches and pious works, and in the contributions for the Holy War, on which much emphasis had already been laid in the Koran. The principle of the retention of pre-Islamic legal institutions under Islâm was sometimes even explicitly acknowledged, as in the following passage of Balâdhurî (ninth century A.D.):

> Abû Yûsuf held that if there exists in a country an ancient, non-Arab normative custom (*sunna*) which Islâm has neither changed nor abolished, and people complain to the caliph that it causes them hardship, he is not entitled to change it; but Mâlik and Shâfiʿî held that he may change it even if it be ancient, because he ought to prohibit [in similar circumstances] every lawful normative custom which has been introduced by a Muslim, let alone those introduced by unbelievers.[5]

Both opinions presuppose the retention of pre-Islamic legal practices as normal.

Hand in hand with the adoption of existing administrative institutions went the reception of legal concepts and principles by the intermediary of the cultured converts to Islâm who had enjoyed the advantage of a liberal education, that is to say, the education in Hellenistic rhetoric which was the normal one in several countries of the Near East conquered by the Arabs. It invariably included some training in the rudiments of law, which was considered necessary for the orators and useful for the members of all learned professions. These educated converts brought their familiar ideas, including legal concepts and general legal maxims, with them into their new religion. (That the early Muslim specialists in religious law should consciously have adopted any principle of foreign laws is out of the question.) In this way, concepts originating from Roman Byzantine law, from the canon law of the Eastern Church, from Talmudic law, and from Sassanid law infiltrated into the nascent religious law of Islâm during its period of incubation in the first century of the hegira. Among those elements which were adopted, we may mention methods of legal reasoning and disputation, including the criterion of the "consensus of the scholars"; the maxim that *pater est quem nuptiae demonstrant* (*al-walad lil-firâsh*); the juridical construction of the contract of *ijâra* in which, following the model of the Roman *locatio conductio*, the three originally separate transactions of *kirâʾ* (corresponding to *l. c. rei*), *ijâra* proper (corresponding to *l. c. operarum*) and *juʿl* (corresponding to *l. c. operis*) were combined; the change in the concept of *rahn* from the old Arab and Koranic one, of which I have already spoken, to one corresponding to the Roman *pignus*. Others of these foreign concepts were, after a period of trial and error, finally rejected, for instance, earnest money (*ʿurbân* = *arrha*);[6] pecuniary penalties for theft; adultery as an impediment to marriage; and, finally, the concept of codification.[7]

All these infiltrations occurred in the first, or early in the second, century of the hegira, and it is interesting to note in passing that Mohammedan religious law shows no traces of foreign influences that might have touched the Arabs in pre-Islamic times, although they were then in superficial contact with the Byzantine administration of justice. More than one Arab must have had experience of Byzantine criminal prosecution, and it is not surprising that the Greek term for robber, *lēstēs*, entered the Arabic language as a loanword, *liṣṣ* (with the variants *laṣt*, *liṣt*, and *luṣt*). But though the

Koran, and after it Islamic religious law, knew the crime of highway robbery, this word was not used as a technical term for it, but only the Koranic *qaṭ*ᶜ *al-ṭarîq*. Again, the Arabic verb *dallas*, "to conceal a fault or defect in an article of merchandise from the purchaser," is derived from Latin *dolus*. It entered Arabic through the channel of commercial practice at an early date but did not become a technical term in early Mohammedan law. How slight, after all, the acquaintance of the Arabs in Mohammed's time was with the exact meaning of Byzantine administrative terms appears from the Koran (21:104), where *sijill* = *sigillum* denotes the scribe instead of the document.

The agent that blended these several ingredients until they became fused into one homogeneous whole was the activity of the early specialists in Mohammedan religious law at the end of the first and at the beginning of the second century of the hegira in Iraq, Syria, and Medina. By these I mean not technically trained professionals but persons sufficiently interested in the right Islamic way of life to have given the subject in their spare time serious thought, either individually or in discussion with like-minded friends. They surveyed all fields of contemporary activities, including the field of law—not only administrative regulations but popular practice as well. They impregnated the sphere of law with religious and ethical ideas, subjected it to Islamic norms, and incorporated it into the body of duties incumbent on every Muslim. In doing this, they achieved on a much wider scale and in a vastly more detailed manner what the Prophet in the Koran had tried to do for the early Islamic community of Medina. As a result, the popular and administrative practice of the late Umayyad period was transformed into the religious law of Islâm. The resulting ideal theory still had to be translated into practice; this task was beyond the power of the pious specialists and had to be left to the interest and zeal of the caliphs, governors, *qâḍîs*, or individuals concerned. Though it is true that the *qâḍîs* came increasingly to be recruited from the specialists themselves, the circumstances in which Mohammedan religious law came into being brought it about that it developed, not in close connection with the practice, but as the expression of a religious ideal in opposition to it. Mohammedan religious law, too, is dominated by the antinomy of the "great tradition" and of the "little tradition."

As the groups of pious specialists grew in numbers and in cohesion, they developed, in the first few decades of the second century of the hegira, into the so-called "ancient schools of law," of which those of

Kûfa and of Basra in Iraq, of Medina and of Mecca in Hijaz, and of Syria are more or less known to us. The differences between these schools were conditioned essentially by geographical factors, such as the difficulties of communication between their several seats and local variations in custom and practice. Variants of doctrine therefore existed, but they were not based on any noticeable disagreement on principles or methods. Do the differences reflect different stages of society? The answer must be qualified. In many cases it is obvious that the teaching of the Iraqis represents the result of a considerable doctrinal development and that of the Medinese an earlier, less developed stage. This would agree with our general idea of the relative speed of social development in Iraq and in Hijaz, respectively, during the period in question. But it must not be forgotten that the Medinese solutions are often attested as the starting point of the doctrinal development in Iraq as well, and it can be shown that the Medinese are regularly dependent, with a certain time lag, on Iraqi opinions and solutions and that the scholars of Iraq maintained, over a considerable period, an ascendancy in the development of religious law and jurisprudence in Islâm. The difference would therefore reduce itself to one of scholarly activity; but this, of course, is a social phenomenon, too.

Parallel with the tendency of the early specialists to Islamize, to introduce Islamic norms into the sphere of law, went the complementary tendency to reason and to systematize. Reasoning was inherent in Mohammedan law from its very beginnings. It started with the exercise of personal opinion and of individual judgment on the part of the earliest specialists and *qâḍîs*, and moved from vague beginnings, without direction or method, toward an increasingly strict discipline. Owing to the success of the movement of the Traditionists in the first half of the second century of the hegira, most of what originally were arbitrary decisions of scholars was put into the form of "traditions" and put into the mouth of the Prophet. The Traditionist movement was the most important single event in the history of Mohammedan religious law in the second century of the hegira. The Traditionists continued and completed the process of introducing Islamic norms into all aspects of life, including the sphere of law, and, in addition, by attributing the outlines and many details of what was the result of a long and complex development to the Prophet himself, imposed upon the various material elements that had contributed to the making of Mohammedan religious law a formal unity, fictitious but impressive and, what is more, after some hesitation accepted and indorsed by the Muslims as a whole. The Traditionists once more attempted to subordinate the legal subject matter to moral considerations. In this, they were not quite successful, and the legal subject matter has retained, within the framework of the religious duties of the Muslims, part of its own technical character.

By the middle of the second century of the hegira, the religious law of Islâm had acquired its essential shape. It became what it is, not merely by the mechanical process of introducing material considerations of a moral or religious kind into the field of law, but by the much subtler process of organizing and systematizing this field as part of the religious duties of the Muslims. It possesses an integrating principle, which has imposed a rational structural order on the varied raw materials out of which it is built, but this principle is not formal and autonomous—it is material and Islamic.[8]

In 132 A.H. (A.D. 750) the Umayyads were overthrown by the Abbasids. In conscious and exaggerated opposition to the policy of their predecessors, the Abbasids made it their program to establish the rule of God on earth. As part of this policy they recognized the religious law, which was in the process of emerging, as the only legitimate norm in Islâm and set out to translate the ideal theory into practice. But just as the pious specialists who had formed the vanguard of the Islamizing tendency under the Umayyads had been ahead of realities, so now the early Abbasids and their religious advisers were unable to carry the whole of society with them. They failed to achieve a permanent fusion of theory and practice, and it was not long before their successors lacked not only the will but the power to continue the effort. What the early Abbasids did achieve was the permanent connection of the office of *qâḍî* with the sacred law. The *qâḍî* was not any longer the legal secretary of the governor but was normally appointed from the center, and, once appointed and until he was discharged, he had to apply nothing but the sacred law. But this independence of the judiciary remained theoretical, and the *qâḍîs* not only were subject to dismissal at the whim of the central government but had to depend on the political authorities for the execution of their judgments. They soon lost control of the administration of criminal justice, the greater part of which was transferred to the police.[9] Ostensibly in order to supplement the deficiencies of the *qâḍîs'* tribunals, special courts of complaints were set up by the political authority, and their jurisdiction became to a great extent concurrent with that of the tribunals of the *qâḍîs*. This institution derives from the administrative tradition of the Sassanid kings and received, in due course, theoretical recognition. The courts of complaints were the first of those administrative tribunals which ever since have coexisted with the tribunals of the *qâḍîs* in practically the whole of the Islamic world. All this shows the breakdown, to a large extent and at an early period, of the administration of justice by the *qâḍî*.

One of the administrative institutions that had survived under the Umayyads from Byzantine times was the office of the "inspector of the market" (*agoranomos*), who had a limited civil and criminal jurisdiction. The early Abbasids maintained its function and superficially Islamized it by appointing its holder to discharge the collective obligation, enjoined in the Koran, of "encouraging the good and discouraging the evil," making him responsible for enforcing Islamic morals and behavior on the community of Muslims and giving him the Islamic title of *muḥtasib*. It was part of his duties to bring transgressors to justice and himself to award summary punishments, which came to include flogging and even mutilation; but their eagerness to have these punishments of the sacred law enforced made the rulers commonly overlook the fact that the procedure of the *muḥtasib* did not ordinarily comply with the safeguards on which the same law insisted. These several aspects of the office of the *muḥtasib* exemplify the nature and extent of the adoption of the ideal system of the religious law of Islâm under the early Abbasids.

We saw that under the Umayyads the administrative-*cum*-legislative activity of the government had originally lain outside, and was only gradually being brought into, the orbit of nascent Mohammedan law. Under the Abbasids, however, when the sacred law had come to be recognized, in theory at least, as the only legitimate norm of behavior for Muslims, the caliph himself had to be incorporated into the new official system. This was done, not by giving him the right to legislate (it would have been difficult to acknowledge this right of the ruler in a system of religious duties which had been formulated in opposition to the practice of the government), but by endowing him with the attributes of a religious scholar and specialist. The caliph, though otherwise the absolute chief of the community of the Muslims, had not the right to legislate but only to make administrative regulations within the limits laid down by the sacred law. This doctrine effectively concealed the fact that legislation on the part of the caliphs of Medina and particularly of the Umayyads had to a great extent, directly by being approved and indirectly by provoking contrary solutions, entered into the fabric of Mohammedan religious law. The adoption of this doctrine did not even lead for the future to a clear division between legislation and administration. The caliphs and the other secular rulers often had occasion to legislate, but they used to call it "administration" and maintained the fiction that their regulations served only to apply, to supplement, and to enforce the sacred law and were well within the competence of the political authority. This was the theory; what happened in practice was that the rulers provided by virtually independent legislation for matters of police and taxation and for the administration of criminal justice. This legislation and, indeed, the whole of administrative justice dispensed by the sovereign directly or through his political instruments of government, as opposed to the sacred law which was administered by the *qâḍî*, is called *siyâsa.*

In the early Abbasid period, too, the ancient schools of religious law, which had been conditioned by geography, transformed themselves into the later type of school, based on allegiance to an individual master. In their relationship to one another, these schools have most of the time practiced mutual toleration. This attitude goes back to the time of the ancient schools, which had accepted the original geographical differences of doctrine as natural. Disagreements on principle, which arose only as a consequence of the creation, by Shâfiʿî, of a theory of religious law on a formally Traditionist basis, resolved itself in a compromise, and since then the consensus, which acted as the integrating principle of Islâm, has succeeded in making innocuous those differences of opinion that it could not eliminate. The several schools, then, are equally covered by consensus; they are all deemed to translate into individual rules the will of Allâh; their alternative interpretations are all equally valid; their methods of reasoning equally legitimate—in short, they are all equally orthodox. In this way, the "catholic instinct of Islâm" achieved unity through variety in the field of religious law.

The early Abbasid period finally saw the end of the formative period of Mohammedan religious law, a process of which the formation of the "personal" schools was a symptom. The whole sphere of law had been permeated with the religious and ethical standards proper to Islâm; the sacred law of Islâm had been elaborated in detail; the principle of the infallibility of the consensus of the scholars worked in favor of a progressive narrowing and hardening of doctrine; the theory of religious law was taking on its final form; and, a little later, the doctrine which denied the further possibility of "independent reasoning" or *ijtihâd* sanctioned officially a state of things that had come to prevail in fact. The transition from *ijtihâd* to *taqlîd*, the unreasoning acceptance of the final state of the doctrine as laid down for each school in its recognized handbooks, came about gradually, and there was no sudden break. For the last thousand years of its existence, down to the present generation, Mohammedan religious law has been, or perhaps I should say was, dominated by the principle of *taqlîd*. The doctrine of the sacred law became more and more scholastic and rigid, but this very rigidity guaranteed its stability and enabled it to survive, without the backing of a strong political authority, the decay of the political institutions of Islâm.

From time to time there have appeared, it is true, scholars who claimed that they fulfilled the incredibly high demands which the theory lays down as a qualification for "independent reasoning." But these claims have remained theoretical, and none of the scholars who made them has actually produced an independent interpretation of the sacred law. It was against *taqlîd* rather than in favor of *ijtihâd* that the eminent Ḥanbalî, Ibn Taimiyya, followed by his disciple Ibn Qayyim al-Jauziyya, made his protest of principle. Ibn Taimiyya did not claim for himself the right to *ijtihâd*; but as a consequence of his narrowly formulated idea of consensus he was able to reject *taqlîd*, to interpret Koran and "traditions" from the Prophet afresh, and to arrive at novel conclusions concerning many institutions of religious law.[10] The Wahhâbîs of Arabia, who constitute the great majority of the present followers of the Ḥanbalî school, have adopted, together with Ibn Taimiyya's theological doctrines, the whole of his theory of the sacred law, including his rejection of *taqlîd*; but at the same time they have retained, unchanged, the positive doctrines of the school as they had been developed before Ibn Taimiyya, apparently without being troubled by the resultant discrepancy. Under the direct or indirect influence of the Wahhâbîs, the various schools of thought that are known as "modernism," from the last decades of the nineteenth century onward, reject *taqlîd*. Some modernists in the present generation combine this with extravagant claims of a new, free *ijtihâd*, and we shall have to consider the results of their efforts later.

Whatever the theory might say on *ijtihâd* and *taqlîd*, the activity of the later scholars, after the "closing of the door of independent reasoning," was no less creative, within ever narrowing limits, it is true, than that of their predecessors. New sets of facts constantly arose in life, and they had to be mastered and molded with the traditional set of tools provided by the science of the sacred law. This activity was carried out by the *muftîs*, whose decisions on new problems, as soon as they were recognized as correct by the common opinion of the scholars, were incorporated in the recognized handbooks of their respective schools. Already the earliest specialists in religious law were essentially *muftîs*, and their concern with it was mainly cautelary; it was their function to advise interested members of the public on what was, in their opinion, the correct course of action from the religious point of view. In the second half of the second century of the hegira, this cautelary and advisory element is clearly discernible in the work of Mâlik. The same concern inspired the authors of the works on *ḥiyal* and of legal formularies, on which I shall have to say something in a moment.

Taken as a whole, Mohammedan religious law reflects and fits the social and economic conditions of the world of Islâm in the early Abbasid period. But the administration of the state and the sacred law drew apart again, and the increasing rigidity of the scholastic doctrine prevented it from keeping pace with the later developments of state and society. The antinomy between a religious ideal and the changing demands of everyday life was indeed inherent in Mohammedan law from its very beginnings. One of the most important means of bridging the gap between theory and practice were the *ḥiyal*, or legal devices, which are attested from early Abbasid times onward; already Mâlik presupposes their existence. I will first give an example from family law which, being based as it was to a great extent on explicit prescriptions of the Koran, as a rule conformed to the theory.

Until quite recently, morganatic marriages have been customary at a number of native courts on the continent of India and in the East Indies. The ruler is married to the full number of four legal wives and besides, by proxy, to any number of young women. From the dagger, which is produced at the ceremony by the proxy as a token, this union is called "marriage of the kris" and, needless to say, is regarded as a great honor by the young woman and her family. But the parties know that this union is not regular, and, when any of the young women becomes pregnant, the ruler concludes a regular marriage with her so that the child may be born legitimate (this is not correct in Mohammedan law, but one chooses to overlook it), then divorces her afterward, and she returns to her former status. But, being already married to four wives, the ruler has to get rid of one of them for the time being; he could divorce her, but, after doing it three times, he could not marry her again until after she had been married to, and had intercourse with, another man. Therefore the wife has to ask for a separation against a monetary equivalent, a kind of divorce which does not become a bar to a subsequent remarriage; and, in order to be prepared for all contingencies, it is customary for the youngest wife to ask for a separation against a monetary equivalent immediately after her marriage to the ruler; and this request is, so to speak, kept in cold storage and only acceded to when the occasion arises.

The law of contracts and obligations was ruled by a customary law which respected the main principles and institutions of theoretical religious law but showed a greater flexibility and adaptability. It, too, was brought into agreement with the theory by the *ḥiyal*, by using legal means for achieving extralegal ends—ends that could not be achieved directly with the means provided by the theory, whether they might or might not be in themselves illegal. For instance, the Koran had prohibited interest, and this religious prohibition was strong enough to make popular opinion unwilling to transgress it openly and directly, while, at the same time, there was an imperative demand for the giving and taking of interest in the commercial life that developed in the great urban centers of Muslim civilization. In order to satisfy this need, and at the same time to observe the letter of the religious prohibition, a number of devices were developed. One of them consisted of the future creditor's buying from the future debtor any object for the amount of the capital, payable in cash, and the debtor's, immediately afterward, buying the same object back from the creditor for a greater amount, representing capital and interest and payable at some future date. There were hundreds of these devices, many of them highly technical, but all with a scrupulous regard for the letter of the law. Many specialists in sacred law, starting with the great Ḥanafî authorities, Abû Yûsuf and Shaibânî, elaborated such devices and put them at the disposal of the public.

It had been the aim of the early specialists to review the current legal practice and to advise the Muslims which of its institutions they might use with a good conscience and which they ought to avoid. If the practice developed transactions that formally observed the religious norms as they had formulated them, norms which were essentially heteronomous, there was little or no reason why they should object; and the validity of the *ḥiyal* was, in fact, recognized by the great majority of the scholars. The interested parties, the merchants, felt the need for these devices and presumably thought out the first and simplest *ḥiyal* themselves, but it was quite beyond them to invent and apply the more complicated ones; they had to have recourse to specialists and professionals, to scholars learned in religious law. Once the system of religious law had been elaborated, the religious zeal of the first upholders of the Islamic spirit in all spheres of life was gradually replaced and superseded by the not less sincere, not less convinced, but more technical, more scholastic interest of professionals who took pride in inventing and perfecting and making work small masterpieces of legal construction. The inventors of *ḥiyal* had to calculate the chances of legal validity to a nicety, if the *qâḍî*, who was bound to the sacred law, was not to upset the real effects of the business transaction that their customers, the merchants, had in mind—effects which depended upon the validity of every single element in an often complicated series of formal transactions under the sacred law. The activity of the authors of *ḥiyal*, catering for the practice, shares this advisory and cautelary character with that of the early specialists who first elaborated the ideal theory. The early specialists warned their contemporaries against acts incompatible with the Islamic way of life; the authors of *ḥiyal* helped theirs not to conclude contracts which would be considered invalid by the fully developed system of Mohammedan law.[11]

A further feature of customary commercial law was its reliance on written documents. I mentioned earlier that Mohammedan law, at a very early period, diverged both from an explicit ruling of the Koran and from current practice by denying the validity of documentary evidence and restricting legal proof to the oral evidence of witnesses. Written documents, however, proved so indispensable in practice that, notwithstanding their persistent neglect in theory, they remained in constant use, became a normal accompaniment of every transaction of importance, and gave rise to a highly developed branch of practical law with a voluminous literature of its own. Theory continued to reason as if there were no documents but only witnesses, possibly helped by private records of their own; practice continued to act as if the documents were almost essential and the "witnessing" only a formality to make them fully valid; and professional witnesses came, in fact, to exercise the functions of notaries public. Again, the authors of the practical books of legal formularies were themselves specialists in the sacred law; they and the "notaries" themselves acted as advisers to the parties concerned and provided forms of documents for all possible needs and safeguards against all possible contingencies. Here we have again the advisory and cautelary tendency. Finally, even strict theory deigned to recognize the existence of written documents and to admit them as valid evidence, the Mâlikîs to the widest extent, the Ḥanafîs and the Ḥanbalîs[12] with more hesitations, whereas the Shâfiʿites continued to reject them on principle; but the actual use of written documents was equally extensive among the adherents of all schools.

Written documents often formed an essential element of *ḥiyal*. The more complicated *ḥiyal* often consisted of several transactions between the parties concerned, each of which was perfectly legal in itself and the combined effect of which produced the desired result. Each transaction was recorded and attested in a written document as a matter of course. Taken in isolation, a document recording a single transaction or a declaration made by one of the parties might be used by the other party to its exclusive advantage and for a purpose contrary to the aim of the whole of the agreement. In order to prevent this happening, the official documents were deposited in the hands of a trusted intermediary or umpire, together with an unofficial covering document which set out the real position of the parties in relation to one another and the real purport of their agreement. The umpire then, acting on the contents of the covering document, handed to each party only those pieces to which it was entitled at any given stage and prevented an unauthorized use of any document by producing, if necessary, the document of a compensating transaction or declaration which had been prepared beforehand for this very purpose. The whole phenomenon of customary commercial law is of considerable importance for the legal sociology of Islâm in the Middle Ages.

Mohammedan religious law as a whole ignored custom as an official source of law, however much customs of varied provenance had contributed to forming its raw material. Most of these elements, it will be remembered, had been effectively disguised and clothed in an Islamic garb by the Traditionists. But late Mâlikî jurisprudence in the Maghrib took a little more notice of the conditions prevailing in fact, certainly not by changing the theoretical doctrine, but by recognizing that the actual conditions did not allow the strict theory to be translated into practice, and that it was better to try to control the practice as much as possible than to abandon it completely, maintaining a kind of protective zone around the sacred law.

Late Mâlikî doctrine in the Maghrib therefore recognized a number of institutions unknown to the strict theory.

All this shows the great assimilating power of Mohammedan religious law, the power of imposing its spiritual supremacy even when it could not control the material conditions. One might say that the sacred law of Islâm more than made good what it lost in control over the acts of its followers by what it gained in spiritual power over their minds. This spiritual power still asserts itself today and sets the background for contemporary movements of opinion. In the way described, a balance established itself between legal theory and legal practice; an uneasy truce between the specialists in religious law and the political authorities came into being. The sacred law could not abandon its claim to absolute theoretical validity, but, as long as it received formal recognition from the Muslims as a religious ideal, it did not insist on being carried out in practice.

These general and normal conditions were occasionally disturbed by violent religious reform movements (e.g., that of the Almoravids, A.D. 1050–1146; that of the Fulanis in the western Sudan in the nineteenth century; that of the Wahhâbîs in the nineteenth and in the twentieth century), as well as by efforts to enforce the sacred law fully in existing Islamic states (e.g., in the Ottoman Empire in the fifteenth and sixteenth centuries; in the Mogul Empire under Alamgir, A.D. 1658–1707). But these efforts were essentially ephemeral, and, after a period of strictness, a new balance between theory and practice tended to establish itself. The few exceptions only confirm the rule.

The impact of European ideas on the Islamic world in the present century, however, has brought about effects of a vastly different, unprecedented, and irrevocable kind. Or, at least, so it seems to us, whose view of the present is unavoidably distorted by the lack of historical perspective. Be that as it may, legal modernism cannot be left out of account in any survey of Mohammedan religious law.[13]

Only in the present generation has the ground been prepared for legislation by Islamic governments on family law, the law of inheritance, and the law of *waqf*—subjects which have always formed part of the central domain of the sacred law of Islâm. This legislative interference with the sacred law itself, as opposed to the silent or explicit restriction of its sphere of application by custom or by legislation, presupposes the reception of Western political ideas. A modern sovereign, a modern government, and particularly a parliament are placed with regard to Mohammedan law differently from a traditional Muslim ruler and even the former Ottoman caliph. The legislative power is no longer content with what the sacred law is prepared to leave to it officially or in fact but wants, itself, to determine the sphere which is to be left to the sacred law, to restrict it, and to modify according to its own requirements what has been left. This leads to an unprecedented relationship between religious and temporal law.

This modernist legislative interference with Mohammedan law started modestly with the Ottoman family law of 1917, which was later repealed in Turkey but remained valid in some of the Ottoman succession states. Then, from 1920 onward, most of the modernist legislative movement took place in Egypt. As a result, all subject matters in which the sacred law was still being applied in practice have been modified in Egypt more or less deeply, and the institution of *waqf* in particular has been changed beyond all recognition. These modifications of the sacred law have evoked much interest in the other Islamic countries of the Near East and have served as a model for several laws in Lebanon and Syria, which occasionally even went further than their Egyptian prototypes. The whole subject is very much under discussion in the countries concerned.

The method used by the modernist legislators savors of unrestrained eclecticism: the "independent reasoning" that they claim goes far beyond any that was practiced in the formative period of Mohammedan law; any opinion held at some time in the past is likely to be taken out of its context and used as an argument. On the one hand, the modernist legislators are inclined to deny the religious character of the central chapters of the sacred law; on the other, they are apt to use arbitrary and forced interpretations of Koran and traditions whenever it suits their purpose. Materially, they are bold innovators who want to be modern at all costs; formally, they try to avoid the semblance of interfering with the essential contents of the sacred law. Their ideas and their arguments come from the West, but they do not wish to reject the sacred law openly as Turkey has done. The present conditions are essentially the same as those that prevailed in the period of haphazard infiltration and indiscriminate borrowing in the first century of Islâm. The process of discriminating, assimilating, rejecting, and fusing the approved elements into a new whole is not even in sight, and it may be a long time before anything of this kind happens.

In any case, the Muslims cannot get away from the spiritual ascendancy and the deeply ingrained influence of their religious law.

The idea of a religious law—the concept that law, as well as other human relationships, must be ruled by religion—has become an essential part of the Islamic outlook. The same, incidentally, is true of politics and even of economics; it explains the recent attempt to hold an Islamic economic congress in Pakistan. Because they cannot face the problem, because they lack historical understanding of the formation of Mohammedan religious law, because they cannot make up their minds, any more than their predecessors could in the early Abbasid period, on what is legislation, the modernists cannot get away from a timid, halfhearted, and essentially self-contradictory position.

Parallel with the tendency to modify the existing doctrine of traditional religious law goes a seemingly opposite trend: the desire to construct modern laws on the foundations of the basic principles of the sacred law, that law which reflects the conditions of early Abbasid society. This is called "temporal Islamic legislation"—a contradiction *in adjecto* in the light of history. Those who propose to do this are to a great extent the same persons who advocate modifying the religious law in those fields in which it is still being applied in practice. All this goes to show how firm a hold the idea of a religious law has got on the legal thought even of modernist Muslims. The common aim underlying both programs is to express modern ideas, which have been borrowed from the West, in a traditional medium, but it hardly seems to have been realized that the two programs are mutually contradictory.

The central and essential feature that makes Mohammedan religious law what it is, that guarantees its unity in all its diversity, is the assessing of all human acts and relationships, including those that we call legal, from a religious, ethical point of view. This implies the duplicity of legal subject matter and ethical organizing principle. This feature brings with it as its necessary corollary a cautelary and advisory attitude. Mohammed himself, the early specialists who elaborated the central core of Islamic normative rules, the scholars who elaborated the detailed system as we know it, the *muftîs* all through Islamic history, the astute technicians who refined the *ḥiyal* and the formularies of legal documents, and the Ottoman draftsmen of administrative law who pretended that they were applying the sacred law were all of the same kind. The second lesson we can draw from the development of Mohammedan religious law is that the impetus that provoked new developments came regularly from outside, from the practice, and that the theory followed suit, either by accepting or by rejecting these developments, in any case bringing its spiritual ascendancy to bear upon them. To grant to the practice the function of an arbiter over the theory would mean going straight against the very nature of Mohammedan religious law. The problem that confronts the Muslims in the modern world, if they are to preserve their millennial concept of a religious law—and it is obvious that they cling to it with all their hearts—is to arrive at a new synthesis, to do the same, with different materials, that their predecessors did in the first, and at the beginning of the second, century of the hegira. If this synthesis is not to be a break with their past, if it is to be true to the whole history of their religious law, it will have to be neither a mechanical and arbitrary reshaping of their traditional sacred law nor the erection of a temporal structure concealed behind an alleged Islamic façade; it will have to be the evaluation of modern social life and of modern legal institutions from an Islamic religious angle. The real problem poses itself at the religious and not at the technically legal level. Mohammedan law, belonging as it does to the Middle Ages, can be either an inspiration or a stumbling block.

DISCUSSION

Mr. von Grunebaum opens the discussion by pointing out the eclecticism which presides over the foundation of Islamic law. Then he mentions Professor Ameer ᶜAlî, of Ḥaidarâbâd, India, who, by interpreting some famous passages of the Koran (9·36 f.) so as to establish that Mohammed provided for a complete solar year, paves the way to a calendar reform (*Journal of Calendar Reform* [June, 1953], p. 63)—this, of course, to make the reform acceptable to Muslims.

Mr. Lewis sees indeed a tendency in Muslim circles to try to justify their innovations with religious motives. He mentions as instances of this the Turkish movement for revival of religion and the attempts of the nationalists to show that true Muslims have always been nationalists and republicans.

M. Brunschvig has two remarks in connection with Mr. Schacht's paper, the first with regard to legal maxims: among them we can distinguish different types, one "learned," the work of scholars who wanted to condense their legal ideas into a concise form, often with didactic intentions; the other popular, consisting of proverbs and sentences which have become part of the accepted corpus of law. Often we find coexisting contradictory legal maxims just as we find contradictory proverbs within one society. A certain light may be shed upon this complex state of affairs by a comparative study of legal maxims in different civilizations. It would be interesting, not only for Islâm but for the study of any civilization, to separate the learned and the popular elements and to inquire into their respective roles in the formation of law.

A second problem is that of the sociological side of the divergences of certain prescriptions of the different *madhhabs*. M. Brunschvig cites as an example the fact that the age of majority is defined in one case by the attainment of physical puberty, in another by an age limit of fifteen years. The second solution seems to be the sociologically more "progressive" one. In one system certain pre-emptive rights are reserved to relatives, in another they are shared by neighbors as well. When, in the case of a slave's being slain by a free man, one *madhhab* prescribes the *talio* and another does not admit it, this again indicates a sociological difference between the two.

NOTES

1. In formulating my ideas, I have to a certain extent drawn on my contributions to an as yet unpublished collective work, *Law in the Middle East*, Vol. I. [The volume was published in Washington, D.C., 1955, with Mr. Schacht's contribution on pp. 28–84.—Ed.]

2. *Revue historique de droit français et étranger*, Ser. 4, XXVIII (1950), 23–34.

3. See *Encyclopaedia of Islâm*, s.v. *Ribâ*.

4. E. Tyan, *Histoire de l'organisation judiciaire en pays d'Islam* (Paris, 1938–43), I, 101–4.

5. *Liber expugnationis regionum*, ed. M. de Goeje (Leiden, 1865), p. 448.

6. This ancient Semitic institution did not survive in the customary law of the Arabs; its place had been taken by the pre-Islamic *rahn*.

7. On the problem of foreign influences in early Mohammedan law, see my papers in *Journal of Comparative Legislation*, Parts 3/4 (1950), pp. 9–16 (also in the *Proceedings of the 3rd International Congress of Comparative Law*); in *Archives d'histoire du droit oriental et revue internationale des droits de l'antiquité*, I (1952), 105–23; and in *Histoire de la médecine*, No. V (1952), pp. 11–19.

8. See J. Schacht, "Notes sur la sociologie du droit musulman," *Revue africaine*, XCVI (1952), 318–22.

9. E. Tyan, *op. cit.*, II, 352–435.

10. H. Laoust, *Essai sur les doctrines sociales et politiques de ... B. Taimîya* (Cairo, 1939), pp. 226–50, and his *Contribution à une étude de la méthodologie canonique de ... B. Taimîya* (Cairo, 1939), *passim*.

11. See "Notes sur la sociologie du droit musulman," pp. 322–27.

12. Cf. the manuscript *fiqh ḥanbalî* 70 in the Ẓâhiriyya Library, Damascus.

13. See J. Schacht, "Šarîʿa und Qânûn im modernen Ägypten," *Der Islam*, XX (1932), 209–36; and my *Esquisse d'une histoire du droit musulman* (Paris, 1953), pp. 84–89.

LITERARY TENDENCIES

FRANCESCO GABRIELI

We obviously mean by "Islâm" here the whole "Muslim civilization" which developed, with its own physiognomy, from Central Asia to the Atlantic, in faith in Mohammed's message and in the wake of the Arab diaspora. Chronologically this civilization appeared in the seventh century and lasted until, ceasing to be autonomous after having ceased to be fruitful, it entered a crisis and was transformed, at the touch of the West, at about the end of the eighteenth century. Religious faith unquestionably furnished to this civilization not only its common denominator but also its axis and fundamental aspect. All other aspects of life—material and spiritual, political and literary, economic and social—bear this religious element's mark, take color from its reflections, and develop under its influence. Islâm, it has been said, is more than any other a totalitarian religion, and it encompasses the whole man, not his religious consciousness alone.

While holding strictly to these premises, it is legitimate, however, to seek to distinguish the other factors making up the historical picture of Muslim civilization, along with the religious factor that influenced them. We want to speak of the literary factor here, not as a purely aesthetic element—which would lead to a study of distinctive personalities standing out against the background of a tradition—but as the study of the tradition itself or, rather, of the several changing and contrasted traditions that reflect the antinomy, "unity and variety of Islâm," in the literary field. Such an antinomy forces itself on anyone who comes into contact with this civilization: behind the rigorously uniform façade of religion, law, and social custom, we can guess, and now and then perceive, that multiplicity conditioned in space and time that gives us the concrete reality within the abstract schema—the live organism behind the stylized expression of the statue. Of course it is a very hard and delicate thing to grasp this life and the secret reality which is masked under the smooth uniformity of the external facies. Where the literary field that occupies us here is concerned, the undertaking is exceedingly difficult and practically hopeless if we aim to come upon cases of "individuality" submerged in the tradition; it is easier, on the other hand, if we can limit ourselves, as we have set out to do, to bringing out the contrasts and varieties of the literary traditions as indexes of the variety within the fundamental unity of the civilization we are studying.

Limiting oneself to these contrasts of traditions also lessens an author's presumption when he extends his judgments to more than one literature, as anyone must do who wants to study this phenomenon, at least in principle, over the whole area of Muslim civilization. We have still another and perhaps better excuse in the fact that over this whole area a single language and a single literature, the Arabic, held predominance and absolute power for some time. Moreover, even where this language and literature lost their primacy in the course of time, their influence did not come to an end, at least within the chronological limits we have indicated. For this reason it is perhaps not so grievous for an Arabist to be speaking here about tendencies and contrasts "in Islâm," rather than an Iranist or a Turkologist, for the Arabic literary contribution is in the forefront of our picture by its proportions in space and time and by its intensity of tone and color; the Arabist speaking in general terms about Islâm might even—to his detriment, certainly, but without getting beyond his depth—somewhat neglect the other two master literatures of the Muslim world, but every informed person knows how inconceivable would be the contrary procedure. Thus Arabic literature (or, better, literature "in Arabic") figures pre-eminently as our subject; and, next, Persian literature, which comes immediately after the Arabic in historical richness and importance but which equals it and perhaps surpasses it in artistic value. When we come to studies referring to the last leg of the "tripod," Turkish literature and its dependencies, both the competence of the present writer and the absolute and relative importance of the subject in the hierarchy of Muslim literatures decline.

Let us now look at this Arabic literature, which came into being, in an already fixed and stylized language, before Islâm itself, and which has furnished a common denominator to our studies. No one can fail to recognize the bonds existing between the literary heritage of pre-Islamic Persia and its later elaboration in the Muslim period; further, it is impossible not to notice the ties, albeit looser and more exceptional, between pre-Muslim Turkish literature, or rather folklore, and the Turks' first timid literary efforts inside Islâm. Neither the Persians nor the Turks, however, continued in the Muslim period to cultivate, except perhaps in certain forms of popular art, any literary products such as had existed in their pre-Islamic period; this is just what Muslim Arabic poetry did, on the contrary, borrowing its forms and its themes from pagan Arabic poetry over a period of centuries as from a model that for a long time seemed incomparable. Along with this poetry, the Sacred Book of Islâm, revealed in Arabic (*Qur'ânan ʿarabiyyan*), the very Word of God which was afterwards felt to be uncreated, forever sanctified the religious and literary primacy of Arabic within Islâm. Arabic was subsequently spread as the language of the believers and conquerors, from the Jazîrat al-ʿArab to the Mediterranean Basin and to Hither Asia. Less than a hundred years after the Prophet's death, it was the official, dominant, if not exclusive, language of government as well as of literature, and it was so from the banks of the Tagus to those of the Jaxartes; so true was this that verses were written in the same Arabic, according to the metrics, diction, and style of the oldest desert poets, at Cordova and at Kairouan, at Fusṭâṭ and at Damascus, at Kûfa, at Merv, and at Bukhara. The cultures that were old national possessions, or that previous history had transplanted into countries where Muslim conquest now extended, rapidly withered or even disappeared altogether before the new Arabo-Islamic culture, which, from the day it arose, conquered and absorbed all pre-existing elements. Latin, Greek, Coptic, Syriac, Armenian, and Pahlevi weakened and tended to disappear as living languages before Arabic's advance; and, when the Abbasids substituted their theocratic and supernational empire for the Arab national state, Arabic nevertheless remained the master language, used even by those who fought the cultural hegemony of the Arabs. The great Abbasid culture in Iraq, during the second and third centuries of the hegira (ninth and tenth centuries A.D.), which marked the apex of Arabo-Muslim intellectual effort, was at the same time the heart and the crucible of Arabic classical literature, which extended its influence from the extreme west to Transoxania. In these two centuries this literature created all its art forms, discussed its vital problems, was opened to the influence of prior great cultures, beginning with the Greek, and thus wrote the most brilliant page in medieval Islamic civilization. In the beginning of the eleventh century of our era, the heartbeats of Arab culture grew weaker in Iraq, only to stop altogether after the Mongol invasion, while the peripheral centers, which were Syria and Egypt, the Maghrib and Spain, burned with the brighter light. The fourteenth century, as is now commonly admitted, saw the end of

Arabic literature as a creative force, after a life of at least seven centuries. Even more rapid in development, its younger sister in Persia had already had its finest classical period by the time of our Renaissance, while the Turkish Osmanli and Chaghatai literatures, the last to appear, began at just this period to live on the hand-me-downs of their two elder sisters—in the most artificial kind of hothouse existence, to the point of total captivation.

In this long and vast cycle of the pre-eminent Islamic literature, what distinctions, groupings, or contrasts can be brought out? The purely formal problem of a historical-scholarly division takes on new meaning if we consider it in the light of the criterion we have adopted here, that is, investigating variety in the literary field: a succession and a contrasting coexistence of tendencies within an apparently static civilization. It is obvious that divisions which are simply chronological or geographical (literature of east and west) cannot suffice, although they contain, in addition to their practical usefulness, undeniable elements of reality. It is necessary to integrate them into an *ab intus* analysis of the Arabic literary process.

Islâm at its origin found a national poetic tradition that was already stabilized and blossoming. The Prophet's own rather slight inclination and competence for poetry, and the traces of polemic which as a result remained in the Koran itself and in Tradition,[1] did not prevent him from recognizing the social value which poetry had long had for the Arabs and from utilizing it for his ends. But although recent studies have weakened the old thesis of the total impermeability of the ancient poetry to the Islamic message,[2] there remains nonetheless the fundamental fact of the contrast, analyzed masterfully by Goldziher, between *muruwwa* and *dîn*—between the pagan ideals, of which the antique poetry had become the vehicle, and Mohammed's Islamic ideal, which the first generations of Muslims developed.[3] Islâm's totalitarian character, which we mentioned above, should logically have led to the condemnation of poetry as a frivolous and even impious foe of revelation, a living witness to vanquished paganism, a diabolic inspiration of the jinns. If this did not happen at all, and if poetry continued undisturbed on its way (with sporadic concessions to the new faith but keeping its themes, motifs, and images intact, as well as its power to fascinate even the minds of the pious), this was due not only to the art's "charm"—a charm that Plato recognized when he banished the art from his Republic—but also to the unbroken continuity among the first Muslim generations of a specific national awareness and pride which the new religion never succeeded in removing completely from their souls. The "Muslim" never succeeded in killing the "Arab" in these men, for whom poetry had constituted the sole means of expression, the sole affirmation of spirituality, and, according to the well-known definition, the record of his pageantry, the living memento of his past. Thus it was that the old poetry survived the *metanoia* of Islâm and was saved from oblivion, gathered into collections, and studied. It has been said that this was done because the ancient poetry contained documentary material for the exact understanding of the Holy Book, and this is partially true; but the whole archaic period of imitation of pre-Islamic poetry, which was pursued in the first century of Islâm and which was to constitute one of the poles of the "Ancients-Moderns" quarrel under the Abbasids, proves that this poetry was nevertheless experienced not only as a means but as an end, with an artistic and historic dignity of its own. The Ancients par excellence, the *mutaqaddimûn*, were the pagan poets, and the fact that two centuries after the end of the *jâhiliyya* they could still be considered by erudite Muslims as an unparalleled model to imitate reveals in our opinion not only a nearsighted classicism—a narrow, archaic, and scholastic notion of poetry—but also a tenacious and perhaps unconscious survival of what we might, "with a grain of salt," call the "humanism" of the *jâhiliyya*—a scale of values, a stylistic and poetic tradition which Islâm might well have been able to eject and which yet maintained itself with an astonishing vitality.

It was not accidental, indeed, that Goldziher, in his analysis of the motives which in the Abbasid period favored the appearance of the "new school" of the *muḥdathûn*, gave a leading place to an element which was neither literary nor ethnic but religious, that is, the growing devaluation of paganism and its ideals in favor of the Muslim *dîn*.[4] But to be consistent, this reversal of values should have led to a revolt not against the antique poetry alone but against all poetry, admitting at most gnomic and ascetic versification of Abû al-ᶜAtâhiya's type. The "Moderns" movement, on the contrary, seems to have been the most daring attempt to renovate the poetic themes and forms which the antique Arabic literature had known—a renovation which was, to be sure, inspired not by rigorist conceptions but by love of the art, by a more fully developed aesthetic awareness, by complex and delicate exigencies of a social kind. We wish to point out that the new literary currents of the Abbasid period and the polemics which they entailed, although abandoning the myth of the *jâhiliyya*—and in this agreeing with pietistic tendencies—did not, however, abandon but rather enlarged the humanistic ideal involved, brought over from the life-styles of pre-Islamic Arabia to the urban society of Iraq in the ninth and tenth centuries and to that of other urban centers in medieval Islâm. As a whole, the fundamental contrast, which nobody then dared explicitly to formulate but which we can today see more clearly, was not so much between "old and new poetry," between Ancients and Moderns, as between, let us repeat, *muruwwa* and *dîn*, between anthropocentric humanism and theocentric religiosity, between Arabic poetry and Muslim piety. Strictly speaking, indeed, the incomparable Revelation, with its *iʿjâz* which was considered even formally perfect, should have depreciated and undermined every other effort at artistic expression; so true is this that a theologian and cultivated literary man of the tenth century, al-Bâquillânî, having undertaken to test Koranic *iʿjâz* in style itself, submitted to equally close criticism an Ancient and a Modern poet, Imruʾal-Qais, and al-Buḥturî.[5] Happily for mankind, poetry never died out and resisted even the most hostile imputations, whether theological or philosophic, explicit or latent.

In purely literary terms, the struggle of the new Abbasid school to consolidate itself against the antique tradition undoubtedly constitutes the most interesting episode in the history of Arabic literature during its classical period. The weapons with which this battle was carried on and its progressive victory during the tenth century are the subjects of Goldziher's study cited above: from Ibn Qutaiba, who remained halfway between correct historical intuition ("No age has a monopoly of poetry; every ancient was modern in his time") and the crushing weight of tradition (forbidding the Moderns to adapt the canonical framework of the *qaṣîda* to the new conditions of life), all the way to the Maghribî school of al-Ḥuṣrî and Ibn Rashîq and to the gifted Ibn al-Athîr, we are able to follow a liberation of literary criticism from the classicist yoke, up to the affirmation of the superiority of the *muḥdathûn* over the venerated *fuḥûl* of antiquity. But to this victory in criticism there did not correspond any true and lasting victory in practice, which would have led to the total shattering of the consecrated frames. It has been noted that, in large part due to al-Mutanabbî's work (d. A.D. 965), a new classicism tainted with preciosity (the most questionable heritage of the "Moderns") weighed upon Arabic poetry after the tenth century and definitively ossified it. It had already been known to what straits this poetry was reduced, at least in the east, after the year 1000; and recent study on the poets of the lesser period now confirms this, as witness Rikâbî's study on the Ayyubid poets.[6] For these, the artistic renovation and the critical labors of the great Abbasid period—the work of a Jâḥiẓ (d. 869) or an Ibn Qutaiba (d. 889), not to mention the isolated efforts of the Hellenist Qudâma (first half of tenth century)—had been in vain, and a saddening neoclassical formalism penetrated their *dîwâns*. Individuality, always in doubt and menaced by tradition in oriental literatures, becomes completely imperceptible from then on; lonely, bent upon his solitary labors, sometimes contradictory and vague, perhaps even deliberately so, and himself paying a very large tribute to tradition, the exceptional figure of Abû al-ᶜAlâᵓ al-Maᶜarrî (d. 1058) rises in this age of decadence.

The battle of the Abbasid period having ended in this way, medieval Arabic poetry was fossilized for centuries in the entire east. It is to the Maghrib, to North Africa and Spain, that the credit goes for introducing some new elements, which were both formal and conceptual, into this literary "unity" now grown terribly monotonous.[7] Let us note, above all, how the lesson of the "Moderns," soon lost in the east under the dominant neoclassicism, seems to have left more lasting traces in the west, in a valuable Alexandrinism and fragmentarism, which is emphasized still more by the anthological collections (Ibn Bassâm, Ibn Khâqân, etc.) and which perpetuates in the west the new taste of Ibn al-Muᶜtazz (d. 908), al-Ṣanawbarî, and others of the *muḥdathûn* of Iraq and of Syria. But beyond this more marked faithfulness to the "new school," the west brought two great innovations to medieval Arabic poetry: the strophic form and the use of the vulgar tongue, the *muwashshaḥa* and the *zajal*, which are a center of interest today for Arabic and Romance studies. The Andalusian origin of strophic poetry, whatever the uncertainty of names and dates for its beginnings, is at the same time affirmed by the whole Muslim historicoliterary tradition. Whatever may have been its possible but highly doubtful oriental precedents, the breaking-away by the Blind One of Qabra, or whoever it was, from the monorhymed scheme of the *qaṣîda*, and its articulation into the more supple strophic form with multiple rhymes, represented more than a purely metric novelty, and fresh blood began to run in the veins of the old poetry of the Arabian deserts. Opposed to the antique *qaṣîda* and its fixed scheme, there appeared not only the free erotic, descriptive, and bacchic *qiṭʿa* of the *muḥdathûn* but also a new type of composition which, in the play of its strophes, in its relaxation of the rules of classical poetry, and in its tendency to use the vulgar tongue, shortened the distance between art and life—a distance which had already been dangerously widened in Muslim society of the Middle Ages. The diffusion of the new art from the Maghrib, where it arose, once more stimulated the rapid and continuous circulation of Arabic culture; the extension of the vulgar tongue from the *kharja* (where according to the learned it had made its first appearance) to all of poetic composition, that is, the step from the *muwashshaḥa* in literary language to dialectical *zajal*, which was carried out we know not by whom or where (Ibn Quzmân [d. 1160] is the most important but neither the only one nor the first of the *zajjâlûn*), constitutes the most daring realistic effort in medieval Arabic poetry, with all the linguistic, literary, and social consequences which we are now in process of analyzing. This realistic attempt did not, however, succeed in breaking the domination of classical language and forms in the high literature of the Arabic-speaking world. As is demonstrated by many indications (Ibn Quzmân's *dîwân* copied in Palestine, the little treatise on the *muwashshaḥa* by Ibn Sanâʾ al-Mulk, the attempts at *zajal* contained in the anthologies by the "orientals" al-Ḥillî and al-Ḥamawî),[8] the Arabic east was highly interested in these Maghribî novelties but did not dare to develop them to the full, arrested as it was, at least so far as the *zajal* is concerned, by the prejudice against literary use of dialectical tongues. The valuable Andalusian innovation thus did not have anything like the revolutionary importance it might have had, that is, elevating to a literary level the Arabic dialects even outside the Maghrib. The divorce between cultivated literature and the spoken tongue was thus accentuated at the end of the Middle Ages and was imposed for good.

An examination of the evolution (or the involution) of Arabic prose leads us to similar conclusions, although it followed a different process. In the absence of literary usage in the pre-Islamic period, or at least of evidences which would demonstrate it, this prose at first attained a high prestige with the Koran and the oldest *ḥadîth* (which was historical and normative) and was spread over the whole of the Arabic world no less rapidly than was poetry. The Holy Book held a special position, naturally, whatever may have been the early and sacrilegious attempts at imitation. But the elaboration of profane prose by the Umayyad and Abbasid *kuttâb* created classical Arabic prose in the first two centuries of the hegira, with its principal center, like that of poetry, in Iraq: the prose of Ibn al-Muqaffa^c (d. *ca.* 757), of al-Jâḥiẓ, of al-Tauḥîdî (d. 1023), and of al-Tanûkhî (d. 994), the sources of the *Aghânî* and of Ibn Qutaiba. As in the case of poetry of the classical type, it would be useless to seek any regional characteristics here, so great was the unity from the center to the periphery of this Arabo-Muslim culture, of this *adab* in the Arabic language which was open to influences from the great foreign cultures, Hellenistic, Iranian, and Indian. The great new formal innovation in Arabic prose cannot be traced back to local variations, but rather can be traced to the appearance in the ninth century of precious prose and its unfortunate victory in literary art. Modern Arab critics have sought to attribute this corruption of the simple, bold, and limber prose of the first two centuries to "Persian influence."[9] Now it is well known that artificial prose was equally widespread, to the point of excess, in the Iranian literary domain; but it seems difficult to attribute the cause of the evil to Persia exclusively or in large part. It was actually an Arab, Ibn Duraid, to whom is attributed the origin of the *maqâma*, on account of his scenes of Bedouin life in the precious style; Arabs also, by blood and culture, were Ibn Nubâta (d. 984) and al-Khwârizmi (d. *ca.* 1000), al-Hamadhânî (d. 1008), and al-Ḥarîrî (d. 1122), those great virtuosos of the *saj*^c, who made a game and a head-splitting exercise out of the literature of the *adab*. From Ibn Ḥayyân (d. 1076) to Ibn Bassâm (d. 1147), Arab also were all those western prose writers who produced in the new style, forcing into their rhythmic cadences and their word-plays the most interesting historical and literary material. Even if we admit some foreign influence as possible, we cannot fail to consider precious prose as a spontaneous degeneration of the innate Semitic tendency to parallelism and to rhythm, a tendency which was already present in the ancient *khuṭba*, sporadically and moderately employed by the great eighth- and ninth-century prose writers, but overflowing in their successors to the point of drowning all content in verbal music. After the year 1000, only the new style of scientific, philosophic, and religious prose was saved from the contagion (and that not always), or the dry chronicle without pretensions to *adab;* but a literature of the *adab* which escaped the precious style is henceforth, from Mesopotamia to Andalusia, an exception. What is most surprising is the fact that the old style gave up without a struggle and without polemics, contrary to what happened in the battle of the old and the new poetry. It became the new fashion to attack the old style arrogantly (the scornful judgment of Hamadhânî of Jâḥiẓ as a writer is very significant here),[10] but no counterblows came from the opposite camp. The very writer who did not succumb to the lure of the *saj*ᶜ felt neither the need nor even the possibility of expressly affirming his position, and no Arab rhetorician, so far as I know, opposed rhetorical excess from a theoretical standpoint. The diffusion of the most authentic product of the new style, the *maqâma,* not only in the whole Arabic linguistic territory but into the other Muslim (Persian and Turkish) literatures and even to non-Muslim neighbors (medieval Hebraic literature), gives the measure of the victory of a tendency which is so strange to us today but to which the most widely separated and varied minds of the Muslim Middle Ages gave their loyalty. If other phenomena point to the unity of "Arabic" culture, that of precious prose—although certainly Arabic in origin, as we see it—imposed itself, across the linguistic barriers, over the whole territory of Islâm.

Passing from form to content (which that form ended by practically destroying), we can isolate other more concrete influences in medieval Arabo-Islamic prose—influences which sometimes reveal local cultural aspects and currents. Such, in the west, are the traces of Hispanic epic and history, uncovered by Ribera in the most ancient Arabo-Spanish chroniclers,[11] to which can be added those still more fragile traces, recently discovered by Levi Della Vida, of contacts between the Arabic culture in the west and the Latin culture of the low period (Orosius' histories).[12] At the same time also, in Abbasid Iraq in the golden centuries, the stream of foreign cultures was spread through the translators and adapters from the Greek, the Syriac, the Pahlevi and, for the Indian world, through the solitary grandeur of al-Bêrûnî (d. 1048). But these cultural goods, transfused into the heart of the caliphate, rapidly became the common possessions of the whole Muslim world. Aristotle was studied by Avicenna in Persia as well as by Averroes in Morocco and in Spain, just as, in the realm of reading for entertainment, the *Kalîla and Dimna,* once it was introduced by Ibn al-Muqaffaᶜ into Arabo-Muslim literature, traveled from one end of the *dâr al-Islâm* to the other, only to return to Persia wearing the inevitable dress of precious prose. But the work whose peregrinations perhaps show the unity and variety of medieval Arabic culture best is, as everyone knows, the *Thousand and One Nights.* A uniform Muslim patina has for centuries covered this classic of world literature, but, beneath this, modern criticism is able to perceive the various Arabic and non-Arabic layers in its immense material: first, traces of the Abbasid phase and more evident ones of the Egyptian phase which gave the celebrated collection its final outward form; while, from beyond the Arabic world, criticism also reveals evident traces of its distant Indian origin, and, still more surprising and suggestive, traces of the Hellenistic world, according to Von Grunebaum's recent studies. With these last might be associated not only the elements that have already been revealed in "The Voyages of Sindbad" but also a large group of love tales which recall, in the intrigue related, in their style, and in exposition, well-known models in the Alexandrian novel.[13]

Arabic literature, in its centuries-long course and over the whole enormous territory through which it extended, was born from the reciprocal influence—sometimes harmonious, sometimes clashing—of two elements: a national, indigenous, and, although intellectually rudimentary, humanistic element, which was at the same time tight and exclusive in its racial pride; and a second, religious, international, universalist element, open because of these qualities to contacts and exchanges with other civilizations. The coexistence of these two elements in our opinion confers on Arabic literature all its breadth, the wide gamut of its interests, and its primacy within the world of Islâm, of which it was and remains the most direct and the most authoritative expression.

During the first two centuries of the hegira (practically until the middle of the ninth century A.D.) Islâm knew no literature other than the Arabic. The appearance about this time of neo-Persian literature is important not only for the history of Iran, which thus reaffirmed its national individuality, at least linguistically, but also for the whole Muslim civilization which with it begins to try out, alongside its mother-language, a new means of expression. The rapid and splendid blooming of this second Islamic literature is interesting, not only from a literary point of view, but also from the social and religious ones, for it breaks for the first time the close bond between Arabism and Islâm and opens new possibilities of spiritual affirmation to non-Arabic Muslim peoples. The well-known fact that the religious, juridical, and philosophic sciences for a long time continued to be treated in Arabic in Persia here remains secondary; what count are the literary and artistic means of expression, suited to expressing a different ethos, a national characteristic, a more than linguistic "variety" within the common Muslim culture. According to the terms of our problem, we can then ask the following question: What did neo-Persian literature bring to Islamic civilization that was new, what did it borrow, what did it prolong, what did it modify in Arabic literature, and what did it add that was original from its own ethnic and cultural background?

Persian literature's debt to the Arabic literature which preceded it and, so to speak, introduced it into the Islamic sphere certainly cannot be underestimated; to be convinced of this, it is only necessary to emphasize here the well-known linguistic phenomenon of the gradual and irresistible invasion of quite foreign structures into the Iranian language from the Arabic vocabulary and even from Arabic phraseology. To the linguistic integrity of the epic and, in less measure, of the oldest lyric poetry, to a certain abhorrence which the Persians at first had for gathering too many Arabic words into their tongue (an abhorrence which is shown to exist as late as the second half of the tenth century),[14] there succeeded in the eleventh century the massive expansion within Persian of this Arabic vocabulary, which was to give and still gives its clearly composite character to that tongue. But it was not only a part of its lexicon that Arabic literature gave to Persia, but also literary kinds and rules, stylistic themes and models, metrics and rhetoric, a scientific and artistic terminology. Where the erotic and courtly lyric of the first stages is concerned, the most elementary chronological consideration obliges us to reverse the traditional thesis which explains the birth of the Arabic poetry of the Abbasid *muḥdathûn* by "Iranian influence" and to see in it, on the contrary, the model for the Persian poetry of the courts of Khurâsân and of Transoxania. Daudpota's study showed twenty years ago to what degree the poets at these courts followed the traditional Arabic models (the *nasîb*, in the first place, and sometimes even the archaic *nasîb* of Bedouin poetry),[15] just as the images and concepts of the Abbasid *badîᶜ* reappear, more or less happily copied in the new tongue. It is understood of course that, once neo-Persian literature was established, the influence became reciprocal within a culture that was often bilingual, a fact which did not prevent the first models from being offered by the already mature Arabic art to the just emerging neo-Persian literature. At the same time, even in this realm, Persian literature certainly did not restrict itself to slavish imitation and immediately introduced novelties in form and content (the creation of the autonomous *ghazal* following detachment of the traditional *nasîb* from the rest of the *qaṣîda*,[16] of the *rubâᶜî* which was destined to receive the eternal imprint of Iranian genius, and of the *mathnavî* immediately consecrated by the epic), just as Persian literature infused new life into even the most commonplace elements (the bacchic theme and the gnomic-pessimistic theme, both brought to a high perfection by Khayyâm), thanks to the splendor of a rapidly stylized repertory of images and to a language which reached no less rapidly an unmatchable fluidity and harmony.

And yet it is not in lyric, courtly, and erotic poetry that Muslim Persia made its most original contribution to world literature but, as everyone knows, in the heroic and romantic epic. The Arabic muse which had inspired it elsewhere failed it here, and the Iranian spirit really drew upon its own resources and created absolutely original works which did not depend in the least on the patterns and products of the elder literature of Islâm. Even if we abstain here from any aesthetic appreciation of the writers, we cannot fail to recognize in Firdausî (d. *ca.* 1020) and Niẓâmî (d. 1203) the most eloquent spokesmen of the national tradition in their poems, which became perfect models for Persian literature and for all those who were inspired by it in this respect. With the heroic and knightly *mathnavî*, Iran produced an indubitably original note in the orchestra of Muslim literature. Only an abstract consideration of content, however, can fail to see in Niẓâmî and Firdausî the links that join them to medieval Muslim civilization, which they were both dependent upon and which is more or less clearly revealed in their works. The *Shâh-Nâma* has been called by turns pagan and Zoroastrian, foreign to Islâm; and certainly its matter is quite extra-Islamic and the poet's emotional adherence to the heroic and distant world he celebrates very sincere. Nonetheless, it remains true that the social and cultural reality of an already Islamized Iran sometimes shines through even the archaic Firdausian poem[17] and does so even more in Niẓâmî's various exquisite romantic poems, all impregnated, although to different degrees, by Muslim culture and piety, as anyone must be aware who has truly read the *Khamsa* in the original. These remarks, brief as they are, are intended as a reaction against the tendency which certain historians of Persian literature have shown (and I must recall here the illustrious name of my compatriot Italo Pizzi) to detach the epic and the romantic Persian poets from the social and religious atmosphere that surrounded them—to make them, as it were, champions of an "Aryan" tradition which, if it ever existed in a pure form in Persia, perished at the same time as did the Sassanid state and civilization. Islâm's imprint, once made upon a people, is never effaced, and the great Persian poets, even when they treat material anterior and exterior to Islâm, carry its stamp no less.

Persian literature was to make a still more direct and fecund contribution to Islamic spirituality with its mystic poetry when it vied in this field, according to its own genius, with Arabic literature and soon exceeded it by its inventive talent and its variety of exposition, perhaps even by its speculative depth. Lyric poetry, the apologue, and mystic meditation constitute the field in which the two great Islamic literatures took one another's measure, and the palm goes without any contest to Iranian literature. Ṣûfism, born in the Arabic world and counting its theoreticians, visionaries, and saints among the Arabs by the hundreds, never succeeded in expressing itself in Arabic except by an abstruse and turgid so-called "lyric," if we make an exception for the few but unforgettable verses of al-Ḥallâj (d. 922), and by a very rich ascetic output of only moderate literary worth. The Persian genius alone gave to Muslim mysticism the glory of a luxuriant poetic bloom in which the innate aptitude of the Iranians for narration and the sentence combined with the energy of a highly stimulated emotionality and with the audacity of the most unbridled esoteric speculations. It is from this that there came, again without equivalents in Arabic literature, the poems of Rûmî (d. 1273), of ᶜAṭṭâr (d. *ca.* 1230), and of Jâmî (d. 1492), the religious outpourings of Abû Saᶜîd (d. 1049) and of Rûmî himself, the refined gnomicolyric embroideries of Saᶜdî (d. 1291) and of Ḥâfiẓ[18] (d. *ca.* 1390)—the most brilliant pleiad in the Persian poetic firmament. The voice of Islamic Ṣûfism seems far more appealing in the works of these Persians than in the very vast asceticomystic Arab literature, which goes from the austere sentences of Ḥasan al-Baṣrî to the obscure *qaṣîdas* of Ibn al-Fâriḍ; and all the great minds of the West, from Goethe to Hegel, who sought to approach this aspect of Muslim spirituality, actually took as their guides not the Arabic ascetics or doctors but the great Persian poets we have just named.

As recompense, if it was one, for this contribution to the religious poetry of Islâm, Persian literature received from Arabic literature during these centuries, if what we have suggested about the origin of precious prose is correct, the seeds of degeneration of its prose style. Surely the Iranian literary genius must have been predisposed to the malady, so easily did the disease capture it, spoiling the vigor and freshness of the prose of its beginnings and reducing it to that hybrid, undigested mixture from which only the contemporary period has begun to liberate itself—and that, not without some difficulty. For lack of space we must restrict ourselves to this comment. In concluding these few observations on what Persia brought to Islamic culture during the classical period, it seems to us that this can be defined by certain original aspects in profane literary creations (epic and narrative) and by the intensity and the brilliant color of religious expression (Ṣûfî poetry). We might also recall, in a field involving prose but one more scientific than literary, the work of the great historians of the Mongol period, which surpasses by far the Arabic historiography of the same centuries.

For obvious geographical and linguistic reasons Persian literature remained foreign to western Islâm, while from the beginning of the thirteenth century it began to fertilize the spiritual life of the Islamic peoples east of the Mediterranean. Three ethnic groups underwent the religious and cultural influence of Islâm through Persia as intermediary: the Hindus, Mongols, and Turks. It is only among the last named, however (leaving aside the not very important Hindustani literature), that the Persian influence manifested itself in their own national language or languages. The group of Turkish Islamic literatures, primarily the Chaghatai and the Osmanli, depends much more closely on the Persian model than Persian literature had ever depended on the Arabic; these literatures, indeed, add nothing to their model that is new in either spirit or form, while we have seen the importance of what Persia brought to the literary patrimony of Islâm. True, the Turks also possessed a crude and strong folklore of their own, which they brought along with them on their migrations from the heart of Central Asia; but this pre-Islamic background, in contrast to those of the Arabs and of the Persians, was almost totally abandoned by the Islamized Turks, who were immediately attracted by the two great full-grown and refined Muslim literatures, especially the Persian. The few surviving monuments of Turkish epic and national folklore, like the recently restudied *Dede Qorqut*,[19] clash sharply with the customary background of Islamized Turkish literature. The latter, from its first efforts (the *Qudatqu Bilik* of the eleventh century and the other minor writings belonging to the period and the environment of the Qarakhânids of Central Asia), leaned directly upon Iranian models—on the "Mirrors for Princes" and the treatises on government of the Seljuq epoch—thus already taking on its character as a courtly, conventional, and imitative art. The same is true for the whole Chaghatai literature (which culminates at the end of the fifteenth century with Nevâʾî at the court of the Tîmûrids) and for a good portion of the Osmanli literature, which appeared in Seljuq Anatolia in the thirteenth century and was carried on, with Istanbul as its center, until the crisis of the last century. Admirers of literature conceived as the authentic expression of the soul of a people, of those *Stimmen der Völker* which appear also in Arabic and Persian literature although narrowed into the most rigid stylization, are likely to regret that such voices were so rapidly killed in Turkish literature, stifled as they were by the cold artistic literature—by that *divan edebiyyati* which today's Turks regard with boredom and scorn. The spontaneous popular current which, with Sultan Veled (d. 1312), Yunus Emre (first half of fourteenth century) and the other older poets, took a spark from the great fire of Persian mysticism and caused it to glow in simple and innocent forms in their national tongue, was quickly extinguished before the artificial current which dominated Ottoman literature for four centuries. The pattern of the Persian poetic world is stamped upon it to the point of the most exhausting monotony, from romantic poems in the manner of Niẓâmî to the courtly and aristocratic poetry, as well as to the burlesque satires where, at the most, one may find some few happy touches of realism. This whole "literature," in the worst sense of the word, follows the rising and then falling curve of the last Muslim empire and collapses, with that state's medieval structure, during the nineteenth century. It is not by chance that, of the three master literatures of Islâm, Turkish literature was the first to go into a crisis upon contact with the West and to move forward daringly and even radically on the way to a total remodeling. This most artificial organism, bred upon foreign models and values, fell almost without any resistance under the innovating shock of European thought and art.

The modern and contemporary phase of Muslim literatures is outside the limits which we have set ourselves in this article, which had for its object summarily to touch upon the principal currents and contrasts; it is outside our scope for the very reason that the modern period saw the weakening of the common denominator of the Muslim civilizations, against the background of which we have seen the three master literatures by which this civilization was expressed, bound to each other in a chain, so to speak. In the years closest to us, as the religious bond has been relaxed and the *dâr al-Islâm* has dissolved into touchy nationalisms (whatever may be the federalist efforts of the type of the Arab League), Islâm's unity was broken up, even in the literary realm; each of these literatures, indeed, reacted in a different way to the preponderant influence of the West, seeking to conciliate it or to repudiate ancient values in its favor. But this concerns history in process, while our analysis is devoted to history which took place long ago.

If we may make one last observation, which joins the past to the present of the three Muslim literatures, we cannot fail to remark on the differing fates of their respective languages. In Persia and in Turkey the national languages, even when they were in the past twisted into a very rigorous literary stylization, kept their character as living languages, and the spontaneous inclinations of many modern writers, sometimes helped and sometimes hindered by governmental undertakings to "purify" the language, have little by little filled in the gap between the written and the spoken tongue. In all the Arab countries, on the other hand, as everyone knows, the general phenomenon of the split between written and spoken language long ago ended in bilingualism. We cannot elaborate here the complex problems of a literary, political, and social order that this duality raises in the modern Arab world. We must, however, notice that this Arabic bilingualism has reversed the relation existing between literature and life, as it marked the three Muslim literatures at their start and for some time. Arabic literature, in which at the outset this relationship was the closest and the most fruitful (one need only think of the origins of Islâm, of the whole Umayyad period, of the golden age of the Abbasid caliphate), has seen this gap widen, as a result of bilingualism, to the point of the disconcerting hiatus in modern times, which the more lively contemporary forces are trying, more or less successfully, to fill. The Persian and Turkish literatures, on the contrary, although courtly and aristocratic from their birth, and expressions of social and intellectual elites, have, because of the single fact of having maintained the substantial unity of the linguistic instrument, been able—first in the case of the Turkish and, recently and more slowly, of the Persian—to go toward the people, to turn to their needs and interests, without in the process breaking all continuity with the national literary tradition. Whatever the position of each of us may be on the theoretical problems of language, we cannot fail to appreciate the enormous literary and social importance of such differing situations among the different Muslim nations. This is the latest case of variety in the long-wavering unity of the old *dâr al-Islâm,* a variety which our statement could not pass over in silence.

DISCUSSION

Mr. von Grunebaum begins the discussion with an observation about the development of strophic forms. It is due to a different attitude toward the phenomenon of the popular as such. There were rudiments of that form in the east (Muslim ibn al-Walîd, 747 [757]–803, and the love strophes of Abû Nuwâs, 747 [762]–806 [814]), but the east, being, so to speak, ashamed of the popular, moved away from it, whereas in the west the yielding to popular impulses was never eliminated.

He then raises the question of who won in the conflict, which was a sort of quarrel of Ancients and Moderns. Certainly the Ancients. He adds that neoclassicism became somewhat meaningless and quotes a passage of Abû al-ᶜAlâ᾿ al-Maᶜarrî (978–1058) wherein Ḥassân ibn Thâbit (d. 674) is chided for using a traditional erotic and bacchic *nasîb* in a panegyric of the Prophet (*Risâlat al-Ghufrân*, ed. Dr. Bint al-Shâṭî [Miṣr, 1950], p. 128). The introduction of such classical elements is no longer understood.

Mr. Gabrieli thinks that neoclassicism annulled only a part of the results of the Abbasid reaction. The lesson of Modernist poetry had its effects in the west. Most of the poetry of this part of the Islamic empire has come down to us in anthologies of single verses and fragments. Mr. Gabrieli sees in this dissolution of the classical unity of the *qaṣîda* one of the most important results of the quarrel of the Ancients and the Moderns.

Mr. von Grunebaum mentions the reference by Ibn Khaldûn (1332–1406) to the existence of strophic forms (*Prolegomena*, trans. W. MacG. de Slane [Paris, 1862–68], III, 402 ff., 422 ff.).

M. Abel wants to draw attention to the popular literature of the age of the Crusaders. He would like to call it an epic literature, because it was conceived to rouse the national conscience of the Arabs against the Christian invaders. The ᶜ*Antar Novel* represents the Ayyûbid tendency against the Crusaders; the romance of the *Banû Hilâl*, which is a pamphlet against the "Franks," is now being recited publicly in Syria—there are three modern editions of it. Finally there is the *Sayyid Baṭṭâl*, whose development has been illuminated by M. Canard. It was created in very early times, utilized in a nationalistic and enthusiastic way by the early Seljuqs, and reutilized in the moment of the fall of Jerusalem by the Ayyûbids.

Mr. Lewis thinks that there was a kind of reaction against the verbiage of flowery prose. An abridgment like the one Abû Shâma (1203–68) made of ᶜImâd al-Dîn's (1125–1201) *Fatḥ al-Qussî* . . . shows a sort of stylistic sensitivity which speaks for this. Mr. Lewis also sees some new and distinctive qualities in certain Ottoman historians.

Mr. Spuler remarks here that at first a gulf seems to exist between the Arabic and Persian historians, but, if we know them well, we can observe a certain development in the manner of organizing facts, from Ṭabarî (838–923) to Juwainî (1193–1283), and from Ibn al-Athîr (1160–1234) to Rashîd al-Dîn (*ca.* 1247–1308) and to the Turkish historiographers Selânîkî (d. before 1566), Pechevî (1574–*ca.* 1650), Râshid (d. 1735), etc.

M. Brunschvig recalls Ibn Khaldûn (1332–1406): we still do not know anything about his antecedents. He uses his own method—search for reasons, organization of facts in a way more significant than chronological sequence—successfully only in the more contemporary parts of his history, perhaps because his chronology was insufficient for the earlier times.

Mr. CASKEL mentions the excellent survey of Spanish history written by Ibn Khaldûn (*ᶜIbar* [Bûlâq, 1867], IV, 116–85) as a proof of the historian's power of organization.

Mr. GABRIELI recalls that for the older history of the east Ibn Khaldûn has nothing very original to offer.

Mr. MINORSKY warns of the danger of dissociating the literary form from its contents. He cites Gobineau: "La croyance musulmane et l'épopée persane ont constitué le fond de la pensée nationale des Persans," and insists upon the Persian spirit of the *Shâh-Nâma*. It was an aristocratic poem with a royalist outlook, but it contains certain episodes which appeal to all the Persian people in the dark moments of their history.

Mr. GABRIELI does not see that the *Shâh-Nâma* reflects a national Persian, anachronistic, and pre-Islamic spirit. Its subject matter clearly is pre-Islamic; but can we dissociate entirely its form, its spirit, from the Persian environment, Islamized two centuries earlier, in which it grew?

Mr. MINORSKY would like to dissociate it. He draws attention to certain poems of extra-Islamic inspiration which have been preserved, like the *Vîs u Râmîn* (*ca.* 1048, by Fakhr al-Dîn Asᶜad), or lost, like the *Vâmiq u ᶜAḏrâ*, and he states that he does not see any Islamic trend in the *Shâh-Nâma*, except right at the end when the Muslim conquest is mentioned.

M. DUCHESNE-GUILLEMIN adduces a new publication (H. Ringgren, *Fatalism in Persian Epics* [Uppsala, 1953]) which shows that the fatalism of the Persian epic is much older than Islâm and is connected with the belief in the stars—*falak, spihr*—and has nothing especially Islamic about it.

Finally, Mr. SPULER mentions a Polish publication (Tadeusz Kowalski, *Studia nad Szah-name* [Cracow, 1952]) which contains French summaries.

NOTES

1. The most striking texts are Koran 26:224–26 and 36:69, with the well-known *ḥadîth* (Ibn Ḥanbal, *Musnad* [Cairo ed., 1313/1895–96], II, 228) which calls Imruʾ al-Qais "the first of the poets on the road to Hell." Also to be remembered are Ibn Hishâm, *Sîra*, ed. F. Wüstenfeld (Göttingen, 1860), p. 882, where the Prophet quotes a verse and lames the meter, and the wretched little poem that Tradition attributes to him (*anâ n-nabiyyu lâ kadhib . . .*); cf. T. Noeldeke and F. Schwally, *Geschichte des Qorans* (Leipzig, 1909), I, 35–36.

2. O. Farrukh, *Das Bild des Frühislam in der arabischen Dichtung* (Leipzig, 1937).

3. I. Goldziher, *Muhammedanische Studien* (Halle, 1888–90), I, 1–39 (*Muruwwa* and *Dîn*).

4. I. Goldziher, "Alte und neue Poesie im Urtheile der arabischen Kritiker," in his *Abhandlungen zur arabischen Philologie* (Leiden, 1896–99), I, 122–74 (see esp. pp. 150–51).

5. G. E. von Grunebaum, *A Tenth-Century Document of Arabic Literary Theory and Criticism: The Sections on Poetry of al-Bâqillânî's "Iᶜjâz al-Qurʾân" Translated and Annotated* (Chicago, 1950).

6. J. Rikaby [Rikâbî], *La Poésie profane sous les Ayyûbides et ses principaux représentants* (Paris, 1949).

7. The development of a Maghribî and, particularly, Andalusian literary consciousness, in opposition to the east, is a fascinating theme which we should like to see treated exhaustively by a specialist like García Gómez or Pérès (in the meantime, cf., by this same Pérès, *La Poésie andalouse en arabe classique au XIe siècle* [2d ed.; Paris, 1953], pp. 40–55). Such a consciousness seems still to have been missing in the tenth century, when the currents of Abbasid science and of the *adab* turned toward Andalusia; it remained for the great cultural upsurge of the century of the Taifas to engender literary nationalism in the west, which developed in the following centuries and led finally to the opposition between *Maghâriba* and *Mashâriqa*, which is so often argued by Ibn al-Khaṭîb and Ibn Khaldûn.

8. Cf. W. Hoenerbach and H. Ritter, "Neue Materialien zum Zacal," *Oriens*, III (1950), 266–315, and V (1952), 269–301. The *Dâr al-ṭirâz* of Ibn Sanâ˒ al-Mulk was edited by J. Rikâbî (Damascus, 1949).

9. M. Kurd ˓Alî, *Umarâ˒ al-bayân* (Cairo, 1937), I, 9 ff., declares himself in favor of the non-Arabic origin of rhymed prose. For the other side see Zakî Mubârak, *La Prose arabe au IV siècle de l'hégire (X siècle)* (Paris, 1931), pp. 49 ff., and our *Storia della letteratura araba* (Milan, 1952), pp. 201–2.

10. Hamadhânî, *Maqâmât* (Beirut ed., 1889), pp. 69–75 (*Maqâma Jâḥiẓiyya*).

11. J. Ribera, "Épica andaluza romanceada," in his *Disertaciones y opúsculos* (Madrid, 1928), I, 93–150.

12. G. Levi Della Vida, "La Traduzione araba delle storie di Orosio," *Miscellanea G. Galbiati* (Milan, 1951), III, 185–203.

13. G. E. von Grunebaum, "Greek Form Elements in the Arabian Nights," *Journal of the American Oriental Society*, LXII (1942), 277–92, and *Medieval Islam* (2d ed.; Chicago, 1953), pp. 294–319.

14. See the evidence from Ibn Jinnî (d. A.D. 1002), cited by U. M. Daudpota, *The Influence of Arabic Poetry on the Development of Persian Poetry* (Bombay, 1934), p. 14.

15. Daudpota, *op. cit.*, pp. 33 ff., with examples drawn chiefly from Mînûchihrî, one of the ancient poets who was most sensitive to the influence of classical Arabic poetry.

16. E. Bertels, "Persidskaya poeziya v Buchare X veke," *Trudi Instituta Vostokovedeniia, Akademiia Nauk S.S.S.R.* (Moscow and Leningrad, 1935), Vol. X.

17. The *Yûsuf u Zalîkhâ*, whose authenticity is in great dispute, is not being spoken of here; cf. on this question, most recently, S. Naficy [Nafîsî], "Le 'Yûsuf et Zalîkhâ' attribué à Ferdowcy," *Archiv orientální*, XVIII (1950), 351–53.

18. Ḥâfiẓ' name requires us to recall that the mystic interpretation includes only one aspect of this poet's personality, while another view in modern exegesis sees the expression of a pure lyricism in his work, free of all exoterism (which henceforth seems almost certain for ˓Umar Khayyâm). The best-founded opinion, in our view, is the one that sees the possibility of two interpretations, both equally valid, for Ḥâfiẓ' poetry, with an ambiguity that the poet himself desired. Cf. H. H. Schaeder, *Goethes Erlebnis des Ostens* (Leipzig, 1938), pp. 105–22 ("Lebensansicht und lyrische Form bei Hafis"), and H. R. Roemer, "Probleme der Hafisforschung und der Stand ihrer Lösung," in *Akademie der Wissenschaften und Literatur, Abhandlungen der Klasse der Literatur*, Vol. X (1951).

19. E. Rossi, *Il "Kitâb-i Dede Qorqut": Racconti epico-cavallereschi dei Turchi Oguz tradotti e annotati* (Città del Vaticano, 1952).

INTERACTION AND INTEGRATION IN ISLAMIC ART*

RICHARD ETTINGHAUSEN

THE unique character of Muslim art is a commonly known fact, which is experienced even by people who know hardly anything about this civilization. The main normative force which created this phenomenon was Islâm itself. Though as a religion Islâm had not allied itself with the arts in a way comparable to Christianity and Buddhism and set but few specific tasks for the artists, it nevertheless created a way of life and attitudes which deeply influenced its architecture, the range and character of its iconography, the treatment and type of ornament, and the choice of material everywhere in its domain.[1] Yet, in spite of the apparent uniform character of Islamic art, everybody who becomes familiar with its various aspects realizes more and more the tremendous variety in the different regions and even in the changing periods within a single territory. These differences are so marked that if we take, for instance, pottery, one of the commonest decorated materials, we can date within a century, sometimes within a half or a quarter of a century, any archeological site where sherds have been found, and gain at times also information about influences of trade or of migratory workers. Even in instances where we have not been able to establish specific dates or places of origin for certain objects, we are confident that we will be able to solve these questions once we have become familiar with more material and have discovered documented examples. Thus, after only fifty years of systematic studies by a small group of scholars, the various styles in Islamic art are generally understood. What is actually more intriguing, yet more difficult to establish than this general state of diversity, are the various factors

* This essay, written in lieu of a lecture, tries to show certain trends and forces in Islâm and illustrates them with examples selected at random. It is in the nature of such a limited study that these examples can never fully describe the entire extent of each phenomenon, but it is hoped that they will, nevertheless, demonstrate its character. Since the explanatory remarks on the various unpublished objects can only be very short, the writer will present more fully documented studies for most of them at the earliest possible moment.

The author is grateful to Professor Ernst Kühnel for having read the manuscript of this article and for having offered some helpful suggestions.

which, through interaction and integration, constantly helped to reinforce the strongly felt universal aspect of Muslim art. It is therefore this specific problem with which we shall primarily deal in this essay.

After the main expanse of the Muslim world had been established through conquest, a period of integration within the enormous caliphate began; this formative stage reached its height in the ninth century A.D. The earliest standing Muslim building in Iran, the Mosque of Dâmghân, dating from the second half of the eighth century, still uses Sassanid construction forms and techniques, though the concept and purpose of the building and its plan are Arabic and Muslim. About a hundred years later, in 876–79, when Ibn Ṭûlûn built his Great Mosque in Cairo, most of its structural and decorative features were derived from mosques in Iraq, particularly from those in the caliph's capital, Sâmarrâ. This adaptation of the universal style is especially evident from the use of un-Egyptian piers, instead of columns, and from a new style of stucco decoration.[2] Indeed, this special decorative style from Sâmarrâ was applied in all countries of the caliphate; it is found in east and west, in Turkestan as well as in Tunisia (Pl. I*a*), thus demonstrating the universality which the new civilization had attained. With the dismemberment of the caliphate and the rise of independent rulers in the various regions, this universality was broken. Indicative of the changed condition is the appearance, in the eleventh century, of a new, peculiar type of Iranian mosque, which, by using an older architectural Sassanid prototype, places a huge dome above the sanctuary. From the early twelfth century on, a further development leads to a mosque type characterized by the domed sanctuary and four large *eyvâns* in the center of each side of the court.[3] In the thirteenth century we see the rise of specific Turkish forms of mosques which, after the conquest of Constantinople and the strong influence of Santa Sophia, led to further variations of the Ottoman mosque.[4] Later on we can speak also of a Mogul version, and so on. What has been said about the general plan of the sacred buildings and the sanctuaries can be stated in even stronger terms about less vital parts such as the minaret, which differs in shape from region to region and also, usually, in the different centuries.

Next to the mosque the most sanctified and therefore *eo ipso* conservative and universal element in Islâm was Arabic writing. Yet, from the second half of the tenth century on, we find a new angular type of Kufic, developed in Khurâsân,[5] and this is at once used for

Koran manuscripts. From the early twelfth century we have a secular paper document, a bill of sale in Persian which reveals, already, the characteristic hanging character of the cursive Persian hand, although in its formalized calligraphic manner it was not evolved until about 1400.[6] Just as characteristically different is the Maghribî manner of writing, of which an early example is a paper Koran of 238/852 in the University Library in Istanbul (No. A 6753). These are just three of the many new varieties of writing used for religious inscriptions and Korans.

What brings about the great variety in Islâm is the underlying ethnic and cultural diversity of its constituent people and the fact that the patrons of the arts were secular, usually being the members of the ruling dynasties and families. Once the central and universal power of the caliphate was on the wane, rulers of more distant regions who had made themselves independent permitted and even instigated new styles which thus express new political situations, especially secessions. Older local traditions or tendencies therefore became compounded with the special predilections and interests of a demanding patron. All this naturally led to the development of varied and often geographically restricted styles or techniques. Thus we have, for instance, a special school of ivory-carving in tenth- and eleventh-century Spain and of rock crystal carving in Fâṭimid Egypt (Pl. I*b*).[7] Other factors which had a divisionary effect on the body of Islamic art are the faculty of reacting quickly to political changes and the comparative ease with which foreign influences could be absorbed and used in a positive manner. To cite an extreme case: while the Mongol invasion was a tremendous catastrophe for Islâm as a whole and for Islamic learning in particular, it nevertheless had certain enriching effects on Muslim art, especially in regions where the Mongol rulers settled. The extraordinary development which Persian miniatures took from the late thirteenth century on is based on ideas and forms brought in by that momentous historical event. The same applies to silk-weaving, which was also greatly changed. Indeed, nearly all eastern Islamic decoration was affected in various degrees by the Mongol invasion, and its influence was felt even in regions which were not directly touched by it.

In considering the forces which help to counteract the rise of the many regional styles, we have to consider first the range and effectiveness of trade within the Muslim world. The extent of commercial transactions is well indicated by the excavations made in Fusṭâṭ, where large amounts of Spanish and Chinese pottery were found, besides the local products or those from neighboring Syria;[8] also by the products of the kilns from Turkestan and Transoxania, which have been found in Iran and India,[9] by Iraqi luster pottery of the tenth century, which has been discovered in Madînat al-Zahrâ᾽, near Cordova;[10] and by Near Eastern bronzes found in Kashgar or in Spain.[11] Indeed, a list of transactions of this sort which have been revealed by research or archeology would be very long. Sometimes the original products shipped in by trade have been lost, but we can nevertheless still notice their effect, because we can observe local imitations brought about by the fashion-creating imports. Thus, tenth-century lusterware from Iraq must have been brought to Turkestan, where it was imitated in a different technique, as demonstrated by still existing examples (Pl. II*a*). The silks from the Abbasid capital, on the other hand, were copied in Spain, even to the point of including the original inscriptions within the decoration, giving the place of manufacture—Baghdad.[12] A shape for a candleholder evolved in one region, in this case the Persian Caucasus, was copied in Egypt.[13] Even an official institution such as the *ṭirâz* could be affected by foreign models, *vide* the *ṭirâz* fabric of Hishâm II (976–1009),[14] which must have been inspired by Egyptian prototypes. Sometimes the effect of one potent source was felt in several different and distant countries, e.g., a certain type of fourteenth-century Iranian pottery—in itself influenced by Far Eastern designs and color schemes—was imitated in Syria and among the Golden Horde on the Volga.[15]

Another great source of dissemination of artistic ideas in other countries, and often distant ones, were the migrant workers, either trying to find work wherever it was offered or deliberately flocking to a renowned court. An early example of this is the Baghdad tileworker who in 862 made some tiles in Kairouan for the *miḥrâb* of the Great Mosque there.[16] To judge from the style, artists from Baghdad must have painted some of the finest animal pictures in the *Manâfiᶜ-ye ḥayavân* manuscript of the Morgan Library, written in Marâgha at the very end of the thirteenth century.[17] Another group of such artists working far away from their own shores were the Near Eastern metalworkers in Venice who, in the late fifteenth century, fashioned all kinds of inlaid vessels in the Islamic manner and signed them with their good Muslim names.[18] Then there was Aqâ Riḍâ, an artist from Herât, who came to the court of the Mogul heir-apparent, later called Jahângîr, and helped decorate some of his manuscripts.[19] A particularly good source of information about this phenomenon of migratory artists and artisans is the building inscriptions, which often give the names of architects who came from great distances to erect a particular monument. One of these is on the Nilometer in Cairo, which in 861 was built by a mathematician and astronomer from Farghâna, the same man who is known as Alfraganus in Western medieval literature and in the early printed books.[20] In Diyârbakr part of the Great Mosque (1155) is the work of an architect from Gurgân, while the two minarets of the mosque of the Amîr Qûṣûn in Cairo (1329) are by an architect from Tabrîz. The Great Mosque at Ephesus was built in 1375 by an architect from Damascus, and the mausoleum of Tîmûr in Samarqand (1404) by an Iṣfahânî. Finally, to give one more example at random, the mausoleum of Aḥmad Shâh Bahmânî in Bîdâr, in Hyderabad State (about 1434), was built by an architect from Qazvîn. While many such artists sojourned voluntarily, others were forced to do so by grave historical events, particularly wars and invasions. For instance, the *minbar* of the Mosque of Aḥmad Shâh at Divrigi was carved in 1240 by a craftsman from Tiflis who had probably fled from that town prior to its siege and capture by the Mongols in 1241.[21] It is also assumed that the famous school of metalworkers centered in Mosul was driven away from this city by the Mongol invasion. While we still have a fine signed ewer of 1232 made in Mosul itself, later signed pieces giving a place of manufacture state that a Mawṣilî artist had worked in Damascus and others had still later moved as far as Cairo.[22] This applies also to architects, one of the best-known instances being that of the three Christian architects from ᶜUrfa (Edessa) who built the fortifications and particularly the gates of Cairo from 1087 on; it is assumed that they had fled before the Seljuq armies which had captured ᶜUrfa in 1086.[23] The Mosque of Aḥmad Shâh of Divrigi was built in 1228 by an architect from Akhlâṭ who had left his home town when it was besieged by the Khwârizmshâh, either in 1226 or in 1228–29.[24] Finally, we can explain in this manner the spread to other regions of a very specific North Syrian marble marquetry with entrelacs; owing to the pressure of the Mongol armies, the stonemasons left their workshops in Aleppo to take up residence in Seljuq Konya and Mamlûk Cairo.[25]

In all periods, but especially in the early one, we encounter the institution of conscript labor, which brought qualified artists from various countries to the main centers for specific work: Greek and Coptic craftsmen from Syria and Egypt were sent by the Caliph al-Walîd to his governor in Medina for the reconstruction of its mosque, in 707–9. The Aphrodito papyri tell us of the dispatch from Egypt of skilled workmen for the building of the mosque at Damascus in the period between 706 and 714. Finally, to quote one more celebrated example from the Umayyad period, the styles on the walls of Mshattâ indicate that besides Syrian workers there were also others from Iraq and Egypt active on this desert castle.[26] The rapid construction of the Abbasid capital, Sâmarrâ, was feasible only by means of large groups of conscript labor. Yaᶜqûbî singles out marbleworkers from Antioch and other coastal towns in Syria, glass-blowers, potters, and mat-makers from Baṣra, potters also from Kûfa, "and from other countries artists of every type and artisans of every craft. They were settled with their families . . . and bazaars for these craftsmen were opened in town."[27] This mixing of what must often have been a heterogeneous group of artisans affected not only Sâmarrâ and Iraq but the whole caliphate, as the resulting new styles were transplanted to and imitated in the various provinces. The transfer of workmen from a distant province for a special use in the capital continues also in later times, *vide* the order of the Ottoman Sultan Murâd III, dated 1585, in which he instructed the *begler beg* of Cairo to send him eleven carpet-weavers with a specified large amount of colored threads to be used for an assignment in the capital.[28] Naturally the travels of all these artisans must have influenced the work in the bazaars of the towns where they were active.

Another category to be considered here is the artists captured by invading armies or brought to the capitals which the victorious rulers wanted to embellish. Tîmûr is a typical example:

> During all his conquests wheresoever he came he carried off the best men of the population to people Samarqand, bringing thither together the master-craftsmen of all nations. Thus, from Damascus he carried away with him all the weavers of the city, those who worked the silk looms. Further, the bow-makers who produce those cross-bows which were so famous; likewise armourers; also the craftsmen in glass and porcelain, who are known to be the best in all the world. From Turkey he had brought their gun-smiths who make the arquebus, and all men of other crafts wheresoever he found them, such as the silver-smiths and the masons. These all were in very great numbers, indeed so many had been brought together of craftsmen of all sorts that of every denomination and kind you might find many master-workmen established in the capital. . . .[29]

This fact is borne out by the monuments and objects connected with Tîmûr. The same policy was followed by the Ottoman sultans. This induced Shâh Ismâᶜîl to hide the celebrated painter, Behzâd, and his favorite calligrapher, Shâh Maḥmûd Nîshâpûrî, in a cave before the battle of Châldirân in 1514, so that they would not fall into the hands of Selîm I.[30] This was a fortunate move for the Iranians, because the victorious sultan took away to his capital many artisans when he occupied Tabrîz.

Less directly endangered than the actual refugee artists were those men who had been working in a court studio which was being disbanded or who were replaced by artists of a new dynasty, with different tastes and artistic intentions. In this category belong the potters and particularly the makers of luster pottery, who are thought to have gone west and east after the fall of the Fâṭimid dynasty and to have brought the carefully guarded secret of their trade to Málaga, Raqqa, and Rayy.[31] Another example is the exodus of painters from Herât after the defeat of the Shaybânids by the Safavids in 1510. It was the course of these events that brought Behzâd to Tabrîz, the capital of the Safavids, where he was eventually appointed director of the Royal Library.

So far we have spoken only of migratory artists, but a movement of artistic ideas can also come about through dynasties which have moved their capitals. An excellent example of this phenomenon is the importation of artistic ideas first found in the mosque in the erstwhile capital of the Fâṭimid dynasty in Mahdiyya in Tunisia (i.e., the monumental gateway and the placement of towers at the corners of the entrance wall) and which appear later on in Egypt, in the Fâṭimid mosque of al-Ḥâkim, and then in the mosque of the Mamlûk Baybars al-Bunduqdârî.[32] An earlier, related example is Ibn Ṭûlûn's shift from Sâmarrâ to Egypt, which must have induced many Iraqis to follow; this influenced the way of building private houses in the Egyptian capital, the new style being that which was customary in Iraq and Iran.[33]

Sometimes rulers brought about a spreading of artistic ideas through their representatives and in particular through their ambassadors. It will be recalled, for instance, that in 921 Ibn Faḍlân went with a mission from Baghdad to the Volga-Bulgars, pursuant to a request of the king of the Ṣaqâliba, for advice about the building of a mosque and a castle and the construction of a *minbar*. The caliph also sent gifts for this king, his wife, children, brothers, and generals, all of which demonstrates the importation of artistic ideas to the northern fringes of the caliphate.[34] Cultural influence of a different sort was the result of the embassies sent in the fifteenth century by Shâhrukh and other Tîmûrids who went to China and were accompanied by merchants and also by at least one artist,

Ghiyâth al-Dîn.[35] Here we find actually a strong reflection of this political and cultural exchange, in the style of the contemporary miniatures and in the sudden use of silk for some of these paintings.

Even the fact that a ruler had to go into exile and leave the country of his birth could have a noted artistic effect. When ᶜAbd al-Raḥmân, the sole survivor of the Umayyad dynasty, established himself in Spain, he named his newly built palace "Ruṣâfa," to remind him of Syria; later on some elements of the greatest monument of Hispano-Moresque architecture, the Great Mosque of Cordova, reflect Syrian features, among them, for instance, the striped masonry.[36] Another example, though of a much later time, is the exile of the Mogul emperor, Humâyûn, in Iran. When he finally recovered his throne, he brought Mîr Sayyid ᶜAlî and Khwâja ᶜAbd al-Ṣamad, two well-known Persian miniature painters, with him, thus starting a new school of Muslim painting in which ultimately a blending of Persian, Indian, and European elements produced a new style.

Less definitely to be established in time and space than the movements of artists or dynasties are the movements of whole ethnic groups which were displaced by historic events or which were seeking other areas on account of natural misfortunes, such as drought, etc. To this category belong certain nomadic and seminomadic groups, e.g., the Turkomans, whose special style of carpet-weaving and patterns occurs in more than one place.

Besides the continued process of interregional artistic exchange, we have to consider also the relationship between various, often centrifugal, forces within one region. The population in a given area is practically never culturally homogeneous. There is always one group representing the new standard of Islâm, which demands universal acceptance and is being opposed by the status quo forces which defend the older but now repressed tradition of the civilization superseded by Islâm, with all its manifestations in religion, literature, and art. If we take a country like Iran, the new and old patterns exist side by side after the Arab conquest, although they can also fuse, as we have seen in the case of the mosque in Dâmghân. The play of the two forces is particularly revealing in the Samanid period, when, shortly after the time of the greatest Islamic integration in the caliphate, a first Persian renaissance took place. The tomb of Ismâᶜîl, the first ruler of the dynasty, follows a true Sassanid architectural form, though modified by novel secondary features.[37] Here the use of such a pre-Islamic prototype was facilitated, as Islâm has no prescribed orthodox sepulchral form. The mid-tenth-century silk of Saint-Josse, with the name of the Qâʾid Abû Manṣûr Nejtekîn, reveals a strong dependence on Sassanid patterns, but these have now undergone stylization in the Islamic manner, and the prominent display of an Arabic inscription adds another Islamic note to the Persian setting.[38] In the field of pottery the influences of the two forces is even more evident. We find vessels which represent the caliphal style, as they are local imitations of the finest wares developed in Iraq (Pl. II*a*). Then there is an original local form to uphold the Islamic concept within this civilization; it is represented by many vessels, perhaps some of the finest produced in Iran, which rely solely on Kufic writing, in the form of Arabic proverbs, as decoration (Pl. II*b*).[39] On the other hand, there are also certain wares which use elements of the Sassanid repertory; one is particularly interesting in that it avoids the primary forms of the old decorations, such as representations of the king or animals, but is satisfied with the secondary patterns of framing and space-filling motifs, which in no way could offend a Muslim conscience (Pl. II*c*).

In the second half of the twelfth century, Persian and Arabic inscriptions begin to appear together on objects and buildings. This is the period when another new revival of ancient Iranian forms takes place. This is demonstrated by pottery bowls decorated with a scene in which Ahuramazda presents to a Sassanid king the symbol of royalty, a subject obviously copied from Sassanid rock reliefs,[40] or with a *Shâh-nâma* scene or scenes.[41] While it is not known for which particular clientele these anonymous objects were made, we have more precise evidence for a large aquamanile in the form of a cow nursing a calf, dated 1206, which is reminiscent of related objects from the Sassanid and post-Sassanid periods. Its mixed Arabic and Persian inscription states that the owner of the piece was an Iranian grandee with the title of *Shâh*, and at least one of the two makers an Iranian. Here we have at least some definite proof that a member of the native aristocracy still revered the ancient forms, which he wished to revive.[42] There are many other moments in Iranian history when we come across such a reversion to ancient Iranian norms; indeed, the phenomenon can be said to be endemic in Iran. To quote some examples: In the audience hall of the Ghaznavid palace of Lashgarî Bazar on the Helmand River, the idea of lining up the military guards on the painted walls has its closest parallels in the reliefs of the Persian and Median guards in the palaces of Persepolis.[43] On the other hand, Ghaznavid metalwork, probably from

Maḥmûd's other capital, Ghazna, shows a marked imprint of the Sassanid tradition, which is combined with Muslim trappings in the form of Kufic writing, garbled though it may be. This is demonstrated by a brass bowl showing a royal reveler attended by two dignitaries and surrounded by musicians and dancers placed in arcades; even a third element of Sassanid royal iconography, the king's hunt, is indicated by the fleeing animal in front of the throne (Pl. III*a*).[44] To pass on to much later times, the Qâjâr Fatḥ ᶜAlî Shâh represented himself in various rock reliefs, thus taking up a tradition widely practiced before him by the Sassanid kings.[45]

While the examples so far quoted represent isolated instances in which the old tradition merged into and enriched the new norm, some cases can also be adduced in which the effect was much broader, and this even though the source was the art of the lowest social level and not the ancient court art. There is nothing more characteristic of the Islamic architecture of Iran from the thirteenth century on than the rich use of colored tiles on the outer surfaces, especially in the form of faïence mosaic. This architectural technique started with the insertion of very small glazed units, usually in the form of borders, and as such is nearly lost in the large ornamental ensemble.[46] So far, it has not been established where the inspiration for this use of bits of bluish glaze in the earth-colored architecture came from. It is, however, not impossible that it is derived from unpretentious forms of decoration on the folk level, since we find simple pottery vessels from the late Sassanid and the Islamic periods in which small fragments of turquoise glaze were inserted to provide a few bright spots in the clay surface or, in more ambitious cases, to give a necklace-like band around certain parts of the vessels (Pl. III*b*). The writer has observed houses near Salmân Pâk in Iraq where blue-glazed pottery fragments were placed in the mud-brick wall, usually above the door, in the same manner as the bits of glaze were inserted in the earlier pottery from Iran. Since in both instances the chosen color is blue, one probably does not go wrong in assuming that the age-old magic remedy against the evil eye was used. In the later complex faïence mosaic the original meaning was probably lost sight of, yet blue continues to be the preferred color.

While this technique found brilliant application in Iran and Anatolia and only occasional use in other Muslim countries, another Iranian institution which also rose from a lower level to the highest found universal acceptance. We are referring to the *eyvân* of the private house, which had also been used for the palace architecture

Courtesy North Carolina State Museum, Raleigh, N.C.

a) Stone Lamps, Said To Have Been Excavated in Tunisia. Ninth to Tenth Century

Courtesy Kevorkian Foundation, New York

b) Fâṭimid Rock Crystal Vessel in Later European Mounting

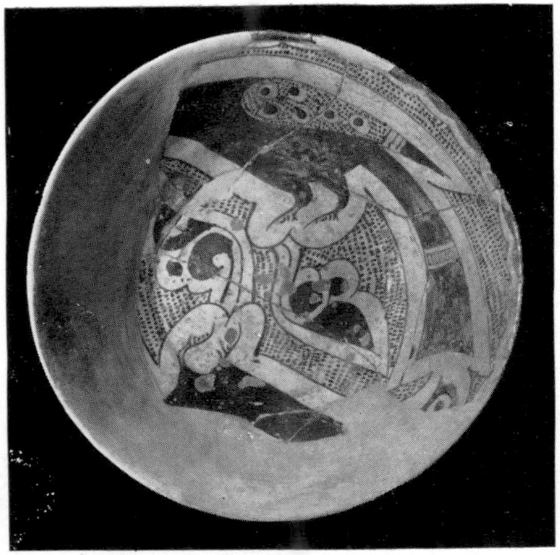

a) Bowl with Slip Decoration Imitating a Luster Design. Eastern Khurâsân, Tenth Century. Private Collection

Courtesy City Art Museum, St. Louis

b) Plate with Arabic Proverb in Persian Kufic. Eastern Khurâsân, Tenth Century

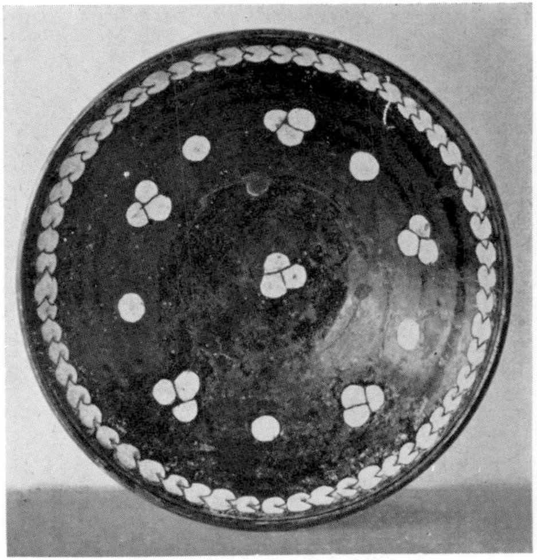

Courtesy Victoria and Albert Museum, London

c) Bowl with Slip Decoration. Eastern Khurâsân or Transoxania, Ninth Century

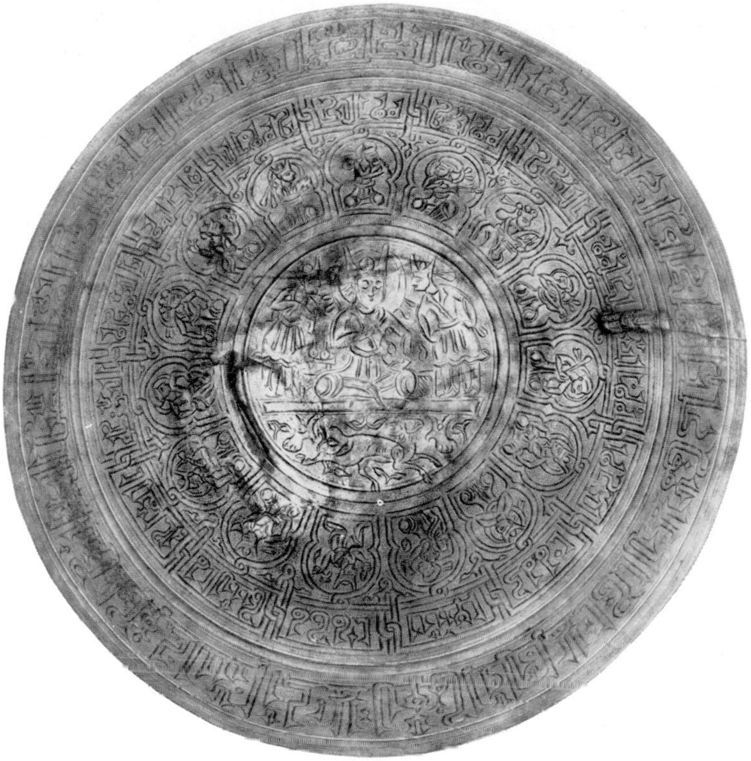

Courtesy Kevorkian Foundation, New York

a) Brass Bowl with Royal Scene and Kufic Inscription. Probably Ghaznavid

Courtesy Dr. E. F. Schmidt and the Museum of Fine Arts, Boston

b) Unglazed Pottery Pot with Inlaid Glaze Pieces. From Rayy. Early Islamic

PLATE IV

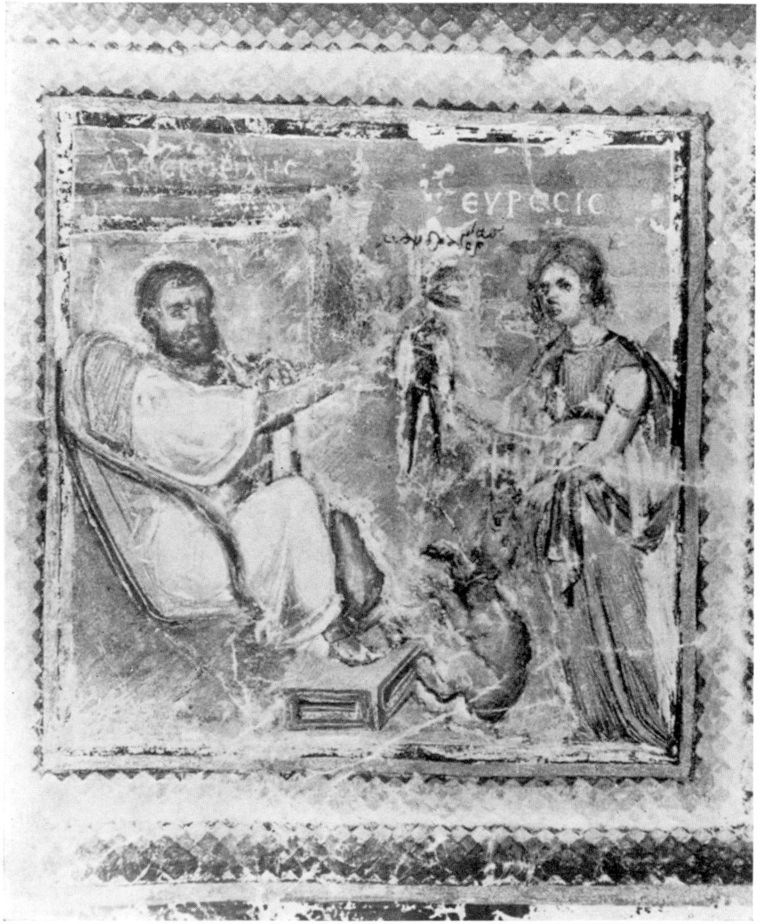

a) "Dioscorides and Heuresis" from the "Vienna Dioscorides" Manuscript. Early Sixth Century. (After Buberl)

Photograph Courtesy Prof. A. Süheyl Ünver

b) "Dioscorides and Student" from a Dioscorides Manuscript, Dated 626/1229. Library of the Topkapu Sarayi

PLATE V

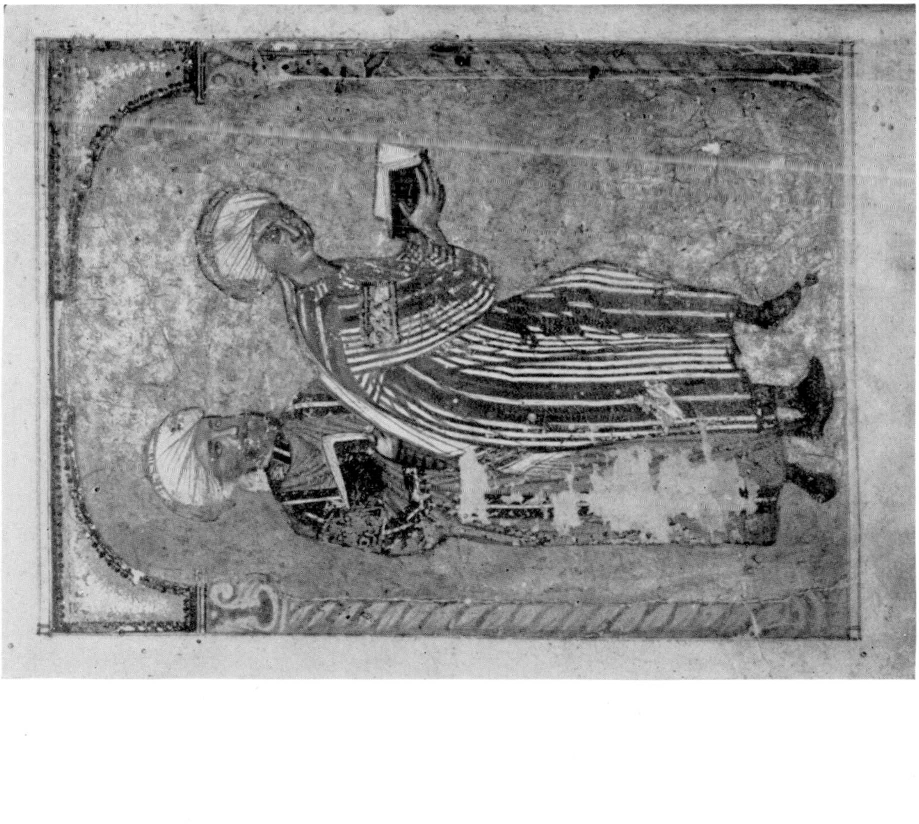

Photographs Courtesy Prof. A. Süheyl Ünver

DOUBLE FRONTISPIECE MINIATURE FROM A DIOSCORIDES MANUSCRIPT (SEE PL. IV*b*)

a) One Side of Double Frontispiece of a Mubashshir Manuscript. Probably Thirteenth Century. Library of Topkapu Sarayi

b) Picture of Seven Physicians or Pharmacologists, from the "Vienna Dioscorides." (After Buberl)

a) One Page of the Finispiece of the Mubashshir Manuscript (see Pl. VI*a*)

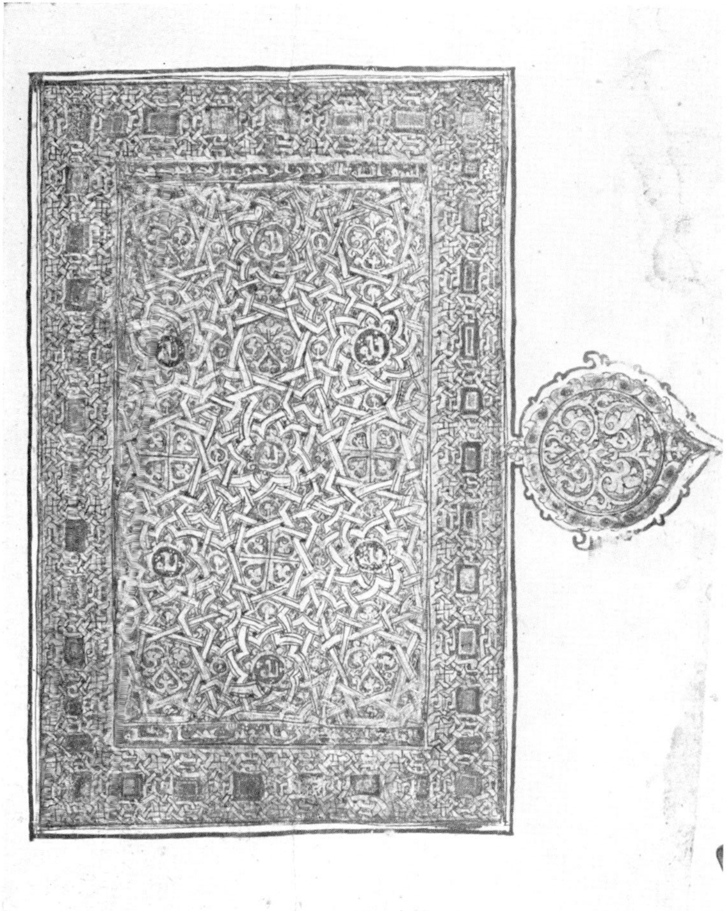

b) Illuminated Frontispiece of a Koran Manuscript Dated 427/1036. British Museum, Add. 7214

PLATE VIII

Photograph Courtesy M. A. Godard

a) Imâm Riḍâ with Believers, Dîvs, and Angels. Nineteenth Century. Imâmzâda at Amol

Courtesy Heeramaneck Galleries, New York

b) "Baraka" in Zoomorphic Kufic on Pottery Bowl. Tenth to Eleventh Centuries

a) "Al-ᶜIzz wa-'l-Iqbâl wa-'l-Daula wa-'l- . . ." from a Bucket Made in Herât in 559/1163. Leningrad, Hermitage. (After Vesselovski)

Courtesy Cleveland Museum of Art

b) "Al-ᶜIzz wa-'l-Iqbâl wa-'l-Daula" from a Persian Footed Bowl. Late Twelfth Century

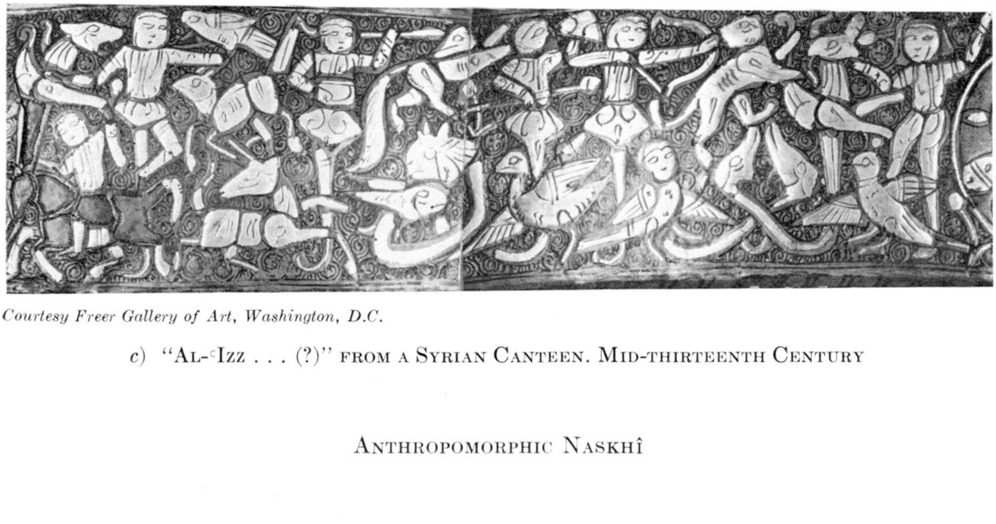

Courtesy Freer Gallery of Art, Washington, D.C.

c) "Al-ᶜIzz . . . (?)" from a Syrian Canteen. Mid-thirteenth Century

Anthropomorphic Naskhî

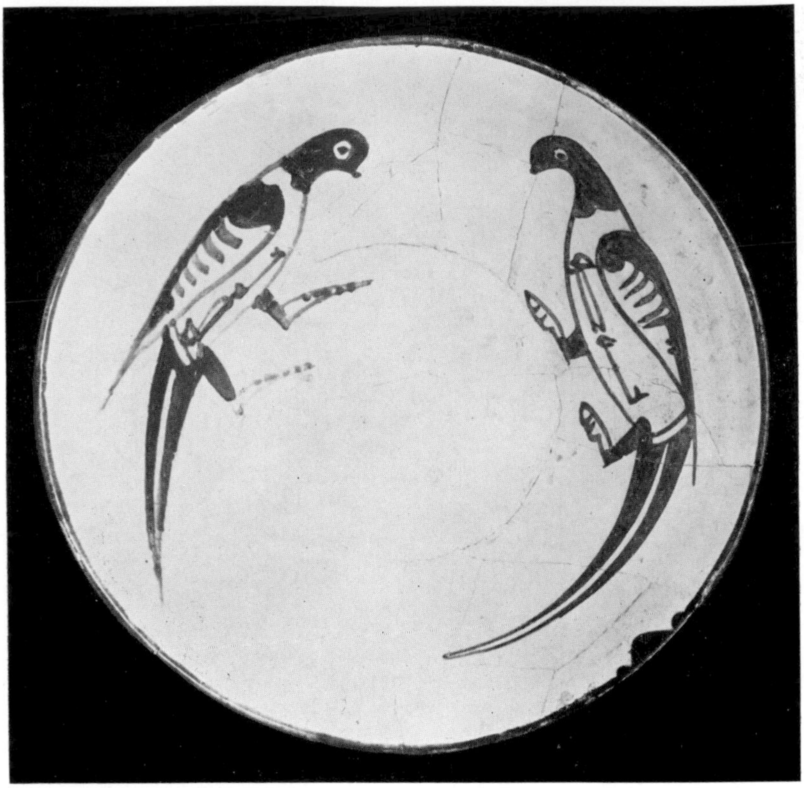

Courtesy Heeramaneck Galleries of Art, New York

a) POTTERY BOWL FROM NÎSHÂPÛR. TENTH CENTURY

Photograph B. V. Bothmer

b) WOOD CARVING OF MUSICIANS, TUMBLER, AND EQUILIBRIST IN FÂṬIMID STYLE. FROM THE CONVENT DAIR AL-BANÂT. EGYPT, ELEVENTH CENTURY. CAIRO, COPTIC MUSEUM

Courtesy Art Association, Montreal

a) SCENE (ORIGINALLY INLAID WITH SILVER) ON THE OUTSIDE OF THE LARGE BRASS BASIN OF AL-MALIK AL NÂṢIR ṢALÂḤ AL-DÎN ABÛ 'L-MUẒAFFAR YÛSUF. SYRIA, MID-THIRTEENTH CENTURY

Courtesy Victoria and Albert Museum, London

b) BRASS BASIN WITH INLAID SCENES. MAMLÛK, SECOND HALF THIRTEENTH CENTURY

Courtesy Kevorkian Foundation, New York

a) "ALEXANDER AT THE VALLEY OF THE DIAMONDS," FROM A NIẒÂMÎ MANUSCRIPT. SHÎRÂZ, 922 AND 927/1516 AND 1521

Courtesy Walters Art Gallery, Baltimore (W. 652, fol. 179)

b) "RHINOCEROS LIFTING AN ELEPHANT ON HIS HORN" FROM AN UNIDENTIFIED PERSIAN POETICAL MANUSCRIPT. KHURÂSÂN, 1022/1613

as early as the Parthian period and was adapted for the madrasa in the second half of the eleventh century, and then for the Iranian mosque and caravanserai.[47] From Iran the idea of the four-*eyvân* structure was taken to other parts of the Muslim world, where it developed a brilliant architectural history in Iraq, Syria, and Egypt.

As we turn from Iran to Egypt and Syria, other phenomena present themselves, although it should not be implied that there are not similar parallels also to be found in Iran. The special situation of Egypt and Syria is the continued existence of a great many architectural monuments and objects from the preceding civilizations; likewise, also, of communities which regarded these monuments and objects as the embodiment of their noblest traditions. The interplay between these two cultural strata runs the whole gamut of possibilities, from opposition to penetration.

If we begin with the stage in which the Islamic norm vitally opposes and disregards the claims of the earlier civilization, we can refer to the many instances where Christian churches have been used as mosques. This happened especially in early Islâm and then again when Crusader churches were taken over, an example for the first being the Great Mosque in Ḥamâ, which was a fifth- or sixth-century church,[48] and for the latter the Great Mosque in Beirut, which was built as a French church in the first half of the twelfth century. Even more negative was the use of ancient monuments as quarries for the structures to be erected for the glory of the new religion. Pharaonic temples, Roman temples, and Greek churches have thus been incorporated into mosques, and not only in the country where they were found, since materials from Egyptian churches were used in Sâmarrâ[49] and a Gothic doorway from ᶜAkka was placed in the Madrasa of Nâṣir Muḥammad in Cairo.[50] It is necessary to emphasize here, however, that this despoiling of ancient monuments was not restricted to Egypt, as we find the use of Classical columns, bases, and capitals in nearly all the early mosques within the old Classical world. On the other hand, in Iran, Achaemenid architectural elements were employed in the mosques of Qazvîn and Iṣṭakhr,[51] while in the Great Mosque of Delhi one finds columns from Hindu temples.[52] The will to disgrace the art and symbols of a defeated civilization is perhaps nowhere better illustrated than in the Crusader period: Saladin turned the large cross, which was on the Dome of the Rock in Jerusalem, upside down, while the famous prince and historian Abû 'l-Fidâᵓ reversed Crusader columns when he placed them in the *miḥrâb* of the Jâmiᶜ Nûrî in

Ḥamâ. The purpose of these actions was to perpetuate the victory by sympathetic magic, and this was done in a manner that had already been practiced in the Near East thousands of years before.[53] However, even in the same periods of which we have spoken, another more latitudinarian attitude is apparent: when in 691–92 ᶜAbd al-Malik built the Dome of the Rock as a shrine to commemorate Mohammed's ascension, he used the traditional plans of certain Syrian churches.[54] Again, the square minaret found in Syria is derived from various tower structures of the pre-Islamic era, and it remained the standard form in that region until the early thirteenth century. Outside Syria it was brought to western Islâm, where it is used in Kairouan and Cordova, and, indeed, became the norm in the Maghrib.[55] Still another example of a more conciliatory attitude is provided by the fact that both ᶜUmar and ᶜUthmân covered the holiest shrine in Islâm, the Kaᶜba, with *Qubâṭî* (that is, Christian) cloth.[56]

The slow processes of amalgamation are well illustrated by a series of textiles. Those of the Fayyûm, of the ninth to tenth centuries, show patterns which are particularly close to the Coptic textiles, yet we find there simulated Arabic, perhaps even imitating the *shahâda*, together with Coptic texts and, slightly later, efforts toward more carefully executed Kufic inscriptions, which, however, are still garbled and often in mirror writing.[57] These Fayyûm textiles represent a product of a more provincial origin, but echoes of Coptic stylization are to be found in the early *ṭirâz* textiles manufactured for the Fâṭimid court.[58] Coptic textiles are also the prototype and norm for the brilliant development of Mamlûk carpet-weaving.[59]

In these examples we have the slow rising of the degraded tradition. We have also the opposite tendency, namely, an influence from the high level of Islâm to the lower one of the non-Muslims. The stucco decorations of the Coptic monastery of Dair Sûryânî of 914, in the Wâdî Naṭrûn, were rendered in the universal Abbasid style, and, when in the Fâṭimid period wooden doors were carved for the Church of Sitt Barbara, they were in style not distinguishable from the wood carvings used in Muslim houses or palaces.[60]

The final interpenetration of two civilizations is reached in monuments and objects in which the figures or patterns of the older civilization are fully accepted by the representatives of Islâm and, with a slight Muslim veneer, or even without it, become part of the Muslim scene. It is best to illustrate this process first with secular examples, and among these perhaps the most instructive ones are those which demonstrate the Islamization of Classical themes. In a famous Byzantine Dioscorides manuscript, now in Vienna, written for an imperial princess, Anicia Juliana, before 512, we find as an "author picture" at the beginning of the volume the seated figure of the herbalist stretching out his hand toward the female figure of *Heuresis*, the personification of scientific investigation and research, who is holding the magic, human-shaped mandrake; to the latter a dog is tied, as, according to late Classical superstitions, his help is needed to extricate the root (Pl. IV*a*).[61] This motif occurs again in a Dioscorides manuscript of 626/1229 from northern Mesopotamia, written by a Mawṣilî scribe, in the Topkapu Sarayı Library (Pl. IV*b*). Now the figures are no longer clothed in Classical garments, but their appearance, up to the turbans, is Muslim. However, this transformation goes deeper: in this Islamic version there is no place for the figure of a woman, especially not one with an unveiled face and with blonde hair at that, to be connected with the doctor; the relationship has been changed to the true Muslim one of teacher and student, *shaikh* and *murîd*. The figure of the unclean dog is also left out, indicating that the fantastic stories about the cutting of the root (which were not included in the text of Dioscorides) finally have been eliminated. Indeed, were it not for the general setting of the scene and an iconographically related one on the preceding double frontispiece (Pl. V), where for the figure of the sage and author we find the same kind of gesture, garment, chair, and footstool as in the Byzantine version of Vienna, one would not have thought that the scene of the teacher and student had any non-Muslim antecedents. Yet one more point should be stressed, even in this brief reference to these miniatures, namely, that the Muslim manuscript is apparently not directly dependent on the earlier Greek version in Vienna. A detail such as the bulging folds over the middle of the botanist's body in Plate V, which is lacking in the sixth-century manuscript, might seem unimportant; the fact that it occurs, however, on a very specific group of other author pictures, namely, those of evangelists placed at the head of Gospel manuscripts (such as on the figure of John, seated on a similar chair, in the eleventh-century Gospel of the Vatican, Cod. Gr. 364) indicates that there must have been one or more other intermediary Greek models for the Muslim artist, who is thus another link in the long chain of borrowings and transformations of Classical forms.[62]

Our second example is contained in a manuscript of Abû 'l-Wafâ Mubashshir's *Mukhtâr al-ḥikam wa-maḥâsin al-kalim*, which contains biographies and sayings of Greek sages.[63] The manuscript (in the same library) is preceded by a double frontispiece in which we can discern seven persons in various attitudes or occupations in each of the two pages (Pl. VI*a*). They can be assumed to be pictures of authors, again with a parallel in the Vienna Dioscorides manuscript where we find two such cycles, each with seven physicians or pharmacologists (Pl. VI*b*). These pictures are reflections of a literary type established by M. Terentius Varro in 39 B.C., in which he dealt with seven hundred famous persons, who were represented by one hundred pictures, each of which showed seven persons.[64] In the Mubashshir manuscript we thus have a final representation of a Classical idea, but instead of the more realistic *mise en scène* of a council with a presiding doctor, as in the Vienna manuscript, the figures, now clothed in Muslim costume, are set in a characteristically Muslim geometric framework in which they appear not unlike so many inserted ornamental panels of a wooden door. Pictures of authors occur again in the double finispiece, only we have now six, instead of seven, figures in each of the two pages, an indication that the tradition of the seven-author unit had become rather tenuous (Pl. VII*a*); here the geometric layout is perhaps even more Islamic, since the configurations created out of straight and circular lines of ever changing radius and center positions are now combined with more realistic plant-like rinceaux. The final Islamization of this idea is shown by corresponding decorative pages from Koran manuscripts, some of which are even earlier than the Mubashshir paintings. Thus, in the interlaced design of the Koran of 1036, in the British Museum, the places which in the secular pages had contained pictures of authors now show invocations of Allâh, again placed seven times within the trellis work (Pl. VII*b*).

If we now proceed to the incorporation of Christian religious subjects into the Muslim pattern, we could point to the representation of a St. George–like dragon killer on the gate of the caravanserai between Sinjâr and Mosul, called al-Khân and built by the Zengid Luʾluʾ between 1234 and 1259. This building was near a medieval village populated by Christians, one of whose sacred images was obviously borrowed, though its meaning probably took on a Muslim aspect; there is al-Khiḍr, a Muslim patron saint of travelers, and his apotropaic picture could thus have served as protection for people resting in the *khân*.[65] St. George was, however, also fully accepted in this region; already Ibn Jubayr (d. 1217) visited a mosque in Mosul dedicated to Nabî Jirjîs, and this building is still in existence.[66] Another very striking example of this acceptance of the older tradition is presented by a magnificently inlaid basin, once owned by the Duke of Arenberg on which two types of inscriptions designate the owner as the Ayyûbid Malik Ṣâliḥ Najm al-Dîn Ayyûb (1240–49), sultan of Egypt and at times also of Syria. The figural imagery of this royal piece is not restricted to standard scenes of the courtly repertory, such as hunting or playing polo, but includes also Christian themes. There are other metal objects of that period which show Christian subject matter, but here it is included in an official piece that once belonged to one of the more important rulers of the time who (ironically, in this context) died in a campaign against the crusading Louis IX of France.[67]

The question of figural scenes, which has come up at various times in this essay and comes up again now, brings us to one of the most challenging issues in Islamic art. Representations of human figures and animals were perhaps the most characteristic and, in view of religious connotations, also the most controversial heritage of the preceding civilizations. Faced with this issue, Islâm as a whole, and in particular Islâm as a religion, took an anti-iconic attitude. The painter is officially regarded as an impostor who, though doomed to failure, is blasphemously trying to compete with God's creative power, while the owning of pictures is like letting an unclean dog in one's house, so that both Mohammed and angels are said to have refused to enter such a place.[68] Yet, in the course of time, the opposite belief was also accepted:

> How well the brocader's apprentice said, when he portrayed the ᶜ*anqâ*, the elephant, and the giraffe.
>
> From my hand there came not one form, the pattern of which the Teacher from above had not first depicted.

As made clear by Saᶜdî in the following verses, he wished to say that God is the source and inspiration of everything, including the figural arts. Jalâl al-Dîn Rûmî also uses the symbol of the painter when he tries to elucidate the problem of how evil can come from God:

> And if you say that evils too are from Him, (that is true), but how is it a defect in His grace?
>
> (His) bestowing this evil is even His perfection: I will tell you a parable, O respected one.
>
> A painter made two kinds of pictures—beautiful pictures and pictures devoid of beauty.
>
> He painted Joseph and fair-formed houris, he painted ugly afreets and devils.
>
> Both kinds of pictures are (evidence of) his mastery: those (ugly ones) are not (evidence of) his ugliness; they are (evidence of) his bounty.

He makes the ugly of extreme ugliness—it is invested with all (possible) uglinesses.
In order that the perfection of his skill may be displayed, (and that) the denier of his mastery may be put to shame.
And if he cannot make the ugly, he is deficient (in skill): hence He (God) is the Creator of (both) the infidel and the sincere (faithful).
From this point of view, then, (both) infidelity and faith are bearing witness (to Him): both are bowing down in worship before His Lordliness.[69]

The painter is thus no longer a questionable member of society; his work is no longer looked at with displeasure or reproof but is now recognized as having didactic values in explaining God.

The actual monuments bear out this dichotomy in the Muslim world with regard to figural representations. With few exceptions, mosques never displayed representations of living forms. It is also true that in ever so many representations of living beings made by Muslim artists the eyes were later gouged out by an iconoclast, or the heads cut off by a symbolic stroke through the neck or scratched off entirely. The pre-Islamic statues and figural paintings fared even worse; for instance, the great rock-carved Buddhas of Bamian have been bombarded by the artillery of Aurangzîb and Nâdir Shâh.[70] Yet, in spite of this hostile attitude throughout the ages, it is noteworthy that we do find representations of living beings even in a sacred context. Thus animals appear on the *miḥrâb* columns given by Sultan Malik al-Muẓaffar II Taqî al-Dîn (1229–44) to the Mosque of Nûr al-Dîn in Ḥamâ, and this at a time when the general attitude of the country was rather antagonistic toward figural representation in public.[71] Snakes, usually associated with evil forces, occur on the mausoleum of Imâm Bâbir, erected in Mosul by order of Luʾluʾ and in conjunction with basic religious invocations.[72] Animals, particularly birds and dragons, become quite common in Safavid tile decorations of Iran and especially in those of mausoleums.[73] Finally, we have whole picture cycles from the Shîʿite sacred history on the walls of late Iranian mosques and *imâmzâdas* (Pl. VIII*a*);[74] here, usually on the popular level, the once spurned image has returned, not only as a fully recognized form of artistic activity but even with a didactic purpose in a religious monument.

Next to the mosque the most sacred institution in Islâm was Arabic writing. Allâh himself was said to have taught it to Adam and thus to mankind, and He swore "by the pen and what they write" (Koran 68:1). Writing was the vehicle of the Koran, the basis of the whole religion and civilization. Its characters follow a well-established canon based on mathematical principles, and they have thus been described as "a difficult geometry."[75] In view of the anti-iconic attitude of Islâm, nothing would have seemed more unlikely than to have this pure vehicle of thought tainted by figural decorations of a fanciful nature. Yet this is what happened and even earlier than is generally assumed. The pottery from Nîshâpûr of the tenth century already shows zoomorphic features in the applied writing and this, not only in what may possibly be the signature of the potter, but even in the word *baraka,* which invoked the blessings of Allâh on the owner of the piece (Fig. 1 and Pl. VIII*b*). A more elaborate development is noticed from the second half of the twelfth

FIG. 1

FIG. 2

FIG. 1.—"Aḥmad" in zoomorphic Kufic from a pottery bowl found in Nîshâpûr. Tenth century. Teheran, National Museum.

FIG. 2. *Basmala* in the form of a bird. Formerly in collection of Professor F. Sarre. (After E. Kühnel, *Miniaturmalerei im islamischen Orient.*)

century on, when the hastae of *naskhî* letters are composed of the upper part of human figures with gesticulating hands, or when letters are made up of near-complete human figures for the hastae and animal figures for the lower parts (Pl. IX*a, b*). This development led to forms in which the writing is practically submerged among these anthropomorphic and zoomorphic figures (Pl. IX*c*).[76] On the other hand, we find also the opposite tendency, namely, the intrusion of Arabic writing into animal figures with which they have a priori no obvious connection. An early example is a pottery bowl from Nîshâpûr from the tenth century, in which a word in Kufic letters (*baraka*) is placed within each of the two birds (Pl. X*a*). In later centuries even the *basmala* was occasionally written in the form of a bird (Fig. 2),[77] and this custom has persisted, as one can still buy modern prints of a *basmala* in bird form in the bazaars and stationery shops of Iran.

After this discussion, first of the interaction among the arts of various Muslim regions and then between the older civilizations and Islâm, at least one more aspect of the integrative process should be taken up, namely, the phenomenon of how and when one social class becomes aware of the lives of others and is stimulated to depict their specific activities in its own art.

In the well-known bucket in the Hermitage dated 1163, which was given as a present to a merchant, the inlay worker made use of some of the imagery connected with the court, namely, throne scenes, warfare, and hunting.[78] On the other hand, artisans employed by the higher classes of Egypt in the eleventh and twelfth centuries, if not by the Fâṭimid house itself, had already used scenes representing more lowly persons, although these acrobatic entertainers (Pl. X*b*) or keepers of strange animals were probably attached to or performing for the court.[79] However, from about A.D. 1200 on, everyday activities of the peasants became subjects of interest to artists working for savants and members of the higher classes, *vide* the miniatures of the *Kitâb al-Diryâq* of 595/1199 (Bibliothèque Nationale, arabe 2964), and the scenes on a ewer of 620/1223 and a candlestick of 622/1225.[80] Even at a royal court genre-like activities appear at this time, such as the one showing the filtering of wine on the Syrian basin with the name of al-Malik al-Nâṣir Ṣalâḥ al-Dîn Abû 'l-Muẓaffar Yûsuf (Pl. XI*a*);[81] or we find an elaborate boat scene (Pl. XI*b*),[82] though the usual repertory deals with human activities on land. The art of the upper level of society was also enriched when certain motifs from lower types of literature entered scientific compendiums or poetic *dîvâns* and were then illustrated. For instance, whole stories of the *Arabian Nights* were apparently not illuminated until the seventeenth century, and then only very rarely, because this literary genre served merely for the entertainment of the lower, uneducated classes. However, when, for instance, an appealing tale such as the one of how the diamonds were taken from the Valley of the Serpents, in Sindbad's story, was included by Niẓâmî in his *Iskandar-nâma*, the subject became socially acceptable, and the manuscripts of the poet's *Khamsa* now contain miniatures of this scene (Pl. XII*a*).[83] The same happened when another sailor's yarn from the Sindbad story, the one of the rhinoceros lifting the elephant on its horn, was introduced into a scientific handbook such as Qazvînî's *ᶜAjâᵓib al-makhlûqât* and into other texts. From that moment on the subject was artistically proper and appears in the iconographic repertory (Pl. XII*b*).[84]

In view of the constant process of integration which we have so far discussed, it is not surprising that an art came into being whose uniquely Muslim character was recognized within the Muslim world. There are occasional statements of Muslim writers showing an awareness of the nature of their buildings and objects and, in particular, of their differences with respect to non-Muslim art.[85] There are also other testimonies which represent perhaps an even higher form of recognition, as they identify the arts with the spiritual aspects of Islâm. Ibn Marzûq, for instance, sees in the monuments the glorious expression of the religion, so that their neglect and ruin will have to be accounted for on the Day of Judgment.[86] For al-Ghazzâlî a beautiful painting or building reveals the inner beauty of the artist and is thus testimony of a moral life and the knowledge of Allâh.[87] And, finally, for the mystic Jalâl al-Dîn Rûmî, "the external form [of the artist's work] is for the sake of the unseen form; and that took shape for the sake of another unseen [form]. Count up these corollaries to the third, fourth, or tenth in proportion to [your] insight."[88] Thus for the knowing ones the arts served even more than their immediate purpose; they became symbols of Islâm.

NOTES

1. For further details, see the writer's "The Character of Islamic Art," in *The Arab Heritage*, ed. Nabih A. Faris (Princeton, 1944), pp. 251–67.

2. K. A. C. Creswell, *Early Muslim Architecture* (Oxford, 1932–40), II, 355–56.

3. A. Godard, "Les anciennes mosquées de l'Iran," *Athâr-é Îrân*, I (1936), 187–210.

4. A. Gabriel, "Les Mosquées de Constantinople," *Syria*, VII (1926), 353–419; M. Aga-Oglu, "The Fatih Mosque at Constantinople," *The Art Bulletin*, XII (1930), 179–95.

5. Fehmi Edhem Karatay, *İstanbul Üniversitesi Kütüphanesi Arapça Yazmalar Kataloğu* (Istanbul, 1951——), Vol. I, p. 3, No. 8 and Pl. V, dated 361/971.

6. D. S. Margoliouth, "Early Documents in the Persian Language," *Journal of the Royal Asiatic Society*, 1903, 761–65. The date of this document, found in Khotan, was originally read as 401/1010, but it has been reread as 501/1107 by M. Minovi (V. Kratchkovskaya, "Ornamental Naskhî Inscriptions," *A Survey of Persian Art* [London and Oxford, 1938–39], II, 1772, n. 6) and, independently, by V. Minorsky ("Some Early Documents in Persian [I]," *Journal of the Royal Asiatic Society*, 1942, 186–87).

The creator of the Nastaʿlîq script is supposed to have been Mîr ʿAlî Tabrîzî, a contemporary of Tîmûr Leng (C. Huart, *Les Calligraphes et les miniaturistes de l'Orient musulman* [Paris, 1908], pp. 207–8).

7. José Ferrandis, *Marfiles árabes de occidente* (Madrid, 1935–40); C. J. Lamm, *Mittelalterliche Gläser und Steinschnittarbeiten aus dem Nahen Osten* (Berlin, 1929–30), I, 177–237 and II, Pls. 66–86; K. Erdmann, "Islamische Bergkristallarbeiten," *Jahrbuch der preussischen Kunstsammlungen,* LXI (1940), 125–46.

8. E. Kühnel, "Loza hispanoárabe excavada en Oriente," *Al-Andalus,* VI (1942), 253–68.

9. Such fragments have been found at Susa (R. Ghirshman, *Rapports préliminaires I. Cinq campagnes de fouilles à Suse [1946–51]* [Paris, 1952], p. 4) and at Brahminâbâd in Sind (R. L. Hobson, *A Guide to the Islamic Pottery of the Near East* [London: British Museum, 1932], p. 8, Figs. 16 and 17).

10. A. W. Frothingham, *Lustreware of Spain* (New York: Hispanic Society of America, 1951), pp. 4–6, Figs. 1–2.

11. F. Sarre and F. R. Martin, *Meisterwerke muhammedanischer Kunst* (München, 1912), Vol. II, Pl. 153 right; Manuel Gómez-Moreno, *El arte árabe español hasta los Almohades ...* (Madrid, 1951), Figs. 390 upper right, 391 right, 394, etc.

12. D. G. Shepherd, "Hispano-Islamic Textiles in the Cooper Union Collection," *Chronicle of the Museum for the Arts and Decoration of the Cooper Union,* I, No. 10 (1943) 365–73, Figs. 5–7.

13. D. S. Rice, "Studies in Islamic Metal Work—IV," *Bulletin of the School of Oriental and African Studies,* XV (1953), 500–502, Pls. VIII–IX.

14. H. Glück and E. Diez, *Die Kunst des Islam* (Berlin, 1925), Pl. 355.

15. Compare Hobson, *op. cit.,* Figs. 68–71, with *La Céramique égyptienne de l'époque musulmane* (Bâle: Musée de l'art arabe du Caire, 1922), Pls. 93, 101–4, 109–11, and R. Ettinghausen, "Islamic Art and Archaeology," in *Near Eastern Culture and Society,* ed. T. Cuyler Young (Princeton, 1951), Fig. 24.

16. Ibn Nâjî, *Maᶜâlim al-imân* (Tunis, 1320 A.H.), II, 97, quoted in G. Marçais, *Les Faïences à reflets métalliques de la Grande Mosquée de Kairouan* (Paris, 1928), pp. 9–10, Pls. I–XXVI.

17. F. R. Martin, *The Miniature Painting and Painters of Persia, India and Turkey* (London, 1912), Vol. II, Pls. 22–23.

18. F. Sarre, *Erzeugnisse islamischer Kunst, Teil I: Metall* (Berlin, 1906), pp. 43–45; G. Migeon, *Manuel d'art musulman* (Paris, 1927), II, 96–101.

19. *The Tûzuk-i-Jahângîrî or Memoirs of Jahângîr,* trans. A. Rogers, ed. H. Beveridge (London, 1909–14), II, 20; J. V. S. Wilkinson, *The Lights of Canopus, Anvâr i Suhailî* (London, n.d.), p. 15 (with further bibliographical references), Pls. III–V, VII, and XXIX.

20. This and the following examples are from a list of migratory architects published by K. A. C. Creswell, *The Muslim Architecture of Egypt* (Oxford, 1952), I, 163–64.

21. Max van Berchem and Halil Edhem, *Corpus inscriptionum arabicorum, Asie Mineure I* (Paris, 1917), pp. 81–82; K. A. C. Creswell, "The Works of Sultan Bibars al-Bunduqdârî in Egypt," *Bulletin de l'Institut français d'archéologie orientale,* XXVI (1926), 182.

22. E. Kühnel, "Zwei Mosulbronzen und ihr Meister," *Jahrbuch der preussischen Kunstsammlungen,* LX (1939), 10–11.

Actually, the earliest of these vessels made in Syria by a Mawṣilî artist is a signed ewer made for an Ayyûbid sultan as early as 629/1232 (D. S. Rice, "Studies in Islamic Metal Work—II," *Bulletin of the School of Oriental and African Studies,*

XV [1953], 66–69). This piece has recently been acquired by the Freer Gallery of Art.

J. Sauvaget has pointed to the parallel case of a Damascene workshop for the production of unglazed molded pilgrim bottles, whose technique and decoration are typical for the valley of the Euphrates, and in particular for Raqqa, so that the potters must be regarded as refugees from that region who had settled in the Syrian capital (*Poteries syro-mésopotamiennes du XIVe siècle* [Paris, 1932], pp. 2–7).

23. Creswell, *Muslim Architecture of Egypt,* I, 161–63.

24. Van Berchem and Edhem, *op. cit.*, I, 70 ff.; Creswell, "Works of Sultan Bibars," pp. 181–82.

25. Creswell, *ibid.*, pp. 184–86; E. Herzfeld, "Damascus: Studies in Architecture—II," *Ars Islamica,* X (1943), 61–62, Figs. 83–85; "Damascus—III," *ibid.*, XI–XII (1946), 16, 17, 61, Figs. 20–22, 83, 104.

26. Creswell, *Early Muslim Architecture,* I, 97, 101, 403.

27. Yaᶜqûbî, *Kitâb al-buldân,* ed. M. J. de Goeje (*Bibliotheca Geographorum Arabicorum,* Vol. VII) (Leiden, 1892), pp. 258 and 264, quoted by E. Herzfeld, *Geschichte der Stadt Samarra* (Hamburg, 1948), pp. 97 and 117. Herzfeld points to similar working conditions in Susa under Darius.

28. F. Sarre, "Die ägyptische Herkunft der sogenannten Damaskus-Teppiche," *Zeitschrift für bildende Kunst,* XXXII (1921), 75–82; see also K. Erdmann, "Kairener Teppiche, Teil I," *Ars Islamica,* V (1938), 179, 187–88.

29. Clavigo, *Embassy to Tamerlane, 1403–1406,* trans. Guy Le Strange (New York and London, 1929), pp. 287–88.

30. A. Sakisian, *La Miniature persane du XIIe au XVIIe siècle* (Paris and Bruxelles, 1929), p. 105, quoting Muṣṭafâ ᶜÂlî, *Manâqib-i hünervarân* (without page reference).

31. Frothingham, *op. cit.*, pp. 12–15; A. Lane, *Early Islamic Pottery* (London, 1947), pp. 37–38.

32. Creswell, *Muslim Architecture of Egypt,* I, 5, 8–9, 68–70, 90–102; "Works of Sultan Bibars," pp. 156–61.

33. Creswell, *Muslim Architecture of Egypt,* I, 121–28.

34. *Ibn Faḍlân's Reisebericht,* trans. A. Zeki Validi Togan (Leipzig, 1939), pp. 2–4.

35. E. Quatremère, "Notice de l'ouvrage persan qui a pour titre Matla-assaadeïn ou Madjma-albahreïn ... ," *Notices et extraits des manuscrits de la bibliothèque du roi et autres bibliothèques,* XIV (Paris, 1843), 304–6, 387, 425.

36. Creswell, *Early Muslim Architecture,* II, 138–39, 156–57.

37. *Ibid.*, pp. 367–69.

38. G. Migeon, *Mussulman Art: The Louvre Museum* (Paris, n.d.), Vol. I, Pl. 39.

39. The inscription in Samanid Kufic on this plate in the City Art Museum of St. Louis reads: *al tadbîr qabl al-ᶜamal yuᶜminuka min al-nadm,* "Deliberation before action protects you from regret." Pottery plates of this and similar series probably represent the earliest extant collection of Arabic proverbs from Iran. The first piece of this type to be recognized was a plate in the Musée du Louvre (S. Flury, "Ornamental Kûfic Inscriptions on Pottery," *A Survey of Persian Art* [London and New York, 1939], II, 1752 and Pl. 560A); since the start of the excavations at Nîshâpûr many more such vessels have been found, although most of them are still unpublished.

40. F. Sarre, "Die Tradition in der iranischen Kunst," *Mémoires, IIIe Congrès international d'art et d'archéologie iraniens* (Moscow and Leningrad, 1939), p. 228, Pl. CIV. A turquoise glazed bowl of this type is in the Freer Gallery of Art (No. 06.40).

41. G. D. Guest, "Notes on the Miniatures on a Thirteenth-Century Beaker," *Ars Islamica,* X (1943), 148–52, Figs. 1–13; *Musée arabe: Exposition d'art musulman, février-mars, 1947* (Le Caire, 1947), No. 101, Pl. XXI; Muḥammad Muṣṭafâ, *Matḥaf al-fann al-islâmî. Dalîl mûjaz* (Cairo, 1373/1954), Fig. 40.

42. M. Wiasmitina, *L'Art des pays de l'Islam. Catalogue, Musée des arts de l'Académie des Sciences d'Ukraine* (Kiev, 1930). "Supplément épigraphique" by V. Kratchkovskaya, p. 114, No. 390 (in Ukrainian).

43. D. Schlumberger, "Le Palais ghaznévide de Lashkari Bazar," *Syria,* XXIX (1952), 264, Pls. XXXI–XXXII.

44. I owe the photograph of this piece to the kindness of its discoverer, Mr. A. F. Mackenzie.

45. F. Sarre and E. Herzfeld, *Iranische Felsreliefs* (Berlin, 1910), Figs. 114 and 115 and Pl. L.

46. D. N. Wilber, "The Development of Faïence Mosaic in Islamic Architecture in Iran," *Ars Islamica,* VI (1939), 30–33, Figs. 2–6.

47. A. Godard, "L'Origine de la madrasa, de la mosquée et du caravansérail à quatre îwâns," *Ars Islamica,* XV–XVI (1951), 1–10; Schlumberger, *op. cit.,* pp. 255, 269, Fig. 3.

48. Creswell, *Early Muslim Architecture,* I, 14 and Fig. 4.

49. *Ibid.,* II, 231, quoting Severus b. al-Muqaffaᶜ.

50. Creswell, "The Origin of the Cruciform Plan of Cairene Madrasa," *Bulletin de l'Institut français d'archéologie orientale,* XXI (1922), 52–53.

51. Creswell, *Early Muslim Architecture,* I, 14; E. Herzfeld, *Iran in the Ancient East* (London and New York, 1941), p. 276.

52. J. A. Page, *A Guide to the Quṯb, Delhi* (Delhi, 1938), p. 2.

53. Herzfeld, "Damascus—II," pp. 46–47, Figs. 18 and 77.

54. Creswell, *Early Muslim Architecture,* I, 70–78.

55. *Ibid.,* pp. 39, 329.

56. R. B. Serjeant, "Material for a History of Islamic Textiles up to the Mongol Conquest," *Ars Islamica,* IX (1942), 64; XIII–XIV (1948), 88.

57. P. Britton, *A Study of Some Early Islamic Textiles in the Museum of Fine Arts, Boston* (Boston, 1938), pp. 40–43, Figs. 17–19.

58. E.g., A. F. Kendrick, *Catalogue of Muhammadan Textiles of the Medieval Period* (London: Victoria and Albert Museum, 1924), Pl. III, No. 869.

59. E. Kühnel, "La Tradition copte dans les tissus musulmans," *Bulletin de la Société d'Archéologie Copte,* V (1938), 79–89; K. Erdmann, "Kairener Teppiche, Teil II," *Ars Islamica,* VII (1940), 56–59.

60. Hugh G. Evelyn-White, *The Monasteries of the Wâdi 'n Natrûn. Part III: The Architecture and Archaeology,* ed. Walter Hauser (New York, 1933), Pls. LXVI–LXXI; E. Pauty, *Bois sculptés d'églises coptes (époque fatimide)* (Le Caire, 1930), Pls. I–XVI. For another Fâṭimid-style wood carving in a Coptic monastery, see Evelyn-White, *op. cit.,* Pl. LXXXVI.

61. P. Buberl, *Die byzantinischen Handschriften. 1. Der Wiener Dioskurides und*

die Wiener Genesis ("Beschreibendes Verzeichnis der illuminierten Handschriften in Österreich") (Leipzig, 1937), pp. 5, 22.

The superstitions about the miraculous cures of the man-shaped mandrake, the danger of its extraction by hand, and the alleged trick of using a dog tied to the plant to pull it from the ground—all these beliefs still existed in the Muslim world (at least among the lower classes) in the second half of the thirteenth century. This is shown by the speech of an itinerant herb vendor (who calls himself a pupil of Dioscorides) at an Egyptian fair in Ibn Dâniyâl's shadow play ᶜ*Ajîb wa-gharîb* (G. Jacob, "Ein ägyptischer Jahrmarkt im 13. Jahrhundert," *Sitzungsberichte der Bayerischen Akademie der Wissenschaften, Philosophisch-historische Klasse*, Jahrgang 1910, Heft 10 [München, 1910], p. 16).

62. The Dioscorides manuscript (Ahmet III, No. 2127) was first published in Süheyl Ünver, *Umumî tĭb tarihi: bazĭ resimler ve vesikalar* (Istanbul, 1943), Figs. 16–19, and *İstanbulda Dioscorides Eserleri* (Istanbul, 1944), Figs. 5–8. I am much obliged to Professor Ünver for putting the photographs of this manuscript at my disposal.

For parallel evangelist portraits see A. M. Friend, Jr., "The Portraits of the Evangelists in Greek and Latin Manuscripts," *Art Studies*, Vol. V (1927), Figs. 99, 106 (Vatican, Cod. Gr. 364), 107, 124, 128, 131, etc. Professor Friend discusses also the earlier history of the picture of a seated author with a standing woman who inspires him, and which goes back to Hellenistic and Roman scenes of poet and muse (*ibid.*, p. 141).

63. I wish to thank Professor Franz Rosenthal for having drawn my attention to this manuscript (Ahmet III, No. 3206), whose miniatures I shall discuss in a separate article. The manuscript is undated, but from various indications its style seems to be that of the first half of the thirteenth century.

64. Buberl, *op. cit.*, p. 20.

65. Max van Berchem, in F. Sarre and E. Herzfeld, *Archäologische Reise im Euphrat- und Tigris-Gebiet* (Berlin, 1911–20), I, 13–15; see also Herzfeld's comments, *ibid.*, p. 205.

66. *Ibid.*, II, 236–38; *The Travels of Ibn Jubayr*, trans. R. J. C. Broadhurst (London, 1952), pp. 244–45.

67. Sarre and Martin, *Meisterwerke*, II, Pl. 147; cf. also Max van Berchem's analysis of the inscriptions and historical notes, in Sarre and Herzfeld, *Archäologische Reise im Euphrat- und Tigris-Gebiet*, I, 6–8, Figs. 2–6.

68. Bukhârî, *Les Traditions islamiques*, trans. O. Houdas (Paris, 1914), IV, 132–35, esp. chaps. 88, 92, 94, 95, and 97.

69. *Bûstân*, ed. M. A. Forûghî (Teheran, 1316), p. 161, ll. 3–4 (chap. 5, ll. 135–36); quoted by A. K. Coomaraswamy, "Note on the Philosophy of Persian Art," *Ars Islamica*, XV–XVI (1951), 126; Rûmî, *Mathnawî*, ed. R. A. Nicholson (London, 1925), Book II, ll. 2535–43 (text, p. 387; trans., p. 352).

Recently Dr. Bishr Farès has also drawn attention to a text of Abû ᶜAlî 'l-Fârisî, dated 390/999, which states emphatically that only corporeal representations of God are forbidden, while others—and he speaks specifically of a figure of a calf made of wood or of precious metal—are said not to incur divine anger or the threats of the Muslims (*Essai sur l'esprit de la décoration islamique* [Le Caire, 1952], pp. 25–26).

70. Joseph and Ria Hackin, *Bamian, Führer zu den buddhistischen Höhlenklöstern und Kolossalstatuen* (Paris, 1939), pp. 20, 38.

71. E. Herzfeld, "Mshattâ, Ḥîra und Bâdiya," *Jahrbuch der preussischen Kunstsammlungen*, XLII (1921), 135, Fig. 9.

72. Bishr Farès, *Le Livre de la thériaque* (Le Caire, 1953), p. 52, Fig. 13.

73. A. U. Pope, "Representations of Living Forms in Persian Mosques, *Bulletin of the Iranian Institute*, VI–VII (December, 1946), 125–29; V. A. Kratchkovskaya, *The Tiles of the Mausoleum from the Khânaqâh of Pîr Ḥusain* (in Russian) (Tbilissi, 1946). The author points to the frequent use of animals on these tiles, dated 1283–85, and also on *miḥrâb* tiles of 1307 where they occur with Koranic quotations (see the review by Salomea Fajans in *Ars Islamica*, XV–XVI [1951], 254); the article by Zaki M. Hassan, "Figures and Statues in the Mosques and Mausolea of Iran" (in Arabic), *al-Thaqâfa*, Vol. II, No. 90 (1940), was not available to me.

74. The author is indebted to M. and Mme André Godard for having kindly put Plate VIII*a* from the veranda of the *Imâmzâda* in Amol at his disposal. A picture of such a sacred painting *in situ* is illustrated in F. L. Bird, "Modern Persia and Its Capital," *National Geographic Magazine*, Vol. XXXIX (April, 1921), Fig. on p. 379; see also A. U. Pope, "The Architecture of the Islamic Period . . . ," in *A Survey of Persian Art* (London and New York, 1938–39), Vol. IV, Pls. 509 C, 553 B, C.

75. See the statement of al-Âmulî, in *Nafâ᾿is al-funûn* (India Office Library, Ethé 2221), fol. 6, quoted in Sir Thomas W. Arnold, *Painting in Islam* (Oxford, 1928), p. 2; cf. also F. Rosenthal, "Abû Ḥaiyân al-Tawḥîdî on Penmanship," *Ars Islamica*, XIII–XIV (1948), 9, No. 13.

76. Fig. 1 and Pl. VIII*b* are unpublished; Pl. IX*a* is after N. I. Vesselovski, *A Bronze Vessel from Herat, Dated 559 H.* (*1163 A.D.*) (St. Petersburg, 1910) (in Russian), Pl. 2; the bowl of which Pl. IX*b* is a part of the rim is illustrated in *Metalwork from Islamic Countries*, Exhibition catalogue by R. Ettinghausen (Ann Arbor, 1943), No. 43, Pl. VII; Pl. IX*c* represents a detail from a Syrian canteen of *ca.* 1240–50 published by M. S. Dimand, "A Silver Inlaid Bronze Canteen with Christian Subjects in the Eumorfopoulos Collection," *Ars Islamica*, I (1934), 17–21, and particularly Fig. 3. See also the inscriptions on the pen case of 1210 (E. Herzfeld, "A Bronze Pen-Case," *Ars Islamica*, III [1936], 35–43 and Figs. 1–9) and the holder of a Mamlûk candlestick made between 1290 and 1293, published by G. Wiet (*Objets en cuivre*, Catalogue du Musée arabe [Le Caire, 1932], No. 4463, pp. 125–26 and Pl. XXIV); the difficulty of reading these advanced anthropomorphic *naskhî* inscriptions is indicated by M. Wiet's uncertain remark: "Le col ... est décoré d'une inscription, probablement votive. ... "

77. Fig. 2 was made after E. Kühnel, *Miniaturmalerei im islamischen Orient* (Berlin, 1922), figure on p. 13.

78. Vesselovski, *op. cit.*; R. Ettinghausen, "The Bobrinski 'Kettle,' Patron and Style of an Islamic Bronze," *Gazette des Beaux-Arts*, 6th ser., XXIV (1943), 193–208.

79. See the writer's "Early Realism in Islamic Art" (in press).

80. D. S. Rice, "The Oldest Dated 'Mosul' Candlestick A.D. 1225," *Burlington Magazine*, XCI (1949), 334–40, Figs. 5, 6, and D. As to the ewer of 1223, it has been referred to in the literature and has also been publicly exhibited (*Metalwork from Islamic Countries* [Ann Arbor, 1943], No. 45), but, as far as this writer is aware, no photograph has so far been published. It was originally planned to illustate a detail of this piece in this article, but, in view of a forthcoming article by D. S. Rice (in *Ars Orientalis*, Vol. II), the reader is referred to this publication.

81. For a full view of the piece see *Metalwork from Islamic Countries,* No. 47, Pl. IX. The basin was made for al-Malik al-Nâṣir Ṣalâḥ al-Dîn Abû 'l-Muẓaffar Yûsuf b. al-Malik al-ᶜAzîz, Ayyûbid Sultan of Aleppo (1236–40) and later of Damascus (1250–60).

82. Victoria and Albert Museum, No. 2734-56. I am indebted to Dr. D. S. Rice and Mr. B. W. Robinson for information about this piece.

83. W. Bacher, *Niẓâmî's Leben und Werke und der zweite Theil des Niẓâmîschen Alexanderbuches* (Göttingen, 1871), p. 103. The only known two medieval miniatures referring directly to the Sindbad story, but without descriptive text, occur in Bodleian Library, MS Or. 133 (one is published in Arnold, *op. cit.,* Pl. XV).

84. R. Ettinghausen, *Studies in Muslim Iconography I: The Unicorn* ("Freer Gallery of Art Occasional Papers," Vol. I, No. 3 [Washington, 1950]), pp. 29–30, Pl. 22.

85. See the statements of Muslim travelers about the pre-Islamic buildings of Egypt (*The Travels of Ibn Jubayr,* pp. 45–46, 54; *Ibn Battúta, Travels in Asia and Africa, 1325–1354,* trans. H. A. R. Gibb [London, 1929], p. 53). The explanation of al-Qalqashandî and al-Maqrîzî for the absence of columns in the Mosque of Ibn Ṭûlûn—these can be gotten only from churches, and this ruler is said to have disapproved of them for his mosque—is factually incorrect, but it reveals a consciousness of the different architectural features in this building and Christian ones (Creswell, *Early Muslim Architecture,* II, 333). Finally, see Ibn Khaldûn's correct juxtaposition of Sassanid textiles with representations of kings and other figures, and those made by order of Muslim princes in which the figures were replaced by royal names and words of praise for God (quoted by Serjeant in "Material for a History of Islamic Textiles . . . ," *Ars Islamica,* IX [1942], 60–61).

86. Ibn Marzûq, "Musnad," ed. E. Lévi-Provençal, *Hespéris,* V (1925), 33; quoted by Creswell, *Early Muslim Architecture,* II, vi.

87. *Al Ghasali, Das Elixir der Glückseligkeit,* trans. H. Ritter (Jena, 1923), pp. 158–59.

88. *Mathnawî,* Book IV, ll. 2881–87 (text ed. Nicholson, II, 448–49; trans. Nicholson, p. 431); quoted by Coomaraswamy, *op. cit.,* p. 126.

THE BODY POLITIC

CLAUDE CAHEN

THE problem which I am to introduce to you can, I think, be formulated as follows: To what degree have there existed, on the level of public organization and behavior, specific characteristics common to all of the Muslim peoples as a whole, and to what degree do these characteristics result from their common religion.

It goes without saying that a complete analysis of the problem so formulated is not possible within the limits of this paper. I shall gladly limit myself to the Middle Ages and even, in general, to the period preceding the Mongol period and the origins of the Ottoman Empire. Even so I shall have to be at once too long and too brief: too long, because it is clear that all the facts I shall cite are known to you much more thoroughly than in the summary form in which I shall mention them; too brief, because I shall be obliged to leave aside completely an analysis of the administrative machinery and, what is more serious, to cite without closer examination, treating them as already established, all the economic and social conditioning factors without which it is impossible to understand the development and the differentiation of the Muslim political regimes on which my paper should bear. What I shall try to bring you is a historical bird's-eye view of these regimes, in which attention will be directed to the following points: first, we are to study how the political regime and religion adapted to each other in the course of the developments of history; second, we are to keep constantly in mind that the Muslim world, especially on the level of its material and social structures, cannot be considered in advance as an undifferentiated unity—and therefore we are not to use documents of one place and one time as universally valid but are to compare among themselves the geographical sectors and the moments of Muslim history; finally, we are not to forget that an exact appreciation of the characteristics of a society, of a civilization, cannot be gained without constant reference to the other societies, the other civilizations of a nearly corresponding level, which surround it in space and in time and, consequently, we are to bring in matters relevant to a comparison with them, and in this case more particularly perhaps with Byzantine Christianity. I do not flatter myself, though, that I have succeeded in realizing even this limited program very well, and I hope that in the discussion you will help me to make clearer to myself all that I have not yet succeeded in seeing with the clarity which I would have wished.

I

It is well known that political organization and behavior are not based on the same principles in the Muslim world as in the Christian world. These principles, for that matter, are simply the transcription of different historical circumstances. Christianity was born in the framework of the Roman state. Little by little it built itself a church. Whatever disputes the boundary line between church and state gave rise to, each acknowledged that the other had an autonomous domain and so conceived society as governed by a duality of powers, the temporal and the spiritual. Mohammed, on the contrary, arising in a society without a state, was, in a manner in which only modern minds introduce any distinction, the preacher of a faith and the organizer of a temporal community. Consequently the social law was an integral part of the religious law, and respect for the social law an integral part of submission to Allâh. Revelation was the joint basis of belief and of temporal organization. The community was in itself its state and its church, and neither the one nor the other existed as an autonomous system. Naturally Islâm is not alone in having set out from this point of view, which had been that of the Hebrews of Moses under partially comparable social conditions. Naturally, also, this theoretical unity is a limit which was never reached, or which at least could not be reached concretely without naturalizing, as Muslim, usages which were in fact pre-Islamic. The orientation, however, was categorical, and it was not to disappear very soon from men's minds. It was to have the consequence that the Muslim would require of his political organization a certain perfection; if this was lost, the principle of obedience which he owed to it was also lost. In contrast, the Christian renounced this perfection in advance and yet did not cease to be bound in his capacity as citizen of a state. It can be easily seen how a similar turn of mind among Muslims could cover much more concrete attitudes of withdrawal with respect to the state, whether we think of the traditional Bedouin anarchism or of the other forms of externalization which we meet in the later Muslim world.

In practice, what had been possible in the way of identifying the temporal and the spiritual in the person of Mohammed ceased to be so by his very death. His successors in the guidance of the community could indeed direct the fulfilment of the duties of the believers; but it was not for them to change anything or even to complete anything in a revelation definitively given, unless they accepted, as some were to venture to do later, the possibility of a certain continuation of revelation, which no one then claimed. In the Roman conception law is constantly capable of reformation, development; in the Islamic conception there could be no theoretical foundation other than reference to precedent, to tradition—single and unalterable. This is a state of mind which, for that matter, is not far from that of all peoples who lack the concept of the state, except for the religious aspect in certain cases: the Christian Occident lived for centuries in a theoretical respect for custom, and for a conception of this custom as being derived from precedents. *Mutatis mutandis*, Arabs and Teutons were of the same human age. Only, in practical reality, things did not happen this way. Mohammed could not have legislated for all the problems of the future. The lightning conquests, resulting from undertakings integral to the religious doctrine, even though the social reasons for them are in fact clear, had the effect of making it suddenly impossible to maintain the primitive politico-religious organization. The vastness of the territory, the entirely new institutions of the subjugated populations, of which a blank slate could not be made, forced the heirs of Mohammed to undertake or to tolerate things which went far outside the field of simple modalities of application in the Muslim Law. There were then in fact two domains: that of the Muslim Law, applicable only to the Arabs and more and more inadequate even for them, and that of the non-Islamic laws, preserved almost unchanged for the conquered peoples and, in fact, governing the empire. This division could be felt by the members of the primitive community who had stayed in Medina and had been discarded as "rejects" by the new regime, with a bitterness expressed religiously; unlike the warriors scattered across the world, they did not experience the burden and the temptations of the new ways of proceeding. There is no reason to think that for these latter the transformations in their way of life, which they accepted very readily, were to be understood as a betrayal of their faith or that they found any scandal in the non-Arab and non-Muslim peoples' being governed by non-Muslim laws, if only they worked submissively to the benefit of the Muslim Arabs.

The state which takes rough shape under these conditions comprises, in short, two sectors: on the one hand, a rudimentary central organization around the caliph which governs the Muslims—for war, for the obligations of the cult, for distributing the pensions; on the other hand, an administration the revenues of which go to the new masters, but the norms and the personnel of which, by the force of circumstances, continue to be largely those of the previous regimes. The Arabs, at the start, would have been entirely lacking in the experience required for any other policy, which, besides, would have made the establishment of the empire as difficult as this nonintervention made it easy. For populations which had had to complain of the vexatious interference of an invading state or an official church the policy was a partial liberation. In fiscal matters, for example, the Byzantine taxes and the Sassanid taxes continued. How could it have been otherwise? They were set by the nature of the economy and the social structure and not by abstract doctrines. The gradual clothing of these institutions in Arabic terms like *kharâj* and *jizya,* to which the jurists subsequently tried to give a precise Muslim definition, must not deceive us. The researches of Dennett,[1] among others, have demonstrated very clearly how the facts behind these same names differ in Khurâsân, in Iraq, in Egypt. Once we have left behind the still narrow framework of the central government, it is therefore not, in the life of the population, *one* regime, but *regimes* with which we must deal. The conquerors themselves had implicitly acknowledged the fact. Precisely because they had no conception of a unitary administration, they had made their conquests empirically and had organized them, not according to a general plan, but by a juxtaposition of local measures. Contrary to what has been believed, it was not at all a construct a posteriori when the later jurists distinguished between territories taken by force and by treaties, and within this second category among as many treaties as territories. Such had very naturally been the actual fact. Certainly there was subsequently a labor of regularization, of assimilation, but one must not be deceived: the later fragmentation of the Muslim world would never have been so easy if this labor had been thoroughly accomplished, and we must get rid of the idea that the centralized, bureaucratized state of the following centuries itself ever did anything but bring together local regimes without casting them in the same crucible. There too the Muslim state seems to us to be of the same age as the Western monarchies.

The situation described above became more complicated when to the Arab Muslims were added a number of indigenous converts too large to be incorporated into the still semitribal structure of the Arab society. Here again we have to do with a phenomenon the major reasons for which are only rarely religious but which was to have repercussions as much on the religious life itself as on the conception of the nature of the state in the Muslim religious community. As Muslims, the new converts demanded to be treated according to a Muslim law which should be alike for them and for the Arabs and not according to an Imperial law which kept them in an inferior status. A social demand, certainly, but one which was expressed in a religious form, in that it amounted to demanding, instead of the rule of a people and of a political organization indifferent to Islâm, a new regime involving the equalitarian rule of the adepts of a religion and, consequently, the adaptation of the political organization to the requirements of Islâm. Thus, by an apparent paradox, and more in form than in content, there were united in a common opposition to the regime the traditionalist Arabs, wishing to have back the good old times of the Medinese supremacy, and the natives who had turned Muslim, hostile to the Arab supremacy and more or less obscurely attached to national traditions antedating Islâm.

It is in the light of these explanations that we can understand the various judgments made in their time and afterwards upon the Umayyad caliphs. The Abbasid propaganda, which overthrew them, described them as impious. A gross falsehood, if one were to take that to mean that the Umayyads were supposed to be indifferent to their functions as leaders of the believers, this propaganda was based nonetheless upon the actual fact that the Umayyad state was not designed to fulfil requirements which had arisen later. It was true that the Umayyad state, in all that was not directly a matter of the cult, had no ties with religion. Now that the juxtaposition of peoples was replaced by a fusion through conversion, it became natural that a new state was expected to seek to give a Muslim inspiration to institutions born outside of Islâm. The question is not, at this stage, whether one could call the desired transformations Muslim, nor whether those which took place were so. We will come back to this question. What is important is that equally in Persia and in Barbary it was in the name of Islâm that the natives rose against the Umayyads and that it was a Muslim regime which their Abbasid successors claimed to be organizing.

The opponents of the Umayyad regime had moved in two doctrinal directions which looked quite different, the most clear-cut manifestations of which are to be found in the Shîᶜite and Khârijite movements but which, less sharply focused, correspond to sentiments which prevailed widely outside of these movements themselves. For some, the coupling of religious illumination and command over men, which had been present in the person of the Prophet, must in the normal course of events be capable of continuation. There is a line of men to whom God continues to give such sufficient light that they must not only be the administrators of the community but also be the guides of men's minds: the "imams," in the full sense which was given to this word. Governed by these men, the state would no longer present the spectacle of a divorce from religion. But these men could not be the Umayyads. It was on the descendants or, more vaguely, on the family of the Prophet that Allâh had once for all conferred this privilege. Hence the opposition assumed a dynastic character. It was Muslim in the sense that it had as rallying cry the family of the Prophet. But it is readily seen also how among the native populations, by a simple substitution of persons, it joined in with the ancestral conceptions of semidivine monarchies, of which the Orient had been full: how, in short, it wrapped in a Muslim flag a return to a past far antedating the Muslims.

For the second type of opponents, the Khârijites, the search for a perfect system takes in appearance a diametrically opposite direction. For them, the guidance of the community falls by right to the Muslim who is most irreproachable, who must naturally be rejected as soon as he ceases to be so. No man, no family, has an essentially privileged position, so that the leader is simply a *primus inter pares*. The true sovereignty is that of the community of believers, from which bad Muslims are excluded. It was the ideal doctrine to dress up handsomely the anarchism of the Bedouins or the Berbers. It could also easily be, and likewise among those Berbers, a presentation suitable to an equalitarian revolt. But in practice it could lead to something quite different. For was it ordinary people, busied with earning their pittances, who could claim to know the Law well enough to judge how good or how poor a Muslim standing their leader had? And so there resulted a dictatorship of the learned, a dictatorship of the *ᶜulamâ*ᵓ.

To tell the truth, there could be found a tendency toward this dictatorship of the *ᶜulamâ*ᵓ in the whole of Muslim society. It is customarily stated that there is no Muslim clergy, no Muslim church. In point of dogma that is a matter of course, since Islâm knows no sacrament which would by its nature confer upon those who receive it more light than upon other men to guide them toward Truth and Salvation. But socially this makes little difference if there exist nonetheless men who have won spiritually and materially the power of a church. It cannot be denied that from the beginnings of Islâm there was an inevitable tendency toward such an outcome. The Law was based on tradition. Even the Koran had not been written down immediately—much less the whole body of the words and acts of the Prophet making up the *ḥadîth*, which was for a long time transmitted only by word of mouth. Even written down, who even so in the mass of the people could flatter himself that he knew it? If the state had promulgated official legislation, the need to turn to the light of specialists could have been circumscribed. But the state applied the Law; it was not the state that had created it or could create it anew. Under these conditions, if the Law was in principle under the protection of the entire community, in practice it could only be under that of the specialists. The consensus of these specialists, the *ijmâᶜ*, formed the foundation of the validity of the Law. That is to say, concretely every demand for an Islamization of institutions implied the claim of further influence for the *ᶜulamâᵓ*.

Naturally it would be important to ascertain what these *ᶜulamâᵓ* represented socially. The first of them, if you will, had been the surviving companions of the Prophet, then those who had known them, and so on. The farther one got from the source, the less reason there was for these to be solely Arabs. To be sure, the Medinese claimed a privileged knowledge of the Law, which had had its start among them. But the recent converts also inquired into the Tradition, precisely in order to find there theoretical justifications for their claims. They had the advantage over the Arabs of a long experience with juridical or philosophical deductions. And what control was there which could have prevented them from subjecting the Tradition to the slight jostling necessary to ground an opinion better? It seems, then, that it can be agreed that in this initial phase of their development the *ᶜulamâᵓ* represented the "intellectuals" of the various movements whose convergence, exploited by the Abbasids with a rare gift for confusing the issue, was to end in the fall of the Umayyad regime.

II

The Abbasid state presents itself to us, then, officially, as a Muslim state—Muslim because the caliph now, if he does not descend from the Prophet as a strict Shîᶜism requires, is at least of his family; Muslim because, though the authority which he derives from this relationship remains unprecise and a good deal short of certain further developments of Shîᶜism, there exists all the same a diffuse feeling that in itself this authority confers upon the political structure an assurance of being Muslim which the Umayyads lacked and which the Abbasids underline by adopting, even though in a rather vague sense, the designation of "imam." Above all the Abbasids wanted to give a concrete foundation to their Muslim character, it seems, by associating more closely with their work the *ʿulamâʾ* and, among them, more especially the *fuqahâʾ*, the specialists in the study of the law derived from the Islamic tradition.

Naturally it is not the Abbasids, it must be repeated, who created Muslim jurisprudence. The pressure of the requirements of a more and more complex society necessarily led to it—but not with the same vigor in all fields of study. It is clear that the *fuqahâʾ* were always more interested in the duties of the cult, in private law, in penal law, than in public law and in the organization and functioning of the administration and the character of its heads. These were things upon which it was perhaps prudent not to discourse too much if one did not want to incur some bitter disgrace. They were also things which need not be judged by the *qâḍî*, whose needs often provided the motive for the jurist's work. They were, above all, things strangely resistant to admitting, in any simple way, of being derived from the Tradition. For if, on the level of theory, it was necessary to build an autonomous Muslim jurisprudence, it was not possible for practical purposes to exclude the mass of non-Islamic institutions which were actually operating, survivals of the former regimes or unavoidable innovations. The problem which faced the jurists attached to the Abbasids, then, was not to derive the ideal Muslim government from the Tradition a priori but, rather, to institute a very loose filtering which should permit, at the price of some retouching or else at the price of a few wiles, of a few suggested reforms, the bestowal upon the regime as a whole of its certificate of "Good Muslim" by integrating into the Muslim system whatever did not resist too obstinately. Naturally this integration is presented in such a way that it seems as if there were being deduced from the Tradition institutions actually given in advance. Hence it is sometimes difficult to recognize the true countenance of the process. But all the cross-checking that can be done proves that it would be supremely unjust, at least at this time and in this field, to regard the work of the Abbasid jurists otherwise as abstract and turning the back on reality. We are watching, on the contrary, an attempt, which was hardly to be repeated, at giving a view of the administration at once theoretical and practical. And the luster which the unique work of the Shâfiʿite Mâwardî was later to gain must not make us forget that the essential points of this achievement were the work of the jurists of the school of Abû Ḥanîfa and Abû Yûsuf in the first Abbasid century.

Now, in historical reality what was there specifically Muslim about the Abbasid regime?

Clearly the regime was Muslim if by that is understood that the Muslims as a whole, and no longer with an ethnic distinction among them, held the position of privilege. The sovereign, the heads of the provincial governments, the army, even the great majority of the viziers, were Muslim; the Muslims were in a better position in point of justice and of taxation than the non-Muslims; the other faiths were tolerated, but Islâm was, we might say, the official religion. But, except that the terms were reversed, exactly the same was then true of the Christian states, to the advantage of Christianity. Or rather in Muslim lands there was an infinitely wider tolerance, at this stage of Muslim history, toward the followers of other religions than in the Christian lands. At first in the minority, and always faced with numerous and compact non-Muslim groups, the Muslims could not, quite apart from any question of doctrine, have adopted another policy. Even in the spiritual realm Islâm, as the latest comer, could not treat as nonexistent the great religions already in the field and strongly organized; at the most it could force them to recognize its political supremacy. The situation was quite different in the Christian countries, where the religious minorities were weak, the church was powerful, and the state functioned exclusively with a Christian personnel. One need look for no underlying doctrinal reason for a difference of behavior which the historical conditions suffice to explain.

Once beyond the limits of public law and of the relations among members of the various communities, these latter, as regards their private law and in part their penal affairs, were governed each according to its own law. In short, it was a system of law according to personal status. That also is nothing peculiar to the Muslim world. To a certain degree this system was later extended even among the Muslims themselves, since it was finally recognized that within Islâm four juridical systems were valid, among which every Muslim was in principle free to make his choice. In fact, all states born of conquest have passed through a phase of law according to personal status, whether the discriminating principle was essentially tied to religious affiliation or at the same time, or chiefly, to ethnic contrasts, as in the Germanic states set up on former Roman soil. The same principle governs no less the modern European colonies. What is distinctive in the case of Islâm is the extreme duration of the system, which has not yet disappeared, in contrast to most of the other cases of conquest where in the long run there came about a fusion of peoples, carrying with it that of laws. But even there the European colonies could exhibit some experiences already lengthy enough to serve as parallels to the Muslim experience. The reasons for this durability are naturally to be found in general historical conditions and not in anything peculiar to the Muslim doctrine. Nay, the establishment in the Muslim empire of law according to personal status had been facilitated by a legal development in the Roman-Christian lands. A growing portion of private law, even some elements of penal law, had there been withdrawn from the jurisdiction of the state, which alone administered them in antiquity, so as to be placed under the control of the Church. From that point it was not necessary to extend very greatly the functions of the bishops in Muslim territory to confer on them juridically as regards their flocks a position to which that of the *qâḍî* soon corresponded as regards the Muslims.

Clearly there is in principle an important difference between Muslim justice and that of the Christian states. The creation of law not being within the province of the state, the *qâḍî* was in the end its guardian independently of the state and, if necessary, against it. In practice the difference is less than it seems, on the one hand because the *qâḍî* did not have, as against the state, the material independence which would guarantee his moral independence, on the other hand because the appropriation by the Church in Christian lands of a portion of the law in the name of canon law conferred, in a slightly reduced form, precisely this characteristic of the Muslim system upon the system of the medieval Christian lands. Once again we note that the two societies were at the same human age.

In still another field a limitation upon the power of the state has its parallel in the West and in Byzantium. All that we would call institutions of public service, the direction of which the Classical state shared with private groupings, was, in the Christian society and in the Muslim society, a matter not of the state but of religion, maintained by foundations deriving from the piety of the faithful, which finally constituted an impressive mass of mortmain property. Thus were supported mosques, schools, hospitals, caravanserais, etc., etc. There is no fundamental difference in this respect between Church property in Christian lands and the Muslim *waqfs*, which originally were probably inspired by it. One can say only that Muslim governments were often able to exercise over the *waqfs*, the founding and character of which did not depend upon them, a somewhat more distinct administrative control than the Christian governments, even in Byzantium, where the Church was administrator of its property without any limitation. It did happen, on the other hand, that the *waqfs* were used to assure the independence of the *qâḍî*, who was their administrator; but there was in this matter no regularly observed rule, and this seems rather to have been the fruit of a relatively late development.

Furthermore, it must not be thought that the Muslim state was in fact restricted to its theoretical limits of simple administrator of the Law so strictly as respect for doctrine would lead one to suppose. Experience showed the inadequacies of the *qâḍî*'s jurisdiction: the prohibition against his freeing himself from the traditional Law, which nevertheless could not provide for everything; his inability to make his decisions respected by the powerful; the necessity for an appellate jurisdiction in case of deficiencies in the *qâḍî;* etc. Hence the theoretical recourse to the sovereign and, when he had not the time or the taste to see personally to that task, the juridical organization dubbed that for the *maẓâlim*, for (the redress of) abuses. The jurists took great pains to establish that on the whole it must converge with the other jurisdiction in its respect for religion. But in fact, freed from a literal respect for the law, permitting a considerable range for personal judgment, and moreover tied directly to the wielders of public power, who lent their effectiveness to its decisions, it became, within more limited, less developed forms, a substitute for the governmental jurisdictions known to the Christian societies of the time.

Furthermore, the exercise of administrative power inevitably leads those who govern to take measures which in a Roman-Christian state would have been within the province of the public law, and about which all that a jurist could do was to perform a work of integration a posteriori, or throw over them a decent veil, or, if he was not in the government, to protest. This is particularly clear in the matters of taxes, of recruitment and payment of troops, etc. All one can say is that such measures were perhaps conceived less as definitive laws than as particular measures dependent on the person of the sovereign who took them—and subject to disappearing with him. In practice there was scarcely any difference. Moreover, even in the field of theory we would find a like situation in the Christian West, where the Roman heritage of law was forgotten and there were known only, on the one hand, a custom independent of the state and, on the other hand, particular measures taken by those who wielded authority, which, to be sure, acquired the force of precedents.

Further, one could wonder if the Muslim caliph, by the very fact that he became officially a religious figure, did not acquire a right to desire, as did at the same time the Christian sovereigns, to make himself the arbiter of strictly religious disagreements and impose his interpretation of the faith. The attempt was made, with Muᶜtazilism, but it failed. The reasons for this may lie equally well in the nature of Muᶜtazilism as in a rejection of the role which the caliph arrogated to himself in connection with it. But it is certain that the abandonment of Muᶜtazilism did not mark the passage of the Abbasids to another official doctrine, but the capitulation of the caliphate before the *ᶜulamâᵓ*, implicitly recognized as alone qualified to discuss orthodoxy. The attempt was to be renewed by others later, as we shall see, but under quite different conditions.

III

For in fact the Abbasid regime did not long remain what it had been at the beginning. It is impossible to study here the reasons of every sort which brought about this development. It showed itself at once in a transformation in the nature of the government and in the political breakup of the Empire. We have already emphasized the fact that the formation of the Empire had never signified the establishment of a uniform government over all its provinces; the more distant had in the nature of things always enjoyed an almost total autonomy. It has been said, almost without paradox, that the Empire fell apart because it had never existed. For a number of reasons, some of them connected with the transformation in the nature of the government, these centrifugal tendencies now were increased and, between the end of the eighth and the tenth centuries, resulted in the partitioning of the Muslim world into a growing number of autonomous kingdoms, some of which preserved the ideal of unity through the honorary pre-eminence which they reserved to the Abbasid Caliphate, from which they requested their legitimation, but others of which even rose against the Abbasid Caliphate and broke the unity of the Muslim world at its root. In this *de facto* situation it becomes necessary for us, from now on, no longer to speak simply of a Muslim government establishing a certain unity over the regional diversities, but of a number of regimes, each to be studied independently—though we may ascertain a posteriori their common characteristics, or those common to certain ones among them. Certainly one must not, on the contrary, exaggerate the significance of all this fragmentation. While some of the regimes had reasons which could attract the deep adherence of the population, others answered to the rival ambitions of leaders who found no popular response. Further, it is certain that the sense of Muslim solidarity was a reality independent of the unity or the disunity in the political system. Finally, since the essential points of that in the Muslim Law which concerns daily life were independent of the state, it was quite possible to pass from one principality to another without having in this respect the sense of leaving one's country. From this point of view the characteristics of the Abbasid regime which we have summarized were equally true of any and all of the regimes which succeeded it. There were nonetheless also, and more especially on the governmental and administrative level which here concerns us, distinct cleavages to which we must pay attention.

The first point we must examine is that of the relations between civil and military elements. Originally, the army amounted to the conquering Arab people—the natives, as non-Muslims, being a priori debarred from it, since the war was a holy, Muslim war. The coming of the Abbasid regime had meant the winning, by the non-Arab Muslims of many origins, of the right to military activity at the same time as other rights henceforward common to all Muslims. In practice, because of the actual demilitarization of a part of the Arabs, of the lack of discipline of many among them, and of the support given to the Abbasid regime fundamentally in Khurâsân, the army of the first Abbasids was above all Khurâsânian. Further, it tended to set itself off technically from the mass of the population in that it became partially an army of paid professionals, who were better adapted to the new ways of fighting of the heavy cavalry and more dependable than independent volunteers living on the possible booty and a wage limited to the time of the expeditions. Nevertheless, the frequency of difficulties in Khurâsân soon caused the caliphs to prefer to recruit a growing proportion of their armies among foreign slaves, especially Turks, bought young in the markets of the north to be brought up for this purpose: we are clearly not to liken the way of life of such slaves to that of slaves of private individuals; and, further, when they received a command they could be freed, and in that case had no other relations with their masters than those of clients to a patron or, more realistically, of payees to a paymaster. In the thought of the caliphs, this army was to be their personal property.

In practice they became its prisoners, as the emperors of Rome became those of the Pretorians, since their power depended on the soldiers alone. The impossibility of providing for their needs or for their demands from the normal receipts of the treasury led to alienating provinces to them, and finally even the control of the central government. The army was henceforth an end unto itself. Composed either of mercenaries recruited among special elements of the population (Kurds, Dailamîs), or of Turkish slaves or freedmen, it had the characteristic of being more and more foreign to the population over which it ruled: it was the government of a military occupation, with which the population could not in general feel any solidarity. The fighting among the various leaders or the various corps of this army showed traits in common with that among the leaders of bands, or *condottieri*, at the end of the Western Middle Ages, and the inhabitants were absolutely indifferent to the overthrow of one by another. On their part, an attitude of withdrawal, and of opposition when possible, confronting an attitude of distrust on the part of the military leaders, often characterized henceforward this system of mutual alienation.

It was in Iraq, around the caliphate, that the development was the fastest and, at least at first, the clearest. But the movement was universal. Even, for example, in a principality such as that of the Samanids, the national and social bases of which, at the time of its formation, were clear and solid, it came to that state of affairs at the end of the tenth century, when the leaders of their army were to overthrow them and found the Ghaznavid dynasty. Nevertheless, there were intermediate cases where the cleavage between army and population was not general—where, on the contrary, at the beginning the conquering army had its source in an element of the population—such as the army of the Bûyids, resulting from a rising of Dailam, or that of the Fâṭimids, from the rising of certain Berbers. But that did not keep the Dailamîs from being foreigners at Baghdad, and the Berbers at Cairo, and, in their own countries, the primitive contact with the population from being broken off in the degree to which they became professionals.

Moreover, we have here, roughly, a factor differentiating between the west and the east of the Muslim world. I do not know the Muslim west well enough to speak of it with exactness and certainty, but it does seem to me that it never knew the deep gulf between military elements and civilian elements or, if you wish, between rulers and population which was characteristic, on the contrary, of the Muslim east. In the east the intermediate phase characterized by the Dailamî regime lasted only a while. In the eleventh century it came to the Turkish conquest (we shall see under what circumstances), that is, to the rule of an army which, however welcome it might have been to some, was nonetheless a thoroughly foreign one. In the west, on the contrary, in the course of the fighting among various Berber and Arab groups, there never arose this absolute ethnic and social separation. In the east an employee of the civil service was never in practice chosen from the same race as the members of the army and the political leaders coming out of it; in the west, on the contrary, nothing prevented both groups from coming from the same milieu, it depending quite simply on professional specialization. Certainly in Spain the evolution of the body of Slavic slaves around the sovereign set on foot a development comparable in certain respects to that of the east; nevertheless, it does not seem that there existed between them and the others the thoroughgoing distinction between careers found in the east, nor that in the makeup of the Umayyad regime at Cordova the Slavs had fully won the place which the Turks held in that of the Abbasid regime at Baghdad. In a very elastic sense of the word, the western governments remained national governments when the eastern ones had ceased to be so.

Without its being possible to follow out through all the institutions the consequences of this divergence, it will perhaps be instructive nevertheless to say a word on the conduct of the civil administration. It is hard to see for what reasons, unlike the Basileus of Constantinople, who generally remained the only co-ordinator of his heads of departments, the caliphs of Baghdad took on, in the person of a vizier, a personage who conducted the whole of the administration: much more than a modern prime minister, rather an entrepreneur of government, who brought his own staff of dependents along and recouped himself from the taxpayers. The Sassanid tradition is suggested, in spite of the Arabic etymology of the word "vizier," and certainly that tradition was in fashion under the Abbasids, but remodeled for the needs of the day, which alone, on the whole, decided matters. Nor does it seem that the Sassanid antecedent of the Muslim vizier ever had all his characteristics. In any case, it is quite certain that such a power presented a danger for the caliphate; hence, for example, the dramatic action of Hârûn al-Rashîd against the Barmakids. But the establishment of the military principalities in the east confirmed the existence of a vizierate, subject, to be sure, to the good or ill will of the prince, but within its administration all-powerful. Niẓâm al-Mulk is the extreme example of this. The military leader was often too incompetent, too foreign to the inhabitants, to be able to concern himself with the administration, which was in practice, seen from his point of view, a sort of bureau of native affairs. They gave themselves blindly into the hands of native viziers, only being ready to torture them if things went wrong. The western government was different. There the title of "vizier" had only subordinate significance. The co-ordinating role was played by the *ḥâjib*, that is, by a dignitary attached to the person of the prince, at the top rank among his domestic servants. His role was usually limited. However, when a powerful caliphate was organized at Cordova, the post of *ḥâjib*, although the dangers in it had been seen, acquired a high actual authority. In the hands of Ibn Abî ᶜÂmir it became a sort of Mayorship of the Palace, stronger than that of the Merovingians, and which in practice put an end to the Umayyad dynasty but without succeeding in putting a durable regime in its place. A political fragmentation, as in the east, followed. But it is to be remarked, for our purposes, that neither under Ibn Abî ᶜAmir nor in the succeeding principalities do we witness a breach between the military power and the civil administration. We will find points of similarity to this state of things under the Fâṭimids of Egypt—under very different conditions, to be sure.

The militarization of governments is not a peculiarly Muslim matter. It is characteristic of our Western feudalism as well as of the Byzantine development. It is generals, in Byzantium, who won the throne. There was to be found there, as later in the Western monarchies, the calling-in of mercenaries—Scandinavians, Normans, Turks—culminating in the eleventh century in remarkable synchronism with the Muslim world. Nevertheless, a part of the army remained Greek or assimilated, and in practice all the generals did. Their power in their field developed as in the Islamic lands; it did not go so far, however, as to set up autonomous principalities. Besides, the Empire was small. There was in Byzantium neither a slave recruitment—we cannot study here the reasons for this difference—nor a thoroughgoing cleavage between the military caste and the civilian sector.

The military factor is naturally not the only one to consider. The ninth and tenth centuries were a period of intense social and religious ferment, which we cannot analyze here. During this period the governments seem to have been a priori almost neutral with regard to the various religious attitudes. It was not their function to be anything else. Do not misunderstand: it is quite clear that when the Zaidî propaganda, and especially the Qarmaṭian and Ismâᶜîlî propaganda, led to political risings, action was taken against them, not only in the form of external military measures, but also in that of investigations and repressive measures against their internal accomplices. But all the movements did not take the form of violent revolt. In respect to them the caliphate, in the ninth century, was neutral. It imposed, it upheld, no doctrine. In its offices worked side by side non-Muslim and Muslim officials, Shîᶜites and Sunnites. In the tenth century, power was taken over by leaders who were frequently Shîᶜites: Ḥamdânids and Bûyids in particular. Certainly Shîᶜism profited by this, and it is probable that the accession of these dynasties was due, not solely to the military phenomena which we have mentioned, but equally to the support of the Shîᶜite bourgeoisie; but their practical attitude was fundamentally the same, from the religious point of view, as that of the caliphate. The Shîᶜites concerned believed that since the twelfth Imam, who had disappeared, and while awaiting the advent of the Mahdî, no one knows when, there could be no true sovereign but only substitutes; moreover, if they attributed no authority to the Abbasid caliph, they saw nothing wrong in letting him continue to exist for the religious purposes of the Sunnites, since the latter on the whole allowed him so little religious authority, and since this tolerance would imply in return an obligation on the part of the Sunnites to accept the emirate of a Shîᶜite as legitimately tolerable. Hence they made no effort either to impose an official doctrine or to reserve public office for the followers of their belief. For example, between them and the Samanids, who were generally Sunnites but Sunnites in this same way, there was politically no essential difference.

Over against these states stood the little Khârijite and Zaidî kingdoms and then, above all, in the tenth century, the Fâṭimid state. Here, in forms which had been through a far-reaching development and upon a different social substratum, we witness the revival of the old Shîᶜite hope for a sovereign sprung from the family of the Prophet, who would be leader at once of men's souls and of their bodies. The founder of the dynasty declared that he was the Mahdî. One of his descendants was to be considered by some as the incarnation of an aspect of the Divinity. Certainly the Fâṭimids neither were able nor perhaps even hoped to convert to their doctrine, even under the elementary forms open to the noninitiates, the entire body of their subjects. Nevertheless, they organized abroad an intense propaganda carried on by specialized missionaries, in order to prepare the way for subsequent political successes; they also organized at home official instruction in the doctrine, to which the University of al-Azhar bears witness even today. At last, naturally, they presented themselves not as temporal princes but as anticaliphs, thus breaking the theoretical unity of the Muslim community. This much being said, their temporal administration must not be considered essentially different from that of the neighboring regimes. Its peculiarities were due more to the traditions characteristic of Egypt or the Maghrib than to a special Fâṭimid system. Moreover, the dynastic quarrels of the second Fâṭimid century, which inevitably took the shape of religious schism, in practice ruined the spiritual prestige of the caliph, who became less and less different from his rival at Baghdad.

No more than the latter had he escaped the seizure of power by this army. However, this seizure presented itself with characteristics which combine western and eastern traits in specifically Egyptian conditions. The army, very heterogeneous, included foreign elements, for example Turks and Negroes, but also Arab elements or semiassimilated ones, immigrant Berbers or Armenians. It was leaders of Armenian or Arab contingents who took power. For that matter, the Fâṭimid caliph, like the one in Baghdad, had had a powerful vizierate. The difference between the Egyptian evolution and the Seljuq evolution is that the victorious leader did not content himself with military power and shift the vizierate off onto a native but, being himself native or seminative, also took over the vizierate himself. It was later, still as vizier, that even Saladin, at the head of still another army, Turko-Kurdish this time, had his legal start in the government of Egypt before suppressing the Fâṭimid Caliphate and bringing Egypt officially, without real trouble, back into the bosom of the orthodox community.

It can be wondered why the caliphate, whether in the Abbasid form, or the Fâṭimid, or that of the Umayyads of Cordova, religiously quite inert, did not succeed in keeping the effective power which the Byzantine Basileus, also sovereign of a bureaucratized state, also living in the midst of a sumptuous court, also surrounded by a foreign guard, even also endowed with religious characteristics and rights, succeeded in keeping. Let us note that there were moments when he very nearly did not: at the time of the barbarian generals of the fifth century, or at the time when a victorious general was associated on the throne, in the tenth century, along with the sovereign of the previous dynasty, still there. The truth is, no doubt, that there were ambitious military leaders on the Byzantine as on the Muslim side, but that in Byzantium these simply overthrew the Basileus, if fortune smiled on them, and demanded their legitimation from the Patriarch or, on occasion, the Pope; while on the Muslim side it was more difficult to suppress the caliph, who represented the application of the religious Law and the only possible principle of legitimation. The result was that in Muslim territory the Abbasid dynasty lasted five centuries at Baghdad, and almost three more in Cairo, because it was to no one's interest to do away with a purely theoretical authority, while in Byzantium, if the imperial dignity preserved all its prerogatives, it was at the price of a continuous change of reigning families. And in fact the Muslim dynasties of sultans (leaving aside the Ottomans, who are another matter) did not last any longer than the Byzantine imperial dynasties.

But to return to the Muslim evolution. The progress of heresy naturally disquieted the orthodox there and those who had an interest in the maintenance of orthodoxy. Moreover, there could be discouragements or reversals among precisely those of the heretics who had seen, in the victory of their doctrines, above all the success of social demands—when they became aware that, under the Fâṭimids, for instance, nothing was changed in this respect from the previous order of things. Hence, in every field, a movement of reaction which finally found expression also on the governmental level. This desire was not necessarily the prerogative of the socially secure circles: in the Baghdad of the great Shîʿite merchants the popular outbursts were often directed by Ḥanbalî jurists. Nevertheless, the extremist heretical movements had often been turned not only against the orthodox, religiously speaking, but also against the fortunate of this world, among whom were the orthodox, or at least their leaders, who lived on the revenue of pious institutions founded for them, or on the favors of their sovereigns. Conversely, it was from the orthodox ranks, from the *ʿulamâʾ*, that the most active movement of reaction naturally proceeded. It is certain that under the Bûyids the social opposition could equally well have lined up one against the other the Ismâʿîlîs and the simple Shîʿites; but, as it happened, the Shîʿites, from a sense of their lack of strength or from a remnant of doctrinal similarity, inclined to Ismâʿîlism, or in any case were suspected of doing so. There was not, then, a *rapprochement*, but a growing cleavage between Shîʿites and orthodox, and the leadership of the movement toward reaction was essentially undertaken by the Sunnite cadres. Their desire was now, in the face of the Fâṭimid state with its official doctrine, to see to it that the other states should have a doctrine, not, strictly speaking, a state doctrine—since this doctrine could only be that of the orthodox doctors independent of the state—but should officially uphold this doctrine against heresy and should firmly link their fate to the fortunes of the *ᶜulamâ*ᵓ. Matters were no longer at the stage of a vague Islamization by the state in the face of infidelity but at that of a precise official religious policy in the face of heresy. Nor were matters any more at the stage of the search by the state for an equivocal accord with the *ᶜulamâ*ᵓ, but at that of the domestication of the state by them.

A first manner of reaction that could be envisaged consisted in a regrouping around a caliphate emancipated from the Shîᶜite tutelage. The weakening of the Bûyids, as a result of their intestine quarrels and of the successes of the Ghaznavids and of the Seljuqs at their first appearances, permitted such a thought to be entertained realistically. For the first time in almost a century, about 1040, the caliph had his vizier and to a certain degree took part in the governing of Iraq. It is during this episode that the treatise of al-Mâwardî is to be placed. I do not believe that he intended, as has been said,[2] to write a purely theoretical treatise—nothing, in any case, is farther from this than the last two-thirds of the work, where the concrete picture of the institutions accords exactly with what we know otherwise about them. Nor do I believe he is expressing the point of view of one school among others: he refers indifferently to the Shâfiᶜî, Ḥânafî, and, secondarily, Mâlikî and Ḥanbalî jurists, and when, no doubt in the face of the success of this work, the jurist Abû Yaᶜlâ al-Farrâᵓ wanted to bestow its equivalent on his fellow Ḥanbalîs, he limited himself to copying word for word his predecessor's text, replacing the references to Abû Ḥanîfa, Abû Yûsuf, and Shâfiᶜî with quotations from Ibn Ḥanbal.[3] It seems to me that the first chapters of the treatise have the force of a program, of a proclamation of what a re-established caliphate must be, in the light both of tradition and of the necessities of the subsequent evolution. Nevertheless, in practice, and indeed al-Mâwardî himself seems to allude to this, the caliphate could not regain its position by itself. It was the Seljuqs who, with its full agreement, crushed heresy. But it was they who garnered the chief advantage from this, even morally.

It cannot be said that it was the Seljuqs who devised this policy. The idea that salvation would come from the east had germinated under the Samanids. Maḥmûd of Ghazna had made himself the champion of orthodoxy, both militarily and in his internal policy.

Nevertheless, the Seljuqs were the first to realize it on a large scale and insure its definitive success. But their conquest must not be imagined as a purely military and external phenomenon. That conquest was accepted, and surely often desired, by the orthodox cadres, whose complicity the Turkish leaders for their part knew how to make use of. It was momentarily encouraged by the caliphate. It led to the reappearance, for the first time in several generations, of a unified, vigorous empire, joining together, if not the whole Muslim world, at least all of Muslim Asia with the exception of corners of Arabia. In external affairs it fought both against the Byzantine infidel and against the Fâṭimid heretic; in internal affairs it prostrated this same heretic and, more positively, developed the orthodox institutions. The regime at its start was based upon Turkish force but directed by a personnel of Khurâsânian orthodox.

Mosques, hospitals, caravanserais—these in themselves were only Muslim or social works, without closer specification. Nevertheless, the richer were the *waqfs* that endowed them, the more numerous they were, and the more the personnel which administered them and lived upon them was carefully recruited only among the staunchly orthodox, then the more these personages, essentially the *ᶜulamâᵓ*, found themselves at once materially and morally tied to the regime and in a stronger position in facing the rivalry of the heretics, whose pious foundations were at the same time pillaged. There was more: the madrasas. The idea was pre-Seljuq, but only the Seljuqs gave it its development, the most famous example being the madrasa founded at Baghdad by their vizier Niẓâm al-Mulk, whose name it preserved. There too it was not the case of a school founded by it-matters-not-whom to teach it-matters-not-what but of a school designed to teach exclusively the orthodox learning and founded by the greatest official personages under the auspices of the state itself, which often endowed it with state property. In a few decades Muslim Asia was covered with madrasas, affording a living to professors and students by the thousands upon thousands. Now, this school was not designed for the disinterested education of individuals. It was thenceforth from among its attenders that the officers of the administration were to be recruited. Offices where the heretics worked side by side with the orthodox were done with. Thenceforward the administrative personnel were students of the *ᶜulamâᵓ*. Thus was constituted a regime which in Christian territory we would call "an alliance of the sword and the altar," the Turkish military element and the indigenous element which one would like to call "clerical" supporting each other in an association of interests thenceforth indissoluble.

This is not the place to enlarge upon the aid which could be brought to such a policy by the *ghâzîs* of Central Asia, volunteer fighters in the Holy War transported to the Byzantine front and naturally attached to the idea of a Muslim bloc united without concern for doctrinal subtleties; nor can we enlarge here upon the movement which in the same period brought the official religion and Ṣûfism closer together, in spite of heterodox elements such as might persist in the latter but were no longer felt as oppositional. This *rapprochement* caused the Ṣûfîs, henceforth gathered into orders, to share in the benefits of the Seljuq material support and, conversely, gave the regime the benefit of their credit with the masses of the people. What is essential, from our present point of view, is to emphasize that there was now a fully Muslim state, if by that is understood a state intimately tied to those who officially have charge of orthodoxy. But, a remarkable thing, this state was not the caliphal state. It was the sultanal power, theoretically limited to the care of temporal matters, which had in fact appropriated even the prerogatives of the caliphate in the realm of religious matters. Not that the founders of the regime had not, the better to emphasize their opposition to the Bûyids, surrounded the caliphate with an ostentatious deference and assured the caliph, at the same time as a decent style of living, an administrative independence which was quite as great as that of the Pope at Rome. But in practice the caliphate was drained of its substance, and it was not to it that the defenders of religion turned.

A final attempt, to be sure, was made to revive the caliphate, by the remarkable personality that was al-Nâṣir. But he figured precisely as a heretic. Circumstances had made him master of Iraq and its confines; he wanted to complete this restoration, which only made of him one prince among others, by a revival of the caliphal function. He had the idea, in contrast to the orthodox of the Seljuq states, of grouping under his moral guidance, as if in a synthesis of Islâm, all the movements which shared it among them; particularly distinctive was his adherence to the *futuwwa,* till then considered a popular oppositional organization. But, except perhaps by the common people, he was neither understood nor followed. The orthodox regarded him with disquiet or horror. And then soon after his death supervened the Mongol catastrophe, which in practice put an end to the caliphate.

Then all orthodoxy flowed back into Egypt, already prepared for this role by the Ayyûbids. These, in turn, had given place to their Mamlûk army, which had become the immediate wielder of power. But if the religious orientation of the Mamlûk regime was in the Seljuq tradition, very different was the way in which the power of this army operated. In the Seljuq state it had not been possible to prevent the progressive appropriation of the provincial governments by great officers behaving as autonomous lords there—to prevent a sort of feudalization, that is. In Egypt, on the contrary, the almost inescapable cohesion of the administrative system explains why the officers were never able to do as they wished with the territories from which they drew their revenues: hence the rule of the army was a collective rule, which did not change the unity of the system. For the same reason, in place of one dynasty, from which opponents liberated themselves, there were the successive reigns of leaders who had been able to impose themselves on the army, without a dynasty resulting. Finally, they maintained the suppression of the vizierate, which the accession of Saladin to sovereign rank had in fact meant, and from which the Ayyûbids only rarely departed: among the Mamlûks there were only heads of departments.

It goes without saying that for the regimes of these new types the doctrine of the state, fixed at the level of al-Mâwardî, was no longer enough. He had already alluded to the practical necessity of recognizing powers other than that of the legitimate caliphate. A little later al-Ghazzâlî had bitterly advised bowing before a bad power rather than accepting none at all. Under the Mamlûks, with Ibn Jamâᶜa, this principle was the basis of law: any power being better than anarchy, it is legal to respect a power sprung from force. But in fact there was no question, for the interpreters of this legality, of just any power at all. The fact is that if they could get along so well with this one, it was because it gave them their place—a considerable place. The theory of this is expressed with all desirable clarity by Ibn Taimiyya, who, in the absence of the impossible consensus of all, believes that for a society to be sound there suffices the agreement of the emirate—the army—and of the *ᶜulamâᵓ*.[4] Which also means that there was no further need for a caliph—until it came to be believed, a strange twist, that the caliphate falls by right to the effective holder of power.

I have neither the time nor the ability to bring in a thoroughgoing parallel with the Muslim west. But it is indispensable to emphasize that the same orthodox orientation developed there, with the difference that the jurists there were not Shâfiᶜîs, Ḥânafîs, and

Ḥanbalîs, but Mâlikîs, quite as strict as the Ḥanbalîs. There also the "moral order" was re-established by simple-minded frontier populations just won for Islâm. At the same moment as the Turkish conquest of the east, the conquest of the west by the Almoravids meant the combined rule of a group of Berber tribes and of Mâlikî jurists. The Almohad movement reintroduced for a moment the belief in a *mahdî*, even though not a Shîᶜite one, and, more desirably, incorporated the religious orders into official Islâm, as was being done at the same time in the east. The subsequent regimes continued to repose upon the balance of the jurists, the mystics, and the military forces of the Arab or Berber tribes—a parallelism of evolution with the east, all the more remarkable in that it was accompanied by a perfectly autonomistic attitude toward it.

Gradually convinced of the irremediable character of the political fragmentation of the community, the Muslims could at least take refuge in the hope of a solidarity which should express itself in political co-operation. The sense of this solidarity is a reality which we cannot analyze here. The parallelism of orientation in certain aspects of the policies of all or part of the Muslim states is another, which has been sufficiently emphasized previously. But none of this implies collaboration. Now, it is impossible not to be struck, in the Middle Ages and perhaps in modern times, with the contrast between the incontestable solidarity of feeling and the almost total absence of collaboration among states. The most interesting phenomenon to study in this respect is that of the Holy War, more particularly when it is a question of meeting a threat presented by a strong enemy or by a coalition of adversaries. The state of mind of the *jihâd*, a mixture of faith and of appetites, naturally was alive at the time of the great conquests and, still, in some later conquests made by different elements, particularly those of Spain and of Sicily. Nevertheless, it cannot be denied that very soon the masses of Muslims lost interest in what was happening on the frontiers: they had enough to do in establishing themselves in the conquered countries and arranging their internal quarrels; the poets of Umayyad times who alluded to the war against the infidel were rare. All the more in the following centuries. The notion of, the taste for, a transformed *jihâd* were preserved on the frontiers of Central Asia, of the Byzantine Empire, of the Niger, limited to the populations, often sprung from military colonies, which were given to it. It was no longer a question of conquest, but of *ghazwa;* the aim of the *ghâzî* was to carry out a pillaging expedition against the infidel, to bring back booty, never to occupy a country. These were purely local undertakings in which, from the ninth century on, neither coalitions of forces nor caliphal troops ever again took part. For a certain reawakening to make an appearance in wider circles, a strong foreign threat was necessary: around Saif al-Daula, threatened by the Byzantines, a sense of the *jihâd* reappeared, though we must not be misled as to how general it was by the official literary manifestations. A few allies, who were not well regarded, came to him from Central Asia. A remarkable fact: neither the caliph nor the neighboring Ḥamdânid, Bûyid, Ikhshîdid, or Azerbaijânî princes made a motion; a combined action among them was never envisaged. An almost private initiative indeed resulted once in a levy of volunteers among the poor of Baghdad; before they had left Baghdad they had been used in the fights among factions, and there was no further question of foreign war. Against the Abbasids there was almost an alliance between the Fâṭimids and Byzantium. The great Seljuq adventure set alight again for a moment the enthusiasm for the Holy War, but in practice it was solely the Turks, brought up in the school of the *ghâzîs* of Central Asia, who waged it, and the spirit was not to be kept up except, in specialized forms, among the Turkomans of Asia Minor. Even the resistance to the Crusaders was to have only a limited effect. A certain defensive popular feeling forced some princes to a few coalitions in which they took part with distrust of each other. The posture of champions of the Holy War certainly made easier the territorial consolidation accomplished by Nûr al-Dîn and Saladin. But it is not clear that their action involved, outside their territories, any collaboration other than that of a few individuals. Especially remarkable is the almost complete indifference of the caliph al-Nâṣir. Further, when particularly with the Third Crusade the war was carried on, on the Frankish side, on an international scale, the very most we can do is to cite some diplomatic bargaining by Saladin with the Turks of Asia Minor and the Almohads, with a view to a naval participation on their part; there was no hint of carrying it out. In the west, before the Almohads, the territorial realignment of the Almoravids had been facilitated by the Christian danger, but the Christian danger had not at all moderated the hostilities among Muslims in North Africa. It was a considerable illusion if St. Louis, setting sail for Tunis, supposed there existed a political solidarity in the Muslim world. There was even less than in Christendom. On the other hand, the foreign danger caused the non-Muslims, few enough now so that they were no longer indispensable, to be treated with less and less consideration, and the heretics, accused of favoring the enemy, to be all the more easily hunted down. In short, the *jihâd* became a negative and internal xenophobia, which resulted in reinforcing the orthodox dictatorship.

Having arrived at the point of the Mongol invasion and the eve of the formation of the Ottoman Empire, that is, at the point of the introduction of new factors into a part of the Muslim world, but also of a certain stabilization of the other regimes, we can bring our inquiry to a halt. We can say that there were thenceforth Muslim "states," if we understand by that states which assured a dominant moral influence and an appreciable portion of material comfort to the licensed representatives of orthodoxy and which had reconstituted in this form the union of the temporal and the spiritual for which the believers had felt a nostalgia since the beginning of the caliphate. But it is hard to say that this type of state still had any connection with the primitive conditions of Islâm, or that it expressed any Muslim Law other than the fact of its acceptance by its beneficiaries, who were held to speak in the name of the community, to incarnate its consensus. The evolution which took place can be summarized by saying that it ended in the failure of the doctrine and in the triumph of those who claimed to represent it.

In reality there was no Islamic political doctrine. There was a fervent but vague aspiration, more and more external to the actual states. To the extent that jurists had formulated a few concrete rules, these did not reveal this general aspiration except in form, and, far from having had some sort of influence on the evolution of the actual institutions, they adapted to them somehow or other—and these institutions resulted from the combination of all the historical, social, national, and other circumstances of the Muslim world, which owed nothing to the intervention of Islâm as a doctrine.

Is this to say that there has not been a type of state which, though not owing anything to a pre-established Islamic doctrine, was common to all the Muslim countries and distinguished them from others? Here we must clearly be more precise. There have been in space and in time differences among Muslim states too essential for us to be able to draw in full a picture of one strictly Muslim state; it does not follow that there have not been a certain number of tendencies common to these various states. Only these common tendencies are less peculiar to Islâm than it can seem to a European of the twentieth century: to a certain degree, with distinctive accents and lines of demarcation, they are often common not only to the Muslim countries but also to all the medieval countries, and in this respect what is peculiar to Islâm is only negative; it consists in the fact, the causes of which we cannot study here, that Europe made a new advance in which Islâm did not follow and that Islâm therefore dug a trench around itself which the people of the Middle Ages had no reason to be conscious of. In particular, whereas in Europe the separation between state and church was slowly but surely re-established, in the Muslim world what one would like to be able to call the Muslim "clergy" came to weigh even more heavily upon the whole of public life. This fact is all the more remarkable precisely in that there was no clergy, theologically speaking, and that there was not even a church—just a local corporate life of the *ᶜulamâᵓ*. This weight, as we have suggested, did not originate in the doctrine. It was no heavier than that of the Christian clergy upon the life of medieval Western or Byzantine Europe. But it lasted, which is perhaps its principal characteristic. And the explanation of its lasting is also not to be looked for in the religious characteristics of Islâm but in the general historical circumstances which brought it about that, until recently, there have not been within the Muslim world the forces of general renewal which we have had in Europe and—I ask Mr. von Grunebaum's pardon—in the European colony which is the United States.

DISCUSSION

M. Brunschvig wants to come back to several particular points. He agrees with M. Cahen's view of the so-called "disintegration" of the Muslim Empire. In fact, there never was any uniform empire. The conception of an Islamic unity which was later divided into separate states goes back to Ibn Khaldûn (1332–1406). In reality the variety of treatment of and the diversity of conditions in the different areas at the time of the conquest and of the early Muslim regime were such that it was in itself occasion enough for the subsequent official separation of the different countries.

Speaking of al-Mâwardî (972–1058), M. Cahen has said that the work of the Abbasid lawyers did not ignore practical realities. M. Brunschvig recalls an article by M. Cahen in which the same thought is expressed ("L'Évolution de l'*iqṭâᶜ*," *Annales: Economies, Sociétés, Civilisations,* VIII [1953], 25–52): al-Mâwardî did not write his famous theoretical tract aloof from all reality and as an abstract exercise of his mind; he based it upon the historical reality of his time. This corresponds exactly to the work of the Western legal thinkers: theoretical thought provoked by the challenge of reality.

M. Brunschvig was particularly interested in M. Cahen's remark concerning the other contemporary treatise of public law we possess today in an edition of the Arabic text, that of Abû Yaᶜlâ al-Farrâᵓ (990–1065). It is indeed nearly identical with the work of the Shâfiʿite al-Mâwardî. What differs are small details and the fact that al-Mâwardî cites all kinds of authorities, Abû Yaʿlâ only the Ḥanbalî ones.

M. CAHEN repeats that the documentary text upon which the juridical constructions of both authors are based is the same from one end to the other.

Finally, M. BRUNSCHVIG recalls M. Cahen's conception of the fundamental difference between the Islamic east and west as due to the fact that a foreign military element came into power in the east but not in the west. This would need some qualification in the case of Spain. M. Cahen himself has mentioned the presence of the "Slavs" in Cordova. Also there were the *reyes de taifas:* we cannot call them indigenous people, for they were Berbers and not at home in Spain, quite in the same way as the Turks were foreigners in the older Islamic countries in the Near East.

M. CAHEN rectifies: he sees a difference in the fact that the Berbers assimilated themselves so far as to enter the administrative careers as well as the military ones; this never happened with the Turks before the foundation of states with a preponderant Turkish population.

M. BRUNSCHVIG speaks of the parallelism observed already by G. Marçais between the Almoravid conquest of Spain and the Turkish intrusion into the political life of the east. In both cases we see originally nomadic populations gain the hegemony in an important part of the Muslim territory, both act under the aegis of Sunnism and orthodoxy, and both engage in war with the Christians. With all this there seems to exist no direct connection between the two series of events. Ultimately in both cases we come to the same results: the Arabs cease to command; the dynasties in the Maghrib after the Almoravids are Berber. The Arabic language remained, except in some rural parts of Morocco.

The lack of feeling of expatriation on the part of people traveling between Muslim countries, as mentioned by M. Cahen, requires some qualifications. Even the differences among Arabic-speaking countries were felt. Perhaps we ought not to speak of "expatriation," which after all is an ambiguous term. Ibn Jubair (1145–1217) was certainly surprised by many things he observed in Damascus, in Mecca, and in the other towns of the east. However, he probably did not feel quite a foreigner in the countries of the Near East. On the other hand, Ibn Baṭṭûṭa (1304–77), speaking about his encounters with Turkish and Indian Muslims, gives us the impression that he feels very far away from his own fatherland. When he came back and related his adventures, even with nations and sovereigns who belonged to the *dâr al-Islâm,* people did not readily believe his tales.

Probably there existed a certain connection among the Arabic-speaking peoples, and the feeling of foreignness increased as soon as a traveler crossed the linguistic frontiers, even though he remained in the territory of Islâm.

Finally, M. BRUNSCHVIG has some theoretical considerations which concern the philosophical position underlying M. Cahen's communication. M. Cahen seems to him to present, generally and in a rather systematic way, the religious doctrine as a result of historical, social, and economic conditions. M. BRUNSCHVIG thinks that often religious doctrine is indeed conditioned by those realities, but probably this is not the whole of the story. Even when limiting our outlook to strictly historical realities, we have to make some room for the possible real effect of a religious doctrine or a number of evolving religious beliefs. M. BRUNSCHVIG cannot quite agree with M. Cahen's contention that we should not look for any theoretical difference between the Christian and the Muslim worlds. He believes that Muslim religious doctrine is different, not from Christian religious doctrine—this would be far too general a way of putting it—but from the religious attitude accepted consciously as a religious attitude by Christians and applied as such.

M. Abel feels that there are two religious attitudes in the Christian world, that of Byzantium and that of the West.

M. Brunschvig replies that there are several of them and that he is prepared to distinguish among them; however, what he wants to emphasize here is simply his belief that there are mental attitudes which produce deeds. These mental attitudes can originate from other deeds, or facts, but they exist in a certain moment, they possess a certain autonomy, and they act. Our contemporary history is only too full of illustrations of this order of things.

M. Cahen thinks he can accept this formulation.

M. Brunschvig goes on to say that, consequently, we do not have to limit ourselves to envisaging religious doctrine as an effect; we have to consider it at the same time as a cause, a factor. We are free to say that in a certain number of cases, or in a great many cases, it has no influence upon the remaining factors, or no decisive influence upon them. We could repeat here many of M. Cahen's examples and add others of the same sort. But this does not exclude there being cases in which religious doctrines do display their influences, and this even where we cannot directly observe them at work. They may, for instance, help to preserve mental attitudes and ideals, which sometimes exert their influence over long periods in an invisible but nevertheless effective way. They can work as a factor which slows down and stops short some kind of development. M. Brunschvig believes that the mental attitude of the Muslims, owing to religious indoctrination and schooling during many generations, exerted a certain influence (M. Brunschvig says "a certain influence," not necessarily the predominant one) upon the refusal of the Muslim world to evolve rapidly at the time of the rise of the European countries.

If a civilization is conscious of itself, possesses a doctrine, and is aware of what it considers its values, we cannot appreciate the totality of the effects and causes which make up its evolution without keeping in mind the effect of that continuous tension which exists between the doctrine of that civilization and the reality in which it finds itself. Certainly, there are periods in which the realities modify the doctrines, but there are moments and periods, as well, in which the doctrine influences the realities.

M. Cahen would not quite agree with M. Brunschvig on the philosophical level.

Mr. Lewis believes that the relations between military and local populations in the middle period can be better understood now because of our own experience; they will have been roughly the same as those of a civil affairs officer with the population of an occupied country.

The synchronism between the Turkish and the Almoravid conquests may be explained as answering the challenge of the increasing Christian power in east and west. There are perhaps more connections than generally appear.

Mr. Spuler remarks that the text of al-Mâwardî corresponds to a large extent to the *Ta'rîkh-e-Qumm* (Teheran, 1934) or *Qumm-nâma* (A. Houtum-Schindler, *Eastern Persian Irak* [London, 1898]), a description of the city of Qumm in Iran. This is probably not because al-Mâwardî took over a part of the contents of this book but rather because both sources depict the reality of the times. Consequently al-Mâwardî's work does not contain only abstract theory, as has been maintained.

Mr. SPULER then returns to the subject of religious minorities. He observes that Christianity and Islâm hold different positions in this respect. Christianity did not suffer alien religions in its territory (with the exception of the Jewish). In Islâm there was a cultural interchange between Muslims and non-Muslims; Judaism had no comparable influence upon medieval Christianity. The observed difference may be explained by the fact that Christianity had to witness the rise of a rival religion (Islâm, whose appearance, empirically speaking, contradicted the Christian claim to possess the ultimate revelation). Islâm, having no rival creed not provided for from the beginning by its religious system, could interpret and apply in a liberal way the Koranic prescriptions which touch upon alien religions. In this way the transmission of classical tradition by means of the Nestorians, and the part played by the Jews in Islamic Spain, became possible.

Mr. MINORSKY refers to the situation of the caliphs and their viziers under the Seljuqs. He describes the proceedings of Niẓâm al-Mulk (d. 1092) against the viziers of al-Qâʾim (d. 1075) and al-Muqtadî (d. 1094) and asks M. Cahen if he sees in this treatment an essential difference from the treatment the caliph suffered under the Bûyids.

M. CAHEN replies that the vizierate of the caliph was completely abolished by the Bûyids but was re-established in the time of the Bûyid decline. The Seljuqs did not allow him to act freely, but the office remained, and the dignitary had some administrative rights in Baghdad and in certain parts of Iraq. M. CAHEN compares the situation of the modern dignitaries of Morocco. He also adds that many times the viziers of the caliphs, in order to fortify their position, felt impelled to marry daughters of the Seljuq viziers.

Coming to the subject of expatriation, Mr. MINORSKY recalls the fact that there were always collective and individual migrations throughout the whole Muslim world. He mentions the two Kurdish tribes whose history is written by Ibn Khaldûn (i.e., Lawîn and Babîn; *Histoire des Berbères,* trans. De Slane [Algiers, 1852–56], II, 461; III, 413). They arrived in Morocco with all their original mutual animosity and continued to wage war between themselves. A modern example is the body of emigrants to Turkey after the arrival of Ismâʿîl Pâshâ (1863–79) in Egypt. The Mongols caused the expatriation of quite a number of Turkoman tribes in Syria and Asia Minor. Wanderings of this kind, caused by purely material motives, exist everywhere.

Finally, Mr. MINORSKY expresses his satisfaction at seeing "historians," not "Orientalists," tackling the problems of Muslim history. He thinks that the Orientalist of olden times is going to disappear. It has become impossible to control the whole range of Muslim life, from literature and history to theology, astronomy, medicine, etc. He supposes that Oriental history should be treated by historians who control the Oriental languages. Why should the history of the Iberian Peninsula be written by people belonging to a different discipline from those who write the history of France? Mr. MINORSKY is glad to hear the contributions of the professional historians, and he thinks that much progress in Oriental studies may result from the fact that Oriental history is beginning to be considered as a part of historical research generally.

Mr. Caskel takes up the question of the situation of slaves in the armies of the caliphs. Their legal status when they reached some higher employment is not clearly known.

Mr. Caskel relates an anecdote from Ibn Baṭṭûṭa (1304–77) which tells of an Indian slave who succeeded to his defunct master, an Indian emir. At the beginning of his first official *majlis* the slave took his letter of emancipation from underneath the carpet he was sitting on and handed it to the *qâḍî* of the country. The *qâḍî* and the lawyers read it and did homage to their new king (*Voyages*, ed. C. Defrémery and B. R. Sanguinetti [Paris, 1853–58], III, 164). Mr. Caskel points out the fact that only a free man was a legally responsible person and could hold an office in the state. We do not know if eunuchs were ever emancipated; however, they could not act as parties in commercial contracts, and probably they never possessed complete economic freedom.

Mr. Lewis adds that the legal difficulties for freed slaves in Egypt are well known.

Mr. Stadtmüller reminds us that the eunuchs played a very important part in the Byzantine Empire, but that we cannot define their juridical position.

M. Abel thinks that in order to understand Muslim history we not only have to follow the chain of development inside the system of Muslim government, as M. Cahen has done in such a remarkable way, but we have to look for the reasons which occasion and continue to cause that internal development of administrative technique M. Cahen has traced.

M. Abel believes that we can find those reasons in the successive social and economic positions held by the classes which influenced the internal life of Islâm. At certain times the enormous expenses of the Caliphate, for its troops and for the maintenance of its *dîwâns* and of all the poets and writers it needed for its propaganda, first created a desire in the minor dignitaries for surrounding themselves with a similar apparatus and later produced poverty in certain classes of the population. This poverty resulted in conspiratorial movements. Our sources do not yield much with regard to such revolutionary tendencies, but this results from their rigid conception of historiography. Memorialists like al-Ṣûlî (*ca.* 837–*ca.* 946) inform us that the caliph al-Râḍî reflected upon his situation, saying: "Yes, but I no longer have the ten million dînârs al-Muʿtaḍid possessed!" (*Akhbâr al-Râḍî billâh wa 'l-Muttaqî billâh*, trans. M. Canard [Algiers, 1946–50], I, 182). Or they explain to us how the inhabitants of Baghdad sometimes plotted with the "interpreter" of the Turks, sometimes with their chief himself, in order to instigate those riots in the interior of the town which eventually brought about the destruction of the Caliphate (*ibid.*, pp. 188, 217, 230, etc.).

M. Abel proposes inquiries into the reasons for the impoverishment of those merchants of Baghdad or those peasants of Dailam or of the Maghrib whose discontent led them to back this or that obscure but ambitious official against some vizier whom they held responsible for their poverty. Their action fostered the political confusion and the continuous procession of viziers, high dignitaries, and caliphs which was halted on rare occasions by some exceptionally capable man. M. Abel sees in the growing wealth of the Lebanese merchant, and in the aspirations of the great landholders of Syria, or in the claims to economic independence of a country like Egypt, the deeper reasons for the great movements in the Muslim world.

Mr. Schacht comes back to the question of the status of the slaves. For the time of the Mamlûks we now possess the work of D. Ayalon (*Oriental Notes and Studies*, No. 1 [Jerusalem: Israel Oriental Society, 1951]). Mr. Schacht tells an anecdote he has read in a manuscript of the Qâḍî al-Nuʿmân (d. 974). The Fâṭimid caliph realized one day that all the great men of his state were legally slaves, that they were married contrary to Islamic law, that their children were illegitimate, and so forth. He then proceeded to legitimize this state of affairs. People did not bother too much about purely legal aspects, even in cases in which the religious law was involved. Mr. Schacht, referring to Snouck Hurgronje (*Verspreide Geschriften* [Bonn and Leipzig, 1923–27], III, 220, n. 3), cites further the situation of Ḥaḍramaut, where the warrior-slaves (*ʿabîd*) enjoy a privileged status.

M. Cahen, concluding the discussion, agrees with Mr. Minorsky that Muslim history, in order to make up for its present lagging behind, needs a certain amount of specialization. Everywhere we encounter fundamental problems which have never been attacked. Above all in sociological history, much work remains to be done. This brings M. Cahen back to the problem of the emancipation of slaves. The essay of D. Ayalon is limited to Egypt; in other Muslim societies things may have been different. The "mixed" armies of the Bûyids, of the late Seljuqs, and of the Zangids were recruited half from slaves of servile Turkish origin and half from Kurdish people who were taken away from their parents as children, but who cannot legally have been slaves. However, we do not observe any difference in the treatment the two groups received.

NOTES

(Bibliographical note: The extremely general character of the present essay clearly makes impossible real bibliographical references. One would have to cite everything or nothing. The three or four particular references that were necessary follow. Nevertheless, I would not want to let it be thought that this essay owes nothing to others, whereas it owes them almost everything. I do not doubt that you have recognized at the appropriate point all that belongs, among others, to W. Barthold, M. Gaudefroy-Demombynes, H. A. R. Gibb, Mr. von Grunebaum, G. Levi Della Vida, Mr. Lewis, Georges Marçais, P. Wittek, and to so many others, who are, nevertheless, in no way responsible for the way in which I have made use of them.)

1. D. C. Dennett, *Conversion and the Poll-Tax in Early Islam* (Cambridge, Mass., 1950).

2. Cf. H. A. R. Gibb, "Some Considerations on the Sunnî Theory of the Caliphate," *Archives d'histoire du droit oriental*, III (1948), 401–10.

3. *K. al-Aḥkâm al-Sulṭâniyya*, ed. M. Ḥâmid al-Fiqî (Cairo, 1356/1938).

4. G. E. von Grunebaum, *Medieval Islam* (Chicago, 1946), pp. 168–69; H. Laoust, *Ibn Taïmiyya* (Cairo, 1939), p. 316.

PART IV

REGIONAL EVOLUTIONS

IRAN: THE PERSISTENT HERITAGE

BERTOLD SPULER

ON THE PENETRATION OF INFLUENCES FROM THE SUBSTRATUM INTO THE ISLAMIC CONCEPTION OF THE STATE

M. Cahen has sketched for us an impressive picture of the development within Islâm in the early centuries and therewith provided the framework within which we must try to make up our minds about influences of the individual peoples upon Islâm on the basis of the older cultural and other heritage which they possessed at the time of the intrusion of the new religion.

That the Islamic culture, as the Middle Ages present it to us and as it has further developed in recent times, is composed of numerous elements needs no proof in this group. But if we want to go into this problem further, beyond the results so far achieved by scholarship, it seems to me that it will be necessary to carry on the discussion in several stages. We know that at the cradle of Islâm old heathen Arabic, Jewish, and Christian, and also, within limits, Zoroastrian and perhaps Manichean influences, had already served as godparents. In addition, influences of Roman provincial law and Roman military organization (including the associated technology) had also found their way into the Arabian Peninsula. These influences have been investigated. It seems to me that—as long as new sources do not turn up—we cannot get fundamentally beyond what has been worked out so far.

If we take this complex body of "primitive Islâm," for the moment, as a single given whole in our further reflections, it appears to have endured as a comparatively well-established culture, not so very much changed from without, till about the culmination of the Umayyad dynasty in Damascus, that is, till about eighty years after the hijra (i.e., *ca.* A.D. 700). The impression which the sources for the Umayyad period in Damascus, taken as a whole, give us is that the position of the caliph as *primus inter pares*, the relationship of the *sayyids* to him, the relations of the individual Arab tribes to one another, and the attitude of the Arabs toward the military profession and toward the state were not fundamentally different from what was already the case in the time of the Meccan aristocracy. It does not seem to me very likely, in view of the fact that the original accounts are mostly covered over with pro-Abbasid alterations, that we can reach beyond what has so far been established for the first century to achieve a more exact knowledge of the first consequences of the symbiosis of the Arab ruling class with the natives of the conquered countries.

After the culmination of the Damascus Umayyad times, that is, in the period which Mr. Schacht has shown was the time when the foundations of Islamic law were finally consolidated,[1] the contacts between the Arab ruling class and the indigenous population became closer; they were very greatly reinforced in the Abbasid time, after 750. Now came a far-reaching synthesis of the Islamic and the old indigenous culture. Leaving aside here, according to plan, religious, cultural, and economic questions, it led in the political sphere also to the gradual elimination of the barriers between Arab conquerors and natives. This effected at the same time the gradual dissolution of the Arab tribal organization, which—in part, no doubt, in defense against the gradually reviving national feeling of those subjugated nations which were not assimilated in speech—in time gave place to a uniform Arab national feeling; the discussions in the framework of the Shuᶜûbiyya need only be mentioned here,[2] but it must also be pointed out that the Aramaic or Aramaicized population in Syria and Mesopotamia did not succeed, with some exceptions, in preserving its mother-tongue (and its church). Rather, this branch of the Semites was merged, relatively soon, fairly extensively into the Arab nationality. The prevalence of Arabic as the language of Islâm, and the prayer in that tongue five times each day, as well as—in the case of Mesopotamia—the geographical position of Baghdad in the center of that area, certainly contributed powerfully to this evolution, alongside the immigration of the Arab tribes. Coptic indeed made the effort—as can still be seen in survivals—to hold its ground against Arabic, but, as is known, it was finally laid low even within what remained of the Coptic church: an astonishing fact, as I see it not yet really explained, if it is considered (in comparison with Iran) that it is a question of a language which—in contrast to Aramaic—at least outwardly cannot be recognized as related to Arabic and which was spoken in a thickly settled province, not subdivided by natural barriers, by a population numerically greatly superior to the Arabs that immigrated.[3]

[In a partly private discussion of this fact which followed, it was repeatedly pointed out—among others by Mr. Schacht—that precisely the open landscape may have favored the spread of Arabic. Yet this fact could, on the contrary, just as easily have brought about the assimilation of the Arab settlements and of the later settlers as they arrived in their smaller waves, as was the case even in Iran, which is so very differently articulated geographically. On the other hand, this development may have been brought about by the very limited depth of the intellectual life of Coptic itself; by the need of those who lived in the country around the larger centers to use Arabic in selling their products—compare the "vegetable dialects" (*Kräuterdialekte*) of the truck gardeners around German cities, for instance, but also the relevant African circumstances; and, finally, by the urge of broad classes among the Copts to be employed as *kâtib* and the like; alongside the causes holding for Mesopotamia. Perhaps the extinction of the Celtic dialects in France by the Roman language (also the language of the Church!) can be compared with this development.]

The success of Arabic in Mesopotamia, in the Syrian-Palestinian area, in Egypt, and also in large parts of North Africa and Spain, which went along with a fairly rapid Islamization of the overwhelming majority of the population (except in Spain), created—in spite of the incipient dialectal development—a mass of population still for some time relatively homogeneous, whose relation to the caliphate and the government—definitively after the discontinuance of the state pensions to the Arab warrior caste—was quite uniform. This fact surely substantially facilitated the success of the so-called "Oriental" type of government. It is not for me to set forth here how this type arose: that is essentially the duty of the ancient historian. For Islâm, at any rate, the model, which it knew and of which it was conscious, was the state of the Iranian Great King. How the Abbasids imitated it is well known, and literary sources on which they based themselves are in part available. Even though this fact is to be dealt with separately in the case of the Iranian area, it is nevertheless important to recall that Islâm had brought together two blocs of lands which had been separated since Seleucid times and had been in hostile relations to each other: Iran and large tracts formerly of a Roman-Byzantine character, which were much more effectively Hellenized than the Iranian plateau, although some Hellenic thought had penetrated there too. Through the uniting of these two blocs with a tradition which was likewise completely different in respect to administration, it became possible for so-called "Oriental despotism" to encroach also upon this territory from which it had been largely barred since Alexander. In this way the last remnants of the *polis* system were done away with—that system which had already begun to totter on account of Christianity, rising up from below, which repeatedly (as perhaps in the case of Hypatia in Alexandria) had set the masses against the special conceptions, and thus the special position, of the formerly leading classes, and finally, in Monophysitism, had caused the ideas of the broad native masses to prevail.[4] However, the study of the history of the Oriental city (following J. Sauvaget's example in the case of Aleppo) still remains an urgent desideratum, and we can expect a great deal from the investigations of M. Cahen and Mr. von Grunebaum.

Accordingly, while in the center, at Baghdad, Oriental—more exactly, Iranian—influences predominated in the system of government (to say nothing here of other fields), the East Roman governmental tradition in Syria and Egypt had necessarily to pass into the background. This did not proceed quickly everywhere; and in Syria, so far as I can see, it was faster than in Egypt, which was almost continuously independent after 868 (the accession of the Ṭûlûnids) and hence substantially removed from the immediate influence of Baghdad. In Egypt, as we know, the Coptic official tradition was still transmitting a Byzantine and older legacy for centuries, clear into the Mamlûk period. In the case of Egypt we are, moreover, in the fortunate position that the extant papyri, that is, genuine sources for the local administration and the daily life also, permit us to follow this process in its details. Here, too, a good part of the work has already been done and is known.

In the case of Syria, because of the lack of original documents, this process of the amalgamation of the Byzantine administration, and of the pre-Hellenic element living on in it, is harder to study, and it is likewise harder to say how fast it took place. Many of the questions which are relatively clear in Egypt are still in dispute here and probably in part cannot be solved at all on unambiguous evidence. One need only think of taxation questions, which are still not in the least fully clear. However, French historical research (especially M. Gaudefroy-Demombynes, J. Sauvaget, M. Canard, and C. Cahen) has presented us here with new information, and that still more information is possible in this field seems to me to be proved by the work of D. C. Dennett and F. Løkkegaard, which, to be sure, centers on Mesopotamia, a region which, as the core province of the Abbasid Empire, received more attention than Syria in the early Abbasid centuries in the Muslim theoretical and practical land-rights literature (al-Mâwardî, etc.) as well as in the relevant accounts of the historians. But here the taking-over of pre-Islamic administrative practices is still harder to recognize, because we are provided only imperfectly with source materials from Sassanid times for this area. To be sure, the Greek and Talmudic sources have already been well exploited (most recently by Solodukho);[5] on the contrary it seems that we can still get beyond A. Christensen's *L'Iran sous les Sassanides* with respect to the Syriac and Armenian literature. I think it would be worth while to undertake sometime an exhaustive synthesis of *all* the source data in the various languages, such as N. V. Pigulevskaya has initiated in various works, especially in the case of the Syriac accounts. It would perhaps be able to throw new light upon much that the Muslims came upon and incorporated here. Possibly the origin of the Abbasid imperial administration, the organization of the administrative offices, and the carrying-out of the irrigation, from an administrative viewpoint, can then be even better explained than has so far been the case. In this, M. Cahen's studies of *iqṭâ*ᶜ[6] and Ahmed Sûsa's studies of irrigation conditions[7] will provide valuable vantage points and indicate new paths of investigation.

IRANIAN INFLUENCES UPON THE ISLAMIC CONCEPTION OF THE STATE TILL INTO THE ELEVENTH CENTURY A.D.*

The question whether or not the Islamic conception of the state, in the first centuries of its existence (which here is to be reckoned up to the time when the Seljuq Empire became powerful in the middle of the eleventh century), adapted itself to Iranian views in Persia itself and elsewhere fundamentally requires no discussion. Anyone who is even very superficially acquainted with Islâm knows what Iran meant for Islamic culture as such. He knows that this culture, at least in the Middle East as far as Egypt, was largely only a continuation of the Iranian. In this connection, by pre-Islamic Iranian culture we mean, here and later, the condition under Sassanid rule. We cannot deal with its origin here; that would be a separate proposition.

* The material dealt with is particularly annotated in:

CHRISTENSEN, ARTHUR. *L'Iran sous les Sassanides.* 2d ed. Copenhagen, 1944.

SPULER, BERTOLD. *Iran in früh-islamischer Zeit.* Wiesbaden, 1952.

———. "Iranische Geschichtsschreiber und Geographen," *Handbuch der Orientalistik,* Sec. "Iranistik." (In press.)

Available only after the conception of this contribution:

WIET, GASTON. "L'Empire néo-byzantin des Omeyyades et l'empire néo-sassanide des Abbasides," *Journal of World History,* I (1953), 63 ff.

If it is established, then, that Islamic culture in some respects underwent an influence from Iran to an overwhelming degree, we have here to speak, in accordance with our stated limits, not of this influence as such, but only of its sociological, social, and legal aspects. We shall leave out of account, accordingly, all questions of religion and world view, of language and poetry, representational art, mental culture, and pure science. It will now be well to keep in mind a picture of the political and legal life and to inquire, in detail, about Iran's impression on it.

At the head of the Sassanid Empire stood the monarch, who was, with a very brief exception in the last period of decline, a man. Even when the intruding Islâm eliminated this king, the luster of various great rulers continued to have a lasting effect in the Iranians' imagination—as the later literature, for instance the *Khwadhâi-nâmagh* and the *Tâj-nâmagh*, shows. The continued existence of local principalities, especially in the districts on the south coast of the Caspian Sea and in the east, also offered their contemporaries at least a reflected splendor from the glorious time of the kings.

But presumably neither the general recollections of the people nor the literary tradition of early Islamic Persia, often available only indirectly, would have been able to keep alive the idea of a king. That it survived was a consequence of the fact that at least in the east of the Iranian area, especially in Khurâsân, the social structure of the population was only slightly infringed on. Precisely there the leading families of the landed nobility and the office of a *marzbân* (margrave) persisted almost undisturbed in Islâm too. The obviously rather rapid acceptance of Islâm by the majority of the members of this upper class assured the preservation of their social position and their right of supervision over the tenants, including the control of taxes. At the same time, here as elsewhere, the conduct of the leading circles was a model for other groups, especially those dependent on them. In this way there was a society at hand which fostered the Sassanid royal ideal and which was also interested in its living on in heroic poems and sagas. A decisive share in the final victory of the Persian language over the Arabic in Iran must be ascribed to them; that language gradually succeeded in assimilating other Iranian tongues even as late as a time when it was suffering substantial losses to Turkish in Central Asia.[8]

The rapid Islamization of that class—which naturally did not in the least take place, completely, right away—enabled it to co-operate with the new Arab ruling class—a co-operation which was rendered very difficult at first by obstacles to understanding of all sorts, not only linguistic, and later on also by the internal Arab tribal feuds, which were continued in Khurâsân, with their changing party alignments. These impediments largely disappeared when, after the victory of the Abbasids (749/50), forces came to the helm whom the Khurâsânîs, who had meanwhile also become more familiar with Arabic, had assisted substantially in their success, and who were more closely connected with things Iranian than the Umayyads in Damascus had ever been. Accordingly, as is generally known, the beginning of the Abbasid period became the era of a lasting Iranianization of Islamic culture, and indeed not only in Iran itself but also in Mesopotamia and beyond. The Abbasids quite consciously regarded the Sassanids as their models. This consciousness of taking over a foreign culture is interesting in point of method because, in contrast to the usual difficulties to be found in studying such processes, the borrowing here is actually *demonstrable*. The caliphate orientalized itself from that time forth and adopted that courtly form of a multiply Iranian fashion which had been distinctive of the Sassanids, their traditions and usages being available without difficulty from oral and written sources. It is not possible here to trace back to its Iranian models each particular trait of the Abbasid court organization; that has already been undertaken repeatedly, and nothing substantially new would be gained here unless new sources should also turn up. In the place of the Umayyad *primus inter pares* appeared the absolute monarch of the Abbasid times, who now set at his side the "vizier," instead of the Umayyad *ḥâjib* (i.e., one who refuses admittance), a more technical official. It may be, indeed, that this title must be considered as Arabic, according to S. D. Goitein's latest studies;[9] but its bearer, so far as this is in any way ascertainable, held the position of a Sassanid *vuzurg-framâdhâr* (the dangers of a circular argument, which M. Cahen has mentioned, are to be guarded against here), and his model was supposed to be, alongside of the Koranic Âṣaf (as Solomon's minister), the Sassanid vizier Buzurgmihr—a tradition which, inexact as it may be in defining the functions in detail, yet at least mirrors clearly the public feeling in this matter. The fact that the leading ministerial position was held during about fifty years by the Barmakids doubtless contributed substantially to the Iranianizing of this office, even if in a romantically transfigured form. Along with him the executioner, now living constantly in the caliph's entourage, has been designated as a symbol of the new times. The supremacy of the Arabic *language* in the administration was not infringed by this (it was promoted even by the Samanids); hence instruction in Arabic literature was postulated even for princes, officials' sons, etc. But Arabic did not affect the tenor of the instruction nor the sentiment about the homeland.

By the side of the great vizier were other ministers, having as their departments the *dîwâns*, establishments which imitated corresponding Sassanid ones. Presumably they depended heavily on this model, precisely at the start, in their formation. As we know, however, they were repeatedly reorganized and given new shape as the needs and expediencies of the administration, as well as the gradually shrinking territories of the caliph, required. In the course of this, many distinguishing marks of old Iranian conditions were certainly gradually effaced in the end, and many functions earlier observed in the provinces were transferred to Baghdad. But that is a technical question, which has nothing to do with the principle.

With the administration through *dîwâns* the continued existence of the tools of this administration became necessary, that is, of the "writer" guild—those secretaries who even before the rise of this new central officialdom had been busily at work in the local administrations of the caliphate, which went back in Egypt and Syria to Byzantine traditions and in Mesopotamia and Iran to Sassanid ones, which traditions had probably already mutually influenced each other before the Islamic invasion, not to mention a possible common origin from yet older organizational systems. The name *dibhêr* also persisted in Islamic times as *dabîr,* but in the course of the *naql al-dîwân* under ᶜAbd al-Malik about 696 it was generally replaced by the Arabic *kâtib.* These secretaries, who specialized according to their particular capacities, had for the most part to satisfy the same requirements as had already been made of them in Sassanid times: clarity, quick-wittedness, knowledge of ceremonial and of titles and legalisms, and intimacy with belles-lettres and poetry and with religion and "examples from history." Since the demand was for the drawing-up of artificial documents, interlarded with allusions, which probably played a similar role in Sassanid to that in Islamic times, from which examples of such ingenuity have been transmitted to us in greater numbers, their adroitness and quick-wittedness was greatly enhanced. In this way the caliphate received from its Iranian heritage the guild of secretaries, sociologically so significant, who could also be drawn into administrative tasks of all sorts, diplomatic missions, etc., and who clearly differentiated early Islâm from contemporary Christendom, where the chancery work then (up till the advent of the ministerials) lay substantially in ecclesiastic hands, and where accordingly the intellectual leadership also was much more determined by religious and monkish considerations than in early Islâm.

To be sure, that did not imply any lessening of the religious concern. We can accept it as probable that the greatly respected and honored position of the *faqîh* had its model in the esteem for the mobeds, to say nothing, moreover, in accordance with our plan, of the meaning of Iranian religious (especially dualistic) teaching for the working-out of Islamic dogmatics (the Muᶜtazilites' antagonism against it) as well as of mysticism. That is not to say that the mysticism is of Iranian origin; it is intended only to underline the meaning of the Iranian religious feeling for mysticism, and the approval which this religious position found precisely there. We need, further, only recall that, as was formerly the Sassanid ruler, so now the caliph was regarded as the upholder of the current orthodoxy, although a direct intervention of the ruler in the dogmatic evolution, as in the case of the caliph al-Maʾmûn in favor of the Muᶜtazilites, was felt to be improper and was plainly rejected. Besides this, however, in my opinion, the old Iranian view of the legitimacy of the ruler as derived from his descent probably became significant for the imamate theory of the Shîᶜa. At any rate, it is precisely in the Iranian sphere that currents of thought of this sort met ever and again with a real and lasting echo among the population, naturally without any "influence" of this kind being admitted in the sources, or probably even being consciously felt. When it was supposed that the fourth imam, Zain al-ᶜÂbidîn, was married to Jihânshâh (Arab. Salâfa), a daughter or granddaughter of the last Sassanid ruler, Yazdagird III, this seems to me a clear sign that a union between the Arabic and the Persian, and a transition from the worldly to the religious sphere, was desired and intended. In fact, the doctrine of the *khvarena* (New Persian *farr*) had ascribed to the Sassanid rulers also a certain divine charisma, which, to be sure—as was the case in China, so far as I know, *mutatis mutandis*—abandoned him in case of failure, but which nevertheless, in my opinion, has been of importance in the development, far beyond early Shîᶜite conceptions, of the doctrine of the divine light-substance in the imams. When Hans Hartmann could show that even the linguistic expression of Iranian was substantially influenced and changed through the belief in the power of supermundane powers (among which is *khvarena*),[10] this indicates so deeply ingrained an influence on Iranian thought that the effect of such conceptions on into Islamic times cannot be denied. Another parallel: although elsewhere in Islâm (as almost always among the Sassanids) the rule of a woman was excluded, in *this* transition she is accorded on the Iranian side (through Jihân-shâh) just as significant a role as the Shîʿa had to ascribe to Fâṭima in the absence of any son of the Prophet. Moreover, this legitimacy principle gained visibly in importance again later on in the secular sphere also, when a whole multitude of local or newly arising dynasties traced their descent to old Iranian kings rather than to Mohammed. That even the Seljuqs did this shows the strong Iranianization to which this Turkish ruling house at once succumbed and, at the same time, the unbroken strength of the Islamic-Iranian culture in the time of Firdausî, but also shows how the Iranian tradition had now become the dominant one in comparison with the Islamic one. Still another example from the sphere of government: as Arsacids and Sassanids had already done, later Iranian ruling houses (even of Turkish descent), among them the Îlkhâns and the Safavids, liked to put the crown prince at the head of the highly important province of Khurâsân.

But the imams were not real rulers and accordingly met with no particular failure (unless their whole lives should be counted as such). Therefore we must find our way back from the religious sphere to the governmental. The twofold division of the local administration in the caliphate between a military governor and a head of finances may well go back to older Iranian models, and the activity of the postal officials as bearers of information for the government corresponds to the "eyes" and "ears" of the king as far back as Achaemenid times.

While in the management of the army Iranian influences are harder to demonstrate in detail, and it is rather Arab and, later, Central Asian nomadic usages that come to light here, the Islamic taxation, like the Sassanid, is founded on land and personal taxes, with the latter limited to non-Muslims on a religious basis (*jizya*). Although it is not possible to go into the involved conditions of early Islamic taxation in detail, the knowledge of which has been substantially advanced recently by F. Løkkegaard and D. C. Dennett, it can nevertheless be stated that there can be no doubt that the Sassanid taxation law and coinage system made themselves felt in the first Islamic centuries to the greatest possible extent. Even the Muslims were conscious of this and pointed it out plainly. To be sure, the attempt was made to incorporate this system into the

Islamic theory. In this way arose that early literature on taxation law, which is generally known and the detailed value of which is still being discussed. Alongside the land tax the regulation of agrarian law in general, including the conditions of rent and interest but especially the undisturbed continuity of the water rights, were presuppositions for a regulated functioning of agriculture and at the same time, to a large degree, of the state itself. Details on this persistence of Sassanid conditions cannot always be gotten at easily, for in Iran and Mesopotamia, in contrast to Egypt, we lack papyri as documents of the daily life. But in our context details can surely be dispensed with.

A continuation of old Iranian customs was evidenced also in the ceremonial of the ruler: his seclusion from the outer world, the gradation of the court offices but, above all, the elaboration of court festivals such as the "coronation" with the diadem (*tâj*), a specially Iranian symbol, with which the consciously Iranianizing and anti-Islamic Ziyârids also associated in 929 a golden throne; and then banquets of all sorts and receptions of envoys. The ceremonial of the courtiers, the court musicians graduated by rank, the presentation of credentials, the kissing of foot or carpet, the ceremonial conversations with the inquiry about the health of the sender and the wish for long life of the receiver, and the presentation and distribution of gifts (including the reappearance of general Naurûz and Mihrjân giving) have the character in every way of older Iranian or ancient Near Eastern usages, even though some details probably cannot be verified for Sassanid times. However, it seems to me, on the basis of cursory reading, as if the Syrian and Armenian sources could be exploited for information on the Sassanid times even more than happened in the case of Arthur Christensen. On the other hand, a simple testimony from Firdausî cannot serve as certain evidence, for his representation gives a romanticized picture of the Sassanid state as seen by the *dihqân* class (Hugo Andersen),[11] in which in externals (clothing, etc.) some contemporary material probably crept in.

The titles of individual ruling houses had throughout remained alive in the eastern part of the Iranian plateau and on the south shore of the Caspian Sea among the Zoroastrians there. We know a great number of them, but we also know that one of the grounds for the execution of the victor over Pâpak in 838, Afshîn of Usrûshana, was the fact that he allowed himself to be addressed by his subjects in the traditional way as Bagh Baghân. For Muslims that was naturally blasphemy. In fact, Islâm was able for quite a long time to suppress at least the title *Shâhânshâh.* Only the Bûyid ᶜAḍud al-Daula (d. 983) caused it to prevail again generally, and almost at the same time the word *sulṭân,* from the appellative for "rule," began to become a ruler's title, as indeed the desire for titles made its entrance generally in Islâm then—a desire which is so common a human failing that in this case we can probably not look so very exclusively to ancient Oriental models. This was also the period when for some time (since 821) native dynasties had again been coming to power in Iran, most importantly the Samanids in the northeast (873–999), of which not a few consciously felt themselves to be bearers of Iranian tradition and expressed this, not only in the cultivation of literature and the like, but also in the manner of their rule, as well as in their dispositions according to the long-inherited feudal system of the *dihqâns* and *marzbâns,* along with whom the remaining "estates" from Sassanid times, the priests (with a different religion), the warriors, the secretaries, and the people (i.e., peasants and craftsmen) had maintained their positions substantially intact.

At the same time there grew up even in Iran itself, on the basis of Abbasid and in this way of old Iranian models, an independent synthesis of Iranian and Islamic administration and political conceptions, which came to prevail also in the provincial administration and its organization, in the feudal system with its symbols (flag, sword, robes of honor), and in the documentary authentication of the chancery with its traditional forms, always very tenacious. The now obligatory opposition to pictures, in Islâm, concurrently hastened the development of the script into an ornament, a trait which suited the Iranian sense of beauty also and had already found expression earlier, for instance, in the bookmaking of the Manicheans.

But here we are again impinging on the limits set for us, this time in the direction of the sphere of art, and so we must leave off.

This concise survey of Iranian elements in the early Islamic administration as a whole, but especially at the caliphal court and in Persia, has frequently touched on things which are known to scholarship. But since they are of value as examples of consciously experienced cultural borrowing, it was not possible to avoid assembling them again in the framework of the appointed theme. On the other hand, the second great subject of inquiry, namely, the influence of the Iranian spirit upon Islamic law as such, has not yet been at all exhaustively studied. A young Iranian, Sayyed Taghi Nasr, has declared, to be sure, in his dissertation *Essai sur l'histoire du droit persan dès l'origine à l'invasion arabe*:[12] "From the difference between the Sunnite and Shîᶜite law, the influence of the Iranian spirit upon the juridical thinking of Islâm can be surmised." But beginners commonly know, or at least say, more upon such difficult subjects than experienced scholars (apart from the question of the Iranian component in the Shîᶜa in general). So long as, in the wake of Christian Bartholomae's studies on Sassanid law, no really exact inquiries into this material have been undertaken by a legal historian such as Pagliaro, as a historian one will have to renounce the setting-forth of individual details (such as perhaps the law of marriage, with polygamy, *mutᶜa*, etc.). But that personal, property, and criminal law in many cases of daily life was decided even in early Islamic times according to Sassanid principles can surely be accepted. Unfortunately, we possess in this matter few particular accounts, which are very numerous only for the ways of inflicting punishment (with torture and execution); precisely in this realm many ancient Near Eastern abominations came to prevail (in this case, unfortunately!) even among the Arabs, obviously more humane earlier, and were known as such. Their enumeration, which could easily be made, I may surely spare myself. There need only be mentioned the setting of red-hot kettles on the body and, in Ghaznavid times, the trampling to death by elephants driven to rage.

In the sphere of pure law, accordingly, this sketch must remain uncompleted; here M. Brunschvig and Mr. Schacht can perhaps speak more exactly. But, even so, the share of Iranian political thought, of Iranian statesman-like achievement in the construction of the Islamic empire, can assume a significant and honorable place in the framework of the early Islamic cultural achievement.

DISCUSSION

M. Cahen mentions that for the sake of brevity in his own paper he was forced to omit a good many of the questions on the Islamic social substratum taken up by Mr. Spuler. He then speaks of the problem of the Classical city, which lived on in the Muslim world. M. Cahen is glad that Mr. Spuler has mentioned the problem, because he thinks that a good many rather vague traditional opinions in that field have to be revised. In reality we have no history of the Muslim cities. Notwithstanding M. Cahen's admiration for the work of J. Sauvaget, he does not see in it a history which centers around the social problems of the cities. Sociological history does have a certain part in Sauvaget's books, but it appears rather as a factor called upon to explain the architectural development of the towns than for the sake of its own intrinsic value.

M. Cahen does not think that there is a clear-cut difference between the Classical and the Muslim town—neither in architectural layout nor in general living conditions. We are given an impression of discontinuity, especially because the Muslim lawyer was concerned with the activities of the Muslim people only as far as they had a direct connection with the religious law or with the actions taken by the government. In reality this does not exclude the possibility that a great number of Classical institutions and tendencies, as they existed in the ancient cities, continued to play their part in a more or less private way during several centuries of Muslim history. Proofs for this phenomenon are naturally difficult to establish. However, M. CAHEN, in various studies he has recently undertaken and hopes to complete within a reasonable time, was surprised to find that certain organizations, certain powerful positions as they are found in the Muslim city of the first centuries after the hegira, perpetuate to a large extent what we know of the Byzantine cities of the east before the Muslim conquest. M. CAHEN has no time to enter into particulars; all he wants is to stress the importance of this field of research.

Two more small details: Mr. Spuler has called attention to the caliph ᶜUmar II (717–720). There seems to have existed a fundamental difference between his attitude and that of the Abbasids. ᶜUmar, educated in the pious circles of Medina, seems to have cherished the project of re-establishing the whole of the system of the Medinese retrospective piety, to apply the Muslim law in its integrity. (This naturally proved impossible; even ᶜUmar's own financial activities show that he was confronted with problems which previously had not existed.) The Abbasids, on the other hand, completely renounced the Medinese pietistic ideals; what they aspired to was to obtain Islamic recognition for institutions which previously had not existed and were non-Muslim in themselves.

Here M. CAHEN comes to his second point: the Iranian influence upon the Abbasid state. He recalls that more than a century had elapsed between the fall of the Sassanid Empire and the rise of the Abbasids. The Sassanid tradition may have preserved itself very much alive during that period; anyhow, there is ground for the suspicion that the Sassanid tradition, as it still lived in the minds of people in 750, did not conform exactly to the real state of affairs in 640.

M. CAHEN cites the case of the Sassanid *vuzurg framâdhâr*. A short time ago he wanted to check on the generally stated fact that the Abbasid vizier is a successor to this functionary. What he found in Arthur Christensen's *L'Iran sous les Sassanides* ([Paris, 1936], pp. 108 f.) was, without much exaggeration, roughly as follows: We do not know much about this dignitary; his function is continued by the Abbasid vizier, and, consequently, following al-Ṭabarî (838–923), we can say of him. . . . Here we are clearly presented with a vicious circle. M. CAHEN wants merely to draw attention to the fallacy of similar circular conclusions; he naturally does not deny the existence of an Iranian tradition.

Mr. LEWIS, referring to the question whether pre-Islamic elements in Egyptian administration were stronger than in Syria, mentions the fact that Egypt is much better documented and that this may cause us to assume that foreign elements in Egyptian administration were especially vigorous. Furthermore, he recalls that in a document dating from sixteenth-century Syria the word for taxes collected in money is *demos*. That word was found in the place itself and not brought in by the Ottomans.

Mr. SPULER admits the survival of Byzantine terms like *demos* in Syria, but he reaffirms his impression that the Egyptian administration underwent to a higher degree Byzantine influence than the Syrian one. He recalls the fact that Egypt was detached from Baghdad as early as 868.

Mr. Stadtmüller believes in an Egyptian continuity with regard to administration; in Syria more recent Greek elements may have been introduced at the time of the Seljuqs. He says that political history should not be dissociated from cultural history and that it is significant that Syria has a far more important Arabic literature than does Egypt.

Mr. Spuler mentions the importance of the Coptic officials in Egypt: they may have been responsible for the continuity of Greek administrative techniques in Arabic Egypt.

Mr. Stadtmüller and Mr. Spuler then speak of the puzzling fact that the Coptic language has disappeared whereas the Coptic religion has survived. The contrast to Iran, where things happened the other way round, may be due to the geographical conditions of Egypt, Mr. Spuler suggests; but he is not too sure of the correctness of his own explanation.

With regard to the Coptic language, Mr. Schacht thinks that the accessibility of Egypt is responsible, at least partially, for its disappearance. Conservative Egyptian dialects are found in places difficult of access, exactly as in al-Maᶜlûla in the case of Syria; and in Upper Egypt there is a small enclave, very difficult to reach, where Coptic phrases are used in more familiar conversation (questions such as "How did you sleep?" greeting formulas, etc.), chiefly inside the houses by women and children.

Mr. Spuler adds that the name of this village is *Pi-solsel* and that the article "Ḳibṭ" (by G. Wiet and W. E. Crum) in the *Encyclopaedia of Islâm* gives a highly informative picture of the gradual recession of the language.

NOTES

1. Cf. also Johannes Wilhelm Fück, review of J. Schacht's *Origins of Muhammadan Jurisprudence* in *Bibliotheca orientalis*, X (1953), 196–99.

2. See now Sir Hamilton A. R. Gibb, "The Social Significance of the Shuᶜûbîya," *Studia Orientalia . . . Pedersen* . . . (Copenhagen, 1953), pp. 105–14; and his "An Interpretation of Islamic History," *Cahiers d'histoire mondiale*, I (Paris, 1953), 39–62.

3. Cf. Wm. Marçais, "Comment l'Afrique du nord a été arabisée," *Annales de l'Institut d'Études Orientales, Faculté des lettres de l'Université d'Alger*, IV (1938), 1–22.

4. Here are to be contrasted Max Weber's work, "Die Stadt, eine soziologische Untersuchung," *Collected Works*, Vol. VI: *Wirtschaft und Gesellschaft* (2d ed.; Tübingen, 1925), pp. 514–601, with a study like that of Georges Brătianu, *Privilèges et franchises municipales dans l'Empire byzantin* (Bucharest, 1936), and the good survey of Otto Brunner, "Stadt und Bürgertum in der europäischen Geschichte," *Geschichte in Wissenschaft und Unterricht*, IX (1953), 525–37.

5. Yu. A. Solodukho, "Podati i povinnosti v Irake v III–V vv. nashey ery," *Sovyetskoye Vostokovedeniye*, V (1948), 55–72.

6. "L'Évolution de l'*iqṭâᶜ* du IXe au XIIIe siècle," *Annales: Économies Sociétés, Civilisations*, VIII, No. 1 (1953), 25–52; "Quelques problèmes économiques et fiscaux de l'Irâq Bûyide ... ," *Annales de l'Institut d'Études Orientales*, X (1952), 326–63;

"Fiscalité, propriété, antagonismes sociaux en Haute-Mésopotamie au temps des premiers ᶜAbbâsides, d'après Denys de Tell-Mahré," *Arabica*, I, No. 2 (1954), 136–52.

7. Ahmed Sûsa (Sousa), *The Irrigation System of Samarrah during the ᶜAbbâsid Caliphate* (2 vols.; Baghdad, 1948) (in Arabic).

8. Cf. the author's article, "Die Selbstbehauptung des iranischen Volkstums im frühen Islam," *Die Welt als Geschichte*, X (1950), 187–91.

9. S. D. Goitein, "Origin of the Vizierate and Its True Character," *Islamic Culture*, XVI (1942), 257.

10. Hans Hartmann, *Das Passiv* (Heidelberg, 1954), pp. 154–59.

11. Hugo Andersen, "Sasanidisk Tradition in Firdausis Kongebog," *Øst og Vest: Afhandlingen tilegnede . . . Arthur Christensen* (Copenhagen, 1945), pp. 84–93. See also Kamilla Vasil'evna Trever, "Sassanidiski Iran v Shahname," *Ferdovsi* (Leningrad, 1934), pp. 147–96; Tadeusz Kowalski, *Studia nad Šâh-nâme*, esp. Vol. I (Cracow, 1952), p. 315; Gustave E. von Grunebaum, "Firdausi's Concept of History," *F. Köprülü Armağanı* (Istanbul, 1953), pp. 177–93.

12. Paris, 1933. P. 112.

IRAN: OPPOSITION, MARTYRDOM, AND REVOLT

VLADIMIR MINORSKY

I CONFESS that in preparing my paper I experienced certain difficulties. For one thing, the statement of the program of our Conference reads: "Unity and Variety in Muslim Civilization," whereas the present tendency is rather to treat separately the history of the Arab, Iranian, and Turkish lands and peoples, as we treat the history of the European peoples regardless of the fact that in the Middle Ages they recognized the same authority of the church, and used the same Latin and the same canon law.

Second, since I did not know the exact scope of Mr. Spuler's paper, I could not bring my paper into line with his so that there would be no gaps or overlapping.

Accordingly, I have approached my task from the purely historical side, following the course of the events which were to have repercussions upon beliefs; for religions may be compared to mirrors in which generations, classes, and parties—often very dissimilar—seek their own images to find support for their own aspirations.

The important facts which one must take into account in speaking of Persia are: (1) that before the conquest by the Arabs or, one may say, by the Muslims, this country possessed a long administrative, cultural, and artistic tradition; (2) that this country was conquered by the Arabs quite rapidly in the course of the second and third decades of the hijra and that all that the conquerors could offer the conquered at that stage was the new religion, in a form not yet well adapted to the requirements of settled life, and a poetry which reflected the conditions of the *jâhiliyya* of a nomad people; (3) that apart from some vague indications in the Syrian and Armenian sources, no indigenous documents on the course of the conquest have survived, while the Arab reports recorded much later concentrate on the outward aspect of events. Though we are more or less well informed on the conquest and the occupation of the chief cities, the situation in the countryside remains very obscure.

THE CONQUEST

Historians are more or less in agreement that force did not play a large role in the *conversions*, but that does not mean that the Arabs met no resistance. Many cities were taken only after a struggle. Even in the third century of the hegira a city like Qumm had to be reduced by force, and, according to al-Balâdhurî, "a great many of its inhabitants were slaughtered."[1]

Since the non-Muslims were saddled with heavier exactions than were the faithful, the Arab administration was more interested in finances than in conversions; but, on the other hand, it was this economic disparity which had become the chief incentive for the Iranian nobles to change religion. The degradation of the old landholders under the new masters made for the same results. Speaking of the nobility of Iṣfahân, al-Balâdhurî says they were willing to pay the *kharâj* "but since they disdained to pay the poll-tax, they became Muslims."[2] If at the price of this desertion the nobles retained their lands and their social position, for their part the Arabs also appreciated the advantages enjoyed by the Iranian privileged class. According to al-Wâqidî (quoted by al-Balâdhurî),[3] on their arrival in Azerbaijan the Arabs seized all they could: "some [even] bought lands from the Persians. To these Arabs the villages turned for protection, and these [local] inhabitants became cultivators on behalf of these Arabs."

In principle Islâm is democratic, and, though it admits slavery, it ought to have accelerated the decomposition of the system of classes officially recognized in Zoroastrianism; however, the structure of the Sassanid state remained more or less unchanged, with the class of landholders being paramount and numerous elements staying outside the new dispensation.

THE CALIPHS

From the time of the Umayyads little information on the internal life of Persia has survived, but, when the Abbasid propaganda had unchained new passions and loosened tongues, we hear of a series of great risings directed against the Arab domination: those of Bihâfarîdh (about 750), of Sunbâdh the Magian (756), of Ustâdh-Sîs (765), of al-Muqannaᶜ, "the Veiled Prophet of Khurâsân" (780), and, finally, of the terrible revolt of Bâbak, which lasted twenty years and proved a sore trial to the Abbasid administration.

Externally these rebellions had a religious character, for their leaders are considered as founders of new sects. Theological hatred has distorted the facts provided about their doctrines, which it seems appealed, on the one hand, to the old beliefs of Iran and, on the other hand, reflected the influence of the great divisions within Islâm. One thing is more or less certain: the very names of the leaders and heresiarchs are purely Iranian, and among their confederates no representatives of the nobility are to be seen. Of the rebellion of Bâbak we know for certain that it was supported by the "non-Arabs" (*ᶜulûj*) and directed against the established authorities, that is, against the Arabs and the official orthodoxy. In this case we seem to be able to establish contact with the life of the classes which otherwise stay outside the field of vision of the official sources.

The coming to power of the Abbasids (in 750), organized by the propaganda of Abû Muslim, put an end to the purely *Arab* empire represented by the Umayyads. From the start of the Abbasid rule new elements coming especially from Khurâsân began to find their way into the governmental circles of Baghdad. The theories of the *shuᶜûbiyya* revived the pre-Islamic memories. The accession of Maᵓmûn (in 813), himself the son of a Persian mother, marks a new turning point in the penetration of the Persians into the administration and then into politics.

THE POLITICAL EMANCIPATION

After the period of movements with a religious appearance, the emancipation of Persia took a purely lay and political form. The breakup of the caliphate now proceeded by the falling-away of whole provinces under the aegis of new Khurâsânian dynasties. The breach which divided the Ṭâhirids from Baghdad was scarcely perceptible. The Ṣaffârids, on the other hand, both by their purely democratic origins and by their independent behavior, turned over a new page in the history of Iran. Although officially the Ṣaffârids had to fight against the petty Khârijite leaders, their political activity seems to have been inspired by the radical ideas of those rivals. Some later sources[4] attribute Shîᶜite motives to the Ṣaffârids. In any case the rulers of Sîstân dissociated themselves completely from the authority of the caliph, and, in general, religion played no significant role in their policy. The Samanids of Bukhara re-established the prestige of Sunnite orthodoxy. Their modest attempts at centralization put them at odds with their feudatories. Curiously enough, the Sunnite clergy, suspicious of the tendencies of certain Samanids (who, wanting to widen the basis of their power, tried to rely upon Shîᶜite extremism and the urban classes), showed a complete lack of national ideas and sacrificed the Samanids to the Turkish outsiders.

The caliphate was unable to save the Samanids, for toward the middle of the tenth century a great movement disturbed the situation in central and western Persia and erected a wall between Baghdad and Khurâsân. This movement, which I have called the "Iranian intermezzo," came out of the north, from the Caspian provinces. The Arabs had not succeeded in establishing themselves securely in that region, and Gîlân especially formed an autonomous and hostile enclave, governed by local kinglets and keeping up the memories of the pre-Islamic glories.[5]

It was ᶜAlid-Zaidid refugees who, making their way into Gîlân, converted the population to Shîᶜism (*ca.* 864). From the start the movement had a democratic character. The local princes lost their power, and the new masters, by their justice, inspired great confidence in their subjects. According to Ṭabarî, "the world has never seen justice like that of Ḥasan Uṭrûsh" (*ca.* 914).[6]

The mountainous country above the marshes of Gîlân was called Dailam. Already in antiquity the warriors of this healthy but poor region are mentioned among the mercenaries of Pergamum. The Shîᶜite ideas implanted by the Zaidî sayyids were of a frankly oppositional character, so far as concerned the caliphate. In the mountains of Dailam they amalgamated with the nostalgic memories of pre-Islamic times, and the combination of these tendencies found energetic supporters among the elements who felt hemmed in in their mountain haunts.

About 920 the first bands of Dailamite adventurers appeared on the central plateau. Eight years later the Ziyârid leaders put themselves at the head of the movement but soon had to give place to their former officers of the Bûyid family.

About this time the caliphate had already entered into a period of decline. After 929 one finds the mayors of the palace (*amîr al-umarâ*ᵓ) seizing the reins of government.[7] Strictly speaking, the Bûyid Muᶜizz al-Daula merely continued their line, but with the difference that he, a Shîᶜite, was called upon to be the guardian of the orthodox caliph. The brothers of Muᶜizz had established themselves at Rayy and at Shîrâz, and thus the whole of the Iranian plateau received an independent organization and was lost to the caliphate. Under the aegis of the Bûyids, other less extensive Iranian principalities sprang up in Azerbaijan, Kurdistan, and Mesopotamia.

It must not be forgotten that the Bûyid courts of Rayy and Shîrâz were great cultural centers, that famous ministers, such as Abû al-Faḍl ibn al-ᶜAmîd and Ismâᶜîl ibn ᶜAbbâd, were great protectors of letters and science, and that Avicenna served as vizier at the court of the Kâkûyids, the immediate successors of the Bûyids.[8]

It seems to me, then, that the Bûyid age, which liquidated the Arab rule and organized Persia on bases antithetical to Islamic orthodoxy, was of primary importance for the formation of the national consciousness of the Persians. For a hundred and ten years the Bûyids secured an "Iranian intermezzo" within the long series of foreign occupations. The Bûyid tradition must be taken into consideration not less than that of the dynasties of Khurâsân.

If the *Shâh-nâma* can be considered as an echo of the sentiments of the landed nobility (*dihqân*) in Samanid times, the somewhat heterodox and extremist Shîᶜism of the Bûyids became the second constitutive factor in the formation of the Persian national consciousness. It was a matter not only of doctrines but of the amalgamation of the ideas with emotions and daily practice. Thus, for instance, the strange character of the holidays in Persia, which are for the most part commemorations of deaths and exaggerated mournings, must reflect the customs of the Dailamî mountaineers, who were given to immoderate lamentations, even over themselves in time of sickness.

THE TURKS

Turkish dynasties succeeded to the Samanids and the Bûyids. Among them, the Qara-Khânids did not reach far beyond the Oxus frontier. The Ghaznavids centered on the southern axis leading toward India and its riches, and their intervention in central Persia was of only short duration. Sunnite orthodoxy was officially reestablished by Maḥmûd, who severely repressed the Muᶜtazilism and other deviations which had developed at Rayy under the mild rule of the Bûyids, but until Mongol times Rayy continued to be the center of religious dissensions.

A different matter was the invasion of the Oghuz tribes under the leadership of the Seljuqs. Their axis was aligned from east to west, and, since they traveled with their families and their flocks, they were able to settle among the indigenous population and influence its composition and its language. It is thus that Azerbaijan became Turkish-speaking. A much more serious effort was made to establish Sunnite orthodoxy in alliance with the secular arm of the state, but for all the respect shown the caliph he did not become much more independent than he had been under the Bûyids. Even the choice of his counselors was strictly controlled by the Seljuq viziers, such as Kundurî and Niẓâm al-Mulk.

It is customary to speak of the strong organization of the Seljuq state.[9] In fact, the period of calm and tranquillity covered by the reigns of Alp Arslân and Malik Shâh lasted only three decades (from 1063 to 1092) and was followed by long struggles and wars among the epigones. It is true that under the Seljuqs we find a close collaboration established between the conquerors and the bureaucracy recruited among the Persians. This is a new class, distinct from the Sassanid *dihqâns*. In the *Siyâsat-nâma* of Niẓâm al-Mulk we have a document of first importance setting forth the program which combined the force of the Turks with the administrative methods of the Sassanids and the great Abbasid caliphs. The system of spies, of messengers, and of troops skilfully assorted from different elements was harmonized with the founding of the religious colleges, those nurseries of administrators who were to watch over the rectitude of the path followed by their flocks. "Religion and government are twins, one of which cannot do without the other," said Ghazzâlî.[10]

Behind the screen of orthodoxy, all was not going well in the Seljuq state. Here we must consider the role which Ismâᶜîlism played during this whole period. Barthold regarded its development as a return to Iranian feudalism, apparently as a re-establishment of the particularism of the *dihqâns*. In reality, the resemblance of the fortresses of the Assassins to the strongholds of the former masters of the provinces was purely external. The Iranian barons reflected the isolation of the areas, which were self-sufficient economically, and the opposition of the local interests to the unifying tendencies of the monarchy. On the contrary, the Ismâᶜîlîs did not work for any particularism. Their idea was to unify the country, and even countries, on the basis of a system which would permit the organization of all classes and sorts of people in a single social pyramid built according to the degrees of initiation. Visions of the order established in Egypt by the Fâṭimids haunted their imagination, as we know by the example of Nâṣir-i Khusrau. It is arbitrary to consider the chiefs of Alamût and of the other fortresses as ambitious adventurers. The severity of Ḥasan-i Ṣabbâḥ against the peccadilloes of his sons is a proof of the moral discipline which reigned at Alamût. To a certain point the Ismâᶜîlîs were continuing the Bûyid tradition.[11] It is a noteworthy coincidence that their great center was situated right in the middle of the former territory of the Dailamîs, where the oppositional tendencies must have been still alive. When one looks at the rock of Alamût one is astonished by the slightness of its area. Without the support coming from the country, such a fortress could not have withstood all the numerous and prolonged attacks which were directed against it. So far as we can judge by the names of the Ismâᶜîlî leaders, they represented the classes below the governmental circles, which had not made their peace with the Turkish invaders.[12] There is no reason to believe that the Turks, or even their Seljuq chiefs, would have been received as "liberators."[13] Niẓâm al-Mulk himself quotes a speech of his master, Alp Arslân, saying to his attendants: "We are foreigners in a land which we have taken by force. We are pure Muslims and these Persians [ᶜ*Irâqî*] have a bad religion and *favor the Dailamites.*"[14] The political assassinations of the Ismâᶜîlîs are morally repugnant, but that is the tactic of oppositional movements which fight against the overwhelming force of the public authorities, especially when these latter depend upon foreign conquerors.[15]

The strength of the opposition can be measured by the governmental reactions. A great part of the *Siyâsat-nâma* consists of passionate diatribes against the revolutionary schemings of the heretics. To the same end Ghazzâlî wrote his refutation of the Bâṭinites, which is on a higher plane but which is entirely in agreement with the government, and it is to be noted that at that time Ghazzâlî was professor at the Niẓâmiyya college.

The general attitude of the Sunna toward the government can be illustrated by passages which are found in *Iḥyâ ᶜulûm al-dîn.* On the one hand, Ghazzâlî analyzes there with much reserve the possibility of accepting subsidies from tyrants, for "most of the funds of the sultans in our time are illicit [*ḥarâm*] and the licit [*ḥalâl*] portion of what they possess is nonexistent or rare." On the other hand, the great theologian speaks of the established powers with an almost fatalistic resignation: "A tyrannical and barbarous sultan, so long as he is supported by force and cannot be deposed without difficulty, so that an attempt to depose him would cause a bitter civil war, must of necessity be left [undisturbed], and obedience is due to him such as that rendered to the emirs. . . . The government of our days is the result solely of force [*shauka*], and whoever may be the person to whom the possessor of force owes his allegiance, that person is the caliph." Accordingly "necessity legalizes what is prohibited," he says elsewhere.[16] This frankness illustrates the temporal limitations on the thought of even the most eminent among the Sunnite theoreticians.

MYSTICISM

From Ghaznavid and Seljuq times, the tendencies of Ṣûfî mysticism can be seen growing and spreading in Iran. Since they are foreign to the lyric poetry of the Samanid time and especially to the *Shâh-nâma*—that palladium of the Iranians—and since, on the other hand, they cannot have been brought in by the conquerors, one is forced to explain their recrudescence by certain particular factors acting on the minds of the time.

There exists an enormous literature on Ṣûfism in which mysticism is treated above all as a natural tendency of human nature, and it is true that such an inclination has appeared in all climes and at diverse times;[17] but what remains to be done is to determine its individual sources and, further, its social, political, and even economic background. In any case, if it is true that man is a *zôon politikon*, the ecstatic deviations which carry him to asceticism, visionary isolation, and a breach with his environment and the real world deserve not only descriptive but also psychoanalytic study.[18] On the other hand, in Persia the phenomenon is so widespread that it is hardly possible to attribute it only to the influence of example and propaganda rather than to seek for its roots in the general conditions of the time. As in the case of the emergence of mysticism in the Polish literature after the great emigration, one is tempted to consider Persian mysticism also as a result of frustration in the midst of a life which provided no direct satisfactions.

A great distinction must naturally be made among the types of Ṣûfîs. Some were ascetics who sought forgetfulness in contemplation; at the other extreme, under the cover of Ṣûfism the hedonistic poets preached the *gaia scienza* of *carpe diem;* some Ṣûfîs were militants leading expeditions against the infidels,[19] or ambitious men seeking a wide political following.[20] In spite of this variety of types, the essential and general influence of mysticism set the Persians on the road to quietism and submission and so doomed them to be victims of all comers.

I am not at all forgetful of the superb exotic flowers which charm all those acquainted with Persian literature and which are regarded by the Persians themselves as the chief asset of their literature. But every virtue has its faults, and the Ṣûfî virtues, which at bottom reflected the vicissitudes of Persian history,[21] weakened the robust good sense which forms one of the virtues of Islâm.[22]

Accordingly, from the Seljuq time on we confront: the official religion tied closely to the interests of the rulers, the Shîᶜite opposition associated with numerous movements directed against the established order, and artificial ways of evasion in which the frustration of generations that live in a dead-end age takes refuge.

CENTRAL ASIA AND THE MONGOLS

After the disruption of the Seljuq Empire new ethnic elements made their appearance in Central Asia: Sultan Muḥammad of Khvârazm had first to place himself in a tributary relation to the Qara-Khitai infidels, natives of Manchuria, and then lost his kingdom as a result of the Mongol conquest. The vanguard of Genghis Khân appeared in Khurâsân about 1221, and till 1295—that is, during three-quarters of a century, or three generations—Persia lived under the rule of infidel governors and princes, who made no distinction among the creeds of their new subjects, who used Christian auxiliary troops, and who employed Jewish viziers alongside administrators hailing from the Far East. It was the greatest indignity the Muslims of the Middle East had ever experienced, and it culminated in the sack of Baghdad and the tragic death of the caliph, Mustaᶜṣim, in 1258.

The country was ruined, the hordes of the barbarous conquerors had to be lodged and fed, and it was a long task to absorb the newcomers. On the other hand, from the cultural point of view, the fact that Tabrîz had become the capital of a great empire on the communication routes between the Far East and the West opened new horizons. The Persian miniature underwent the influence of Chinese painting, and a series of great Persian historians created works whose importance far transcends the limits of Persia and even of Islâm. As we have said, the Mongols practiced an absolute tolerance toward the other religions, while their own beliefs, which were vague and primitive, had no chance of success among the conquered population. If, on the one hand, the Mongols put an end to the Baghdad caliphate, on the other, they did the Muslims a notable service in destroying Alamût, which was undermining the life of the Sunnite community. The Sunnites, freed of the internal enemy, made up their losses, and as early as 1282 an Islamized khan occupied the throne of Tabrîz for a short time.

When Hûlâgû Khân arrived in Persia (*ca.* 1256), the number of pure Mongols at his disposal was about 100,000, and in the campaigns waged against Egypt this contingent was seriously decimated. It became impossible to control vast territories and a numerous population with foreign and ethnically alien (Mongol or Christian

Caucasian) troops, and in 1295 Ghâzân Khân made the weighty and inevitable decision to assimilate himself to the majority of his subjects by becoming a Muslim and converting his army to Islâm.[23]

From the start of the Mongol conquest the Persian bureaucracy, accustomed to serving the Turks and intent on keeping their posts, set about collaborating with the Mongols. The famous history of the Mongols written by ᶜAṭâ-Malik Juvainî, himself a representative of a great family of officials, reflects the moral dichotomy of the time. The author sheds tears over the misfortunes of the Muslims, and at the same time[24] attributes to his infidel masters the role of those of whom God said: "They are my troopers through whom I take my vengeance upon the rebels." Still more practical was the attitude of the famous scholar, Naṣîr al-Dîn Ṭûsî, who after having served the Assassins then acted as counselor to Hûlâgû on the Baghdad campaign and ended up happily in the observatory built with funds furnished by his new protectors. Such a flexibility allowed the Persians to come through many trials, but it has not been without its effects on the national character.

About the middle of the fourteenth century the Mongol empire fell apart, and the Persian territories, filled with remains of the successive invasions, did not have time to organize themselves into a political unity. A series of principalities arose in the various corners of the Iranian plateau. Among them the most curious formation was perhaps the republic of Sabzavâr, governed by a succession of energetic leaders professing the Shîᶜa. It was still another example of the democratic traditions with which this form of heterodoxy was inspired on Persian soil.

TÎMÛR

The conquest of Tîmûr swept away the principalities which had been formed on the debris of the Mongol empire. The conqueror himself was a follower of the Sunna, but to the rigor of his doctrines he added an extreme veneration for the saints and the shaikhs supposed to possess supernatural powers. Even more curious among his beliefs were survivals of certain superstitions which he had inherited from his pagan Turkish ancestors. Tîmûr left Persia disorganized and stripped of its artisans, scholars, and artists, whom he had carried off to Central Asia.

Tîmûr's deviations were rectified by his son, Shâhrukh—that model of a "most Muslim monarch." Since for a century and a half the question of the caliphate destroyed by the Mongols had tormented the conscience of the believers, it is interesting to note the attempts of Shâhrukh's lawyers to bring in discreet allusions to the continued existence of the caliphate in the person of their master, on the basis of the Koranic passage according to which God "gives the kingship to whom he will." Consequently, the very existence of a powerful king presupposed the divine blessing. It was another way of approaching the problem of *de facto* power, before which Ghazzâlî had bowed. This theory left traces in the ambiguous style of the kings of Persia—Safavids and even Qâjârs.

In spite of the triumph of the Sunna, even in the time of Tîmûr, Faḍl Allâh Astarâbâdî (1339–93) founded the new secret sect of the Ḥurûfîs. The outward characteristic of his doctrines was the use of the numerical values of words, but apart from this cabalism the Ḥurûfî books which have survived reveal little about their actual mysteries. Tîmûr's son, Mîrân Shâh, executed Faḍl Allâh in 1393, and his lieutenants emigrated to Turkey, where they grafted their doctrines upon those of the Bektâshî order. Even in the east the clandestine propaganda continued. The instigators of the attempt on the life of Shâhrukh in 1427 were accused of Ḥurûfism. If it was not merely a pretext for the accusation, one might conclude from it that behind the abstruse theories there was hidden some political idea which took no account of the prerogatives of the very pious Sunnite king.[25]

THE FIFTEENTH CENTURY

The second half of the fifteenth century is filled with the domination of new conquerors, this time from the west. The Mongols had forced back a number of Oghuz tribes from the Seljuq Empire toward Armenia, Syria, and Asia Minor, and now these Turkomans tried to fill the vacuum left by the weakness and quarrels of the Tîmûrid epigones. From the religious point of view, of the two Turkoman dynasties—the Qara-qoyunlu and the Aq-qoyunlu—the former are more interesting, for, by a path as yet uncertain, Shîᶜism, and even Shîᶜite extremism, had slipped in to their federation of tribes.[26] This problem must be studied along with the popular heterodox movements which in the fifteenth century shook Asia Minor in opposition to Ottoman centralism.

Personally, I think that the sect, or rather the religion, of the Ahl-i Ḥaqq (familiarly called ᶜAlî-allâhî) was definitively formed at this time.[27] One must no longer suppose that its adepts are merely exaggerated worshipers of the fourth caliph and of his descendants. In fact, the sect believes in seven cycles of divine manifestations, and in this scheme ᶜAlî presided only over the second period, while the complete revelation of the Truth (*Ḥaqîqat*) took place in the fourth period, that of Sulṭân-Isḥâq, who fixed the dogmas and established the rites. The sect is interesting as a special parallel to the sects of an extremist Shîᶜite inspiration (such as the Druzes, the Nuṣairî, etc.). The sect—more widespread than it is supposed—is curious for its purely popular character, for it is successful only with the common people—nomads, traders, workers, and servants.

The Qara-qoyunlu deviations may have paved the way for the spectacular rise of the great dynasty of the Safavids.

THE SAFAVIDS

This period (1500–1722) is justly regarded as the great turning point during which the Persian nation retrieved itself and asserted its originality, but paradoxically enough at its initial stage the advent of the Safavids had the appearance of a new conquest. In fact, the instrument of which the founder of the dynasty made use was simply a new grouping of the same Turkoman tribes which the Qara-qoyunlu and the Aq-qoyunlu had used in order to occupy Persia. The difference was in the official doctrine professed by the new regime. It is true that under the Qara-qoyunlu there had already been some deviations from orthodoxy, but now the Safavid partisans were all fervent adepts of a special form of Shîᶜite extremism. It is known that the family of the shaikhs of Ardabîl had been famed for its irreproachable Sunnite orthodoxy, and it is on this basis that they acquired a numerous following among the Turkoman tribes, even as far as Syria and Asia Minor. Only under the grandfather of Shâh Ismâᶜîl had a change taken place in the family. The ambitions of the young shaikh Junaid won for him exile, and for a few years he wandered among the tribes affiliated to his house. The rights of the Safavids to descent from the family of the Prophet were somewhat suspect, but, as it seems, Junaid assumed the role of a living embodiment of the line of imams. Thus he conquered the hearts of the nomads (no less credulous than the Berber nomads), who had little interest in the pious doctrines and practices of the city-dwellers but were enthusiastic at the thought of being able to touch the hand of a being who incarnated the divine holiness and even omnipotence. Supported by the dervishes who sprang from the faithful tribes, Junaid, and after him his son Ḥaidar, tried to concentrate the energy of their followers on raids against the Caucasian infidels. Although by their marriages the Safavids were related to the Aq-qoyunlu princes, these latter were alarmed at the formation of a state within their domain. They were eager to check the military adventures of Junaid and Ḥaidar, and one after the other the father and the son perished in the course of their expeditions. The blood of the martyrs consolidated the Safavid party, and the young Ismâᶜîl, son of Ḥaidar, grew up surrounded by hopes that he would become the avenger of his ancestors.

Independently of the pious legends which describe the visions and miracles of the young prince, we can judge of Ismâᶜîl's claims from the poetry included in his *dîvân*. It is in the Turkoman dialect ("of Azerbaijan") and is meant to be recited by his adepts. In it we find it asserted that the author is the *Fâᶜil muṭlaq* (*Agens absolutus*) and that the *sijda* (prostration before God) is due him. When the travelers of Safavid times declared that the shahs were worshiped as God, these statements were interpreted figuratively, but they should rather be taken literally.

With the aid of his followers, Ismâᶜîl had to reconquer Persia, and we know the excesses committed in carrying out this task and the names of the *émigrés* who had to take refuge in Turkey or in Central Asia.

The state founded by Ismâᶜîl was a theocracy, nearly in the sense which this term bears in regard to Tibet and the Dalai Lama. The state was supported by a religion and by the assistance of the unique party of the Shâhî-sevans ("those who love the shah").[28] Our sources often mention conflicts between the followers of the shah which could not be settled by conciliation. The shah then appealed to the discipline of the religious party (*ṣalâ-yi shâhî-sevanî*), and the followers submitted to such decisions of their supreme head.

One sometimes hears voices expressing regret at the breach in the Islamic community which resulted from the actions of Shâh Ismâᶜîl.[29] But from the point of view of the Persian nation one could maintain the thesis that it is precisely this isolation which saved the Persians. From the west the Ottomans, from the east the Uzbegs, threatened Persia, penetrating farther and farther into it, and Persia would have ended by being submerged in these waves of Turkish assaults. The new religion with its ecstatic character helped to concentrate the central power, and, on the other hand, the new doctrine, which in itself had no connection with the Persian *nationality*, provided the platform upon which the Persian people could maintain its rights against absorption into an abstract Islâm and, in practice, into the Turkish ocean.

We have seen that the chief followers of the Safavids, though immunized by their beliefs against the seductions of their kindred neighbors, were Turkomans.[30] Now, states based on nomadic and tribal organizations lack solidity, and Shâh Ismâᶜîl's successor already ran into difficulties with his Shâhî-sevans. Little by little the shahs found themselves obliged to disperse certain recalcitrant tribes, and a hundred years after the formation of the Safavid state Shâh ᶜAbbâs modernized his armed forces. For the Turkish tribes he substituted troops of fresh Caucasian converts similar to the Ottoman Janissaries.[31] The old ecstatic and anthropomorphist religion gave place to the official Shîᶜism under the influence of theologians from Syria (Jabal ᶜÂmil) and Baḥrain, and finally the new pillar of the state religion, Mîrzâ Bâqir Majlisî, set on foot a persecution of the extremist Shâhî-sevan "Ṣûfîs." The nation, once consolidated, was to change its basis while losing its former *élan*. This development was one of the causes of the fall of the Safavids at the time of the invasion of the Afghans of Qandahâr (1722), to whom the shah could not oppose, as before, the monolithic front of his single party.

As regards the intellectual and artistic life of the Safavids, E. G. Browne had expressed his surprise that this important period did not produce great poets.[32] The explanation of this fact would perhaps be that the mysticism which penetrated the Persian poetry, or gave it a special coloring, was linked to times of distress and frustration. At a time when the people was fighting for its national existence and when possibilities were opening up for useful enterprise and the improvement of general conditions, the mystical routine no longer corresponded to the conditions of the time. Then again the poets, too much tied down by the perfection of their great models, were unable to find a new technique. Even in our times the ascendancy of the past hampers the imagination of the new Persian poets. The creative energy of the Safavid time, on the contrary, found worthy expression in architecture and in miniature-painting, two arts more appropriate to the spirit of the time.

NÂDIR SHÂH (1736–47)

In a dramatic turn Nâdir Shâh retrieved the situation and, following a series of campaigns against the Ottomans, as well as in India and in Central Asia, extended his rule even beyond the frontiers of the old Iran. Nâdir had come from the Turkoman tribe of the Afshârs, which belonged to the Shâhî-sevan confederation. At the start of his career Nâdir himself had taken the name of Tahmâsp-qulî, "slave of Tahmâsp," to show his attachment to the last Safavid. After his brilliant victories and the deposition of Tahmâsp, Nâdir suddenly changed his religious policy and even made it a condition to his accepting the crown that the Persians should abandon the deviations of Shâh Ismâᶜîl. His intention was to reunite Islâm by getting the Sunnites to recognize the Shîᶜites as the fifth orthodox rite (*rukn*, "pillar"), placed under the patronage of the fifth imam, Jaᶜfar the Truthful. The contemporary sources explained this unexpected about-face by purely temporal intentions, especially by Nâdir's hope of incorporating more easily the conquered territories and even by his designs in the direction of the Ottoman Empire. In any case these plans failed lamentably. The Ottoman and Sunnite clergy, probably seeing through Nâdir's essential purpose, categorically refused to rehabilitate the Shîᶜites. Toward the end of his reign, and even after a fresh victory over the Ottomans, Nâdir recognized the superiority of the sultan's rights as "the Caliph of the peoples of Islâm and the luster of the Turkoman race (*dûdmân*)." It was clear that after the general disillusionment produced by such a finale Nâdir could no longer overcome his difficulties. The Shîᶜite clergy, which he had despoiled of its material advantages, especially felt itself wronged. In the Shîᶜite books Nâdir's conduct is described as monstrous, and Nâdir's insignificant successor who restored their sequestered properties to the clergy received the title of "Just" (ᶜÂdil Shâh).

Shîᶜism was accordingly restored, and Nâdir's fiasco shows that that form of Islâm, associated with the memories of Safavid greatness and appealing to the Persians' sentiments, had defeated the attempts to modify it. But the triumphant Shîᶜism was no longer provoking any strife, while it assured the enjoyment of worldly goods to their old beneficiaries.

THE QÂJÂRS (1779–1925)

During the Qâjâr period—up to the Persian Revolution (1905)—the Shîᶜite clergy played an important role in public life, maintaining established privileges and paralyzing the progress of the country.

A single attempt to reform the religious life of Persia under the Qâjârs was made by the Bâb and his followers. In spite of all that has been written upon his religious system by De Gobineau, Kazembek, E. G. Browne, and Nicolas, the main lines of his attempt to recast the elements of Islâm, and especially of heterodox Islâm, remain vague; the life of the new prophet was too short (1820–50) for him to be able to work out an orderly system. It is an interesting fact, however, that the new preaching was addressed definitely to the middle classes, to the petty bourgeoisie, the lesser clergy, and the traders. The Bâb himself belonged to a family of merchants, and it is curious to find among his demands such trifling details as the legalization of loans at interest, the fixing of the monetary standard, and the inviolability of (commercial) correspondence.

In a recent work the activity of the Bâb has been studied with relation to the economic crisis which Persia went through at the beginning of the nineteenth century. Further, the author[33] points out the extremely radical character the preaching took after the arrest of the Bâb. His followers, gathered in Mâzandarân, went so far as to suggest the abolition of private property, which was regarded as a usurpation. The shah's government, relying on the great landed nobility, closely connected with the administration, drowned the revolt in blood, and Bâbism, transformed into Bahâʾism and directed by the new leaders from abroad, then took a vague, humanitarian, and harmless form.[34]

To what has been said about the social and political roots of the Bâbîs one could add that practically the same classes took part in the Persian Revolution which resulted in the overthrow of the Qâjârs, except that the Bâb was still thinking in medieval and religious terms, while in the twentieth century the basic ideas were shifted to a purely lay field. One need only glance at the photographs of the protesters who in the summer of 1904 sought asylum in the British legation to recognize the character of the class which opposed the rule of the princes (among whom must be included the princes of the church) and of the great landed proprietors.

RIZA SHAH

We cannot follow further the vicissitudes of Islâm in Persia. Under Riza Shah Pahlavi the people's attention was turned toward new undertakings and new horizons. The Europeanization of the state was pursued with remarkable zeal, and diversions of a religious type, such as the celebrations of the month of Muḥarram, were looked down upon. The role of the clergy was considerably reduced, so that it was kept out of political affairs.

In the troubled period since the end of the second World War the clergy has begun to regain its former position, but it is best not to come to any conclusion on events which belong to the realm of purely political current affairs.

This survey—inevitably too summary—of the role played by the religious factors in the history of Persia since the Arab conquest allows us to formulate some conclusions, though naturally only approximate ones.

1. It seems improper to reduce the life of the Muslim states simply to the influences of the religious law of Islâm. The conversion to Islâm in many cases, as Mr. Spuler has recently confirmed, was the result of political and economic factors.

2. In the case of Persia one must definitely take account of its pre-Islamic culture and of its extra-Islamic inspirations. For example, at all times, as De Gobineau noticed, the influence of the Iranian epic went along side by side with the "belief in the imams." It already sustained the national consciousness at the time of the *shuᶜûbîs*. It was of service to those kings who plumed themselves on their Iranian origins. All across the Middle East it provided patterns of virtue for the conduct of princes. It formed a counterweight to the quietism preached by the Ṣûfîs.

Some of the most famous Persian poems (the *Shâh-nâma*, the poems of Niẓâmî) are based on traditional Iranian or purely lay subjects. The panegyrics, which form so important a part of Persian poetry, are likewise *Gelegenheitsgedichte* of a nonreligious inspiration. Miniature-painting, that eminently Persian art, illustrates by preference the exploits of the national heroes and only to a smaller degree religious or Ṣûfî themes.

3. It is with a certain justification that Mr. Spuler speaks of the *religious governmental* party which gathered around the official Sunna. Accordingly the Sunna acquired a certain class character. It is certain that the higher bureaucracy, which had quickly ranged itself on the side of the conquerors at the time of the Turkish and Mongol invasions, rendered some service to the people in civilizing the invaders and smoothing the harshness of the barbarous and foreign administration, even though at the same time, by its submissiveness, such administration regularized the position of the conquerors and the subjection of the people.

4. The rule of the foreign conquests weighed heavily upon the lower classes, who in the end had to pay all the additional charges which resulted from the need *to feed* the conquerors and their hordes. Our historical sources reflect chiefly the point of view of the ruling classes, but little by little we are beginning to find and uncover a great many facts on the administrative practices and on the life of the nonofficial classes—an unchanging life, interrupted only by

sporadic uprisings. This documentation is much more abundant and varied than was supposed in the time of the historians "primarily of Islâm." Quite recently one of our colleagues,[35] in a richly detailed work, showed how archaic a system of agrarian relations has survived in Persia across the ages up to our day. It was the cause of the debasement of the masses and often of great dissatisfactions. The official Islâm, with its judges and preachers, rarely placed itself on the side of those affected, for the high clergy itself possessed lands and did not set itself off from the great proprietors, while the middle clergy depended upon the public authorities through the distribution of pensions and other allowances.[36]

5. Under these circumstances the cause of the nonprivileged classes was espoused particularly by the unofficial Islâm, connected at first with the pre-Islamic survivals and later with Shîᶜism. If powerful parties can elaborate detailed systems and maintain purity of line in their doctrines, the opposition, leading a hazardous and hidden life, is forced to accept compromises and varied coalitions. On this account the unofficial Persian Islâm has always preserved traces of multifarious contacts as it became more and more heterodox but more popular and accessible to the masses. Miracles and the presence of living incarnations served to comfort the elements which found no justice at the hands of the ruling classes. Even the moderate and "official" brand of the Shîᶜa contained a mass of well-known associations and allusions which (like the union of the house of ᶜAlî with the Sassanid princess, the sufferings of the martyrs, etc.) made it a much more living force than the cold dogmas of the rigid law of Islâm.

One of our esteemed colleagues[37] has passed a rather severe judgment on the duplicity of the Shîᶜites with their "most unattractive flavor of moral ambiguity" and their emotionalism. However, one must not speak of Islâm and its subdivisions as if these were logical and absolute categories. In fact, their contents and incidence change according to the conditions of Time and Space. In Persia one must above all keep in view the vicissitudes of history. The Persians have rarely been conquerors but often conquered. Leaving aside the periods of an uncertain character, from the Arab conquest up to the year 1800 the Persians passed about four hundred years under indigenous dynasties, against about seven hundred years of foreign rule. This explains their emotionalism and the need to look to secrecy and plotting. From this point of view even the reprehensible practices of the Ismâᶜîlîs served as a check on the conquerors and a corrective to oppression. If then Shâh Ismâᶜîl, with armed might, undertook to break the opposition of the official Islâm, he soon found the path leading to the hearts of the Persians. Not only during the 222 years of Safavid rule, but even up to our day, Shîᶜism, with its overtones and its aroma of opposition, of martyrdom, and of revolt, is matched quite well with the Persian character—a character formed in the course of a long history which is very different from the history of other peoples nearby.

DISCUSSION

Mr. MEIER, referring to Mr. Minorsky's paper, says that it is methodically inadequate to connect the phenomenon of mysticism with Iranian tendencies so long as we do not know anything of a Sassanid mysticism. Mr. MEIER would rather refer to the mysticism of the eastern Christian church (J. Climacus, d. *ca.* 606; Diadochos of Photike, middle of the fifth century, etc.). In its earliest period the Shîᶜa also had no particular connection with Iran. It developed out of ideas such as those represented by the non-Iranian Ibn Sabaᵓ (d. 661 or later) and from political and historical events which were elaborated with the help of archetypical conceptions. The lament over the death of Ḥusain, as a typical motif, may be linked with the lament over Tammûz or over Adonis as well as with the lament over Siyâvush. The breach in the imamate did not appear for the first time with the seventh imam and not only in his case. There were nearly as many imams as descendants of ᶜAlî, but each Shîᶜite recognized only his own imam—he was appointed by *naṣṣ* (nomination)—and we cannot say that the Shîᶜites knew or admitted a division of "khwârena" between different persons.

The old Ṣûfîs, as is shown in the lists compiled by Sulamî (d. 1021), came mostly from Persia, but this does not mean, naturally, that the movement originated there. Mr. MEIER would see the reasons for this Iranian preponderance in early mysticism rather in the fact that the Arabs were a young nation, not inclined toward a secondary form of religiosity, which, on the contrary, may easily have attracted the more differentiated minds of the, culturally speaking, much older Persians

As to the question whether Ṣûfîs alienated religious forces from the government, Mr. MEIER remarks that Ṣûfism usually dissuaded its adepts from mingling with the affairs of the sultan. But this fact in itself, and a number of anecdotes illustrating the contrast between Ṣûfism and the official theology, prove that the Ṣûfîs not infrequently had to do with the government. The cordial relations between Seljuqs and Ṣûfîs are well known; Ghâzân Khân (1271–1304) was converted by a son of the Ṣûfî Saᶜd al-Dîn Ḥamûyî (d. 1252 or 1260). Other Ṣûfîs, like Simnânî, ostentatiously turned their backs on the government.

Mr. SPULER thinks that the concept of the illuminating spark (*khwârena*) did penetrate into the earlier Shîᶜite doctrine through Persian adepts.

Mr. CASKEL, referring to Mr. Spuler's paper, remarks that Shâh Ismâᶜîl (d. 1524) had already introduced the Twelver Shîᶜa into Persia as a state religion; but he himself and his court retained their extremist religious views. The Shîᶜa was accepted by certain big tribes, like the Tekelu, Ustâjlu, Shâmlu, and Afshâr, which—adds Mr. MINORSKY—are usually said to have been seven, but in reality were more, and consisted of many splinter groups from the great nomad tribes.

Mr. Caskel asks further if the teaching of the Basran and Kûfan philologists did not influence the idea of the state as it was conceived by the sons of the early Abbasid caliphs.

Mr. Spuler does not believe so and argues from the fact that the reinstatement of Arabic as the governmental language by the Samanids did not influence their Iranian conception of the state.

M. Brunschvig thinks it would be worth while mentioning the coincidence of interest between the Persian state and Shîᶜism in these last centuries. It finds its expression in the creation of sanctuaries belonging specifically to Persia. We know that the kings of modern Persia fostered national shrines of pilgrimage in order to divert as far as possible the stream of Shîᶜite pilgrims which went yearly to Iraq in Turkish territory. Such conjunctions of political and religious interests are always a very important phenomenon and well worth a detailed analysis. The Shîᶜite places of pilgrimage are unique in Islâm; they are incomparably more important than the North African sanctuaries.

M. Le Tourneau confirms that no North African sanctuary attracts people from all over the Maghrib. That of Mawlây Idrîs at Fez counts practically only in northern Morocco, and that of Sidi Oqba near Biskra is very modest.

Further, M. Brunschvig continues, the cleavage pointed out by Mr. Minorsky between painting and literary expression, which seems to manifest itself in Persia at the beginning of modern times, is very significant. We ought to make similar observations in other sectors of Muslim history, and it would be quite easy to find links in this particular matter with other civilizations. M. Brunschvig recalls some interesting passages of J. Huizinga about the same phenomenon (*The Waning of the Middle Ages* [London, 1924], pp. 252 ff. and 279 ff.).

Mr. Gabrieli adds that in Italy too we observe the same contrast; the decline of art does not coincide with the decline of literature. Italian literature of the *quattrocento* is essentially poor; the same century is probably the greatest of all in painting.

M. Brunschvig goes on to say that he thinks this contrast is worth keeping in mind. It is not enough to state that "culture flourishes" in a certain epoch; we have to try to analyze its different elements. The different media of expression do not always correspond in sincerity, in their capacity of conveying the sentiments, the social realities of the times, or even in their aesthetic values. We ought to try to apply similar criteria to the different places and moments of Muslim history.

Mr. Minorsky adds to M. Brunschvig's first point that the importance of the national sanctuaries was intentionally stressed by documents such as the description of the pilgrimage of Shâh ᶜAbbâs I (1557–1628) in a special chapter of the official history of the Shâh, thanks to which we have today the list of all the stations and of the parasangs between them. The Safavid architectural activity has to be viewed in the same light.

As to the second point: E. G. Browne observed the same phenomenon and was very much intrigued by it. He even wrote to his Persian friends and asked them for their explanations. Mr. Minorsky sees the reasons especially in a certain rigidity of literary form which went so far that it did not admit any new developments.

M. Cahen is interested in the conversion of the Mongols. There is no question that the Mongols in Islamic territory accepted the religion of the majority of their subjects, but why did the Russian Mongols become Muslim and not Christian? Certainly general conditions must have been quite different in the two countries. In all questions regarding level of civilization, participation in the administrative life of the state, etc., we cannot compare the Russian subjects of the "Golden Horde" to the Iranian subjects of the Mongols in the Middle East. Nevertheless, M. CAHEN asks himself if we should not rather say that the Mongols accepted the religion of the majority, not of their subjects, but of their fellow-nomads. It seems probable that the masses of the Mongol people had contacts and cultural intercourse more with the Turkoman tribes, who led the same kind of life as themselves, than with their sedentary subjects.

Mr. MINORSKY does not agree: The Mongols in Russia lived absolutely apart from their Russian subjects, their capital was outside the borders of ancient Russia, and their revenues were collected by Russian princes. The situation in Russia and in Persia was different.

M. CAHEN goes on to enumerate the elements which intervened in the formation of the Persian nation. One part was played by the regions of the north and northeast, incorporated in the Samanid state; another part was played by the Shîᶜites from whom the Bûyid dynasty arose. Was there not a third element constituted by the Kurds?

Mr. MINORSKY replies that the Kurds at first joined hands with the Bûyids. This happened in an epoch which is generally given too much consideration. It was a time of general confusion in which the tribes, liberated from the Arab hegemony, organized themselves in their own way. We cannot separate the Kurds too well from the other Iranian tribes of the time. Practically all of them marched in the same direction. The Kurds have never been interested in the Shîᶜa; they are Sunnites even today, but they once inclined toward Khârijism. Their great leader, Daisam (d. 956), was of Mesopotamian origin and belonged to a Khârijite family. In the seventeenth century the Kurds were mostly opposed to the Safavids.

M. CAHEN asks about the vizieral office of Avicenna (980–1037). Is this an established fact? As far as he knows, it is attested only in Avicenna's autobiography. This is certainly an important testimony, but, on the other hand, it was rare that princes accepted as viziers people who had not risen in the administrative career from the very beginnings. M. CAHEN was surprised to see that no chronicle seems to allude to the fact, or is there any mention of Avicenna's vizierate in our historical sources?

M. DU BOIS answers that Avicenna was a vizier for about ten years, according to Ibn al-Athîr (1160–1234), who, by the way, considers him a heretic.

Mr. MINORSKY adds that Ibn al-Athîr insults Avicenna in the most terrible way. We do not, in fact, know much about the philosopher's religious outlook. One thing is evident: from the very beginning he never wanted to associate himself with a Turkish dynasty. His wanderings from Bukhara to a petty prince in Khwârizm, then to Mâzandarân, to the emir Qâbûs (d. 1012), the Bûyids, and finally to the court of ᶜAlâᵓ al-Daula (d. 1041) show this clearly. It is very significant also that he never went to Baghdad; probably with the ideas he held he would not have obtained a visa to that place, if visas had existed in his time! Today all nations claim him as one of their great men—the Arabs, the Persians, even the Turks. We know one thing for sure: as soon as the Seljuqs arrived in the town of Avicenna's temporary residence, he fled to some other small indigenous prince. Concluding, Mr. MINORSKY speaks of the great wave of enthusiasm which seems to distort somewhat the real character of Avicenna. He has even been made into a moralist, although his autobiography shows us very different traits.

NOTES

1. *K. Futûḥ al-Buldân*, ed. M. J. de Goeje (Leiden, 1866), p. 314.
2. *Ibid.*
3. *Ibid.*, p. 329.
4. Already in Niẓâm al-Mulk, *Siyâsat Nâma*, ed. Ch. Schefer (Paris, 1891–97), p. 11, not to speak of the late (1010/1602) and very Shîʿite *Majâlis al-muʾminîn* of al-Shushtarî (Teheran, 1286).
5. As late as A.D. 1020 one finds in Mâzandarân Pahlevî inscriptions on tombs of Muslim princes.
6. *Taʾrîkh*, ed. M. J. de Goeje *et al.* (Leiden, 1879–1901), III, 2296.
7. About 329/941 one already finds among them a Dailamite called *Gôr-angêj*, "hunter of wild asses."
8. It must not be forgotten that the range of the Iranian Renaissance was extensive, and great men such as Firdausî (d. *ca.* 1021) and Bêrûnî (d. 1048) were contemporaries of Avicenna (d. 1037).
9. For example, bills drawn on the shores of the Oxus, and payable in Syria, etc.
10. *Al-dîn wa-l-mulk tauʾamân fa-lâ yastaghnî aḥadu-humâ min al-âkhar.* See M. al-Ghazzâlî, *Iḥyâʾ* (Cairo, 1346/1927), II, 123.
11. The grand master of Alamût, Ḥasan b. Muḥammad, was married to a descendant of the former Bûyid princes; see Juvainî, *Taʾrîkh-i Jahân Gushâ*, ed. M. Qazvînî (London, 1937), III, 239.
12. B. Lewis, *The Origins of Ismâʿîlism* (Cambridge, 1940), p. 92, writes that Ismâʿîlism was "the natural expression, in the theocratic milieu, of the depressed classes, Persian and Semite alike."
13. "Erlösung," as B. Spuler expresses it in his *Iran in frühislamischer Zeit* (Wiesbaden, 1952), p. 129.
14. *Siyâsat Nâma*, p. 140.
15. One must keep in mind the manners of a time when governments themselves turned to the professional services of the Assassins when it was a question of liquidating some distant enemy.
16. The first passage is to be found in *Iḥyâ*, p. 124, and the second is concealed in *Al-iqtiṣâd fî-l-iʿtiqâd* (Cairo, 1327), p. 98, l. 10: *wa-lâkinna al-ḍarûrât tubîḥu al-maḥẓûrât.* My attention has been drawn to these passages by H. A. R. Gibb, *Islamic Society and the West* (London, 1950), p. 31.
17. In his *Literary History of the Arabs* (2d ed.; Cambridge, 1930), R. A. Nicholson writes (pp. 384–85): "No doubt the origin and the growth of mysticism in Islam, as in all other religions, ultimately depended on general [internal?—V. M.] causes and conditions, not on external circumstances." He admits the existence of such factors as the political anarchy under the Umayyads, the skeptical tendencies under the first Abbasids, and the arid form of Muslim theology, which by opposition provoked tendencies toward quietism, spiritual authority, and emotional faith. Nevertheless, toward the end Nicholson repeats that mysticism "was not called into being by any impulse from without" (pp. 384–85). I desire to make it clear in this regard that I am not speaking of psychological reasons for the phenomenon but of its generalization and spread.
18. I know only of one work of a medical specialist who stressed the problem of Ṣûfî psychology. Dr. Kazansky wrote on the basis of his professional observations

in Turkestan, and his curious and rare publication (*Mistitsizm v Islame*) appeared in Samarkand in 1906. He treats mysticism as a morbid attitude of the human mind toward the phenomena of the outer world. Some of the characteristics of the mystic are: prolixity in speech, florid language, symbolism, depression, ecstasy, or asceticism. Dr. Kazansky explains these states by the psychological law of "dispersed excitement." Persian Ṣûfism triumphed over Arab asceticism. "A Ṣûfî's progress to Truth has the appearance of a clinical demonstration of hypnotism." The specific psychological action exercised upon the dervish by his master (*murshid*) consists in the weakening of his will and in leaving in his consciousness only a minimal number of ideas, capable of provoking ecstasy. Through the continuous practice of prescribed exercises (*dhikr*) a dervish easily falls into a hypnotic state and, like some hypnotic or hysteric subjects, can empirically guess the treatment indicated for some illness, sense at a distance the specific "smell" of the sex, age, etc. The *dhikr* affects the normal condition of the body (acceleration of the pulse, perspiration, involuntary movements, dilated pupils). When a whole group of dervishes carries out identical movements, an individual dervish becomes subject to imitative nervous fits. A dervish believes in his superiority over other men and places himself outside the recognized rules of social conduct, etc.

19. Of whom Abû Isḥâq Kâzrûnî converted 24,000. The Bûyid governor of Fârs tried to moderate his cruelties to the Zoroastrians. See F. Meier, *Die Vita des Scheich Abû Isḥâq* (Leipzig, 1948), pp. 20–22 ("Glaubenskrieg") and 39.

20. Like some of the masters of Ardabîl.

21. For the sake of illustration one could cite the time of Abû Saᶜîd ibn Abî al-Khair when the Iranian Renaissance was already shaken by continuous struggles and the approach of the Turks (immediately after the death of the shaikh the invaders destroyed all his foundations); the flight of Jalâl al-Dîn's family before the Mongol hordes; the charged atmosphere at the time of Saᶜdî, who compared the state of affairs in his time "to the tangled hair of a Negro"; and the interminable fighting and crimes of the kinglets of Shîrâz with whom Ḥâfiẓ was contemporary.

22. Speaking of the abuses resulting from the authoritarian ways of the shaikhs, the same eminent specialist, R. A. Nicholson, wrote (in connection with Abû Saᶜîd of Meyhana): "Stories of the type showing the saint as a minister of divine wrath and vengeance must have influenced many superstitious minds. The average Moslem's fatalism and belief in clairvoyance lead him to justify acts which to us seem desperately immoral" (*Studies in Islamic Mysticism* [Cambridge, 1921], p. 42).

23. In this he was following the advice of his Muslim emir, Naurûz, and this latter had more success than the Arab shaikh who, according to Montholon, made similar suggestions to Napoleon, promising him the obedience of the millions of his fellows.

24. *Jahân-gushâ* (Leiden, 1912), I, 17.

25. The Nuqṭavî ("cabalists") are mentioned as late as the time of Shâh ᶜAbbâs (see *ᶜÂlam-Ârâ*, pp. 324–25 [under 1002/1593]) as materialists who do not believe in the resurrection of body and bones. Nevertheless, the identity of their teaching with the doctrine of Shaikh Faḍl Allâh is not quite certain. See now Ṣ. Kiyâ, *Nuqṭaviyân yâ Pasîkhâniyân* (Teheran, 1320/1941), and H. Ritter in *Oriens*, VII, No. 1 (1954), 1–54.

26. See V. Minorsky, "Jihân-shâh and His Poetry," *Bulletin of the School of Oriental and African Studies*, XVI, No. 2 (1954), pp. 271–97.

27. In the old khanate of Mâkû the canton bearing the name of Qara-qoyunlu (which I visited in 1904) is inhabited exclusively by Ahl-i Ḥaqq.

28. Here the word "shah" has a double meaning, for it designates not only the shah "king" but also ᶜAlî, who bears the title *shâh-i vilâyat,* "the Shah of Holiness" (or perhaps "of relationship to the Prophet").

29. See, for instance, A. Toynbee, *A Study of History* (London, 1934–54), I, 392, who makes use of the idea of an "Iranic society" including Persia and the neighboring lands: "This schism of the Iranic Society, on the moral and religious as well as the political plane, severed all the threads that previously knit the Iranic social fabric together."

30. The tribes *Shâmlû, Rûmlû,* "those of Syria, those of Asia Minor."

31. About the end of the seventeenth century the former Shâhî-sevans served only decorative ends and were relegated to their *tauḥîd-khâna* where they practiced their *dhikr.*

32. See in E. G. Browne, *Persian Literature* (Cambridge, 1924), IV, 27, the very significant letter of M. Qazvînî, for whom the only poetry worth considering was the Ṣûfî poetry.

33. M. S. Ivanow, *The Bâbî Revolts in Irân* (*1848–52*) (Moscow, 1939) (in Russian); see *Bulletin of the School of Oriental and African Studies,* XI, No. 4 (1946), 878.

34. I recall the question I once posed to a Bahâᵓî leader on the life beyond. The answer was: "Every day our opinions on this point become milder [*mulâyimtar mîshavad*]."

35. Ann K. S. Lambton, *Landlord and Peasant in Persia* (London, 1953).

36. I expect to publish soon the account by an author of the fifteenth century of the tempest raised in his time among the clergy by the decision of a pious vizier who wanted to restore the ways of primitive Islâm. (To appear in *BSOAS,* Vol. XVII, No. 2 [1955].)

37. G. E. von Grunebaum, *Medieval Islam* (2d ed.; Chicago, 1953), p. 191.

SPAIN: INTERNAL DIVISION

ARMAND ABEL

It was the internal division of Spain which determined, in 711, the Muslim intervention in the peninsula. It was a manifold division, which went far back in time and which the arrival of the conquerors only aggravated.

A province at the far end of the Roman world, Spain had known under the Empire an activity, a wealth, and a vitality of which a thousand testimonies have come down to us.[1] In Baetica alone there were one hundred and seventy *oppida*, centers of as many ethnic and economic groups. These *oppida*, like the groups of which they formed the point of support, were generally of ancient origin, previous to the Roman conquest. When they came under the Imperial protection, they had often been rebaptized. Forty-six of them, at the time of Pliny, had received either quite simply their freedom, or Latin rights, or a treaty carrying with it privileges and exemptions.

Besides the *oppida*, peopled by the ancient inhabitants of the peninsula, Baetica had seven colonies of veterans and eight municipalities. Latin culture penetrated there profoundly, and, if it produced as early as the time of Cicero poets whose fame had reached Italy, it was especially under the Later Empire and up till under the Arab occupation that literature flourished there in the language of Caesar in the fields of eloquence, history, theology, and even philosophy.

At the time of the Germanic invasions, the Latin language had become that of the entire people, whose thought was impregnated with the Latin contribution. Neither the Germanic of the Alans, Vandals, Suevians, and Visigoths, nor Arabic, was ever to succeed in supplanting it, however great was, at any time from the eighth to the fourteenth centuries, the importance with which Arabic may have been invested. And from the first, in a study on the history of Muslim Spain, this fact must claim our attention.

Everywhere, in fact, where the conquests by the Arabs took place their language spread and became established. The instrument at once of a high culture and of all forms of the administration, it gave rise to a popular literature at the same time that it eliminated the language of the conquered. Neither Greek nor Pahlevi, nor Aramaic nor Coptic held out against it. Only Berber and Latin persisted; and the resurgence of a national language in Persia constitutes a phenomenon which is parallel to this survival only at certain points. It is not without interest to point out that in Muslim Spain recourse to the language of the people remained, at the time when colloquial literature was producing the *zajal*, a favored picturesque element, while the literature of popular tales perpetuated the use of the language of the Romans, in which as late as the ninth century rebels like Eulogius and Alvaro composed their works, exchanged their letters, addressed the Christian communities, and polemicized, for the edification of their coreligionists, against the religion of the Arab occupiers.

And immediately two other traits of the Latin heritage must strike our attention. One is, in the social sphere, the existence of an organization based above all on the existence of the great landed properties which extended and perpetuated the latifundia system. The second is, in the administrative sphere, the tendency to division, to decentralization, with all their consequences on the mentality of the citizens and on public spirit.

Though the Republic and the first period of the Empire had organized a state in Spain made up of two regions, as early as the time when Pliny gives us his picture of Spain it clearly appears that still another subdivision was tending to be introduced into this disposition. The Edict of Diocletian consecrated, as it were, this fragmentation, delimiting the provinces in a system which, in the time of Honorius, included Baetica, Lusitania, Galicia, Tarraconensis, the province of Carthagena, Tingitana, and the Balearic Islands.

This division had something organic in it which, corresponding to demographic and economic realities, was to weigh profoundly upon the future and which the Islamist has not the right to be unaware of. Baetica, especially, which was to include the provinces of Granada, Seville, and Cordova, formed, as it were, the heart and soul of Roman Spain—its most thickly inhabited region, and its most cultivated. It was distinguished, says Pliny, by its culture, by the beauty of its landscapes, and by its fertility. Its particular characteristics, like its geographical position, as well as the fact that the Roman administration extended the province of Spain to the African coast in Tingitana, lay down the lines of traditions which were predetermining in the history of Muslim Spain.

The Roman organization had sanctioned, if not favored, the

particularist tendencies of the ethnic groupings of Spain, upon which, for that matter, the orientation of the rivers and mountains conferred their characteristics in advance. Then Christianity, laboriously built up in Roman Spain, had its hour of powerful originality with the Priscillianist heresy, the echoes of which, in spite of three councils, a rescript of Honorius, and the execution of the founder of the sect, were to resound, as late as 563 in the midst of barbarian invasions, in the habits of thought which it had engendered and within which it propagated and deformed itself freely. When it is considered that in Ibn Masarra[2] Muslim Spain was to produce one of the most original and powerful thinkers of the Middle Ages, it is perhaps not out of place to recall here the orientation which Priscillian had given, through his doctrine, to the average thought of that country, which remained in any case so profoundly pagan in the spontaneous manifestations of its intense religiosity.[3]

The fundamental psychology of Spain seems to us, then, to have been indicated from the time of its origins. The work of the Sevillian Isidore,[4] which is to be placed chronologically at the end of the sixth and the beginning of the seventh century, with his concern to find a mystic sense and an intent even in the succession of the letters of the alphabet, his desire to be deeply versed in the language, his attitude as a passionate and partial historian, is a significant witness of this at the very eve of the invasion.

There is one element in the prehistory of Muslim Spain, however, which is not well attested in the Roman origins and which it will be necessary to look for in the bosom of the Visigothic world: that is, what can appear to us as a total unawareness as regards affiliations and fidelity. It is not a question of a spirit of treason or of perfidy but, it seems to us, of so passionate an attachment to personal causes that the feeling of obligations toward the group—family, religion, nation—is easily attenuated to the point of disappearing in the eyes of every adventurer, of every man of ambition or of action. No country, during the centuries which concern us, brought forth renegades in such great numbers as did the Andalusian countries. This fact is especially striking for one who, having studied the history of the east in Muslim times, is accustomed to behavior based on strict observance and rigorous fidelity—to such conformity that it could even be deduced, it would seem, from the affiliations alone. It is with the passing of the governor Julian into Mûsâ's camp, with the calculated desertion of the sons of Witiza, that the occupation of Spain by the Muslims began. And the preface was to be worthy of the book.

But it must not be supposed that we have to do here with a psychological trait due to some unknown characteristic inherent in the Spanish people or to an excessive individualism. The causes of this sort of passionate reaction, which seems to us hard to explain, must be sought in the incongruous structure, whose character was to be aggravated with time, of Spanish society in the Arabic period.

The Muslim invasion, at first, had not only met with a world in which dynastic rivalries and princely ambitions sowed division and oppositions. The military organization, the social stratification, the incidence in the latter of politicoreligious conceptions, made up just so many supplementary factors of contradiction and division. As early as the fifth century Paul Orosius and Salvian of Marseille, speaking of the Germanic invasions, note with mixed feelings that the population of Spain preferred to be free and poor under the barbarians rather than laden with taxes and oppressed in its everyday life under the Romans, and the situation was to be much more complex two centuries later. The unity which their Roman character had conferred upon the population had lost all significance in the face of Islâm, in view of the presence of Germanic sovereigns who had not been slow, there as in all Europe, to become a good deal more oppressive and more greedy than had been the imperial fisc. The maintenance, furthermore, of the rural system of the latifundia sufficed to preserve the heterogeneous character of the social structure, still more aggravated by the coexistence of the descendants of the former nobility, humbled or ruined, by the side of that which the occupiers had formed as they became, with time, the sovereign class in the state.

In another respect, the organization of religious *power*, the collaboration of the episcopacy with the Visigothic nobility and with the royalty, had made, of a spiritual authority which had once still been a liberating one, a factor of division and oppression. The shift in 587 of King Reccared and his Visigoths from Arianism to Catholicism emphasizes this union but takes away henceforth from the immense servile population all hope of finding a support in the church, fostered as it was by a political regime which the introduction of statute labor, a Germanic institution, had made more burdensome yet for the people on the land and all laborers. The consolidation of rule, moreover, which resulted from this drawing closer of the ties among the ruling classes—the traditional church and the new state—reinforced, finally, the practice of hereditary servitude on the soil.

The measures which the Church had induced the kings to take against the Jews had, from 616 on, introduced another element of disorder into a society already too much divided. Forced conversion, the unheard-of decision of the fourth Council of Toledo that the children of the Jews should be taken away from them to be brought up in the Christian religion, the stipulation of the sixth Council that no king could enter into his royal functions without having sworn to put in practice the edicts against "that abominable race"—all this had made of the important Jewish colonies, which had remained rich and vital in spite of everything, places of resistance and revolt.

King Egica, seventeen years before the Muslim invasion, had in collaboration with the seventeenth Council of Toledo denounced a plot of the Spanish Jews, who were said to have planned with their Berber coreligionists to make of Spain a Jewish state. The bishops, crediting this denunciation, or pretending to do so, had decided that the whole Jewish nation should be reduced to slavery—as was the immense majority of the people of the Christian countryside—and that their goods should become the property of that weak and violent majority which held power.

This power could maintain itself only in time of peace. From the day when, the system of conscription of the inhabitants of the realm coming into play,[5] it was necessary to arm the serfs, Christian or Jewish, or else call to arms the city people whom Germanic usage bound to their service as the peasant was bound to his serfdom, the society could not hold up. And when in addition the king was, like Roderick, a usurper, whom his own nobility abandoned, the conquest was secured in advance to any invader whatsoever.

But we must pay attention to the meaning of this term "conquest." If the Visigoths, the latest of the barbarian invaders from the north, had in the end become sovereigns, in the proper sense of the term, it was because they had been able gradually to eliminate the old aristocracy either by murder or by impoverishing it or by assimilating it; it was, besides, because the Church had preserved its *raison d'être* by giving them its support, which was reciprocated; and, finally, because there had been formed a homogeneous ruling class whose unity only a betrayal, like Roderick's conspiracy, could break.

But the Muslims, here as in many other places, did not conquer the country at first but received its submission and occupied it. And this was due both, as it happens, to the state of disunity of what they had found facing them and to the rules which they observed with regard to the peoples who submitted: due, that is, not to their laws—still in the course of elaboration in 711—but to their customs. Now in the case of Mûsâ and his associates these customs were, in the most artless way, those of warlike and pillaging nomads. Their reputation as such had preceded them so effectively that the nobles who plotted with the sons of Witiza to abandon Roderick on the field of battle, in order to bring about his discomfiture, had drawn their deductions from it and considered the coming of Ṭâriq as a pillaging expedition without any possible political consequences.[6] And in the eyes of this nobility, for which its privileges alone made up the whole law and which could not help confusing the notion of country with that of domain, the invasion of the Arabized Berbers was hardly a conquest. Tinged with Islâm, the companions of Ṭâriq and of Mûsâ were content to levy tribute, allowing their subjects to retain their laws and customs, among which was included retention by the traditional hierarchy of its position, provided there was no armed resistance. It was, at a distance, the history of the conquest of Egypt and of Syria repeating itself.

But it was an invasion carried out at an infinitely greater distance from the cradle of Islâm, with auxiliaries as its chief participants, namely, the Berbers, whom their individualism and the sense of their own continuing existence led only too readily to become a clearly individualized force, capable of forming a party over against the Arabs themselves.

The entry of these Islamized Berbers had been favored by the temporary and voluntary exile of Roderick's partisans and, especially, of a significant part of the ecclesiastical authorities, after the battle of Wâdî Bekka. But this accident was strictly limited in its effects: as is known, Spain immediately regained a moral armament among those very ones whose desertion and then collaboration had favored the designs of the new arrivals. It would not be too venturesome to maintain that, in the years that separated the coming of Mûsâ himself from the establishment at Cordova of the Umayyad ᶜAbd al-Raḥmân, it was precisely the rivalry among the Berbers, the Arabs of the conquest, and the Medinese party which not only gave the Andalusians the sense of their national existence[7] but, in addition, obliged them, in order to defend themselves in the economic field, to rediscover themselves and form themselves into a party.

It would be imprudent to try to measure exactly what part was played by the direct influence of Damascus, that is, of the Umayyad princes, upon Spain between the beginning of the conquest of that province and the establishment of ᶜAbd al-Raḥmân at Cordova. The fact that the defeated and exiled Medinese could find refuge there after the battle of al-Ḥarra seems to bear witness that the allegiance of that province to the caliphate of Damascus was scarcely profound.[8]

There had indeed occurred, between 724 and 742, the attempt of Hishâm to eliminate the near-schism of the Berbers, who, with Munûsa, had gone so far as to ally themselves against the Arabs with the Frankish governor of Aquitania. But if the governor appointed by Hishâm, ᶜAbd al-Raḥmân b. ᶜAbd Allâh, had eliminated Munûsa, he had also been the sorry hero of the so-called "Battle of Poitiers." And his defeat in Gaul had been followed shortly by the dreadful battle of Wâdî Nauᶜâm, which marks, with Maisara, the recovery of the Berber opposition.

It can be inferred from all this that the energetic reforms which, with ᶜAbd al-Malik and Walîd, had indicated in the east the way to assimilation of the tributary population had only the role of preface to the conquest of Spain, in that they helped to define, for the moment when this province was to be conquered, the notion of tribute in a clearer way than it had been formerly for Syria. But no more than the proscribed Medinese did Balj's Syrians, after the "Day of the Nobles," bring to Spain what would make for an assimilation to Islâm. The consequence of this was that at the time of his arrival in the country the fugitive Umayyad pretender received only, as the result of the first forty years of the occupation of Spain, a heritage burdened with the heavy mortgage which the already existent division of the population into parties had imposed on it.

The arrival of the Medinese and the Syrians, their need to arm themselves against the Berbers on the one hand and then against the Andalusians, and the stupid tribal and racial pride which they had carried into the conquered country had built between the native population and the Arab occupiers a wall which was to become still more solid with time and events. There is, in fact, a noticeable difference in the psychology of the relations of the Muslim sovereigns of the east with their subjects, on the one hand with the Spanish Arabs, and on the other with the Andalusians. This difference appears especially in the behavior of the occupiers toward the converts. Everywhere else, in fact, the converts, once having accepted the religion of the victors, found themselves treated as Muslims and equals, and the mention of their relation of clientage with one or the other great Arab clan became for them only one more form of dignity. In Spain, on the contrary, whether they were Kalbites or Qaisites, the Arabs never *adopted* the natives. And as late as the tenth century, at least, they gave to the terms *ᶜibâd* and *muwallad,* which they applied to the converts, all the pejorative sense which these terms could carry.

It is not astonishing then that, just as the clan rivalries among Arabs, Medinese or Syrian, were freely pursued under the eyes of the Andalusians and Berbers and even sometimes—exceptionally—in alliance with them, the national quarrels were settled by force of arms and without the least regard for religious considerations.

This inconstancy of Andalusian Islâm appeared continually in the history of the Umayyad caliphate, but there is hardly a time when it appeared more obviously than during the long struggle which Ibn Ḥafṣûn, the rebel in the hills of Bobastro at the very gates of Cordova, carried on at the end of the ninth century by turns against the caliph and against the Arab nobility. No episode of the history of Muslim Spain, perhaps, brings out more clearly the structure of this incongruous society. Ibn Ḥafṣûn, a convert—*muwallad,* to call him by the name which was that of his caste—belonged to that class of Spanish landholders which the Muslim invasion could not deliver from the difficult condition which the structure of the country, agricultural as well as economic, irresistibly imposed on them. This class was at the same time the one which was to represent, at least till the eleventh century, the Andalusian nation. It was eked out, in the cities, by the class of artisans and merchants, both Christian and Islamized.

When a leader was at their head, Andalusian Christians and Muslims marched together, either against the caliph or against the representatives of the "Arab nobility." Their poets then hurled defiance against those of the Qaisites and the Kalbites. It is not without interest to consider all the implications of a verse of the Andalusian poet, al-ᶜAblî,[9] who, even while adopting the touch of the traditional tribal poets and the provocative insolence customary with them, emphasized broadly all that separated the Islamized Andalusians from the descendants of the conquering Arabs.

This verse was composed on the occasion of a massacre perpetrated in 889, in the reign of the Umayyad ᶜAbd Allâh. It celebrates with savage delight inexpiable grievances, which appear as a holy revenge. "We have," says the Spaniard, "brought down their pride. Those they called *base rabble* have cut away the foundations of their power. *For how long have their dead, whom we threw in this well, awaited an avenger in vain?*" All the hatred which race can inspire, with the feeling of the traditional blood vengeance, resounds in turn in the retort which the poet, Saᶜîd b. Jûdî, made to this insolent verse after the so-called "Battle of Jaᶜd" several months later. The Spaniards are there called contemptuously "sons of whites," "sons of slaves," and find themselves opposing, in the classical manner, "a renowned leader, born of the purest blood of Nizâr, more than any other the support of his tribe."

And when shortly after the Arabs of Qais and of Kalb, united for a moment, had gotten the better of their adversaries, at the battle of Elvira, the same poet had above all this significant verse: ". . . sprung from a race of champions, *whose blood has never mixed* with that of a foreign race, he attacks his enemies impetuously, *as befits an Arab,* a Qaisite especially, and *he defends the true religion* against every miscreant."

The conversion of the Andalusians to Islâm mattered very little, as can be seen, in the eyes of the Arabs. Nor had it mattered much more in the face of the exclusive considerations of race and blood at the time of the frightful massacre of the Spaniards of Seville, of Carmona, and of the countryside, by the Banû Khaldûn and the Banû Ḥajjâj in association with the Arabs: ". . . sword in hand we have exterminated these *sons of slaves* . . . their number was prodigious before, we have made it trifling. . . . We, sons of Qaḥṭân, we number among our ancestors the princes who once reigned in the Yaman, but they, those slaves, have only slaves for ancestors."[10] The epic of Ibn Ḥafṣûn and then of his sons, aimed now against the Arab nobility and now against the caliph, and the struggle of cities such as Seville and Toledo, erected into veritable democratic republics led by an indigenous patriciate whose patronymics often recall their Christian if not Roman origin, were the most outstanding evidence of the character of the indomitable resistance which the old Andalusian people made against its conquerors till the beginning of the tenth century – and that, without failing to take part in the intellectual activities which the development of Islâm implied. In this respect it is useful to recall, in the reign of ᶜAbd al-Raḥmân II, the melancholy terms which Alvaro used,[11] at the time of Eulogius' outburst, to describe the taste of his people for Arabic letters: "My coreligionists [the Christians of Cordova]," he says in his *Indiculus luminosus,* "love to read the poems and tales of the Arabs. They study the writings of the Muslim theologians and philosophers not to refute them but *to acquire a correct and elegant Arabic diction.* All the young Christians who stand out by their talents know only the Arabic language and literature." (We are in the middle of the ninth century.) "They collect at great expense immense libraries of it, and declare everywhere that that literature is wonderful."

In the reign of ᶜAbd al-Raḥmân II, the splendor of which marks a first peak in Spanish civilization under the Muslims, two of the men who particularly helped to make it brilliant—the singer Ziryâb, disciple of Isḥâq al-Mauṣilî, and the royal physician, who bore the *nisba* al-Ḥarrânî—bear witness, by their origin, that Muslim Spain, thoroughly dismembered as it was, had in the general framework of Arabic civilization become a favorite province even of the east. For, if it is true that Spain was the farthest march of the Muslim world toward the west, it is also true that up to the end its thinkers, its philologians, its mystics, its theologians exchanged their ideas and doctrines with the thinkers of the east. After ᶜAbd al-Raḥmân this was, for that matter, to become accentuated. From the tenth century on, the current of men and ideas flowed uninterruptedly from the east to Spain, on the one hand, and from Spain to Egypt and Iraq, on the other.

It is in the tenth century that the Umayyad emirate of Spain attained its full power and all its glory, after the cruel period of humiliation and dismemberment accompanying the struggles and revolts of which that of Ibn Ḥafṣûn marked the climax. It is then (A.D. 929) that can be noted, in the general political system of Spain, the appearance of a certain number of formulas attesting outwardly to the deep evolution which had taken place in the course of this critical period, and no doubt as its consequence. In the first place, ᶜAbd al-Raḥmân III, who restored the unity of Spain, retook Toledo, once more in revolt, and extended the activity of his armies as far as Pamplona, absolutely ceased to count on the Arab immigrants, whose evil role and tenacious prejudices we have emphasized.

It was in Spain itself that he sought human resources, and it was also from Spain that he drew his economic resources. In this respect Andalusia, with its agriculture rich in traditions and resources, its long tradition in the realm of technique and commerce, offered him considerable means. It was then that the Mediterranean ports of Muslim Spain, Almeria especially, began the regular growth which was to make of them the natural middlemen for Marseille, Genoa, and Palermo, and which prepared for the expansion especially of the important western branch of the silk and gold commerce.

But though he protected the *muwallad*, sometimes with a bit of affectation, and extended this protection to the Christians and Jews, though he encouraged their industries and even favored the diversity of their thought, it is elsewhere, following the example of the caliphs of the east, that ᶜAbd al-Raḥmân went to seek his armed forces. Just as the eastern caliphs recruited Turks, the caliph of Cordova would recruit Slavs, that is, whatever could be found as soldiers in that corner of the world, possessing fair skin and eyes—Aquitanians, Aragonese, Burgundians, Franks, and perhaps even Slavonians and Normans—whom the attraction of a wage could put at the disposal of whoever paid well.

It will doubtless never be known what defeats and desertions this innovation cost the caliphate of Cordova, that emirate at the mercy of war, as can be seen right away at the battle of Simancas, in 939, where we witness still another downfall in the history of that Muslim Spain where for a long time no battle ever brought a decision, and where at every defeat we witness a happy reversal of fortunes, to the point of seeing victory desert a prince in the midst of his ascendancy.

Things continued this way as long as the great body of Islâm continued to exist, beyond Tangier, and as long as it preserved a relative cohesiveness. For it was there that the Muslim kingdom of Spain went to seek each time, even in opposition, new sustenance and strength—a regenerative sustenance, serving as a shock. For in that Andalusian Spain, perpetually in a state of anemia and in addition socially very old, the contribution of Tingitana, now become the Maghrib, underneath its armor of God's warrior is only the stimulating contribution of barbarism.

The taste for luxury, for softness, and an intellectual curiosity were the results of individualism and of a tradition of culture which had its twofold source in the permanent contacts with the east, both by land and by sea, at least as much as in the Roman tradition, which latter was constantly kept alive by contacts with that Languedoc which knew no retreat until after a pope and a king had united their forces to ruin it. When after the second Spanish Umayyad renaissance, under al-Ḥakam II al-Mustanṣir (A.D. 961–76), Spain saw flocking around the library of Cordova and around its twenty-seven schools architects and decorators, philosophers, authors, and poets, physicians, and the translator and commentators of Dioscorides, it was indeed time to be prepared for the direct economic consequences as well as for the remote social effects of this cultural growth and this diffusion of knowledge.

The weakness of the state then made its appearance, with its essential characteristics: encumbered finances and rivalry between the mercenary army—repository of the material power and of force—

and the administration, within which this rivalry produced, at last, unity among the Arabs, the old Andalusians, and the Berbers, which last had been permanent auxiliaries in the past and were to be the final hope in the future.

As is known, Spain owed its restoration, at that moment, to the prime minister of the phantom caliph Hishâm II, the Berber Ibn Abî ᶜÂmir, the "Great Almanzor" of the Western chronicles. The memory of his military activity, which involved the taking of Barcelona (A.D. 985) and of Santiago de Compostela and the total ruin of that already famous sanctuary, is on the same footing with the destruction of the books of the profane sciences and philosophy preserved in the library of ᶜAbd al-Raḥmân III. That was a necessary satisfaction given to the men of law and the jurists, Moroccans and Berbers when not sprung from the common people, whose support was indispensable to the prince in order to retain Muslim public opinion—the only basis, yet always threatened, of his power in the face of the faltering or rebellious Slav mercenaries. This auto-da-fé beyond the call of duty harmed only an elite, and no head of state has ever hesitated to strike a blow at intelligence to make sure of the support of numbers, indispensable to his very continuance in power.

It was at most a relative permanence, for that matter: al-Manṣûr died in 1002; his brother and successor was executed in 1009! Then took place for half a century the great Berber-Slav *fitna*, during which civilization experienced a time of remarkable luster both in the oligarchic republics—Cordova or Seville—and in the little kingdoms of the *reyes de taifas*. It must be said that there were no longer great armies to support, that the level of expenses was in keeping with possible income, and that the situation in the neighboring Christian principalities, the only rivals and the only possible danger, corresponded, in division and impotence, to the state of the Muslim emirates.

The principal form of power beyond Spain, for that matter more economic than military, was at this time the activity of the ports—Málaga, Almeria, Denia. The latter, which was put into dangerous prominence by its geographical position at the farthest point of what was organically the zone of expansion of Spanish Islâm,[12] then gained enough importance so that Pope Alexander II undertook to lead, by land, a veritable Crusade against it (A.D. 1063). Twenty years later, Saragossa and Toledo were threatened. It was again time to appeal to the Berbers.

Once again the cycle which constitutes the history of Muslim

Spain ran its course. Yûsuf b. Tâshfîn, the Almoravid prince, was called on for help by one party in a Spain once more divided. Once in the country, he stayed there as conqueror, extended his influence in this mountainous land mass that devours armies, and established his dynasty there. The latter, which had established itself at first in a spirit of sobriety and good will, in the guise of the popular Muslim, as much opposed as possible to subtleties of intelligence—and thereby assured of receiving the support of the *fuqahâ*ᵓ—found its rigorism crumbling away, the purity of its doctrine being perverted, and the morals of its adherents corrupted at the penetrating contact with this refined civilization.

This time it was no longer just the books of profane sciences and philosophy which were to be burned. Rigorous, formalistic Muslims like Ibn Ḥazm and enemies of free thought and lay knowledge like al-Ghazzâlî also had their books delivered to the purifying flames. This calls for certain observations.

The Berbers of Yûsuf b. Tâshfîn caused religious simpleness and an intellectually egalitarian rigorism to prevail, inspired by their revolutionary religiosity, their attachment to their spiritual guides, and their spontaneous distrust of whatever could derogate from it. But they were not the first in Spain to commit the pious ravages of their dull-witted ignorance. Ibn Ḥazm's career, so distressing in many ways, bears witness to this. It is also, and especially for us, an example of the feeling of opposition which sprang up spontaneously from the Andalusian milieu in the face of spiritual oppression. Ibn Ḥazm can be accepted as a well-known representative of the Andalusian milieu: of Spanish origin, he belonged to the aristocracy of Umayyad Spain, that of the caliphate of Cordova. Son of a high personage, he passed his youth on the family estates at Manta Lishâm. In 1013 the Berbers bore into power, for the second time, Sulaimân al-Mustaᶜîn, against Hishâm II, whom the Slav party had just caused to taste anew the anxieties of the throne. In the course of the troubles which accompanied this change the prince, perhaps, lost his life, but Cordova was given over to pillage. The books of Ibn Ḥazm and the house of his father underwent the common fate. It was in the far north of the caliphate, then, at Jativa, far from the Berbers in the midst of a region dominated by the "Slavs," that the poet sought refuge, as he was to do again in 1027 when, after having been minister twice and having twice been in prison, he gave himself a little relaxation before becoming, under Hishâm al-Muᶜtadd, minister for the last time.

It was there at Jativa that, dipping into his memories as a young poet, he composed, in the face of the "Shepherds" whose shadow was extending, slowly as yet, over his country, a curious pamphlet: the *Ṭauq al-Ḥamâma.* He presents it as the work of a pious Muslim, an abstract book, almost mystical in spots, furiously passionate in others, in which he illuminates with chosen anecdotes the various theses he upholds on love. The order of the chapters and their import make it a treatise of courtly love,[13] the purity of which is, however, curiously spattered by the scandalous tales which the author sprinkles through it. This incongruity awkwardly jolts the reader taken with the preface and what it leads him to expect from the book.

But we need only reflect on the conditions in which men then found themselves—and the author's contemporaries, members of his class and his caste, could not think of anything else in that year when the way was being prepared for the prince to come to power in whom were centered the last hopes of the Umayyad party—to understand that the ill-assorted tales, as well as the inappropriate reflections, were to take on a very different meaning for the reader.

We need only leaf through the book. Suddenly this work, which makes itself out to be harmlessly conformist, strikes us by the number and the frequency of its attacks upon the Berbers. To begin with, it paints them from life—as plunderers and murderers: Ibn Ḥazm recalls the taking and the pillage of Cordova,[14] of his own palace and that of his friend ᶜAbd Allâh al-Tamîmî, an accomplished young man.[15] And when the reader has become indignant at these undeserved misfortunes, the author obligingly recalls the injustices of which he was the victim after the assassination of the Umayyad prince,[16] perpetrated "with the complicity of all the adventurers and all the rebels from every corner of Andalusia."

In contrast to the noble victims, he depicts for us the devout Berbers, coarse or clumsily tricky, or their allies, those popular *faqîhs* whose wiles are on the level of the *Thousand and One Nights:* they make a vow of *tauba* (pious and repentant return to God), provided they are allowed to fornicate at leisure when they want to.[17] And so that no one can miss it, Ibn Ḥazm dwells on the matter and tells with many details the story of the *faqîh* fallen into debauchery,[18] to match which he soon after tells of the outrageous adventure of the pious women who "on their return from the pilgrimage, having already renounced the world . . . pious and zealous in their devotions . . ." indulge, without resistance but not without hypocrisy, their animal inclinations.[19] All these tales, if looked at closely, are ranged about a single sentence one might say, which contrasts the Andalusian aristocrat, the educated, the cultivated, man to the fanatical brutes upon whom power had then devolved: "... a soul which rejects amusements and pleasures through wisdom, in obedience to God Most High, or else *to gain consideration in this world, and become famous as an ascetic....*"[20]

How should the educated reader, the intelligent Andalusian, have failed to recognize immediately in these hypocrites greedy of consideration the Berberizing *faqîhs?* In contrast to all that, all the delicacy, the chastity, the refinement are ascribed to laymen,[21] the Andalusian nobles[22] and the descendants or members of the defunct Umayyad dynasty.[23] If it is still in doubt that this book is of the nature of a political pamphlet—it seems we do not possess it in its complete form—the bitter ending should be reread: "I know that *my fanatical adversaries* will reproach me for having written such a book, and will say he has violated his principles and turned aside from his course.... I am no partisan of hypocrisy and do not go in for foreign piety (*lâ ansuku niskan aʿjamiyyan*). When one has fulfilled the obligatory religious duties, when one avoids transgressing the divine prohibitions, when one does not forget kindness in his relations with his neighbor, one can be called a good man. And may I be left in peace as regards the rest. God suffices me."[24]

With the reign of the Almoravids—a half-century after Ibn Tâshfîn, just time enough to allow their revolutionary faith and freshness to be corrupted—something found a place in the sensibility of Muslim Spain which had remained foreign to it up till then. Religious fervor, as we have seen, had always been rather slight there, to the point of not making felt what is the first effect of a common affiliation: the brotherhood of the faithful. Neither had the tragic struggles which the east had seen over the question of the imamate ever troubled the religious life of this country. These problems were foreign to Spain. And, if something can be inferred from a symptom which seems rather slight, it is remarkable that Spain, alone in all classical Islâm, had a popular romance of Alexander-Dhû al-Qarnain, whereas everywhere else in Arabic literature the story of the conqueror-prophet became a reserved domain and found its place in the *qiṣaṣ al-anbiyâʾ*, that supplementary literature of piety.

The tradition of such an attitude as regards the faith, and the sentence with which Ibn Ḥazm ends his book, would bear witness in any people to a humanistic aspiration, to a detachment to which, for that matter, the freedom of mind, carried sometimes to obliviousness, among the princes and their associates bears witness. Now it is into this country that the Kabyle "Shepherds," crossed with Senegal Negroes, came to contribute their valor against the Christians of the north who were preparing an assault upon Andalusia—valor which was the direct result of their religious sincerity, of their fanaticism, which fell in with the fanaticism, swelled with the long rancor of a sad history, which the common people, those eternal victims of the Andalusian landholders and the Arab nobles, could feel.

The arrival of the Berber liberators, and their rigorism, marked a time of sudden arrest in the history of Spanish thought. There were fifty years of struggle, when the object of thought left the sphere of gratuitousness to take on its essential, functional aspect.[25] The irritation of a learned and pious man before the summary dogmatism of the Almoravids, which reduced the realm of juridical knowledge to the *furûᶜ*, proscribed inquiry in dogmatic matters and adopted altogether an anti-intellectual attitude,[26] engendered the energetic doctrinal reaction of the Almohads, which found in the fiscal oppression of the conquerors a natural support among the formerly privileged classes of the population. And Spain, which in happy times had produced—at the start of the tenth century, under ᶜAbd al-Raḥmân III—the active teaching of Ibn Masarra, reacted once more in an imposing manner.[27]

Yûsuf b. Tâshfîn died in 1107. In his own reign and under his immediate successors there flourished, at Seville and Granada, Ibn Bâjja; at Granada and then in Morocco, Ibn Ṭufail; and finally, under the Almohads, the greatest of the Arab philosophers, the one who was able to find a place in the universal history of thought, Averroes. The intellectual vigor of that country, which could no longer hope to gain liberty by itself, asserted itself then. But the more the mind found scope for itself there, and the higher the elite carried its reflections, the more the people were alienated from it and drew apart from them.

After Ibn Ḥazm (d. 1064), who lets us sense what Andalusian refinement had conceived and put in order in the field of amorous mystique and of courtly refinement of sentiment—the love of great hearts and distinguished persons—Ibn Quzmân, a lowborn fellow, will describe for us what might be called uncourtly love—gross, cynical, and deliberately offensive. Here are adventures which foreshadow a Villon, and the same world besides. For the laudatory poetry addressed to great lords by the Arabic poets infatuated with classicism and fine language, Ibn Quzmân substitutes pieces in a paradoxically composite language addressed to bourgeois—and not always very rich ones it seems. The great lady for whom one can die of love is now only a crafty vulgar woman, and the sentiments she inspires are appropriate to her. When one thinks what the glory of Ibn Ḥazm was to be a half-century after his death, at a time which in all respects marked his revenge, it seems impossible, in the face of this contrast, to fail to think that there is in this naughty Ibn Quzmân an intention to offend, rising not out of popular theological circles with regard to an aristocracy thought to be lax, but out of popular circles in which moral laxity was the rule, as a hateful caricature.

As the adventures of the Spanish nation unfolded, new factors intervened to guide them. The formation of an intellectual proletariat played its role in this. And, as later in the fifteenth century in Paris, we find the great schools at Cordova and Granada casting into society, among the multitude of students, a number of mediocre and limited theologians whom hunger carried into adventures, and a smaller number, but doubtless not negligible, of dubious men of letters, of whom Ibn Quzmân is only an example. Thus knowledge itself contributed its share to the dissension in this world in the course of decline. It was a slow decline doubtless, but slow only in appearance. Spain under the Almohads was no more than a land protected by a foreign power, as it had been under the Almoravids. But the actions of those in Morocco who set about carving out principalities from the remains of the empire of a moment, that of the Almohads, ended by depriving Spain of that security which it had received from outside.

The Almohads had not yet been expelled from Spain, the emirate of Granada was not yet established, when an Andalusian writer provides us with the last testimony of the rivalry which for centuries had set the Spaniards and their invaders against each other. The imminence of the catastrophe still did not put an end to it. This testimony is the *Risâla* of al-Shaqundî. And it is in some ways the testament of a culture.[28]

This work, a veritable repertory of the glories of Andalusian literature, contrasts the merits of Spain, in the realm of mind and manners, to those of the Berbers. The translators of this epistle have already emphasized its general characteristics. One of them has seen in it a composition inspired by the ethic of the *mufâkhara,* or contest for pre-eminence. If we will keep in mind what has been said in the preceding pages, we will find much more in it than a game conformable to the traditions of the desert Arabs, heightened with the prestige of erudition. As against the Almohads the Andalusians had several reasons to feel humiliated and offended: subject to foreigners, the Almoravid Berbers, it was to other foreigners, the Almohad Berbers, that they owed their liberation. But this liberation had not, for all that, restored to Muslim Spain the mental picture which the Andalusians had of their country: in the cities of Spain as well as in the countryside the Almohads and their clients reigned and could say, as al-Shaqundî mentions at the start, "Kingship and merit come only from the Maghrib."[29]

These considerations were complicated by the fact that the Almohads, in Spain as in Morocco, could justly plume themselves on being superior to the picture which the Almoravids had formerly given of the Berbers, they whom it had even been possible to accuse of *tashbîh*.[30] Religiously rigorous, educated, and austere, and, in addition, occupying the respectable position of Maecenases—in particular for al-Shaqundî[31]—it was a delicate matter for him to attack them. Accordingly it is to the vaguer theme of the pre-eminence of the Maghrib with reference to the men whom the Almoravids had imposed upon Spain, who were still remembered, that the polemicist limited his strokes. Within these limits he could talk freely enough: the Almoravids, those stupid Berbers, had been the enemies of the Almohads also. And where about a century and a half earlier Ibn Ḥazm had attacked the liberators, become the oppressors, of his country, by treating of an apparently harmless subject, al-Shaqundî, taking up the even more classical theme of literary pre-eminence, indulged in the same type of attack against the very race of the new liberators and protectors of his country, become, if not oppressors, at least very much in the way.

Al-Shaqundî's *Risâla*, by its more direct manner, bears witness to the difference. And it is the same ideas that recur. The Andalusians do not lack any of the virtues on which the Berbers plume themselves: if the Almohads are pious, the Umayyads and the ᶜÂmirids, those Andalusian princes—all the *fitnas* are henceforth forgotten—were no less so; they respected knowledge and pious men, but their generosity gave them an overwhelming superiority over the formalistic niggardliness of the men of law and of religion.[32] The examples which our author cites, though they go back to the ninth century, would only the more readily incite informed people to observe the parallelism with the twelfth century, when the tyranny of the contemporary *faqîhs* and their narrowness of mind made the gracefulness and vivacity of the Andalusians stand out all the more.

To better make his meaning clear, the author, after his praise of the *reyes de taifas,* cruelly ridicules Yûsuf b. Tâshfîn, the most glorious of the Almoravids.[33] And it is not by accident, no doubt, that he insists on the orthodoxy and the fidelity of these very kings, children of cultivated, free, and intellectual Spain, in whom nothing —except their levity and their vanity, but this is a truth unavailable to al-Shaqundî—merited the miserable fate which befell them. In his sympathy al-Shaqundî is not satisfied to quote Ibn Ḥazm; he borrows from him, in addition, the theme of the affected chastity to find which he goes to one of those Umayyad court poets[34] who were proscribed and utterly out of place in the opinion which ruled under the virtuous Almoravids, representatives of the spirit which was no doubt the most hated in the history of all Spain. And of course, as in Ibn Ḥazm, this affected chastity, the refinement of a decadent society, is subtly contrasted to the scarcely defensible erotic passion of a pious *qâḍî* of the very time of ʿAbd al-Muʾmin.[35]

Since this is not enough for his aggressive spirit, the polemicist passes, with an almost tragic insistence, from allusion to direct insult by quoting the verses of the poet al-Yakkî: "The Almoravid is miserly with his gifts, but prodigal with his women. He carries on his face the trace of everything ugly that happens to him; hence he veils himself with the *lithâm.*" One can feel in the background all his hostility against the Moroccans—those whom he outrages openly and those whom their doctrinal position, like their acts, leads to listen to these outrages—not without their suspecting that they might take it personally. For if the Almohads felt themselves to be and wanted to be very different from the Almoravids, and indeed were historically their opponents, the national feeling of the Spaniards ranged both within the same nation, and in the same category of human values.

The whole collection, designed to celebrate the literary glory of al-Andalus, is of course not devoted only to a polemic against the Berbers. There is to be found in it, as in a testamentary epitome, a statement of all that the Andalusians could find in themselves in the way of merits, or could consider such. There are in it claims which make us smile, but which upon reflection are to be ascribed to a certain audacity of purpose, such as that which consists in claiming as a title to fame for Spain, that lighthearted and trifling Umayyad

Spain, that it gave the Maghrib all the musical instruments which the latter knew.

Al-Shaqundî does not have the reasons which we might suppose for dissimulating or passing over in silence what we might consider a blemish. He is not ashamed of the levity and trifling; on the contrary, in the face of the dismal Berber puritanism he seems to make a parade of it. Nothing bothers him: neither the daring quotations of the erotic verses of Abû al-Ḥasan b. Bassâm,[36] nor the mention of the dancing girl–jugglers of Jaen,[37] nor even the most daring descriptions, when he celebrates the valley of the Guadalquivir with the words, "The valley of the Guadalquivir is favorable to happiness because it does not lack any joy. No musical instrument is disapproved there, nor the use of wine. Those of the governors of Seville, *zealous partisans of religion*, who wanted to put an end to these ways of living could not suppress them. The Sevillans have the liveliest wit, and are the most naturally inclined to tell racy anecdotes, the most given to joking, even joined to the grossest insults. They are used to this, which has become a custom among them, to the point that those of them who are not constantly given to it and do not utter curses are detested by them and considered dull-witted."[38]

We will not insist on the quotations he makes, as an aesthete, of love poetry, of which the least one can say is that it must have curiously scandalized the religious and rigorous Berbers.[39] Al-Shaqundî for that matter is so thoroughly the son of his time and of his people that he emphasizes from the beginning of his epistle, and as a kind of glory, even of honor for his people, their incapacity on any level whatever to understand the needs and the conditions of existence of a unified empire, as well as their taste for appreciating much more the splendor of a reign, and the verses of a poet celebrating the generosity, or the prodigality, of a prince, than what could make for the durability or even the continued existence of the empire.[40] It is appropriate to conclude with this trait.

The store of ideas which Islâm had brought with it was very slight. It had to develop subsequently with the ideological contribution of the lands where it prospered. But these contributions came from former elites which political and still more often economic reasons had rallied to the party, and sometimes to the religion, of the conquerors, and whose assimilation took place only gradually. For a long time, even in the east near the cradle of Islâm, the ideas of these elites, as much in their substance, foreign to both the language and the usages of Islâm, as in the form which they finally took in Islâm, remained more secular than religious. And when the development of the intellectual riches of the conquered peoples had become an Islamic matter, the Arab world properly so-called long felt itself a poor relation before the progress of philosophy and the sciences.[41] What gave Islâm, from the ninth to the eleventh centuries, a marvelously increased power was the popular pressure in the realms of dogma and of opinion, that which set in motion the Ḥanbalîs and the Ashᶜarites, and that of the popular Ṣûfîs, commanding respect from intelligence as early as the reign of Maᵓmûn, which furnished Ghazzâlî with the means of eliminating at last the philosophical and humanistic tendency which was still shining in the twelfth century in eastern Islâm.

In Spain the more or less Romanized Gothic people whom the Muslims found before them at their arrival did not have the culture of the Syrians or of the Chaldeans. Those first conquerors, moreover, had nothing to contribute in exchange for the subjection which they imposed. Immediately the antagonisms showed themselves on the only possible level, that of the most elementary emotional hostilities, which the most barbarous men feel: hostilities of language and race. Religion, as we have seen, was not to play any role except by fits and starts and in a generally secondary way. Assimilation to Islâm was essential neither to the conquered Spaniards nor to their conquerors.

The persistence through the centuries of the Romance language and habits of mind did not allow any form of assimilation before the arrival of the Umayyads. These, moreover, bringing with them the Syrian tradition from before the great creative period of the Arabic theology—which was to be the work of the Abbasids—likewise could not found a popular tradition of strict observance nor inspire in their subjects that simple, unquestioning faith which makes it possible to have armies, to lead crowds along, and to carry out persecutions against the heterodox by sublimating rivalries and making use of the hatreds and envy of the humiliated classes of the people, which find a certain dignity in claims made in the name of the faith and the law.

The "libraries in the gardens" peculiar to Umayyad and ᶜÂmirid Spain were not favorable to long theological or even philosophical meditations. The example of Ibn Masarra, going to found a hermitage for his disciples and himself far from the city, is significant in this connection. These gardens were almost exclusively the preferred resorts of the poets. It is interesting to notice in passing that when the Andalusian elite gave birth to a great theologian, Ibn Ḥazm, he showed himself as far as possible an opponent of the subtleties of the eastern theologians, and that even in the spirit of the doctrine he followed; but he remained a great stylist after having been a poet. It is no less worthy of notice that Spanish Islâm left traces only in the poetic vision, even the modern one, of the lands it occupied.

When the Almoravids invaded Muslim Spain and caused the Christians to withdraw for three centuries, they destroyed these libraries. This act marked for the first time the passing of religion to the foreground in the concerns of Spain. But this act was that of the foreign Caliban, an act which challenged the vigilant and fervent spirit of an immediately and openly rebellious people. The caricature of greatness and the gross laxness of the last Almoravids only gained for them still more scorn on the part of the Andalusians, who had for the first time after the passing of the ᶜÂmirid dynasty grasped the meaning of their unity. The effort of the Almohads, in the time that followed, was henceforth fruitless. The Spaniards, who had at last assimilated the Arabs, thenceforth felt as a result only the more lively aversion to the liberators from across the sea. And their local or personal rivalries, subtly used, offered too many temptations to these proud men, traditionally infatuated with particularism. Islâm lost in the end then, in Spain, a match which it had never begun to win.

NOTES

1. Pauly-Wissowa, *Realencyclopädie der classischen Altertumswissenschaft* (1894 ff.), Vol. VIII, partic. cols. 2038–43.

2. M. Asín Palacios, *Encyclopaedia of Islâm, Supplement* (French ed., pp. 99–101).

3. It will be remembered, for example, that in the second half of the sixth century Martin of Braccara, in the northwest of Spain it is true, was combating paganism (*de correctione rusticorum*) while he was multiplying his moral warnings and teachings for the Christians of the cities (*formula vitae honestae*). Cf. Pierre C. de Labriolle, *Histoire de la littérature latine chrétienne* (Paris, 1920), p. 432.

4. Cf. Pauly-Wissowa, *Realencyclopädie*, Vol. IX, cols. 2069–80.

5. R. Dozy, *Histoire des Musulmans d'Espagne*, revised by E. Lévi-Provençal (Leiden, 1932), I, 265–66 and 267.

6. *Ibid.*, pp. 272–74; and esp. his *Recherches sur l'histoire et la littérature d'Espagne pendant le Moyen-Âge* (3d ed.; Leiden, 1881), I, 1–83.

7. As in the east the rivalries among Muslim Arab parties had brought forth among the Christian Arabs, on the one hand, and the Christians of the cities, on the other, the sense of their distinctiveness over against the conquerors and had engendered a reaction, whose chief argument lay in points of language, custom, and institutions, which was led from 730 on by a man such as George of Boṣra, Bishop

of the Arabs (cf. *Actes du XXe Congrès des Orientalistes, Bruxelles, 5–10 septembre 1938* [Louvain, 1940], p. 326).

8. It was this way for a long time with the whole of the Maghrib. When Idrîs created his independent state in Morocco, Hârûn al-Rashîd thought of sending an army to put him down, but "when he thought about the distance and the obstacles which separated the east from the west, and the lack of support which the armies of Iraq would find in going to Sûs . . . he gave up that project" (Ibn Abî Zâr, *Rauḍat al-Qirṭâs,* in E. Lévi-Provençal, *Extraits des historiens du Maroc* [Paris, 1948], p. 18).

9. Dozy, *Histoire des Musulmans d'Espagne,* II, 25.

10. *Ibid.,* II, 52.

11. *Ibid.,* I, 317 ff. Eulogius of Cordova, sprung from an old Christian family, led the life of a novice in the convent of St. Zoilos, where he studied the Christian sources and the lives of the saints. Then he entered the monastery of Cutelar, where he was influenced by the priest Spera-in-Deo, author of a Latin refutation of Islâm. Eulogius, going back into the world, was to be found everywhere in the Christian circles of Cordova, himself composing a polemic which insulted the Prophet. He even obtained in Muslim circles the conversion of a girl to Christianity. The little group that surrounded him strained their wits to become martyrs. He himself, before undergoing the fate which he desired, found the time to write a curious *Apology for the Martyrs,* which reveals to us that these extremist demonstrations shocked and disturbed the Spanish Christians themselves. He died in 859. His friend, Alvaro, whom he had known at Cutelar, wrote his biography. Cf. *Patrologia Latina* (Paris, 1852), Vol. CXV, cols. 731–870.

12. That is, that in which the continuity and density of the occupation had made possible the continuity of the exchanges and influences which give unity to a civilization.

13. *Al-ḥubb al-ᶜudhrî,* which had already been extolled by Ibn Dâwûd al-Iṣfahânî in his *Kitâb al-Zahrâ* and celebrated in Spain itself by the courtier poet, Abû ᶜUmar al-Farrâj (d. 976), under al-Ḥakam II (cf. E. García Gomez, *Al-Šaqundî: Elogio del Islâm español* [Madrid, 1934], p. 63, n. 80).

14. L. Bercher, *Le Collier du pigeon* (Algiers, 1949), pp. 272–73.

15. *Ibid.,* pp. 304–5.

16. *Ibid.,* pp. 306–7. See also, on the sorrows of the time, the touching story, pp. 280–85, of a beautiful and good girl and of the noble family whose fate she shares, suffering the loss of her beauty in the hard tasks of poverty.

17. *Ibid.,* pp. 320–21.

18. *Ibid.,* pp. 334–38.

19. *Ibid.,* pp. 344–45.

20. *Ibid.,* pp. 272–73.

21. *Ibid.,* pp. 200–201.

22. *Ibid.,* pp. 268–69, 268–71, 312–15.

23. *Ibid.,* pp. 378–79.

24. Ibn Ḥazm took elsewhere a militant position, now in the defense of the fundamental worth of his compatriots (*Kitâb Faḍl al-Andalus*), now against the doctrinal position of the Almoravids in point of law (*Masâʾil uṣûl al- fiqh* and *Kitâb al-uṣûl wa al-furûᶜ min qaul al-aʾimma*).

25. That is, we witness at first the departure in some numbers of the scholars

for the east, and those who do not become secretaries or *faqîhs* are reduced to the rank of flatterers with the dangers which accompany this. A very interesting example is that of Abû Naṣr al-Fatḥ b. Khâqân al-Qaisî (C. Brockelmann, *Geschichte der arabischen Litteratur, Supplement* [Leiden, 1937–42], I, 339).

26. *Handwörterbuch des Islam*, ed. A. J. Wensinck and J. H. Kramer (Leiden, 1941), p. 134, col. 2, and *Encyclopaedia of Islâm, s.v.* "Almoravids," "Almohads."

27. Brockelmann, *GAL Suppl.*, I, 378–79, and above, p. 209.

28. Cf. Maqqarî, *Nafḥ al-Ṭîb*, II, 126. Translation, with introduction and notes, in Gomez, *op. cit.* Cf. also A. Luya, "La Risâla d'al-Šaqundî," *Hesperis*, XXII, No. 2 (1936), 133–34.

29. Luya, *op. cit.*, p. 143.

30. *Encyclopaedia of Islâm, s.v.* "Almohads."

31. See the introduction to the translation of the *Risâla*, *Hesperis*, XXII (1936), Fasc. II, 143.

32. Luya, *op. cit.*, p. 169; Gomez, *op. cit.*, pp. 101–3.

33. Luya, *op. cit.*, p. 148; Gomez, *op. cit.*, p. 54.

34. Luya, *op. cit.*, p. 152; Gomez (who calls in the poet Abû ʿUmar b. Faraj), *op. cit.*, p. 63.

35. Luya, *op. cit.*, p. 164; Gomez, *op. cit.*, pp. 63–64.

36. Luya, *op. cit.*, pp. 158–60; Gomez, *op. cit.*, pp. 76–78.

37. Luya, *op. cit.*, p. 172; Gomez, *op. cit.*, p. 107.

38. Luya, *op. cit.*, p. 167; Gomez, *op. cit.*, p. 96.

39. Luya, *op. cit.*, pp. 163, 172–73; Gomez, *op. cit.*, pp. 87, 109–10.

40. Luya, *op. cit.*, pp. 145–46; Gomez, *op. cit.*, pp. 48, 49–50.

41. And this can have played a role in the origin of the defeat of humanism in Islâm.

NORTH AFRICA: RIGORISM AND BEWILDERMENT

ROGER LE TOURNEAU

BEFORE studying what Maghribî Islâm is today, it appears indispensable to suggest in very broad strokes a few essential facts of its historical development, because in this very conservative country the past not only explains but often closely controls the present.

Of the establishment of the Muslim religion in North Africa, it must be confessed that we know almost nothing. The first conversions of the inhabitants cannot have been prior to the foundation of Kairouan (Qairawân) by ᶜUqba b. Nâfîᶜ, the generally accepted date of which is A.D. 670. The chroniclers assert, on the other hand, that in 711, when the Muslim troops left for the conquest of Spain, the Islamization of the Maghrib was practically completed; in fact, the Berber contingents, furnished especially by the tribes of northern Morocco, formed a good part of the army of Ṭâriq b. Ziyâd, and then even of Mûsâ b. Nuṣair himself. We also know that, up till the nomination of Mûsâ b. Nuṣair to the government of Ifrîqiya, the resistance of the Berbers to the Muslim conquest was very vigorous. The date of Mûsâ's nomination is controverted: at the two extremes, some place it in 698, others in 705 or 706; if it is accepted that Mûsâ took over his command right at the start of the eighth century, it must have been in barely ten years that he made Islâm triumphant in the whole Maghrib. Now we know exactly nothing about this crucial period, or about the procedures which Mûsâ followed to obtain these massive conversions, or about the doctrinal instruction which was given to the new converts. We may nevertheless suppose as entirely probable that the new believers of the tribes were very ill instructed in their new religion: there would have to have been a veritable army of specialized missionaries to preach the doctrine appropriately, and these missionaries would have had to speak Berber and get themselves accepted by the tribes—just so many practically insurmountable difficulties. It was a different matter in the urban centers created or revived by the Muslim occupiers; there they were in some number and could easily indoctrinate the local population. Thus, from the time of the appearance of Islâm in North Africa, we see it dividing into branches completely distinct from each other—the Islâm of the cities and that of the tribes.

The first is hardly to be distinguished from the Islâm practiced in the east. It was drawn from a good source, since it was often spread originally, if not by the companions of the Prophet themselves, at least by their "followers." Nevertheless, a few superstitions certainly remained, especially in the less-educated urban circles. By reason of circumstances it was the Mâlikî school which soon took root in North Africa, and it very soon produced illustrious masters such as the famous *qâḍî* Suḥnûn, one of the most brilliant doctors of the Mâlikî school as a whole. The light soon went out from Kairouan to illuminate other Muslim cities of the Maghrib; the Mosque of the Olive at Tunis was founded in the first half of the eighth century and probably very quickly became an important center of study. It is not to be doubted that these hearthfires of Muslim learning sent out their rays round about and that the neighboring tribes underwent their influence, but for a long time the cities were few; until the foundation of Fez, one can hardly find any to mention in Morocco except Tangier and Ceuta, which were quite untypical, and Walîlâ, the ancient Volubilis, a Berber hamlet rather than a real city, if one is to believe the *Rawḍ al-Qirṭâs;* in the present Algeria between Tlemcen, still very unpretentious, and Constantine there was an almost completely empty space. Ashîr, Médéa, Miliana, and Algiers were not to be born or reborn till the second half of the tenth century, under the impulse of the Zîrids; the Qalʿa of the Banû Ḥammâd was not to rise from the earth till the beginning of the eleventh century. Only Ifrîqiya had a relatively great urban density. Later, when the cities became more numerous, the habits had been established and the tribes continued to live apart, in the religious sphere as elsewhere.

It is not surprising, then, that the Islâm of the tribes was very little influenced by the Islâm of the cities and that it presented very different characteristics. Having little learning, it was for long very unstable: the Khârijite doctrine was early to take the place of Sunnism in a large part of North Africa; later, Shîʿism, with the missionary Abû ʿAbd Allâh, was to spring up in the confederation of the Kutâma, north of Sétif; in Morocco, as early as the middle of the eighth century, a Berber deformation of the Muslim religion, on which we are imperfectly informed, was to spread through the whole of the important confederation of the Barghawâṭa, between the Bû Ragrag and the Umm al-Rabîʿ. It is certain, moreover, that very strong traces of the old Berber beliefs persisted alongside of or, rather, under the cover of a not very particular Islâm, as they had persisted in the time when the Maghrib was in part Christian. Unfortunately, we are reduced to conjectures on this point as on many others, for the Muslim authors do not broach these subjects, which they consider improper. We do not know, therefore, exactly what these beliefs were or to what degree they were influenced by the Muslim religion. Nevertheless, on the basis of what exists at present, it can be affirmed that there has been no lack of superstitions since the beginnings of Islâm in the Maghrib.

What also deserves to be noted is that, however uncertain, however impure it may be, this Islâm of the tribes took root immediately. It is within the framework of the Muslim religion that all the various forms of belief which have just been mentioned appeared: Shîʿism and Khârijism were Muslim—there is no need to prove it—and even the religion of the Barghawâṭa, so far as we know it, was only a counterpart of Islâm, with its Koran, its prophet, its fasts, etc.; nowhere is to be seen a return to the former paganism, even less to Christianity. The famous text of Ibn Khaldûn on the many apostasies of the Berbers applies only to the period preceding the activity of Mûsâ b. Nuṣair. We are confronted, then, with a faith very variable in its mode of appearance, very poor in point of doctrine, but very tenacious and vital from the beginning—the unquestioning faith of the poor.

For that matter, the Islâm of the tribes did not always remain unconscious of its weaknesses and its inadequacies. It must not be forgotten that the great reforming movements of the Maghrib were born in the tribes and were propagated by them: the Almoravid reform sprang up in the western Sahara and developed among the Ṣanhâjian tribes of those regions before it was carried by them to Morocco, as far as Algiers, and then to Spain; the Almohad reform saw the light among the Maṣmûdian tribes of the Upper Atlas and was propagated by them in the whole of the Maghrib and Muslim Spain. That these movements quickly took a political turn is not what matters here; what is important for us is that the Islâm of the tribes came to feel its deficiencies and to try to remedy them.

With this desire to do better, to behave better in the eyes of God, must be connected the Maghribî mystical movement. Everything proceeded as if the tribes, tired of seeing reform turning inescapably to politics, had sought elsewhere the satisfaction of their religious needs. They found it in people obsessed with the problems of the other world (*ahl al-dîn* in contrast to *ahl al-dunyâ*), unattached to the goods and the affairs of this world (*fuqarâ*ᵓ), and initiated, often on the occasion of trips to the east, into the Muslim mysticism which had long since come into existence. It could not be said, of course, that Maghribî mysticism was the monopoly of the tribes; many city people adhered to this movement, and many mystics of the Maghrib were townsmen and scholars, like the famous Sîdî Bû-Madyân revered at Tlemcen. This did not prevent the mystical movement from having spread widely across the countryside of the Maghrib, as witnessed by the rapid multiplication of the *zâwiya* and the success of the brotherhoods, especially from the fifteenth century on; is it not reported that the brotherhood of Muḥammad al-Jazûlî (*ṭarîqa jazûliyya*) numbered twelve thousand members at the death of its founder (about 1465)? Now his domain was essentially the region which stretches between the present localities of Safi, Agadir, and Shishâwa, where there then existed no city worthy of the name. If certain mystics, like al-Jazûlî, studied in a thoroughgoing manner the traditional theology, others were simple countrymen who, with hardly any contact with the learned of the cities and without having studied the doctrine thoroughly, arrived through prayer, meditation of Koranic texts, and a sort of inward illumination at the religion of the heart which they set about preaching around them or, better, into which they *initiated* the simple folk among whom they lived. A hagiographical collection like the *Ḍauḥat al-nâshir* of Ibn ᶜAskar (third quarter of the sixteenth century) is full of facts which support the principle which has just been laid down. It is probable, although we have very vague information about him, that the famous Moroccan mystic, Sîdî ᶜAbd al-Salâm b. Mashîsh (beginning of the thirteenth century), was one of these country mystics: no one tells us that he went to study in the east or even at Fez; he is shown to us simply as living at the top of a mountain, the Jabal ᶜAlam to the south of Tétouan (Ṭiṭṭâwn), separated from this lower world and devoting his days to meditation and prayer.

Finally, though the descendants of the Prophet (*shurafâ*ᵓ) were everywhere the object of a special esteem, they enjoyed a veritable veneration in the Maghribî countryside; the success, first of Idrîs b. ᶜAbd Allâh among the Aurâba Berbers, then of his son Idrîs b. Idrîs in a part of the present Morocco, does not seem explicable except by the fact that they were descendants of the Prophet. Even more, when the Shîᶜite missionary, Abû ᶜAbd Allâh, settled among the Kutâma, he asked them to embrace the cause of a person of whom he could speak only in vague terms, since he did not know him himself, but, since it was a matter of a descendant of the Prophet, the Kutâma let themselves be won for the cause of this unknown man; it is thus that ʿUbaid Allâh gained power in Ifrîqiya. There is, then, to be found very early among the Berber population of the Maghrib a sort of anthropolatry with regard to the members of the Prophet's family.

The slow infiltration of the Bedouin tribes—Banû Hilâl, Banû Sulaim, and others—and their coexistence with the pastoral Berber tribes might, it would seem, seriously have modified the features of the Islâm of the Maghribî tribes. It did not do so at all. For one thing, the first Bedouins did not arrive in North Africa till the middle of the eleventh century, when the Berbers had long since formed their Muslim habits. Further, it appears that the Bedouin tribes let loose upon the Maghrib by the Fâṭimids of Egypt were very little preoccupied with religious matters. It can even be thought that they were influenced by their new neighbors, the Berbers, in point of religion. If the Hilâlian migration constituted a decisive factor as concerns the Arabization of the Maghrib, the same cannot be said of its Islamization.

The Turks did not play any more important a role. As is known, they did not occupy all the Maghrib, since Morocco always escaped them, and they made their presence felt in southern Algeria only in a sporadic manner. Besides, the Anatolian peasants and the renegades of various origins who made up the greater part of the Turkish occupiers were not zealots in religious matters, if they even practiced the faith at all, so that the only trace in the religious sphere of three centuries of Turkish occupation is the existence of the Ḥanafite rite (*madhhab*) alongside of the Mâlikî rite in the few administrative centers where the Turks were in sufficient numbers.

The presence of a dense Western population since 1830 in Algeria, 1881 in Tunisia, and 1912 in Morocco and Tripolitania has been much more significant. Certainly the Western powers which established themselves in these countries in virtue of various treaties, whether Spain, France, or Italy, all proclaimed their respect for the Muslim religion and their express intention not to harm it in the least. The same formulas, or very nearly, are to be found in this regard in such different texts as the proclamation of Marshal de Bourmont after the capitulation of Algiers, the treaty of Le Bardo between the French government and the Bey of Tunis in 1881, and the treaty of Fez by which the Sultan of Morocco accepted the French protectorate in 1912. The sincerity of those who signed these diplomatic documents in the name of the Western governments cannot be doubted, any more than the good faith of those who applied them. In Algeria the Catholic Church tried to get conversions in Kabyle circles but, meeting with very little success, gave it up; it can even be said that at the present time it accepts only after thorough inquiry and mature reflection a few very rare conversions of Muslims to Catholicism. The attitude of the Protestant missions is nearly the same. It can be affirmed, then, that neither on the official level nor on the religious level nor even, aside from very rare exceptions, on the individual level have the Westerners in North Africa carried out any concerted and conscious action against Islâm.

Some Muslims complain of the way their cult is administered in Algeria, where a non-Muslim government appoints and pays the officers of the Muslim cult. It must be mentioned that these complaints are few, very recent, and inspired by considerations which are as much political as religious; it is known, besides, that the officers of the Muslim cult have nothing in common with a consecrated clergy and that, consequently, the conditions of their appointment are much less important than in the case of priests. If on the level of principle it constitutes an anomaly that a non-Muslim government should take charge of the Muslim cult, it must be admitted that in fact the Muslim community of Algeria accepted this situation without difficulty and that the officers of the cult appointed under these conditions suitably discharge their functions. Besides, it is known that the Algerian Assembly is at present considering a bill for the separation of the Muslim cult from the state.

Finally, in Algeria and elsewhere, the Western governments which were masters of the situation did not content themselves with showing regard and honor for the representatives of Muslim learning and with assuring an absolute respect for religious buildings and ritual ceremonies; they have caused the mortmain goods to be profitable, as in Tunisia or in Morocco, where the yield of the *ḥabûs* properties has considerably increased in absolute value since the establishment of the protectorate, and have restored or built a number of mosques. Recent mosques are numerous in Algeria, for example, the vast Mosque of Laghouat; I have also seen at Murzûq a very beautiful mosque built by the Italian government alongside the old Turkish mosque. It is appropriate to point out also the considerable work undertaken in Morocco by the office of historical monuments, in cooperation with the vizierate of the *Ḥabûs*, to restore to their ancient splendor several mosques or madrasas of Fez, Rabat, Salé, Marrakesh, etc.

In spite of this respect for the Muslim religion which has been announced and practiced, it is not in doubt that the simple presence of hundreds of thousands of non-Muslims and of non-Muslim administrations in the Maghrib is pregnant with consequences for Maghribî Islâm.

To begin with, the frequent personal contacts, often on a basis of trust, with the Westerners have led the Muslims of the Maghrib to open their eyes to the outside world, which they had scarcely done till then. This country, turned in for centuries upon itself and its convictions, has suddenly discovered—in the cities at first and now in many corners of the *bled*—another world of ideas and beliefs. This discovery has led some into doubt; many others, without going so far, have come nevertheless to temper the traditional rigorism of Maghribî Islâm. The contact of the civilizations, so fruitful in so many other spheres, has also had its effects in the religious domain, not so much as concerns the doctrine itself as with regard to the relations between adherents of different beliefs.

Further, the presence of Europeans has brought to life in some Muslims the tendency to Muslim reform: the reactions of the Westerners in the presence of the practice of Maghribi Islâm, whatever direction they took, have convinced certain ardent believers of the necessity for a religious reform. "The Europeans must not," they thought, "be able to make fun of the crude ritual of such-and-such a brotherhood or of the charlatanism of such-and-such a marabout, nor must an informed Islamist be able to point out heterodox practices here and there; the only way to escape such reactions is to return to the pure Islâm of the Koran and the sunna." Others have believed that the European influence was harmful to the believers (women's dress, cinema, drink, mingling of the sexes) and have reacted against it by recalling the essential precepts of Muslim morality.

In another field, the substitution of European administrations for, or their superimposition upon, the traditional Muslim administration has had its consequences in the strictly religious sphere. It has happened that essentially religious officials, like the *qâḍî* and the *muḥtasib* in Morocco, have been deprived of an important part of their functions, not because the administration of the protectorate desired to suppress them, but because it envisaged their role from a purely administrative angle, not a religious one. Of the *qâḍî,* who was formerly the principal religious figure in the city, controlling the *ḥabûs* properties and the religious instruction, that is, all the intellectual life, enjoying a prestige greater than that of the governor (*ᶜâmil* or *qâᵓid*), it has made a simple judge of questions relating to personal status; as for the *muḥtasib*, censor of morals and supervisor of the traditional economic life, he has been transformed into a quasi-parasite, simply a liaison agent with the ancient guilds, and authorized, by virtue of this, to receive as formerly a tithe in money or goods from those under his jurisdiction. These transformations are to be explained by the fact that the European administration, judging matters from its purely practical point of view, without any spiritual concern, saw in the *qâḍî* a judge charged with applying the Muslim law just as a French judge applies the civil code, and in the *muḥtasib* a sort of provost of tradesmen, a temporal head of the guilds. It left to the one only his judicial functions, not realizing that a judge could be at the same time administrator of sometimes considerable properties and the inspector even of religious instruction; it left to the other his economic functions, without taking account of his moral role, which, it must be emphasized, had dwindled some time before the establishment of the protectorate; and, as little by little the artisan activity has entered willy-nilly into the general economic cycle of the country, the technical organizations charged with economic questions have taken artisan affairs under their charge, so that the activity of the *muḥtasib* has gradually diminished almost to nothing.

Furthermore, the European administration, with all the respect that it had for the Muslim religious life, noticeably upset its development. There is an official holiday on the day itself and sometimes on the morrow of the great religious solemnities (*ᶜÎd ṣaghîr*, *ᶜÎd kabîr*, *Maulid*, *ᶜÂshûrâᵓ*), just as the Catholic holy days of obligation give the right to one or two free days (Christmas, and then Easter Monday, the Monday of Pentecost, and All Souls' Day). Now, the Maghribî custom was that the Muslim holidays were the occasion of several days of family rejoicings. If the Western administrations have greatly facilitated the Pilgrimage, they have, on the other hand, greatly interfered with celebration of the fast of Ramaḍân. Formerly this had been a month of greatly slackened activity, which permitted the believers to fulfil the hard obligations of the Muslim fast in the normal course of things. Certainly the administrations or the European enterprises allow some accommodations to the Muslims they employ; even so the practice of the fast becomes a very arduous ordeal for them, which many do not have the courage to face.

Education has completely changed in character. Leaving aside some timid attempts like the foundation of the Ṣâdiqî College at Tunis in 1875 or the organization of a school of engineers at Fez (*madrasat al-muhandisîn*) under Maulây ᶜAbd al-Raḥmân, it can be said that traditional Maghribî education was only religious; sciences like grammar, history, and astronomy were only, as a matter of fact, auxiliary to the only science that counted, that of divine things. The Europeans have introduced to the Maghrib a modern education, provided in the same spirit as it had been in Europe, that is, in a secular spirit. That this secularism was almost always respectful of religious doctrines my North African experience allows me to affirm; it is nonetheless true that in the modern education God does not hold the place which He held in the traditional education. In the territories controlled by France, at least (I do not know exactly what has been done elsewhere), a corrective to this secularism has been introduced: Franco-Muslim institutions have been founded in Algeria, in Tunisia, and in Morocco. As their name indicates, they provide not only an Arabic but an Islamic education: theology, law, and ritual have their place in it. But they are not there alone; by their side mathematics, natural sciences, etc., are taught in a Western spirit. Such an education, however respectful the European teachers are of the beliefs of their students, cannot fail to form young minds in a way very different from the past and to bring about important consequences in the spiritual field.

On the other hand, the development of modern means of communication has greatly facilitated relations between the Maghrib and the Arab countries. The reknitting of these ties, which had been so strong at the start of the Arab conquest and which had much relaxed from the eleventh century on, has had its effect on the political level but also on the religious level. Maghribî reformism has been influenced by eastern theorists like Muḥammad ᶜAbduh and Rashîd Riḍâ; the prestige of the University of al-Azhar and of King ᶜAbd al-ᶜAzîz Ibn Saᶜûd is in fact undeniable.

In short, one cannot insist too greatly upon the importance of the presence of the Europeans in North Africa. However involuntary its consequences often are, in what concerns the Muslim religion they can go very far.

Such are the historical components which it seems to me must be kept in mind by anyone who wants to try to analyze the present situation of Islâm in North Africa. It has been seen that they point in different directions and lead us to expect a very complex reality.

This study, as objective as possible but necessarily too brief, of Maghribî Islâm will not contradict these first expectations.

The first impression which this Islâm gives is one of a great vitality. The Maghrib is profoundly marked by the Muslim religion: to begin with, the landscape, the mosques, chapels, and religious buildings in general are very numerous; then, individuals continually use in their conversation phrases in which figures the name of God (*Allâh ibârek fîk, bâraka 'llâhu fîk, Allâh ijâzîk biʾl-khîr, in shâʾa ʾllâh,* etc.) or quotations from Koran or *ḥadîth;* the manifestations of collective piety are often very impressive—daily prayers in the mosques, the Friday sermon, open-air prayers on the occasion of the canonical holy days, pilgrimages, and, above all perhaps, the fast of Ramaḍân. Finally, Muslim sensitivity remains very keen: it sufficed in 1930 that a few young people, certain of whom were known for their piety, represented the Ḍâhir over Berber justice as prejudicial to the Muslim religion, for two bourgeois cities like Salé and Fez to come out for the first time in opposition to the authorities of the Moroccan protectorate. In 1937 a small group of students of the traditional University of Fez provoked a riot in the Arab-Berber town of Khemisset (80 kilometers east of Rabat) for the same reason. It happens quite often that certain political parties use religious means in their propaganda, especially the Movement for the Triumph of Democratic Liberties (M.T.L.D.) of Messali Hadj in Algeria.

This general impression would have to be corrected and made more precise at many points. It is quite certain, for example, that the religious fervor does not reach the same degree everywhere. It is much less in most of the great cities of Algeria than in those of Tunisia and especially of Morocco; it also varies according to tribes and regions. Further, it would be desirable to see the strength of North African piety measured more exactly, and it is to be hoped that research in the sociology of religion, such as that which Le Bras is undertaking in France in regard to Catholic piety, will be attempted on North African Islâm. The fact must not be overlooked, to be sure, that such investigations will come up against all sorts of difficulties and will provide, at least to begin with, only approximate results, but they will still be worth more than the perfectly vague impression with which we must be contented for the moment. That does not prevent this impression from having its value nor prevent us from affirming the vitality of Islâm in the Maghrib.

Can as much be said of its unity? Here we will not deal with the divisions which have been established since the first ages of Islâm at the time of the caliphate of ʿAlî. The Shîʿites disappeared from North Africa many centuries ago. The Khârijites remain, but in the condition of a tiny minority in the Mzab, at Wargla, in the island of Jerba, and in the Jabal Nafûsa; they form, besides, very vital little groups in the largest cities of Algeria, Tunisia, and Tripolitania, where they emigrate temporarily to carry on trade or follow certain occupations which they have practiced for centuries. The communities of the Mzab and of Wargla seem to be stable; those of Jerba and of the Jabal Nafûsa are being slowly nibbled into by Orthodoxy. On the whole, it can be said that these Khârijites do not pose any important general problems.

When I speak of the unity of Maghribî Islâm, then, I mean the unity of Sunnite Islâm. We will not be dealing, of course, with the division of certain great urban communities of Algeria, of Tunisia, and of Tripolitania into the Mâlikî school and the Ḥanafite school: there is no factor of cleavage there. I am referring to more recent divisions, but much deeper ones, which far from being peculiar to North Africa extend over the whole Muslim world, but which, on account of the particular conditions to which North Africa is subject, take on proportions which are perhaps more strongly marked there than elsewhere. Among the Maghribîs who reflect and are capable of taking a position upon the problems of the hour can be found essentially three tendencies: a conservative tendency, a reformist tendency, and a modernist tendency. It almost goes without saying that these tendencies are hardly to be noticed except in urban surroundings, except for the first, which is quite generally spread over the whole of the country; the second and the third put out only a few rare feelers in certain country districts.

The conservatives get along very well with the present situation in North Africa and, believing it satisfactory, see no serious modifications to introduce into it. In this category are found all sorts of people, but the most prominent are the majority of the traditional scholars (*ʿulamâʾ*) and of the marabouts and heads of brotherhoods. They are all, it must be noticed, people with position and, at least in the case of the marabouts and heads of brotherhoods, with a hereditary position. It is easy to conceive, then, that from the temporal point of view they are hostile to all change. But there are some among them who are able to get beyond these contingent reasons and to wish for the continuance of the present situation for purely spiritual reasons: educated according to the methods practiced in the Maghrib for centuries, they are very distrustful in regard to the modernism which can lead, they think, to the worst adventures; and they have hardly more sympathy for the reformists, who turn up their noses at the whole sum of religious knowledge amassed during almost fourteen centuries by the most brilliant doctors of Islâm, and want to hear of nothing but the Koran and the sunna. This conformism is found not only among the older people who have been educated in the traditional disciplines alone but also among young people who are students either in the venerable mosque universities of Tunis and of Fez or even in the institutions of a mixed culture created in North Africa by the European administrations. I have personally known, and in a great many examples, this type of young people at the Muslim College of Fez, and I have found it also, with a few local nuances, at Tunis and Algiers.

The mosque universities of Tunis and Fez, with their dependent institutions, constitute the very type of the centers of Muslim conservatism in the Maghrib. It will be objected that these establishments have undergone more or less profound transformations since the setting-up of the protectorates. In fact, the curriculum of studies has been regulated, and passing examinations, quarterly compositions, and other items borrowed from the pedagogical systems of the West have been put in force; these last few years have even witnessed the creation of women's sections at the Qarawiyîn Mosque and at the Zîtûna Mosque; quite recently the decision has been made to teach modern subjects (mathematics, natural sciences, philosophy, etc.) at the Zîtûna. All these innovations have their place and will perhaps produce in the years to come a profound transformation in the traditional religious institutions. They have not yet borne fruit, supposing that this must happen. If the form of the traditional instruction has changed somewhat, its spirit remains almost entirely intact. The methods have remained the same: the master continues to teach *ex cathedra*, the students to learn by heart rather than to reflect and exercise their critical spirit; the manuals and the fundamental works have hardly changed, particularly as concerns the *fiqh*, which remains the essential matter; finally, and above all, the spirit in which this instruction is given remains immutable—scholastic logic, unrepentant casuistry, cult of absolute truth in all fields, to the exclusion of any idea of relativity. The students subject to this regimen would have to be endowed with an extraordinary personality not to come out of it as conformist as could be wished. That in the long run the teaching of modern subjects instituted at Tunis will bring substantial modifications into this system is indeed possible, but time will be necessary. I have seen in an important *zâwiya* of Zliten (Tripolitania) an attempt at modernization which seems to me significant: the students educated for long years in purely Koranic studies to the exclusion of every other were having great difficulty in following a lesson of elementary arithmetic; as to the so-called modern course of history, it was quite simply a study of the *Sîra* of the Prophet conducted according to the most traditional forms. For that matter, the students of the Zîtûna demanded the modification of their programs not through a taste for, or simply curiosity about, modernism but rather with the sole concern of pulling themselves up to the same level as their comrades who had studied at the Ṣâdiqî College or in the French *lycées* and *collèges* of the protectorate so as to be able to compete with them for administrative posts with some chance of success. Supposing that in the long run this new instruction runs the risk of modifying the very spirit of the Zîtûna, we shall certainly witness those who hold to tradition, among the students as well as among the professors, rising against it; and heated fighting is to be expected.

The conservatism of the marabouts and heads of fraternities is perhaps even stronger than that of the theologians. Everything considered, the theological education can in theory adjust itself to reformism, if not to modernism, at the price of a serious effort in adaptation, whereas Maghribi mysticism, such as it has manifested itself for centuries, is strictly incompatible as much with the one tendency as with the other; in fact, neither modernism nor reformism admits the idea of a *baraka* transmissible by heredity or by initiation, which is the very foundation of the organization of the brotherhoods and of the *zâwiya*. As is known, reformism sweeps away at one stroke any intermediary between God and the believer, that is, it eliminates all the holy personages who form the skeleton of the brotherhoods and of the marabout centers; as for the modernists, they consider the practices of the mystics pure trickery. It is not, then, astonishing that the association of the marabouts and heads of brotherhoods of North Africa, presided over by the shaikh Sîdî ʿAbd al-Ḥayy al-Kattânî of Fez, adopts a thoroughly conservative position in all fields.

The reformists, whose zeal, as I have indicated above, may have been brought into life by the presence of the Europeans, are to be connected with a tendency common to many religions and in any case abundantly represented in Islâm; they claim to be fighting against all the adulterations which men may have introduced into religious practices and in consequence to go back to the sources of the faith themselves, which by definition are free of the least impurity. If the Almoravid and Almohad movements are to be disregarded as too early, reformism came to flourish only very late in the Maghrib; the Moroccan sultans Sîdî Muḥammad b. ᶜAbd Allâh (second half of the eighteenth century) and Maulây Sulaimân (first quarter of the nineteenth century) were acquainted with the doctrine of the Arabian reformist Muḥammad b. ᶜAbd al-Wahhâb and tried to introduce it into Morocco, but without notable success. It was not until the second quarter of the twentieth century and the influence of the Egyptian movement of the Salafiyya that the reformist seed began to germinate in North Africa, particularly in Algeria with the shaikh ᶜAbd al-Ḥâmid Ben Bâdis and in Morocco with the *qâḍî* Muḥammad b. al-ᶜArbî al-ᶜAlawî and the young shaikh ᶜAllâl al-Fâsî. In both cases they certainly cherished political concerns, but they were also, perhaps above all, at least as concerns the shaikh Ben Bâdis, truly pious men moved by spiritual concerns.

To make their doctrine, which was almost wholly that of the Salafiyya, known, the reformists had recourse to several means. Their preaching came up in Algeria, at least in the Department of Algiers, against serious administrative difficulties, owing to the fact that the actions of the shaikh Ben Bâdis and his friends were not devoid of all political character, owing also to the opposition of the official preachers who did not intend to let themselves be deprived of their monopoly, and all the less since the reformists did not think it wrong to attack the official officers of the cult. The press was another means: the Algerian reformists published two reviews in classical Arabic, *al-Shihâb* and *al-Baṣâᵓir*, of a good standard but not widely circulated. Education was the principal means: the Algerian reformists founded numerous schools (they have at present about a hundred), beginning with the traditional centers of culture—Constantine, the home of Ben Bâdis, and Tlemcen; in Morocco also several reformist schools were founded in the principal cities and in some secondary centers. The instruction is given there in classical Arabic, an important part being given over to religion and morality. Finally, in order the better to co-ordinate their efforts, the reformists of Algeria combined in an association which still exists, and has a considerable influence, the Association of Algerian Reformist Scholars (*Jamᶜiyya al-ᶜulamâᵓ al-muṣliḥîn al-jazâᵓiriyyîn*). In Tunisia the reformist movement has been less pronounced.

On the whole these intellectuals, which the reformists are, have reached only intellectuals, or nearly so. Their following is above all urban and limited to the bourgeois classes: the lowly are not well enough educated to follow them easily in their theological speculations and often remain under the influence of the brotherhoods and marabouts, particularly in rural areas. It is the case, then, of a movement limited in its audience but significant, for it is made up of a good number of truly cultivated people, and also because, thanks to the schools which it has opened, some of which have now been in existence almost a quarter of a century, it is little by little widening its field of action upon solid foundations. It can be wondered, nonetheless, if it will ever be able to reach the masses of the people and to resolve the contradiction which exists between the devotion to the past which its doctrine resolutely affirms and its aspirations for a material revival of the Muslim world based on the use of modern techniques.

There remain the modernists, whom one can also call the "advanced." Most of them have been brought up in European schools, and many have passed through a serious crisis of conscience there. Few, nevertheless, have abandoned Islâm, but most no longer feel at ease in it, as if in a piece of clothing the cloth of which is still good but which no longer fits the body exactly. They are prey to the temptation of secularism. They have learned in the course of their studies and through contact with Europeans the principle of the separation of spiritual and temporal, have found immense advantages in it, and would like to apply it in their own society. They try to do this in their daily life and especially in the political sphere: parties like the New Dastûr or the Democratic Union of the Algerian Manifesto (U.D.M.A.), whose general staffs are made up especially of modernists, resemble Western political parties at many points. But they experience serious difficulties in this, because the troops that follow them are not on the same level as they and freely mix together spiritual and temporal, following the Maghribî tradition. Moreover, the necessities of political action sometimes lead them to make alliances which put them in contradiction with themselves; thus we find the U.D.M.A. often making common cause with the *ᶜulamâ᾽*, although the essential viewpoints of the modernists and the reformists are contradictory, the first seeking to find new formulas, and the latter going back resolutely to the past.

Like the reformists, the modernists are intellectuals, and like them they have a limited influence. Their opportunities, however, seem to be greater, for their number is growing proportionally to the development of schools, that is, at present at an accelerating pace. But it must be noted that their doctrine is nonexistent; however clear cut is their tendency, it is not formulated in a precise way. Swept very early into political action, they have not concentrated the effort of their thought upon the spiritual problems and have not yet seriously posed the problem of the Muslim religion faced with the modern world. In Algeria there is to be noted only the timid attempt of one Mâlik Bennabî, author of a little book on *The Koranic Phenomenon*, which tries to broach the spiritual questions.[1] For the moment, in short, the modernists have nothing to oppose to the immense literature of the traditionalists or to the coherent plan of the reformists. It is probable they will finally give shape to their thought beyond the framework of the political parties, but this has not yet been done.

I have scarcely spoken till now except of an elite, either urban or educated in the cities. Whatever its importance may be, this elite is not all North African Islâm—far from it. Therefore I must try now to distinguish what the Islâm of the masses of the people is.

If I were asked to define it in a single formula, I believe I would light upon this one: rigorism in ignorance. In fact, except perhaps in Tunisia, where matters are more finely differentiated, the Islâm of the Maghribî people still shows the effects of the Almohad rigidity. The doctrine and the political system of Ibn Tûmart did not last, but the moralist who broke the jars of wine at Bougie and the musical instruments pretty much everywhere, who separated the men from the women in public and in family ceremonies, and who did not fear to upbraid the sister of the Almoravid sovereign himself in the streets of Marrakesh because she was parading unveiled on a mule still finds an echo in the North African people: the separation of the sexes, although somewhat mitigated by modern customs and very relative in the countryside, is still strictly practiced in many circles; no Muslim would dare openly infringe the law of the fast in the *madînas* of Tunis, Marrakesh, Constantine, Salé, or even in the Muslim quarters of Algiers; many refuse to continue treatment of injections during the month of Ramaḍân, for they fear to break the fast so; even children can be seen asking to fast before the age, and poor people can be seen setting off on the Pilgrimage without a single penny. Certainly men can be seen also indulging in drink even in public, but many believers hesitate to take beer because it contains a very slight amount of alcohol, and it took some time for Coca-Cola to become commonly accepted, because it was suspected of containing it. In sum, the very great majority of the North African Muslims set themselves to practicing the Law very strictly, to the degree that they know it.

Here ignorance enters in: the poor man who leaves for the Pilgrimage does not know that this duty applies only to those who have the means and leave their families enough to live on normally during his absence but that the poor believer, who risks reducing his family to need by leaving for the Holy Places, does not have the right to do it. The sick man who refuses injections during Ramaḍân does not know that health has priority over fasting according to all the Muslim doctors, supposing indeed that an injection can be likened to the absorption of nourishment or drink. In short, a very large proportion of the North African Muslims knows only scraps of the Muslim law, without much connection between them. There is indeed the Koranic school, but how many went to it, even in the cities, before the coming of the Europeans? How many yet go to it? And, above all, how many learned or yet learn the whole Koran? Since, moreover, there exists in Islâm no established clergy, no one has the responsibility of giving the believers a complete survey of the Law. Even in the bourgeois classes one is surprised at the ignorance of the children (and probably of the parents) with regard to the Law and, even more, the doctrine. An inspector in the Franco-Muslim educational system who has lived in Fez for almost fifteen years undertook an inquiry into the ideas and beliefs of the children in his district: the first results which he got (he plans to present a doctoral thesis on this subject) are sometimes astonishing when it is a matter of the sons of the bourgeois of Fez; legend is closely mingled with doctrine, and many important points are completely unknown. All the more in the lower classes and in the country. In short, most of the Muslims of the Maghrib are living on a fund of oral traditions, distorted by the wasting of time, much more than on a coherent system of authentic beliefs.

That is not all. The anthropolatry which, we have seen, was born under the cover of mysticism is not dead. The *baraka* retains a large part of its prestige among the masses: one need only see the attitude of the Moroccans in the presence of their sultan, a descendant of the Prophet. It is not enough for them to see him and acclaim him; they almost all hope to touch him if they can, or at least to touch the objects which belong to him—his automobile, for example—in order to soak up the Sharîfian *baraka*.[2] To a lesser degree (but only slightly) the holy personages enjoy the same prestige, transmitted hereditarily or revealed by miracles. This anthropolatry is addressed not only to the living but also to the dead: the major and minor saints of the Maghrib are still honored with a very keen fervor, from Sîdî ʿUqba or Maulây Idrîs to the holy patron of the most obscure artisan guild of Fez or Marrakesh. There again it is not enough to perform an act of veneration; one must touch the tomb or the walls of the funereal monument to soak up the almost material grace which emanates from it.

Let us take another step: it is not in just any way that the favor of the "friends of God" or of God Himself is obtained. Fervor and impulsive faith are not enough; it is indispensable to make use of a sometimes complicated ritual, to recite so many times a given series of formulas, in a given posture, to make one or more duly listed offerings. The saints, who after all have been men, may have retained the idiosyncrasies of men, but it seems that the like are also attributed to God; not to speak of certain complicated and complex ceremonies such as those which R. Brunel has described in his *Essai sur la confrérie des Aïssaoua au Maroc*—the *dhikr* of all the brotherhoods, with its formulas arranged in a certain order and pronounced a rigorously fixed number of times, has all the appearances of a pious recipe.

And it is, in fact, a case of recipes, for in North Africa as in many human societies magic and religion are closely intermingled. One does not content oneself with magic formulas to satisfy amorous desires or to discover treasures; one uses them also to conjure the evil powers which wander ceaselessly about people, ready to profit by their weak points if they do not employ the appropriate means against them, those of magic. Here, for that matter, the popular feeling has no great difficulty in fitting into the Muslim belief, since that admits the existence of beings which are immaterial but can at certain times take on a concrete appearance and suffer most of the passions of men—the *junûn* or jinns. This orthodox idea has taken on enormous proportions in the popular belief, where the *junûn* play an essential role, whirling constantly around men, taking an interest in their most secret affairs, ceaselessly ready to intervene among them, rarely favorably. To limit or escape their misdeeds, precautions must be taken: avoiding darkness or the neighborhood of water, where the jinns like to be, throwing pinches of salt, fumigating with certain plants, pronouncing propitiatory formulas, and all this with discretion and privacy, for they are matters which it is not good to publicize. Not only the *junûn* but all sorts of evil powers, or ones which may become so, threaten poor humanity: ogres, the evil eye, and forces of nature, which one must try, if not to conciliate (that is not easily done), at least to neutralize. To succeed in this, the appropriate recipes must be used; they are innumerable and complicated and vary according to the individual and the circumstances. Accordingly recourse is had to initiates who know about these things, God—or the devil—knows how. The fame of the Maghribî sorcerer does not date from yesterday, since we find it very well established in the *Thousand and One Nights*, but it still endures, especially in Morocco, where the people of Sûs retain a great reputation in the matter; they use a highly varied ritual which goes from the Koranic talisman to the chemical preparation, inoffensive or not. Besides these technicians of magic, many of the human groups of the Maghrib (families, villages, tribes) have their recipes, transmitted from generation to generation, for the principal events of life: for birth, for marriage, to get rain or good weather, to make an enemy powerless whom one cannot handle by strictly human means (dolls for sympathetic magic are still used), etc.

It has been seen that besides jinns the forces of nature play a large role in the popular belief. Thus the existence can be established in the Maghrib, particularly in Morocco, of nature cults which are certainly very old and of which there persist only traces without any coherence among them. Caves, high places, springs, and trees (at least certain of them) remain at the present time the objects of a marked veneration. Often these pre-Islamic cults have covered themselves with a more or less transparent cloak of Islâm: thus two venerated thermal springs in the region of Fez are dedicated to Maulây Yaᶜqûb and Sîdî Ḥarâzem. In these two cases the Islamic vesture is visible, but what shall we say of a summit in the Atlas Mountains, almost 3,000 meters high, on the peak of which is a minuscule sanctuary, which bears the name of Lâlla Umm al-Bint, or of that holy personage of Fez, patron of a spring, who is called Sîdî al-Mukhfî? There the Islamic cloth, transparent and anonymous, veils practically nothing. In the cities these traces of paganism are slowly disappearing under what is in fact the joint influence of reformism and Western ideas, but in the countryside they remain very much alive; the marabout trees, on which are hung strands of wool, shreds of cloth, locks of hair, to cause the tree to absorb all the ills with which human beings are overwhelmed, are numbered in the thousands in all North Africa.

If one leaves this completely aberrant sphere, it becomes clear that popular Islâm presents other anomalies. As is known, in many

Berber lands (Kabylia, the Moroccan Atlas, Ahaggar, etc.) personal status is governed not by the Law but by ancestral custom. The Berbers who have recourse to this are practicing, without suspecting it, a sort of separation of spiritual and temporal quite foreign to Islâm. As is known, at least in Morocco this question of Berber custom has taken a political turn since 1930, but the government of the protectorate did not invent that custom: in North Africa, as indeed in many other regions of the Islamic world, are to be found a great many Muslims who do not accept the Law, even while considering themselves genuine Muslims. Most of the Berbers manifest a great attachment to their customary law: the conservatives accept this situation without saying anything much, although they consider it as heterodox; the reformists condemn it in the name of the pure Islâm they would like to revive; the modernists see in it a stagnation, an obstacle to progress which they could not tolerate. Here are seeds of a discord which is perpetually being reanimated, although the custom has a tendency to lose ground under the blows which are struck at it from all sides.

Besides, the masses of the people are still under the domination of the marabouts and heads of brotherhoods to a degree which is impossible to tell exactly but which is nonetheless important. It is known to the officers serving in the North African military units that the Muslim noncommissioned officer is not always the one who has the real influence on his subordinates; it often happens that he is supplanted in fact by a simple soldier who has maraboutic ties. A fact of a political order will emphasize the vitality of the brotherhoods in rural areas: in 1937, at the time when there was being organized in Morocco the Committee for Moroccan Action, directed by Sî ᶜAllâl al-Fâsî, several Berbers of the Middle Atlas, seeing only the religious character of this personage, believed that it was a matter of a new brotherhood, the *ṭarîqa waṭaniyya* (in fact, the members of this party were currently called *waṭaniyyîn*), under the patronage no doubt, in their minds, of some Sîdî al-Waṭanî, and joined it. The brotherhoods no longer play their former social role: the organization of modern means of transportation has considerably reduced their function as lodgings on the road; the pacification of the country has almost entirely eliminated their mission as mediators; the limitation of governmental arbitrariness has restricted their right of asylum. Their spiritual role, which has always varied a great deal according to places and persons and which as a general rule does not seem to have been very considerable, has certainly not increased.

And yet brotherhoods and marabouts keep having their adepts; the festivals of the patron saints continue to be enacted in the presence of often considerable crowds, in spite of the obstacles which have since 1934 been put in their way by the sultan in Morocco; quite recently a large number of heads of brotherhoods in Morocco have dared to stand up against their sovereign, doubtless persuaded that their followers would follow them in case of need; commerce in *baraka* still pays. To what is this vitality to be attributed? Perhaps to the absence of clergy: marabouts and brotherhood dignitaries discharge its functions; they are directors of conscience, or catechists. Besides, they are the spokesmen of a religion which the heart can feel and which the Maghribî population needs; to be convinced of this, one need only read the letter of a young man of Fez about a devotional session of the Derqâwa of Fez, which Émile Dermenghem has reproduced in the "Essai sur la mystique musulmane" which serves as introduction to his translation of *The Praise of Wine* of Ibn al-Fâriḍ, or the story of a popular brotherhood session (*ḥaḍra*) which occurs in the excellent novel of François Bonjean, *Confidences d'une fille de la nuit*. Whereas modernists and reformists carry out a dialectical attack and use their *ratio rationans*, the mystics offer to the simplest believer the exaltation of feeling which he hopes for to escape for a moment the miseries of life, transcend himself, and enter into a spiritual and magnificent world. This is the reason why the mystics, in spite of their faults and their anachronism, keep the hearing of an important part of the masses; to supplant them, modernists and reformists would have to furnish food for the feelings which they do not possess and of which they do not seem to dream.

To end this brief survey of the Maghribî Islâm of today, I owe it to myself to note what is as yet in a state simply of indications, purely of symptoms, but which will perhaps take on larger proportions later. I am referring to a certain halfheartedness, still not widespread, but clearer, it seems to me, than only twenty years ago. It is to be discerned in two very different environments, which are both, however, in frequent contact with Westerners—that of the intellectuals with Western culture and that of the laborers working in European enterprises or who have emigrated to Europe.

The former are certain students or former students of the Western schools or of the universities of Europe. Steeped in a culture which does not know the values of Islâm and which besides is made up of rationalism and of a critical spirit, they are little by little led, if not to doubt (a few, very rare, declare themselves frankly unbelieving), at least to a skepticism which contrasts very strongly with the pietistic atmosphere of traditional Muslim society. This attitude of mind is further reinforced by their constant contact with European companions or colleagues, some of whom profess unbelief. With them the Maghribîs do not want to appear backward and willingly play at being free-thinkers; several cling to this game. It is probably in Algeria that the largest number of people of this sort are found: organizing a trip of Algerian Muslim students in France a few years ago, I arranged for the visit to the Mosque of Paris to take place on a Friday so that those who desired to could take part in that day's prayer. When I informed those affected of the program of the trip, what was my surprise to hear one of them say to me in a tone at once anxious and discontented, "But still we won't have to perform the prayer?" I answered that I was providing them with the possibility of performing it but that I was in no position to oblige them to do it, and it would be as each wished. "That's good," my questioner answered; "we never perform the prayer and would be much annoyed to have to do it on the pretext that we are on an official trip!" None of his companions protested against what he said. From this resolute abstention from practicing to unbelief is a long way, and perhaps this young man will later be numbered among the most fervent Muslims of his city. There is here, nonetheless, a symptom which is worth noting. This religious indifference is not peculiar to Algeria; it can be found also in Tunisia and even in pious Morocco.

As regards the working classes, the causes of indifference are not exactly the same. The North African laborer, whether he works in Algiers, Casablanca, the North African mines, or Europe, is almost always an uprooted person. He is a tribal man who has abandoned, in general temporarily, the surroundings of his origin to look for remunerative work which will permit him to help support his family. Arrived at the place where he is to work, he finds himself deprived of the social armor in which he was living, far from the collective constraint which guided many of his actions, attitudes, and thoughts. Most of the time the physical conditions of his work do not permit him to fulfil his religious obligations easily; the hours when he must be at the factory prevent him not only from going to the mosque for the daily prayers but even from getting off by himself to perform the prayer individually; the effort which is required of him is scarcely compatible with the fast of Ramaḍân, and he rarely has the leisure to return to the country to take part in the great religious ceremonies of the year. From this point of view the conditions in which he lives in Europe are even less favorable than those which he finds in a large city of the Maghrib. There are also the contacts with European companions or foremen, often far removed from any religious concern, who do not always scruple to make fun of the artless believers. Thus estranged from the practice, however concise, which was pivotal to their faith, and plunged into surroundings aggressively indifferent, or hostile, many workers are little by little estranged from Islâm; there are even some who are won by propaganda to purely materialist doctrines. For those who work in Europe there must also be mentioned the influence of the women with whom they live. Most of them come back to the country after a few months or a few years away; many are taken up again into the religious atmosphere which continues to prevail there; some, however, have been too much affected to become again exactly what they were before.

I repeat, this halfheartedness is still not widespread. It has reached only a relatively small number of individuals; it scarcely touches the country and is far from reaching all the urban classes: the innumerable artisans of the traditional cities have no experience of this state of mind. The fact remains, nonetheless, that the intellectuals and workers devoted to modern activities run the risk of playing an essential role in North Africa; they have every likelihood of being the leaven in the dough. It is possible, then, that their attitude in religious matters, if it is accentuated in the years to come, will be an important factor of transformation for Maghribî Islâm.

In the face of this disaffection the supporters of Muslim piety remain as yet quite passive. They are not found trying to fight against it, to get the intellectuals or workers who begin to be estranged from the faith back under control. In a word, in spite of the efforts of the reformists, there is to be found not the slightest impulse to renewal in North African Islâm. It would seem that the reformists are obsessed with the past; they wish for a return backwards much more than for an adaptation and do not try to envisage the future of the Muslim community in terms of modern realities. They are willing to use modern means of communication, like the press or radio, but in a spirit resolutely devoted to the past. As for the conservatives, they do not seem to perceive the danger and content themselves with set couplets upon the impiety of modern youth.

Must it be concluded from this analysis that North African Islâm is quietly passing into a sleep betokening its death hour? Personally, I do not believe so. I have mentioned that in the country at large the attachment to Islâm remains very deep, and I shall not go back on what I have said. The simple, unquestioning faith of the poor has its gaps and its inadequacies, but it presents a considerable reserve power. However imperfectly practiced, Islâm has grown roots in the Maghrib too deep and too strong for it to be regarded as in the course of slow disappearance. It is no less true for all that that the presence of the Westerners has had its influence upon the religious behavior of North African Muslims as on their other behavior. For the moment this influence, quite involuntary and unconscious in most cases, is, above all, deleterious. But it is very possible that this stage will one day have been passed and that the presence of Westerners will produce at once a reinforcement and a lasting transformation of Maghribî Islâm, not in the doctrine, by definition immutable, but in the practice of the Muslim religion and in the behavior of the Maghribîs in their personal life and in their relations with non-Muslims.

DISCUSSION

M. Brunschvig: M. Le Tourneau has emphasized to perfection the need in which we stand today of more developed studies than those which have been made so far in the field of what we should fundamentally like to call "North African sociology of religion." The remarkable essays of Le Bras, which all those who concern themselves with this sort of thing will have in mind, must provide the initial guidance. The field of observation is extremely wide, and it seems to me almost scandalous that ethnographers of the first order have in fact practically never thought of using maps—of placing their inquiries geographically. We have studies made by people of a generation which is already old and even disappearing. I can cite them in the case of those who are dead: Alfred Bel of the University Faculty of Algiers, for example, who was a very good ethnographer in his time, who concerned himself among many other things with the prayers for rain (I am speaking of the popular, not the classical, rites) and those of the midsummer-day fires. He provided us, indeed, with abundant, valuable, and very important information. One could cite names of other authors in whose work there are no supporting maps—we can examine such studies as attentively as we wish, we will not know in the least where the phenomenon in question stops—not only in one or another restricted area of North Africa, but in the great North African countries. It seems to me that it is not too late to go into these studies again, trying to tie down geographically the facts of an ethnographic order, popular rites upon which that whole sociological school laid its stress. I think the geographical distribution of the facts in the case of elements of the official cult itself ought also to be seen. For in the official cult, however fixed it appears to be, however stereotyped it is in principle and in the doctrine, in practice there are usages which are very minor for the unbeliever but sometimes important in the thought or the sentimental reactions of the believer, which, even if they do not affect the deeper feelings of individuals, may be of interest in cultural history because they can help delimit the cultural provinces. In Morocco, for instance, there are divergences among the great cities in the practices regarding sermons on the occasion of Ramaḍân—here I am speaking of the absolutely official cult. Looking more closely into these matters, we would make some discoveries of details and perhaps even in the over-all picture. Thus, in which cities is the prayer of the two great holidays held? Is it held in the mosque or in the open air? In North Africa there are regional differences. If at a given moment the prayer ceased to be held in the *mṣalla,* as we know was done everywhere in the Middle Ages, and was held in the great mosque instead, there must have been something which occasioned this change.

I shall take the liberty of expressing some reservations upon the manner in which M. Le Tourneau presents certain aspects of the Muslim religion as practiced in North Africa in the past or at the present time, not upon the facts, which are perfectly well set forth, but upon M. Le Tourneau's own attitude toward these facts. As regards the past, for example: "Shîᶜism, a deviation." I recall the word "deviation," but there are others which are almost synonymous. I apologize for thinking that it is a hindrance for objective sociologists and historians, such as we should be, to seem to take sides, saying "deviation": this is a Sunnite position.

As to the present facts: "recitations of formulas," "pious recipes," M. Le Tourneau says, speaking of the rituals of the brotherhoods. Personally I believe it is also rather dangerous to set forth matters in this way, when it is a question of a religion to which we do not belong. For I think that, in taking things this way, one is also running the risk of reflecting on some official rituals. It is not for us to decide between a ritual considered as official and a ritual considered as unofficial. We confront the religious phenomenon of ritual. We can indeed say that in certain cases it is ratified by such-and-such a group, such and such an element in the population, and enjoys a certain prestige; that in such-and-such another case, on the contrary, it is attacked. But if we introduce into the account of such facts a formula which is a value judgment, it seems to me that we go beyond our duty as objective historians.

I shall say the same thing again—excuse me for insisting perhaps a bit heavily on this point—on the remark of M. Le Tourneau regarding the Muslim religion in the case of Sîdî Mukhfî. We know that fundamentally all the religions have arisen in this way. What matters is the spirit of the believer. It is not the more or less veiled, more or less overlaid, origin of the thing. Our duty as historians is to emphasize dependences and transitions, but I do not think that we also have to pass a value judgment, such as seems implied in the expressions used.

M. Le Tourneau has very justly emphasized how much the presence of the Europeans—I do not even say their rule or their *prepotenza,* but simply their presence—has introduced modifications of a religious order into the religious practice, without this being deliberately desired at the beginning; for example, in the practice of the festivals. Friday is now a rest day, and that is not in the Muslim tradition. And today there are certainly many young city Muslims who are convinced that it was that way before and that Friday ought to be a rest day because the Jews rest on Saturday and the Christians on Sunday. Finally, as a rule, it is to the fact of the continuing presence of the Europeans and the wish to imitate the Europeans while remaining faithful to their own faith that is to be attributed the desire to see to it that what is a solemn day for the Muslims should have the same dignity as the solemn days for the Christians. Another example: the fast of Ramaḍân is called today in Algeria and even in some circles in Morocco *Carême* (Lent). In the French-speaking Muslim circles it is no longer desired to say "Ramaḍân." Nonetheless, in French everyone, even people who do not know Islâm, understands what "Ramaḍân" means; it appears in French literature. But the Gallicized Muslims no longer care to use the Gallicized term "Ramaḍan," nor even *jeûne* (fast), as was said for a long time. Today they say *Carême*. I believe that began in Algiers; I spotted it there formerly, and I heard it in Fez a few months ago.

M. LE TOURNEAU: I would take the liberty of adding that from the circles which proceeded by conscious imitation, that has been carried into popular classes. In the popular circles of Algeria that speak French the word *Carême* is now used.

M. BRUNSCHVIG: I wonder if it is not of popular origin. I think I have noticed in Algeria that the word *Carême* came in through the women servants who worked in European houses.

M. LE TOURNEAU: Quite so.

M. BRUNSCHVIG: With regard to the present development in the field of education, I must say I was very much struck a few months ago, also at Fez, to observe that there was pressure toward the modern education of Muslim girls; and that, moreover, in the French *Lycée* of Fez, which is at present a mixed *lycée* of secular status, for all classes from the age of six up to the *baccalauréat*. In these last few years the number of Muslim girls enrolled is increasing in astonishing proportions. Muslim girls as old as fifteen or sixteen years, accordingly, find themselves unveiled in class, where there are also Muslim boys and European boys or girls. And this is demanded and sought after by elements which are not in general, properly speaking, "popular." It is a question of a secondary education, which is reserved for the petty and even the middle bourgeoisie. Yet the French administration is not putting on any pressure for it at all. It is not making a lot of noise over it; one must be well informed to know it at Fez. The families come soliciting the education administration to accept their little girls even if they are not quite at the level; they insist on their being accepted. Finally it is a movement which comes from a part of the population of Fez which is interesting from all points of view. You see what it represents. It is the great city of the conservative elements of Morocco.

I do not want to wander off into other considerations, but all things considered I believe that, not for the present but taking a general view over the history of long centuries, it can be wondered at bottom what is specifically Maghribî in the Muslim religion practiced in North Africa—from the intellectual point of view, from instance, and not that of the popular practices. From the intellectual point of view, has North Africa contributed in the course of its history anything really important to Islâm? I think the answer is likely to be rather negative. North Africa has shown itself very receptive to Islâm, and has had its own reactions; but to the degree that it becomes intellectualized—that it expresses itself in doctrines—these are reflections of the east. There is not to my mind any real originality in North African religious thought. The Almohad movement itself has no real originality; I am against the idea that Ibn Tûmart was a figure with truly original doctrinal conceptions. He had a somewhat new combination of eastern conceptions, but I do not think there were any truly new elements of thought that came out of the brain of Ibn Tûmart. Yet it is he who would represent the most original and the most novel that could be found in the history of North Africa.

As for the mystics, there would be room for discussion regarding certain points that I consider very secondary. The great mystical tradition on the intellectual side is Spanish. Sîdî Bû Madyân was an Andalusian settled in North Africa, and even the great Ibn Khaldûn was of Andalusian origin, and all his intellectual education was Spanish. I believe that from that point of view the balance sheet of North Africa is very likely to be negative in spite of the school of Kairouan, which was brilliant for a while; but that also is a reflection of the east, in a period when it is quite difficult to distinguish between what was happening in Tunisia and what was happening in the east.

As for literary criticism, Mr. Gabrieli has very justly referred to the school of the critics and poets of Kairouan. Here I have not personally studied the matter. Is there a real originality in Ibn Rashîq: in the case of ᶜ*Antar* for instance, as compared with the east?

Mr. Gabrieli: There is a development of thesis in the modern poetics. But this poem dates from the eleventh century, and it can be said that there is a flame here.

M. Brunschvig: In spite of a few individual exceptions it cannot be said, generally speaking, that there was a great and really creative literary or artistic talent among the North African people. At any rate, it is certain that if this province is compared to Spain, on the one hand, and to Iran, on the other, North Africa has rather the appearance of a poor relation, from the cultural point of view, in the history of Muslim civilization. What it will be tomorrow we naturally none of us know, but even at the present time it does not seem, in spite of the restlessness which M. Le Tourneau has shown to perfection, that there have been North African voices to bring a really new contribution even today in the present movements. One has the impression that whatever has life and intellectual value comes from the east, is thought of by the east, and is more or less digested in North Africa.

Mr. Caskel: M. Le Tourneau mentioned the two so-called "uprooted" groups of the workers and the intellectuals. By chance I have twice in my life met Maghribî intellectuals, the one a Moroccan, the other a Tunisian, who combined the whole of Arabic and Islamic education with a French education. If these two cases are not unique, I think there is a fund of intelligence and strength which has been sleeping for centuries and which one fine day will be surprising. I have made the acquaintance of many Arabs from Iraq, Egypt, and Syria, and these two persons were much more intelligent, much more sparkling.

M. Le Tourneau: I did not intend to say that all the intellectuals with a modern education were moving in the direction of the lukewarmness of which I spoke. Certain ones retain a very conscious and very solid Muslim faith, in these advanced surroundings; I have known many of them in the institutions of mixed instruction where I have taught myself.

Mr. Caskel: Second, if it is desired to appreciate all these magic rites, etc., in North Africa, I think it must be realized to what degree all these things are widespread even among us. I know a Parisian, a very intelligent and able man, who told me in confidence that his uncle was a sorcerer. This is to be found in Germany also, of course, but was it always to be found in North Africa on such a broad scale? Is it possible that in the Middle Ages these rites and practices were not so widespread as now?

M. Le Tourneau: It is very difficult to say, because our information comes essentially from orthodox authors who scarcely speak of these things. From time to time they refer to them almost involuntarily, but actually we cannot find in them what is necessary for a serious study. All that we can say is that fifty years ago in Morocco, a century ago in Algeria, when curious Europeans arrived on the site and began to study the population, matters stood as I have said. I cannot honestly go any further, for the texts at our disposal do not permit it.

Mr. MEIER asks a question about the celebration of the Friday service: Are the changes of attitude mentioned by M. Le Tourneau not due rather to Egyptian influence than to the presence of Europeans? We do not know much about the celebration in older times, but there is an anecdote of the Kâtib Ibn ᶜAbbâd al-Ṣâḥib (939–95) who, asked about the day of the week, answered, "Yesterday must have been Friday, because I got out of practice [in my writing]."

M. ABEL calls attention to the so-called "pious collections" which are found in many libraries. They always contain a certain number of prayers attached to one of the *madhâhib* and, in the same volume, magic recipes and formulas which all come from the Maghrib and date back to the fifteenth century.

Mr. VON GRUNEBAUM points out that the traditional system of Muslim sciences never discarded magic.

Mr. SCHACHT, speaking about the lack of creativity in the Maghrib described by M. Le Tourneau and M. Brunschvig, sees a certain contribution by North Africa in its very conservatism. Another more tangible contribution would consist of the late development of Mâlikî law in Morocco. There are certain original traits, like the ᶜ*amal* and others, which are not found, even in the Mâlikî schools, in the east. A third detail would be the coexistence of the Mâlikî and Ḥanafite *madhhabs* in Tunis, and after the Turkish conquest and to a certain degree in Algeria. Mr. SCHACHT comments on the Maraboutism mentioned by M. Le Tourneau as an essential spiritual element in the life of the North African masses. It existed too in the east. But the so-called "religious fraternities" have been reduced to insignificance under the impact of modernism and reformism; the result has been a considerable loss for the social life of the east.

M. BRUNSCHVIG answers Mr. Schacht that, speaking of the relative sterility of the Maghrib, he did not mean to deny any activity in minor fields. As to the special developments of Mâlikî law, they may be of great importance when we come to determine the different cultural regions of the Maghrib. M. BRUNSCHVIG again regrets the lack of geographical maps showing the extension of certain religious phenomena in North Africa. He exemplifies with the religious *baraka*, "blessing," attached to the person of the Moroccan sultan. This phenomenon is found only in the western part of the Maghrib.

There is certainly quite a difference of attitudes, actions, and reactions between Morocco and Tunisia. The two opposed centers of attraction are Kairouan and Fez; Algeria constitutes a distinct entity in between, its center shifting sometimes to the north, sometimes toward the south.

Mr. VON GRUNEBAUM considers the North African conservatism a kind of original contribution, but it is older than Islâm. We can discover it in our rather poor Classical sources. The same thing seems to be true for what we may call the second North African contribution to Islâm, its extreme anthropolatry.

Mr. LEWIS asks a question about the part played in the Turkish antinationalist movement by people from North Africa. The leaders of the Tijâniyya seem to be in contact with North Africa.

M. LE TOURNEAU answers that he does not know how the Turkish branch of the order is connected with its African place of origin. He points out, however, that this order has a marked tendency toward decentralization. There is a branch of it in

French West Africa which claims to have originated from Fez and differs considerably from it in its practices and in its cult. Even in North Africa there are at least two quite distinct centers of the order: one at Fez around the tomb of the founder, who died in the nineteenth century, the other in southern Algeria, where a part of his family has settled. They do not maintain close contacts, though communication is very easy today and was relatively so in the past century. M. LE TOURNEAU has no information on their present activity in Turkey.

Mr. LEWIS explains that the Tijâniyya has appeared quite recently in Turkey. One of their heads, by the name of Kemal Pilâvoğlu, was condemned by the penal court of Ankara, and thousands of his faithful gathered to protest. It is a clandestine conservative organization, which sometimes arouses semiclandestine demonstrations. Curiously enough it has appeared in Turkey only since the last war. It is said to have found adherents among the Khalwatîs, but this is not too sure.

Mr. CASKEL explains that the Tijâniyya penetrated into Syria with the French troops in the time of the mandate and the occupation of Syria (1918–46).

Mr. SPULER returns to Ibn Khaldûn. Is there any book which traces his influence upon the later Muslim historians?

M. BRUNSCHVIG answers that Ibn Khaldûn did not have the importance which is attributed to him in modern times.

Mr. SPULER recalls the fact that Ibn Khaldûn has been spoken of in connection with the Turkish historians.

Mr. LEWIS recalls the translation of his work into Turkish.

M. BRUNSCHVIG states that it is certain that Ibn Khaldûn was essentially rediscovered by the Europeans of the past century. From here M. BRUNSCHVIG comes to speak of the values in general which Europeans discovered in Muslim civilization, and he shows how those European discoveries force the Muslim world to reconsider its own civilization. For instance, their own art did not interest the Muslims of the past century; its great monuments have been conserved, relatively speaking, better in Christian Spain than in Muslim Morocco. A sad illustration is the state of the madrasas in Fez.

Mr. VON GRUNEBAUM closes the debate by saying that a mythology of Ibn Khaldûn is just about to develop. Clearly his legend has reached a stage at which there is an authoritative text which is referred to but not necessarily read.

BIBLIOGRAPHY

BEL, ALFRED. *La Religion musulmane en Berbérie.* Vol. I (all published). Paris, 1938.

BOUSQUET, G. H. *L'Islam maghrébin.* 2d ed. Algiers, 1944.

BUSSON DE JANSSENS, GÉRARD. "L'Indépendance du culte musulman en Algérie," *Revue juridique et politique de l'Union Française,* V (July–September, 1951), 305–39.

"Daouhat an-nâchir" de Ibn Askar, trans. A. GRAULLE. ("Archives Marocaines," Vol. XIX.) Paris, 1913.

DRAGUE, GEORGES. *Esquisse d'histoire religieuse du Maroc.* ("Cahiers de l'Afrique et l'Asie," Vol. II.) Paris, n.d.

D'ÉTIENNE, JEAN, VILLÈME, LOUIS, and DELISLE, STÉPHANE. *L'Évolution sociale du Maroc.* ("Cahiers de l'Afrique et l'Asie," Vol. I.) Paris, n.d.

Julien, Charles-André. *Histoire de l'Afrique du Nord,* Vol. II: *De la conquête arabe à 1830.* 2d ed. by R. Le Tourneau. Paris, 1952.

———. *L'Afrique du Nord en marche.* 2d ed. Paris, 1953.

Lévi-Provençal, E. "Un nouveau récit de la conquête de l'Afrique du Nord par les Arabes," *Arabica,* I, No. 1 (January, 1954), 17–43.

Marçais, Georges. *Les Arabes en Berbérie du XIe au XIVe siècle.* Paris, 1913.

———. *La Berbérie musulmane et l'Orient au Moyen Âge.* Paris, 1946.

Naissance du prolétariat marocain. Enquête collective. 1948–1950. ("Cahiers de l'Afrique et l'Asie," Vol. III.) Paris, n.d.

Terrasse, Henri. *Histoire du Maroc.* 2 vols. Casablanca, 1949–50.

NOTES

1. Cf. his interesting *Vocation de l'Islam* (1954).

2. This was true during the reign of Sîdî Muḥammad b. Yûsuf. But since the crisis of 1953 his successor does not enjoy the same popularity.

TROPICAL AFRICA: INFILTRATION AND EXPANDING HORIZONS

J. N. D. ANDERSON

This paper can make no claim to be comprehensive. Its direct concern is with British territories alone—although what is true of Tanganyika and Uganda, and still more of Nyasaland, may be said, perhaps, largely to cover Muslim influences in Portuguese East Africa, the Belgian Congo, and Ruanda-Urundi; and what is said of Nigeria, the Gambia, the Gold Coast, and Sierra Leone is, probably, of fairly general application in corresponding areas of neighboring French (and other) colonial possessions. It is written, moreover, almost entirely from the legal standpoint, although some material of a more general character has been included. Again, it is based primarily on personal observations, necessarily of a somewhat fragmentary character, drawn from a very widespread, but equally rapid, survey of eleven different territories; but a considerable amount of secondhand information has also been incorporated. Finally, it makes no attempt to give any adequate historical background; instead, it is concerned almost entirely with the present, except for an occasional reference to earlier material by way of illustration, confirmation, or explanation.

The situation in East and West Africa, respectively, may be said to represent considerable contrasts. The Islamic influence in the east is strongly centered on immigrant elements—on the Arabs of Zanzibar and the coastal towns of Kenya and Tanganyika (to say nothing of yearly visitors by dhow), on the widespread Indian and Baluchi communities, on pockets of "Nubis" in Uganda, and on that Swahili race and language which represent a fusion of immigrant Arab with indigenous Bantu blood and speech. But it has also spread to some extent among the indigenous peoples, such as the Digo of the Kenya Protectorate, the Yao of Portuguese East Africa, Nyasaland, and Tanganyika, and a considerable number of tribes, subtribes, and individuals in Tanganyika and, to a much smaller degree, in Kenya and even Uganda. Still more, of course, it has spread among the Somali and Galla, for the former (and some sections of the latter) are almost solidly Muslim, but it is somewhat questionable how far they should be described as "indigenous," while the influence of Arabia has in their case been direct and continuous. In West Africa, on the other hand, peoples who, whatever their origin, have now become substantially indigenous to that area—such as the Fulani, Mandingo, and Hausa—represent the core and dynamic of Islamic influence, while the immigrant elements from North Africa, Syria, Lebanon, and India play today a distinctly secondary role.[1]

Again, the Islâm of East Africa originally stemmed largely from Arabia—from either the Abbasid caliphate or its Arab opponents; today it represents in microcosm all the major divisions of Islâm, with Sunnites of both the Shâfiᶜî and the Ḥanafî schools, Shîᶜites of all the chief subsects (e.g., Ithnâ ᶜAsharîs, Ismâᶜîlîs of both the Nizârî and Mustaᶜlî branches, and Zaydîs), Ibâḍîs and Wahhâbîs, to say nothing of Indian Aḥmadîs and their converts—although only the Shâfiᶜîs have made any appreciable impact on the indigenous peoples; it looks to the Near and Middle East[2] as its centers of religious authority; and it expresses itself largely in Arabic or (still more) Swahili speech and literature. The Islâm of the west, on the other hand, stemmed chiefly from Idrîsid Morocco, the Murâbiṭîn, and the culture of the Maghrib; it represents almost[3] exclusively the Mâlikî school of Sunnite Islâm, with its divisions limited largely to the minor differences between the Qâdirî and Tijânî orders; it scarcely looks beyond itself for religious authority, for both the Sultan of Sokoto and the Shehu of Bornu are regarded locally as the titular head of the Muslim community,[4] while elsewhere in West Africa men's eyes turn more to centers of learning in French territories than to the Near and Middle East (except, of course, for the pilgrimage to Mecca); and Arabic is scarcely spoken,[5] although Arabic loanwords abound in a number of West African languages. In the east, moreover, the only Muslim ruler who professes to apply the law of Islâm as the "fundamental law" is the Sultan of Zanzibar, and even there successive sultans have issued a series of decrees which curtail and transcend the application of that law in the most radical way; while in the west the Muslim emirates of northern Nigeria are comparatively rigid in their resistance to any innovations of Western origin. Yet, in the application of the Shâfiᶜî and Mâlikî law, respectively, by the *qâḍîs'* courts of the Kenya Protectorate and of the Colony of the Gambia,[6] for instance, there is a marked similarity; as also, but to a lesser extent, in the treatment by the "native" courts of problems raised by the adoption of Islâm by individuals or family groups in mainly pagan areas on both sides of the continent, in those regions where Islâm and paganism still meet and intermingle.

THE INFILTRATION OF ISLÂM

The processes by which Islamic influences infiltrate a pagan African environment seem to follow a reasonably uniform pattern—wherever, that is, the advent of Islâm is not heralded by the sword. The first phase is commonly for Muslim merchants and "holy men" to visit a country, or even begin to reside there, and for the indigenous inhabitants, without any real understanding of Islâm whatever, to adopt Muslim charms as an adjunct to pagan charms and to have recourse to Muslim holy men as an alternative or addition to visits to their pagan priests (by whatever name these may go). This minor assimilation is everywhere assisted, moreover, by the fact that animists, on the one hand, almost invariably believe in one supreme God—although they commonly ignore Him in favor of inferior but much more imminent and obtrusive spirits[7]—so the Allâh of Islâm is not an entirely alien conception, while Muslims, on their part, readily identify the objects of animistic ritual with the jinn, and scarcely question the efficacy—as distinct, in theory at least, from the legality—of the practices of pagan magic. This phase may be aptly illustrated by some quotations from *Mission to Ashantee*, by T. E. Bowdich (London, 1819), where we are told that "the most surprising superstition of the Ashantees, is their confidence in the fetishes or saphies they purchase so extravagantly from the Moors, believing firmly that they make them invulnerable and invincible in war, paralyse the hand of the enemy, shiver their weapons, divert the course of balls, render both sexes prolific, and avert all evils but sickness (which they can only assuage), and natural death."[8] So much so, that "a sheet of paper would support an inferior Moor in Coomassie for a month."[9] These same "Moors," moreover, "augured from the sacrifice of sheep, with which the King supplied them abundantly, and, excepting those who had made a pilgrimage to Mecca, (of which they told us wonderful tales) did not hesitate mingling the superstitions of the natives with their own, either for their profit or safety. They were tolerably expert in slight of hand tricks."[10] Again, in *The Influence of Islam on a Sudanese Religion*, Mr. Greenberg tells us that the pagan Magazawa include in their list of named spirits, or "*iskôki*," one called "Malam Alhaji," who is depicted as a learned and aged Muslim pilgrim! And I myself observed, in the Gambia Protectorate and elsewhere, how charms and amulets of

Islamic and animistic origin are intermingled with almost complete indifference, while the relatives of one who is seriously ill will often seek the help of some local Muslim savant and of some pagan "ju-ju" priest simultaneously, with little or no sense of incongruity.[11]

The second phase may, perhaps, be said to have been reached when pagans not only make use of Muslim charms but also adopt Muslim prayers. I found several interesting examples of this in both the Gambia and the Gold Coast. Thus in many parts of the Gambia Protectorate, and especially among the Jola, even professed pagans will often attend Muslim funerals, keep Muslim feasts, and say Muslim prayers. Again, in centers such as Kpembe and Yendi, in the Northern Territories of the Gold Coast, a considerable number of pagans regularly recite Muslim prayers. In Yendi, for instance, all the members of the native court whom I questioned affirmed that they did so, but they emphatically denied that they were Muslims, for they "could not read the Koran." When, moreover, I suggested that this presumably showed their desire to become Muslims, they denied this too: their pagan religion still came first in their allegiance, and they regarded their pagan fetish as more powerful than anything that Islâm could boast. They had adopted Muslim prayers only as a sort of insurance policy, since Muslim teachers had assured them that this would guarantee their eternal felicity. Here, too, I found that the Chief (the Ya-Na) regularly appoints Muslim functionaries to perform various duties on his behalf, including participation in his enstoolment and in funeral ceremonies.[12] But at this point an important caveat must be entered, for it is clear that among some of the tribes in these regions of West Africa signs of Muslim influence must be regarded more as the relics of an attachment which has waned than as a new phase in an allegiance which is in course of development.[13] Even so, however, fresh contacts with Muslim traders and teachers may reinforce the influence of the past, as in a center such as Tamale, where I was told that something approaching fifty per cent of the population probably said Muslim prayers, while not more than twenty per cent, at most, had made any genuine break with paganism. And in Nigeria, again, Sir Alan Burns recounts how Afonja, the pagan chief of Ilorin, tried to strengthen his position by inviting a Fulani Muslim *malam*, Alimi, "to join him as his priest,"[14] while C. K. Meek quotes Lander to the effect that the Chief of Bornu used to offer prayers to pagan gods at the Ramaḍân festival, "for he is still a pagan, though he employs Muhammadan priests to pray for him."[15]

In the third phase the people definitely profess to have embraced the religion of Islâm, although many traces of their former pagan concepts and practices remain. Thus Meek informs us that "even today many of the less-enlightened Muslim rulers keep at their court pagan priests to direct and guide them as occasion requires. Traditional pagan rites are frequently observed on ascending the throne," while there "are also Muslim communities (e.g., at Kusheriki) where the Ramaḍân festival is begun and ended with pagan rites."[16] Similarly, J. Greenberg has shown how the Muslim Hausa regard the spirits which dominate the religious concepts of their pagan compatriots (the "Maguzawa") not only as identified with the jinn of Islamic thought but also as divided into "white" or Muslim jinn and "black" or pagan ones; how they see no harm whatever in resorting to such devices as the popular thought of Islâm allows in order to influence these spirits and to effect cures from the diseases, and relief from the disasters, which they are believed to cause; and how they regard those pagan practices designed to these ends which Islâm cannot cover with a veneer of orthodoxy as sinful indeed but nonetheless effective—so that recourse is constantly had thereto in any time of major crisis.[17] Again, the fact that pagan belief commonly localizes these spirits in trees and other objects of nature facilitates their identification with the jinn, whom popular Islâm believes frequently to inhabit just such places;[18] while pagan ancestor worship easily acquires a façade of Islâm through the Muslim belief that contact may still be made with the spirits of dead saints (whether at their tombs or elsewhere) and their aid implored in any time of need.[19]

It is not surprising, then, that to many Negro Muslims the Koran practically takes the place of their pagan fetish. Thus Meek records that "there is the same belief in the magical punishment of the perjurer, and I have known of a comparatively educated court Malam advising a British magistrate to purchase for his court a fresh copy . . . on the ground that the old one had lost its punishing power."[20] This was probably because it had been mutilated or become defective; and I have heard of courts where a Koran with a missing leaf was deliberately kept so that it could, on suitable occasions, be used with impunity![21] To drink the ink with which Koranic texts are written, on the other hand, is a cure for every ill. Again, Muslim prayers for rain partially take the place of the pagan variety—which are themselves sometimes addressed to the one supreme God whom almost all animists recognize but largely ignore:[22] yet, even so, "many so-called Muslims still believe in the power of pagan priests to control the rain supply, and to change the course of Nature in a variety of ways."[23]

Further points which deserve mention in this connection are the superficial Islamization of pagan "naming ceremonies" in the Muslim *ᶜaqîqa;*[24] of pagan rites of initiation, including male and female circumcision, in Muslim circumcision and clitoridectomy;[25] of pagan bride-wealth in the Muslim *ṣadâq* or *mahr;* and of pagan secret societies in the Ṣûfî fraternities of Islâm.[26] Further, the ceremony termed *sadaka* among the Yao, I was told, represents a survival of a pagan funeral feast held at the time of burial and at stated intervals thereafter, which is typically associated with a special dance (*cindimba*) and the brewing of special beer; but it has today been partially Islamized by the performance of the *sikiri* (*dhikr*), which is locally regarded purely as a dance. Again, the prayers and oblations which the pagan Yao used to offer to ancestral spirits are brought within the fold of Islâm by regarding the oblations (offically, at least) as the gift of food to passers-by in order that God may forgive and bless the ancestor concerned, while the prayers are said to be offered not to him but on his behalf.[27] Similarly, again, Meek informs us that "animal tabus are universal in Nigeria, not merely among the pagan tribes, but even among the Muslim communities as well. Muslim families still have their sacrosanct animals." Thus Muslim informants will explain that "the totem witnessed the foundation of the home. They will not usually go so far as to say that their family was actually descended from the totem," although some professing Muslims allow that the totem "contained the spirits of their forefathers." In any case the species is sacrosanct and is never eaten. Thus it is clear that, "in spite of their professed religion, many Muslim tribes retain a strong sense of mystic relationship with their totemic animals."[28] Furthermore, among the Yao, for instance, conversion to Islâm seems chiefly to imply the acceptance of the complete circumcision of the *jando* rite in place of the partial circumcision, or incision, of the indigenous *unyago* or *lupanda* (although it is noteworthy that much of the pagan flavor of the initiation ceremonies and fertility rites of the male *lupanda* and female *ciputu* seems to have survived in the nominally Islamic practices of today); the adoption of a few Islamic prayers and postures with little or no knowledge of their meaning; and, pre-eminently, the observance of the Ramaḍân fast and abstention from pig flesh, or that of any other animal not correctly slaughtered.

THE INFLUENCE AND APPLICATION OF *Sharîʿa* LAW

It seems clear, then, that the influence of *sharîʿa* law on newly converted "Negro" animists is more in the sphere of matters of ritual than, for example, in the law of personal status and family relations. Thus the Yao were much exercised and divided until recently regarding questions such as the propriety of eating cooked food at funerals before the burial, and of singing, dancing, and carrying flags on such occasions; on the suitability of dancing at graves at the yearly visit thereto; and on the legality of eating hippopotamus meat, of building new mosques where one already exists, and of the recitation of certain prayers. Similarly, Baganda Muslims, I found, are still bitterly divided as to whether the ordinary noon prayer should be recited after the Friday *jumʿa* prayer to cover the possibility—or probability—that the exacting conditions stipulated for the validity of the latter by some jurists had not been fulfilled. Yet the Yao commonly conclude their marriages in a purely customary manner, and the bridal pair normally live together as man and wife for some considerable time before they call in a *mwalimu* to recite the *fâtiḥa* and celebrate the wedding by Muslim ceremonial; in matters of divorce I found that the *sharîʿa* has scarcely any influence on the Yao and very little on Baganda Muslims; and in questions of inheritance customary law has made virtually no concessions among either.

It may be said in general, therefore, that in this phase the local varieties of animistic belief and observance are at least partially retained, but Islamized in a superficial way in practice, and systematized to a considerable degree in theory, by the application thereto of the concepts of Islamic thought. At the same time Muslim ritual is largely adopted, and regarded as a matter of primary importance, while the influence of the *sharîʿa* on matters of family law is much less decisive. Among the Mandingo (and some other tribes) of the Gambia Protectorate, for instance, I found that little or no attention is paid by certain chiefs to the Islamic maximum of four wives,[29] and the children of additional wives are regarded as perfectly legitimate. Other Gambia Muslims, on the other hand, pay just enough attention to the *sharîʿa* to limit what they term their "free wives" to four in number, while they allow themselves an additional number of "slave-wives"—that is, women of slave origin, although now, of course, legally free (and these are not necessarily drawn from among the number of their own ex-slaves and their descendants nor of those "given" to them as "slave" concubines by their ex-owners, as is the case in the more orthodox circles of Northern Nigeria, but obtained from their parents for a suitable dower in a regular contract of marriage; so the whole procedure is totally irregular according to the *sharîʿa*). Again, in the Sierra Leone Protectorate, even practicing Muslims often have more than four wives and are frequently married to two or more sisters at the same time. I was told, for example, of an upright and practicing Muslim who died a few years ago leaving at least a hundred wives, including two or three batches of sisters (for the Kissis and certain other tribes have a custom that a man who marries an elder sister may also marry any or all of her younger sisters or half-sisters). Yet in the same Protectorate the relative strength or weakness of Islamic influence may be traced, *inter alia*, by the degree (if any) to which levirate marriage is enforced.[30]

In regard to the application of Islamic law in tropical Africa in matters other than questions of ritual, it is important to distinguish at least three different cases: (*a*) where individuals, only, embrace Islâm; (*b*) where a tribe or community tends to adopt Islâm collectively; and (*c*) where a Muslim government seeks to impose Islamic law.

The simplest case under category (*a*) is where the individual concerned becomes detribalized. This, I found, was true of those very few among, for example, the Giriama of the Kenya Protectorate who had embraced Islâm. Similarly, it is stated in the *Jibana Case* (*East Africa Law Review*, V, 141) that "members of the tribe converted to Islâm (known as Mahaji), having assumed an individual status incompatible with the customary communal tribal life, and in order, no doubt, also to live with members of their own faith, always leave the tribal land and go to live nearer to the coast." Among such, Islamic law is applied in comparative purity: and I found, for instance, that converts from the Giriama pay only a small bride-wealth which is not returnable on divorce unless by agreement, conclude their marriage contracts before the *qâḍî*, and follow the *sharîʿa* rather than tribal custom in regard to inheritance; while one whom I questioned told me that he had left his relatives of his own volition after his father's death, had married before the *qâḍî*, and wished to live "according to Islamic law."[31]

In other cases, however, converts to Islâm do not become detribalized in this way, and it is among such that problems are apt to arise if any attempt is made to apply Islamic law in questions of marriage, divorce, inheritance, etc. True, some native courts (such as that of the Jarawa in the Bauchi Province of Nigeria) are apparently prepared to apply Islamic law, as interpreted by a "Muslim member," in regard to any converts to Islâm—even, it seems, to the extent of allowing the exclusion of non-Muslim relatives from any claim to inheritance. In other cases, again, native courts are prepared to make partial concessions to Muslim principles in regard to Muslim litigants, as is the case in Obuasi (Ashanti), where the members assured me that while two-thirds even of a Muslim's estate must go to the customary successor, one-third would, as a concession, be granted to the eldest son, if himself a Muslim, or would be divided among such sons of different mothers as were all Muslims. But elsewhere, as in the Gambia Protectorate, the question as to whether customary or Islamic law would be applied would turn both on the proportion of Muslims in the tribe or vicinity and on the religion, orthodoxy, and learning of the local chief and court members.

Where, again, the greater part of a tribe or community accepts Islâm it usually happens that a fusion takes place between their previous customary law and parts of the *sharîʿa*. This process can be seen at work in various stages of development among, for example, the Digo of the Kenya Protectorate. Here I found that the "Swahili" Digo of the coastal region have already become largely Islamized and have accepted Islamic law to a considerable extent. Among the more tribal elements further inland, however, marriages are normally concluded in accordance with tribal custom and only regularized later, from the Muslim point of view, by a contract in the Islamic form (in which the original bride-price is usually named as dower). Questions of inheritance are still more complex, and the Digo seem to fall into three divisions in this respect. Their original tribal structure is matrilineal, and the *mjomba* (mother's brother or sister's son) is the customary heir; and this still prevails among the pagan elements and even among large numbers of those inland Digo who have adopted Islâm but who still live according to tribal customs. The fully detribalized Digo, on the other hand, have swung right over to the *sharîʿa* in this matter. And between these two extremes there are other elements, on whom the influence of Islâm has been such that sons are tending to displace the *mjomba* as the primary heirs, and a patrilineal system to replace the matrilineal, but without the more complex niceties of the *sharîʿa*. It must, however, be repeated that none of this has taken place, for example, among the Yao, who have remained solidly matrilineal, although predominantly Muslim.

Another instance where Islâm has been accepted, this time almost exclusively and by a whole people rather than a tribe, is provided by the Somalis; and here Islamic law has largely, but by no means completely, replaced their customary law. Thus customary payments in respect of marriage, such as the *yarad*, the *gabbâti*, and the *ḍibâd*,[32] have survived, and the Islamic *ṣadâq*, while always named, is virtually never paid except on death or divorce. In matters of inheritance, again, Islamic law has largely prevailed in some quarters, while in others females (for instance) are still excluded from their rights. The customary law, moreover, enforced exogamy, but under the influence of Islâm this is tending somewhat to break down; in regard to such questions as the custody of children, "equality" in marriage (*kafâʾa*), and matters of insult (*ḥâl*), the customary law still largely prevails; and much the same may be said concerning, for example, the Somali variety of levirate marriage[33] and the "*qasâṃa*" oaths applicable in cases of homicide.[34] In general, however, it may be observed that in most such cases Islamic law tends to extend its scope little by little—and here it is quite clear that the influence of Islâm has a unifying effect on the multifarious varieties of tribal and local customs.

Where, again, Islamic law is enforced, or enforced in part, by the authority of some Muslim ruler, a yet different situation arises, for here an attempt, at least, may be made to override the customary law of the community, in some respects, in favor of the doctrine of the books, while Islamic law may also be imposed, in some cases, on pagan litigants. The latter phenomenon may be observed in some of the Muslim emirates of Northern Nigeria, but steps have been taken, of recent years, to restrict this tendency. For the rest, however, these Fulani-Hausa emirates provide a splendid example of the degree to which customary law succeeds in modifying the pure *sharîʿa* even in the most professedly orthodox circles, for I found a number of respects in which scarcely a single *alkali* applied the orthodox Mâlikî doctrine in its rigor (even in matters of personal status).[35] But J. Schacht has ably emphasized, in an unpublished paper on Northern Nigeria, how this accommodating attitude tends to be minimized in a protectorate, for the Muslim rulers are apt to take refuge in rigid orthodoxy in order the better to resist any unwelcome suggestions from the protecting power—and I myself found several clear examples of this tendency. It is noteworthy, moreover, that the *qâḍîs*' courts of Zanzibar and Kenya tend to apply the pure *sharîʿa* with rather fewer concessions to customary law—although within a much more limited scope—than the *alkalai* of Northern Nigeria; and this is, presumably, largely attributable to the fact that the

Islâm of the east is more immigrant, and less truly indigenous, than that of the west.[36] Yet again (to take an instance of the imposition of law by authority, even informally, at the lowest level), it is noteworthy how much more completely and rigorously Islamic law is followed, and even "enforced" by headmen, in those villages of the Gambia Protectorate where "Marabûṭ" influence has been strong than in neighboring villages of "Soninki" persuasion.[37]

THE *Sharîᶜa* AND CUSTOMARY LAW

It is, however, a matter of considerable complexity how far the *sharîᶜa* can be, or should be, identified with, and applied as, the "native law and custom" of an African tribe or community. It has been held, for instance, by the Court of Appeal for Eastern Africa (in *Khamis* v. *Ahmed* [1934], I E.A.C.A. 130, at p. 133) that the law of Islâm cannot be described as "native law" for the purpose of Article 7 of the Kenya Colony Order in Council "merely because it is the law applicable to many or even all of the natives of the Kenya Protectorate." It seems possible, however, to interpret this dubious dictum as meaning that it cannot be so regarded merely because a Muslim ruler such as the Sultan of Zanzibar may have sought to impose it on his subjects, rather than that Islamic law can never be so embraced by the people themselves as to influence profoundly or even partially replace their own indigenous customs.[38] There are, of course, obvious objections, to the purist, to regarding a system of law elaborated centuries ago in lands of very different circumstances and culture as the "native law and custom" of African peoples today, yet the fact remains that in some localities Islamic law has become as inextricably combined with indigenous law as has Arabic with some of the indigenous languages (e.g., Swahili). And it is precisely as "native law and custom" that Islamic law is enforced, in Northern Nigeria, more extensively than anywhere else in the world outside the Arabian Peninsula. The true criterion, therefore, seems to be whether it has in fact been recognized and adopted by the native community concerned, rather than any doctrinaire consideration of its historical origin.

In general, however, it may be said that Islamic law is applied today in tropical Africa sometimes as the *fundamental* law, sometimes as the *dominant* law, and sometimes as a *particular* law. In the first case, Islamic law as such is expressly said to be applicable, either (as in Zanzibar) in so far as it has not been ousted by legislative enactments or (as in the Somaliland Protectorate and the

Gambia) in regard to a specified list of subjects; it should, technically, be applied according to the books; and customary law is recognized, if at all, as a different and somewhat parallel system which is tolerated in some respects only.[39] In the second case, Islamic law is extensively applied under the cover of "native law and custom" (as, pre-eminently, in Northern Nigeria); and here the two are in practice fused, and the resultant law is substantially Islamic (and, in most points, rigidly so, as possessed of divine authority) in the more strictly Muslim areas, but substantially, or even wholly, customary in mixed or pagan areas. In the third case, on the other hand, Islamic law is applied, if at all, as a sort of equitable exception to the prevailing customary law, recognized by the courts, to a limited extent, in regard to such Muslim litigants as wish to be governed thereby.

In general terms, again, it may be noted that the range of degrees to which customary and Islamic law may be combined or fused, whether in regard to whole tribes or individual families, is almost unlimited. Marriages which have been arranged on a customary basis, and in respect of which all the customary gifts and payments have been made, are frequently completed in the case of Muslims, for instance, by a form of ceremony at which a small additional payment is made to the bride to represent the specifically Islamic dower (or, in some localities, "minimum dower"); in other localities the previously paid bride-wealth is so named in the contract, or—again—a new sum is named as dower but not actually paid until divorce or death. Thus, in the vicinity of Mumias' trading center in the Kavirondo Province of Kenya, bride-wealth is still paid in cattle to the woman's family, but Muslims add a few shillings as *mahari* for the bride herself;[40] in the Gambia a small sum, probably representing the minimum dower of the Mâlikî law, is commonly paid by Muslims at the actual contract of marriage, in addition to a larger sum which may be partially deferred; among some elements of the Digo the bride-wealth of a prior customary marriage is mentioned as dower at a subsequent Islamic ceremony; and among the Somali the Islamic *ṣadâq* is named at the marriage but not paid before divorce or death (as, also, in the Aden Protectorate), whereas a customary bride-wealth is paid either at once or by instalments. In most such cases, too, Muslim marriages include a formal contract comprising the declaration and acceptance fundamental to Islamic law; this is noticeable, for instance, almost everywhere in the Gold Coast, while the absence of this in many "tribal" marriages in Tanganyika gives rise to a number of problems.[41]

The same situation prevails, too, in regard to questions of divorce. This may be arranged on a purely customary basis between the families concerned, and the return of bride-wealth, of other expenses incurred in respect of marriage, and even of the more specifically Islamic "dower," if any, may be regulated and enforced accordingly. Alternatively, however, the pure *sharîᶜa*, or some approximation thereto, may be applied. Or an almost infinite number of gradations between these two extremes may be found in practice. Even in the strictest areas of Northern Nigeria, for instance, a married woman can always secure a judicial divorce if she is sufficiently insistent and if she or her family are prepared to make suitable repayments; and this is also true in the Gambia and throughout West Africa. In Tanganyika and throughout East Africa, on the other hand, many *liwalis* and *qâḍîs* are much more chary of ordering what amounts to a forced *khulᶜ* (the Islamic term for a dissolution of marriage on the basis of a financial consideration supplied by the woman) where the parties cannot be induced to agree thereto.[42] And the possible variations as to the amount of refund which may be enforced, and the degree to which this is dependent on or influenced by Islamic law, on the one hand (e.g., the presence, or absence, of some recognized justification for judicial divorce), and by customary law, on the other (e.g., the length of time for which the marriage has persisted and the number of children the wife has borne), are almost infinite.

Again, it is noteworthy that in some communities which are solidly Muslim the *ᶜidda*[43] neither of widowhood nor of divorce is observed; in others that of widowhood is respected and regarded but that of divorce ignored; and in others both are habitually enforced. Similarly, the degree to which a divorce in, for example, the triple form, even if uttered in sudden anger, is regarded as final (and as utterly precluding remarriage except after an intervening union), on the one hand, or all divorces, of whatever kind, are held to be susceptible to conciliation and retraction (even, perhaps, after the end of the *ᶜidda* period), on the other hand,[44] varies according to the relative orthodoxy of the area or group concerned; and there are a large number of possible compromises between these two extremes. And just the same is true of such questions as the position which arises when a girl promised in marriage in infancy subsequently refuses the union;[45] the terms (if any) on which a married woman who elopes with a paramour can subsequently be validly married to the latter;[46] the concept of that maximum period of gestation on which the legal paternity of posthumous children or those born subsequently to divorce will not infrequently depend[47]—or, indeed, many other problems of paternity;[48] and rules regulating the right to the custody of the children of divorced or deceased parents.[49] As for matters of testate and intestate succession, customary law proves here, in most cases, to be even more strongly intrenched; while in all that concerns land tenure it usually finds its only real rival in English legal concepts.[50]

In part, it is true, most of these questions turn on such basic considerations as the patrilineal or matrilineal structure of society, on the distinction between individual and family property, and (in many matrimonial causes) on whether restitution of conjugal rights, or "obedience," may be enforced by courts of law.[51] But the fact remains that the variations concerned go far beyond these considerations. They depend, to some extent, on the relative orthodoxy of the tribe or family concerned and on the degree of their attachment to customary practices; they turn, in part, on the relative orthodoxy of the court concerned and on the degree to which it seeks to apply the pure law, the prevailing custom, or some amalgam of the two; and they depend, in part, on a number of *ad hoc* considerations which may themselves vary enormously from case to case.

Nor do the points discussed above by any means exhaust the possibilities of conflict of laws in Africa today. There is, of course, the constant possibility of conflict between colonial statute law, mostly in the form of territorial ordinances, on the one hand, and local customary law, the local variety of Islamic law, or the resulting amalgam, on the other—or, indeed, between the latter and Western ideas of "natural law" or "justice, equity and good conscience." But there are also the perpetual problems raised by the differences between the customary laws of one tribe or community and those of another, particularly in urban life or any circumstances in which persons or groups become detached from their tribal environment. And all this is complicated by the fact that Islamic law, although often applied on a geographical basis under the umbrella of "native law and custom," is essentially and intrinsically a personal law which demands the obedience of every individual Muslim.

These problems are apt to appear insoluble to the European lawyer—except, that is, on the basis of a ruthless application of a number of possible principles of priority or exclusion. But it is just at this point that African institutions and practices reveal their characteristic genius. This is true, moreover, not only of "native" or "local" courts as such but also of those less formal processes of arbitration before some chief, headman, or community council which still account for an enormous volume of actual, or potential, litigation. The essence of this genius lies in the fact that the African conception of the judicial function is not so much the categorical statement and enforcement of certain firm principles of law as a careful and conscientious attempt to reconcile differences, adjust conflicting interests, and restore the social equilibrium. And for such a purpose a conflict between tribal laws, local laws, and religious laws is not nearly so insoluble as it might seem; for in appropriate circumstances two, or even more, of these may all be taken into account in an *ad hoc* "equitable" settlement.

MORE GENERAL INFLUENCES

The profound effects of the advent of Islâm on Negro African life and culture have repeatedly been noticed. Thus Meek goes so far as to say:

> Not only did it entail profound changes in the ethnic composition of the peoples, but it brought with it a new civilization, which gave to the Negroid races the distinctive cultural character which they bear today, dominating their political life and social institutions. . . . Islam has brought civilization to barbarous tribes. It has converted isolated pagan groups into nations; it has made commerce with the outside world possible . . . ; it has broadened the outlook, raised the standard of living by creating a higher social atmosphere, and has conferred on its followers dignity, self respect and respect for others. . . . Islam introduced the art of reading and writing, and by the prohibition of the use of alcohol, of cannibalism, blood revenge,[52] and other barbarous practices, it has enabled the Sudanese Negro to become a citizen of the world.[53]

But the same author has also noted how the adoption of Islâm has always been facilitated by the fact that its "recognition of polygyny, circumcision, the prohibition of certain foods, slavery and various other practices" demands little radical departure from primitive Negro customs. In particular, the Muslim juristic tolerance, and practical encouragement, of the institution of slavery has had a pernicious influence on the history of Negro Africa.[54]

The primary factors which tend to exercise an unifying influence throughout the whole Muslim world (including, of course, tropical Africa) are the rites, the law, and the culture of Islâm. The rites almost always come first, as we have seen, and the local differences in these are generally of minor importance. But even here the influence of the particular variety of animistic ritual previously followed tends at first partially to permeate, or at least affect, Islamic practices.

It has also been noted, moreover, that differences of opinion on points of Muslim ritual are apt to cause bitter controversy in very superficially Islamized communities, and, while this is frequently no more than a matter of personalities, it may sometimes correspond to pre-existing differences. Yet it is significant that Greenberg can justly remark:

> In spite of the local variations that exist in Mohammedan culture, its unity, especially that of its basic religious practices expressed in written form, is so great that although Islam was presented to the Hausa through such diverse media as the Negroes of Mali and Songhai, the white Touaregs of the Sahara, and Arab traders from various regions of North Africa and the Near East, it is still possible to speak of the effect of Islam on the Hausa people as a single coherent process.[55]

Everywhere, moreover, the pilgrimage to Mecca, with the transcontinental traffic this involves, tends to exercise a markedly unifying influence.

Again, we have already seen that the influence of the law of Islâm in matters other than ritual generally comes at a distinctly later date and is apt to extend far more slowly. There can be no manner of doubt, however, that the *sharîᶜa* tends to introduce a common norm of social life throughout the whole Muslim world. The law of marriage little by little succeeds in limiting unrestricted polygamy;[56] the law of divorce tends to increase the power of the husband at the expense of the wife as compared with most forms of customary law; the laws of marriage and inheritance combined are apt to transform a matrilineal, and perhaps matrilocal, community into a patrilineal and patrilocal one; the law of testate succession serves to introduce, or comes to regulate, testamentary bequests; and the enforcement of rules of exogamy, levirate marriage, etc., tends first to decrease and then to disappear.[57] But it is noteworthy that even the modern Aḥmadî missionaries usually concentrate their energies in Africa on points of ritual and dogma rather than social laws, at least in the early stages of their teaching.

The influence of the culture of Islâm may be said to anticipate, to accompany, and also to follow the ritual and the law, for both of these are commonly spread, taught, and maintained by either local or immigrant "scholars" (*malams*, *walimu*, etc.), whatever standard of learning these may have attained. Thus, again to take Northern Nigeria as an example, Meek remarks:

> There are schools in every Muslim town, conducted privately by malams. The children are sent at a very early age—sometimes at three or four[58]—by parents who wish to save themselves the trouble of looking after their offspring. Frequently the children are handed over to the care of teachers who live in a different town, or even

to malams who have no fixed abodes at all, combining trading[59] with their educational work. Ordinarily in the big centres the children attend classes for an hour in the morning and an hour at night. Females also receive instruction. The lessons are generally given before sunrise and just after sunset, so that the boys can work in the fields during the day.[60]

The curriculum in almost all such schools, whatever the locality, is primarily concerned with the prayers and other ritual duties of Islâm, and the children are taught to read and memorize the Koran in Arabic. This they commonly do by writing it out verse by verse on a writing board, or slate, and chanting it in unison in a loud voice. Later, a running commentary is given in the vernacular, while the more advanced pupils take further courses in the traditions, law, and theology of Islâm. But it is comparatively rare for them to gain any deep understanding of their religion or any real knowledge of the Arabic language, and the majority learn the prescribed passages from the Koran purely parrot-fashion. Until recently, moreover, it was true that "even the most learned and cultured *malams*" in, for example, Northern Nigeria were "wholly untouched by any of the liberalism of modern Islâm,"[61] but the secondment of *qâḍis* from the Anglo-Egyptian Sudan to the legal section of the Kano School of Arabic Studies, together with other contacts with the outside world, is now beginning to produce slow but appreciable results in awakening at least an interest in developments elsewhere. And on the east coast, of course, contacts with trends of thought in Arabia, and elsewhere in the Near and Middle East, have always been far more close and continuous. In both East and West Africa there are, moreover, a few outstanding scholars of the traditional type.

The Nigerian *malams*, as is frequently the case in other Muslim lands, are normally paid for instructing the young both by occasional gifts of money and by a present of a sheep or goat at the conclusion of the course.[62] But they also derive an income from combining the duties of a "family physician and family spiritual adviser"—thus proving the natural successors to the pagan priests. It is the *malam* who names the newborn child and provides him with Koranic charms for his protection, who later celebrates his marriages and prescribes medicines for his sicknesses, and who finally presides over his funeral.[63] Many, again, obtain the greater part of their living from exploiting the alms of the faithful. In addition, the *malams* in West Africa and the *walimu* in East Africa are regularly consulted on points of law not only by individuals but by native courts and native arbitrators of every grade and variety, while from among their number are drawn the *qâḍîs, alkalai,* a few of the *liwalis,* and most of the other officials of all Muslim courts. Needless to say, the differences between individual and individual, whether in learning or ignorance, rigidity or tolerance, piety or exploitation, are almost infinite.

In most cases, however, the knowledge of Arabic possessed even by the *malams* (etc.) in tropical Africa[64] is roughly comparable to the knowledge of Latin one might expect from a Roman Catholic priest of no high standing in a country parish in Ireland; that is, he can understand it tolerably well within a very limited range of books and subjects but has extremely little knowledge of it on any wider basis. There is, however, a tendency in some localities for strongly Muslim communities to demand the inclusion of Arabic in the curricula of ordinary government schools, as, for example, in Zaria in Northern Nigeria; while the need for *qâḍîs* and schoolteachers may give an impetus to the founding of schools or institutes such as the School of Arabic Studies at Kano or the Muslim Academy in Zanzibar. Any such developments are bound, of course, not only to reinforce the spread of Islamic culture as such but also to increase the somewhat modernist, and frequently political, influence exercised by the Arabic-speaking countries of the Near East. But this is limited, in West Africa, by the claims of the Sultan of Sokoto, the Shehu of Bornu and, of course, the Sultan of Morocco to the leadership of the whole Muslim community, and by the strongly conservative, exclusive, and self-sufficient attitude which has hitherto prevailed, for example, throughout Northern Nigeria; and, in East Africa, by the fact that the Ibâḍîs stand somewhat aloof from all but their own community, while the Shâfiᶜîs still look more to Arabia than to Cairo for their inspiration.

Although Islâm may no longer be imposed by the sword,[65] there can be no doubt that it is still spreading in tropical Africa. Paganism as a philosophy is always parochial, and, with the growing awareness of a wider world beyond the tribal boundaries, it must inevitably give way to larger faiths or larger skepticisms. On the whole it would be true to say that, where Muslim influences were already at work before the European occupation, Islamic propaganda has tended to extend and consolidate its hold, whereas elsewhere the same sociological factors have helped Christianity to fill the vacuum.[66] In some areas, it is true, the hatred and fear engendered by centuries of slave raiding, combined with a genuine attachment to the old way of life, have enabled islands of paganism to survive within a sea of Islâm. This is particularly true of the Bauchi and Plateau Provinces of Northern Nigeria. Elsewhere, as we have seen, a veneer of Islâm only very partially covers a fundamental paganism, as in parts of the Northern Territories of the Gold Coast. But there are many localities where it is true that "the pagan who goes abroad from his home finds it convenient to adopt the Muslim garb and mode of life,"[67] for it is noteworthy how those from the Northern Territories of the Gold Coast, for instance, almost all adopt at least a façade of Islâm when they emigrate to the Zongos of Ashanti and the Colony. This is one of several ways in which the present-day improvement in security and communications tends to accelerate the expansion of Islâm—an expansion which is also considerably assisted by the fact that local British authorities, particularly in West Africa, so often appear to be biased in its favor.

Elsewhere, of course, Christianity is making a more successful bid for the allegiance of pagan Africa, as is probably true throughout the whole of East Africa except, perhaps, Tanganyika and the Kenya Protectorate, and also in many areas of the more southerly parts of Nigeria and the Gold Coast. Some administrative officers, it is true, go so far as to maintain that Islâm is better suited than Christianity to the soul—and the present progress—of tropical Africa, and it may certainly be conceded that the African, even more than the European, finds it easier to be a consistent Muslim than a sincere and practicing Christian. But, even apart from the basic question of ultimate truth and divine revelation—which must, obviously, be the final arbiter—it seems clear that the adoption of Islâm by a primitive people will unquestionably help them to progress up to a certain, and fairly clear-cut, stage of social advancement, but thereafter inevitably act as a deterrent to any further progress; while the sincere adoption of Christianity, although far more difficult and costly, opens up the possibility of advance to which there are no such limits.

NOTES

1. Thus J. Greenberg maintains, in *The Influence of Islam on a Sudanese Religion* (New York, 1947), that in Hausaland "amalgamation of Moslem and native belief did not take place in the main through intensive contact between peoples, but came about by a process in which the native learned class adapted what they found in the written and printed sources at their disposal to the native situation" (p. 10).

2. E.g., Mecca, Tarim, Cairo, al-Najaf, Qumm, Bombay, Ṣanᶜâᵓ, Nazwa, Lahore, etc.

3. Except, that is, for certain Aḥmadî missionaries and their converts, and the

other immigrant communities mentioned above. Similarly, exceptions to the foregoing generalization may be found in contacts with Libya, Egypt, and the Sudan.

4. Cf. the Sultan of Morocco.

5. Although I was able to converse with most Nigerian *alkalai* in that language.

6. As distinct from the Colony of Kenya and the Protectorate of the Gambia, respectively.

7. Cf. Greenberg, *op. cit.*, p. 27; Sir Alan Burns, *History of Nigeria* (London, 1929), p. 235; and elsewhere.

8. P. 271.

9. *Ibid.*, p. 272.

10. *Ibid.*, p. 273.

11. Cf. my recent survey of the position in British colonial possessions in Africa, *Islamic Law in Africa*, in which many of the points noted in this paper are elaborated.

12. Cf. R. S. Rattray, *Tribes of the Ashanti Hinterland* (Oxford, 1932), II, 559, 579, 584, 586.

13. *Ibid.*, pp. 473, 530, 550; Bowditch, *op. cit.*, pp. 169 ff. Yet I was told that the number of those who say Muslim prayers was increasing in both Yendi and Kpembe.

14. *Op. cit.*, p. 21.

15. C. K. Meek, *The Northern Tribes of Nigeria* (London, 1925), II, 2.

16. *Ibid.*, pp. 3 and 4.

17. *The Influence of Islam on a Sudanese Religion*, pp. 27, 29, 60–61, 67–68.

18. *Ibid.*, p. 62.

19. But Rev. J. Spencer Trimingham's recent researches have surprised him (he tells me) by the absence of the saint-cult among Negroes. It is very active among the Moors of the Sahil; it is present in the defective form of attachment to living holy men among Negro people in the Senegal (particularly the Wolof) and some other borderland regions influenced by Moors; but it is not an integral part of the religious life of West African Negro Muslims. This, Mr. Trimingham concludes, seems to show that there is no necessary affinity between the ancestor-cult and the saint-cult, since the first may disappear but the second (in the form of veneration of holy men after death) not take its place. In the central Sudan the highly developed spirit-cults (e.g., *bôrî* in Northern Nigeria) take the place of the saint-cults.

20. *Op. cit.*, I, 269 (cf. *ibid.*, II, 3). For the pagan attitude and practice, cf. the following summary: "The oath is not normally a solemn asseveration that the speaker is telling the truth—it is a self-imprecation charged with punishing power. It may be sworn by the elemental forces of nature . . . , or by the spirit of some forefather, or by some sacred object charged with magical power, or by some non-sacred object symbolising the kind of punishment that will overtake the swearer if he perjures himself" (*ibid.*, I, 264).

21. I am indebted to Mr. Spencer Trimingham for this information.

22. Greenberg, *op. cit.*, p. 27.

23. Meek, *op. cit.*, II, 4.

24. E.g., in the Northern Territories of the Gold Coast, among the Yao, and elsewhere.

25. Which may still be performed in age-groups, etc., and retain much of their pagan background.

26. Cf. *The Northern Tribes of Nigeria*, II, 6 (quoting Professor Westermann).

27. Cf. also, in this connection, Greenberg, *op. cit.*, pp. 58–59.

28. Meek, *op. cit.*, I, 174.

29. Cf., in this matter, practice in Darfur (and elsewhere).

30. See below, n. 57.

31. Muslim Giriama, moreover, do not (it seems) enforce the levirate marriage otherwise practiced by the tribe.

32. The *yarad* represents the Somali bride-wealth and is payable to the bride's father; the *gabbâti* is an advance payment of part of this; and the *ḍibâd* is a bridal present from the bride's father to his daughter. Both *gabbâti* and *ḍibâd* commonly bear some relation to the size of the *yarad*.

33. In this the first husband's children are regarded as belonging to the second, not vice versa (*Encyclopaedia of Islâm*, IV, Part I, 487).

34. These are taken among the Somali by the accused, not, as in the normal Shâfiᶜî law, by the "heirs of blood." And there are other differences.

35. E.g., in regard to questions of land tenure; certain matters of procedure; talion for wounds; the rate of blood-wit for accidental homicide; systems of marriage gifts and payments; a wife's ability, in all circumstances, to enforce dissolution of marriage for return of dower (if sufficiently determined); the age at which a divorced or widowed woman's custody of her children is regarded as ending; the maximum period of gestation, as commonly reckoned, in regard to the paternity of posthumous children; etc.

36. But it is also due in part to the fact that the Mâlikî law applicable in the west accords a cruelly ill-treated wife the right to a judicial divorce, and also enforces divorce (with or without financial consideration supplied by the wife) when this is recommended by a council of arbitrators appointed to investigate the causes of any grave marital discord; and this is far closer to African customary law than is the more rigid Shâfiᶜî doctrine applicable in the east.

37. Cf. J. M. Gray, *History of the Gambia* (Cambridge, 1940), pp. 328–30, 388–98, 416–30, 444–55, etc. The term "Soninki" is here used neither in its ethnological nor its linguistic sense but as the name locally applied to those whose attachment to Islâm and its observances is, or was, regarded as somewhat lighthearted. "Marabûṭ" is, of course, a corruption of the Arabic *murâbiṭ*, and is here used of the stricter Muslim party.

38. Cf. (both above and below) a discussion of this subject, fuller but in similar terms, in *Islamic Law in Africa*, pp. 3–6.

39. But this is less true, e.g., of Bathurst than of Somaliland, for in the former there has been more fusion of the two.

40. Cf. the *sadaki* payment added by Muslims, throughout most of the Gold Coast, to the customary payments of their pagan compatriots.

41. In such tribal marriages there is unquestionably an agreement to marry between the couple concerned, the consent of the bride's father, the payment of bride-wealth, and the presence of witnesses. Normally, however, there is not that formal declaration and acceptance which constitute the essence of the Islamic contract of marriage, and the absence of this is often made the basis of an allegation, *inter alia*, of the illegitimacy of the children of such a marriage, in any case of disputed inheritance.

42. This is partly because the dominant Shâfiᶜî view never allows a forced *khulᶜ*

at all, whereas the Mâlikî doctrine regularly allows this when recommended by a council of arbitration (although not otherwise). See n. 36, above.

43. The waiting period during which a widowed or divorced woman may not remarry. Where Islamic law prevails in such matters, this is strictly enforced; where customary law predominates, it may be wholly disregarded; and where the two are in competition, the *ᶜidda* of widowhood, alone, is sometimes observed (since this is reinforced either by threats of the anger an immediate remarriage would cause to a dead husband's spirit, or by the observance of some similar waiting time for widows in the local customary law).

44. Here, again, the pure *sharîᶜa* regards a first or second divorce in the single form as revocable, with or without the wife's consent, during the continuance of the *ᶜidda* period, while thereafter the divorce is decisive, although the parties may remarry by mutual consent, a new contract, and a new dower. But any utterance of the triple formula, or any divorce repeated for the third time, instantly and finally dissolves the marriage; and the parties are utterly precluded from remarriage unless or until the woman has consummated a valid marriage with another man and then been widowed or again divorced. Customary law, on the other hand, allows for conciliation, and resumption of the marriage relationship, in any circumstances and without restriction.

45. In the past this would not have been allowed, in many localities, for the acceptance by the parents of prenuptial gifts and payments was regarded as virtually constituting a marriage in customary law. Today, however, a girl who is sufficiently determined can usually, in theory at least, resist the union, but all such disbursements must then be returned. Until this is done, the man who made them may, in some systems, sue any more successful suitor for adultery, or even claim the child of such a union. In the *sharîᶜa* the second suitor is regarded as gravely at fault unless the former promise of marriage has first been rescinded; but the only other question at issue would be how far the various gifts and payments were reclaimable.

46. In some districts this is never allowed; in others it will only be allowed after the former marriage has been duly dissolved and suitable repayments completed (and then by means of a new and formal contract); while in others it can easily be arranged, virtually with retrospective effect, by the agreement of the woman's parents and the refund of the former husband's disbursements. And there are corresponding differences regarding the legal paternity of any child born of the second union in the meantime.

47. I.e., four years in Shâfiᶜî law, and five in the best known of several Mâlikî opinions. But in customary law the paternity of such a child frequently rests solely on the word of the mother, while about a year is commonly regarded as the maximum period of gestation.

48. E.g., the legitimacy of the children of "tribal" marriages, of marriages with pagan women, or of wives in excess of the legal four; of children born to a paramour or "slave" concubine; etc.

49. The mother's right lasts until the child is about seven, in the Shâfiᶜî doctrine, for boy or girl alike (after which the child has an option), and in the dominant Mâlikî doctrine until puberty for a boy and removal to her husband's house for a girl; but the "weaker" Mâlikî opinion which substitutes the age at which first teeth give place to second instead of puberty is much favored, on customary grounds, throughout West Africa, while in a number of widely scattered localities children may be

claimed by the father at any time after weaning. And there are further departures from the strict law in regard, e.g., to whether a divorced mother may take the children away from their father's locality.

50. Even, e.g., in Northern Nigeria, in spite of the lip service paid to Islamic law, even in this respect, in certain purist circles.

51. This is not normally allowed today, either in East or in West Africa. As a consequence it is much easier for a wife to induce an unwilling husband to agree to a dissolution of marriage on repayment of dower, since, otherwise, he will neither profit from her society nor, perhaps, be in a position to contract another marriage.

52. But this is an overstatement, and it would be preferable to substitute, e.g., "human sacrifice."

53. Meek, *op. cit.*, II, 1, 4, and 5.

54. For although the Muslim may point with satisfaction to the fact that domestic slavery has frequently proved quite a humane institution in Muslim lands, no such plea can be admitted in regard to the slave raids and slave trade which provided so large a part of the wealth of Muslim African princedoms: on the contrary, the misery, suffering, and loss of life involved were prodigious.

55. *Op. cit.*, p. 11.

56. In spite, that is, of the various devices regarding "slave" wives or concubines mentioned above.

57. The first development in regard to levirate marriage is, commonly, for the new union to be accompanied by a new contract and even a new (but decreased) dower; then any such union becomes increasingly dependent on the free consent of the widow concerned, but bride-wealth is returnable if she refuses it; and, finally, the widow is regarded as free to remarry as she chooses without any obligation or repayment.

58. But this is probably younger than the normal practice, which seems to be between five and eight (Greenberg, *op. cit.*, p. 64). And outside the main towns it is only a minority which receives any formal education at all.

59. Or, indeed, agriculture, in which the pupils provide the labor except at those hours, or seasons, when the claims of the fields give way to those of learning.

60. Meek, *op. cit.*, II, 8.

61. *Ibid.*, p. 9. This is also largely true of East African *walimu*.

62. *Ibid.*

63. Greenberg, *op. cit.*, pp. 66 and 67.

64. Except, that is, on the coast of East Africa (including Zanzibar).

65. In the past the sword was, of course, one of the major means of Islamic expansion, in Africa as elsewhere. In general, African Muslims conducted campaigns less from proselytizing zeal than from a desire for territorial expansion or slave raiding—and it was partly in an attempt to secure immunity from the latter that many pagans embraced Islâm.

66. Cf. R. Oliver, *The Missionary Factor in East Africa*, (London, 1952), pp. 202–7. But a further factor in some localities is that Islâm is regarded as offering the attractions of a comparatively lofty theology and world-wide brotherhood without either the exacting morality of Christianity or its European associations.

67. Meek, *op. cit*, II, 7.

INDONESIA: MYSTICISM AND ACTIVISM

G. W. J. DREWES

WRITING about life in Mecca in the latter part of the nineteenth century, a distinguished authority remarked that the Indonesian pilgrims behaved in the holy city in a much more modest way than pilgrims from countries that had once played an important role on the stage of Islâm. It was—he said—as if with every step the Indonesian wanted to give expression to the conviction that his share of the blessings of Islâm was utterly undeserved, as it had not been earned by his own labor!

And, indeed, Indonesia with her more than sixty million Muslim inhabitants may freely boast of being one of the largest Muslim states in the world. But her conversion to Islâm set in when this religion had already achieved its definitive form. In the gradual absorption of many a thing for which the Islamic religion stands, Indonesia has shown great receptivity and an amazing faculty for adapting newly acquired ideas to her old basic pattern of thinking, but she has not displayed any creative impulse. In matters of religion the Indonesians have always been good followers; they have never taken the lead.

But however modest the contribution of Indonesian theologians to the sacred literature of later times may have been, it has not been nonexistent. For in every century there has been in Indonesia not only a certain number of scholars whose knowledge was equal to that of theologians in other regions of the Muslim world but even some who did not cut a poor figure in the centers of Muslim learning.

From their pens came the Indonesian commentaries to Arabic texts and the textbooks adapted from foreign sources for the needs of the Indonesian believers in general, not to mention the innumerable mass of small tracts and pamphlets they wrote on their own initiative, prompted by the current needs of Indonesian society. A host of less important writers and copyists followed in their wake. Some of these authors, who during a prolonged stay in an Arab environment had acquired proficiency in Arabic, wrote in this language and saw their books published by the printing presses of Mecca, Cairo, and Istanbul. Even Malay works were sometimes published in these centers of Muslim learning. Numerous unpublished religious works in various Indonesian languages are still to be found in collections of Indonesian manuscripts, especially in the Jakarta and Leiden collections. Although a complete survey of this literary activity is not yet available, dependence upon Arabic sources will undoubtedly prove one of the main characteristics of this kind of literature. It would, however, be unjust to reproach the Indonesian writers on religious subjects with their lack of originality, in view of the well-known fact that in Muslim religious literature a writer who faithfully reproduces an approved model may lay claim to the highest merit.

Modest again appears at first sight the place of Islâm in Indonesian society. One might even say that one of the most conspicuous traits of Indonesian Islâm is its inconspicuousness. Whoever knows Islâm only as it appears in North Africa or in the Near East can, on visiting Indonesia, at first hardly believe himself to be in a Muslim country at all. And not only passing visitors but even people who have been living in the country for a considerable time will tell you first and foremost about Borobudur and Hindu-Javanese temples, about Javanese and Balinese dancing and stage performances. In short, they can inform you about all kinds of non-Muslim aspects of Indonesian life, but most probably they will never have seen the inside of a mosque. Nor is this surprising. Magnificent structures that bear witness to the skill of Muslim architects are completely lacking in Indonesia. Nearly everywhere daily worship takes place in the most inconspicuous of buildings, barely and sometimes almost shabbily furnished. The famous religious schools of old (*surau; pĕsantrèn*), mostly situated in the interior, were simplicity itself, and the contemporary schools for religious instruction, commonly called madrasas, equal the old schools in simplicity of design and furnishing. Therefore, in these remote regions of the *dâr al-Islâm* nothing is to be seen of the outward splendor of Muslim civilization in its prime.

Nevertheless, Islâm has prevailed to a remarkable extent over the inner man. It was this result that was envisaged by Snouck Hurgronje when he wrote that the victories gained by Islâm in Indonesian territory were on a par with the triumphs won by this religion in earlier centuries.

These words should not be misunderstood. Nowhere has the triumph of Islâm meant that it succeeded in extirpating pre-Islamic ideas root and branch. On the contrary: everywhere something of the old has remained, but among some peoples the remnants of pre-Islamic ideas and institutions are more numerous and more noticeable than among others. The same holds true for the population of Indonesia. Certain ways of thinking that were peculiar to the Indonesian mind in pre-Islamic days seem to be so fundamental that even sustained contact with Islâm has not changed them, and in many regions the indigenous culture has held its own to a very considerable extent.

Nor, I need hardly add, has the triumph of Islâm entailed a complete reception of Islamic law. For, as we all know, everywhere in the old Islamic countries the application of Muslim law has been restricted to certain well-defined domains of life. This was the prevailing practice at the time Indonesia became converted to Islâm, so how could it have been otherwise there? Moreover, in several parts of Indonesia the new religion penetrated to the higher strata of society from below and not the other way round. Therefore, there is nothing amazing in the fact that Islamic law is mainly operative in the sphere of family life. Even here, however, exceptions are found. Succession is almost everywhere based upon customary law (*ᶜâda*), not upon Islamic law (*sharîᶜa*), and this is even the case in religious circles. Social institutions seem to have undergone little change, the principal innovation being the establishment of the mosque as the center of religious life, which was used not only as a place of daily worship but for the adjudication of cases considered as coming under religious law.

However, from the religious point of view many of the time-hallowed institutions in Indonesian society were quite contrary to Islâm. A most striking example of an institution that in Muslim eyes can only be anathema is offered by the typical matrilineal social organization of Minangkabau, in the western part of central Sumatra. Here a perpetual struggle of varying intensity between *ᶜâda* and *sharîᶜa* has been going on, and similar conflicts on a smaller scale occurred from time to time in several places where social institutions or popular beliefs and superstitions gave rise to criticism from the Muslim point of view. As a matter of fact, the Islamization of Indonesia is still in progress, not only in the sense that Islâm is still spreading among pagan tribes, but also in that peoples who went over to Islâm centuries ago are living up more and more to the standard of Muslim orthodoxy. A third stage in the development of Indonesian Islâm was reached with the spread of reformist ideas. Then orthodoxy became engaged in battle on two fronts: it had to combat both conservatives and reformists. The latter, however, joined forces with orthodoxy in denouncing all that was considered incompatible with Islâm, however dear it might be to Indonesian hearts.

Of course we can mention here only a few points of this long story; much must go unreported. One may say that in the course of time the struggle of *sharîᶜa* versus *ᶜâda* has become only one of the manifold problems with which Indonesian society has been confronted by the intellectual and social evolution of modern times. All these problems have this in common: that they arise from the desire for emancipation from the shackles of tradition. Former generations strove to give expression to their enhanced sense of individuality and, sometimes, of self-importance, in the obvious terms of Muslim orthodoxy. Among the present generation many still try to do so in the terms of reformism, but for an ever increasing number of Indonesians these too no longer suffice for that purpose.

As is well known, Islâm reached Indonesia by the same channel through which in earlier centuries Indian civilization and Indian religions had been transmitted: the southeast Asian trade route from India to China along the coast of the Malay Peninsula. It is to the proselytizing efforts of Indian merchants who had settled in the ports of Malaya and northern Sumatra that Indonesian Islâm owes its existence. Hence the fact that the Indonesians belong to the school of law of al-Shâfiᶜî, which is likewise predominant on the Coromandel and Malabar coasts. But Islâm as preached and practiced by these Indian merchants had passed through Persia and through India, and it showed unmistakable traces of that long passage. According to the formula coined by Snouck Hurgronje, it laid more stress upon thinking than upon acting: to have the right ideas about the relation between God and the world and about the place of man in the universe was considered much more important than what Allâh had ordered His servants to do.

Now, speculations as to the value of life and the character of the phenomenal world, the Absolute and the Transitory, were already a common feature of Indonesian religious thinking in pre-Islamic times. Moreover, it appears from medieval Indonesian inscriptions and literature that various yoga practices were in use to bring about the extinction of human individuality and to insure the merging of human existence into the Unique Being. It is not too bold a supposition that these teachings of the Shivaite and Mahayana Buddhist sects that were in vogue in Java and Sumatra before Islâm prepared the soil for the reception of the seed of Islamic heterodox mysticism.

For it was this kind of mysticism that was brought by the Indian merchants when Indonesia got its share for the second time of the spiritual treasures of the Indian continent.

Perhaps one could argue that the esoteric teachings of Shivaism and Buddhism had most likely not affected the ideas of the common man and that, therefore, the mass of the population had maintained its autochthonous way of thinking. Even then the attraction for the Indonesian of heterodox mysticism with its doctrine of All-Unity may find a plausible explanation in the affinity between mysticism and so-called "primitive" religion. Primitive religion derives from the conviction of the unity of all life. There is an internal coherence between macrocosmos and microcosmos, between the universe and its epitome—man. Man participates in universal life, and this participation is something he demonstrates in various actions and tries to experience in different ways; it is not an abstract idea acquired by reasoning.

One may suppose that a new religion in which the mystical element was as prominent as it appears to have been in medieval Indian Islâm was likely to appeal to the Indonesian mentality. But of course other factors too may have been operative. The new faith, laying claim to being a universal religion, was perhaps particularly appealing to those Indonesians who lived in the cosmopolitan atmosphere of the Malayan ports and had outgrown the fabric of their hereditary social and religious system. It seems that they were easily attracted by the new and the unknown, and gratefully appropriated the feeling of superiority to "idolators" that Islâm imparts to its adherents.

However this may be, at the end of the thirteenth century the propagation of Islâm among the Indonesians had set in. We have very scanty information about the first centuries after its appearance, as the oldest documents available go back to the end of the sixteenth and the beginning of the seventeenth century. They contain either mystical poetry and mystical tracts or attacks on heterodox mysticism.

There is a marked difference between the texts from Java and those from Sumatra. The literature of Sumatran origin reveals a number of striking personalities: Hamzah Fansuri, Shamsuddin, Nuruddin arRaniri, AbdurRauf of Singkel. The Javanese writings, however, bear the impersonal character that in general is peculiar to most Javanese literary works.

Hamzah Fansuri and his pupil, Shamsuddin, were adherents of a school of mysticism that by its adversaries was disparagingly called "heretical *wujûdiyya*"; its popular name is the "Seven Grades" (*měrtabat tujuh*). It may be characterized as a doctrine of emanation that derives from and bears close resemblance to the existentialist monism of Ibn al-ᶜArabî. Ibn al-ᶜArabî taught that all things in the universe necessarily emanate from divine prescience—in which they pre-exist as ideas—as a flux evolving in five stages. In man, who represents the sixth stage of emanation, this evolution may be undone, as the soul can reintegrate the divine essence by seeing through the false outward appearance of plurality. Man has to become conscious of the fundamental truth that the existence (*wujûd*) of created things is nothing but the very essence of the Creator; hence the name of this doctrine: *wujûdiyya*.

As is well known, there is no unanimity among Muslims about the orthodoxy of Ibn al-ᶜArabî. Although he belonged to the Ẓâhirî school of law and enjoined upon his followers the strictest observance of the prescripts of Islâm, this did not mislead his opponents. With infallible instinct they diagnosed the heretical character of his teachings and accused him of emanatism and monism. The same charges were brought against the Sumatran mystics, Hamzah and Shamsuddin.

One is inclined to suspect that apart from discrepancies in doctrine —which might be forgivable if not ventilated in public—it was the outspokenness of Hamzah in his rapturous poetry that provoked the indignation of his enemies. Moreover, although Hamzah kept up the appearance of ritual obligations for the common believer, it is highly improbable that he himself clung to the observance of outward religious duties, as he proclaimed prayer and fasting superfluous for the accomplished mystic who knew how to free himself from the shackles of this illusory phenomenal world.

After Hamzah's death his pupil, Shamsuddin (d. 1630), rose to the position of dignitary at the court of Achèh. His most illustrious pupil was the sultan himself, Iskandar Muda, the most famous of all the rulers of that northern Sumatran bulwark of Islâm. At the death of Iskandar Muda (1636) the influence of Shamsuddin immediately came to an end. Reaction, sponsored by the court, set in, and an Indo-Arab scholar from Rander in Gujarat, Nuruddin, who had learned to write in Malay, became instrumental in the re-education of the population on orthodox lines.

During the seven years of his stay (1637–44) this man set himself the task of inculcating in the Indonesian mind a greater knowledge of the tenets of Islâm and more respect for the main points of orthodox belief. Probably he was of the opinion that what the Indonesians needed most of all was the genuine Muslim fear of the Last Judgment and of Hell. Therefore he wrote a book on eschatology that became very popular and was widely read even centuries later. But to insure the success of his program he did not hesitate to take more drastic measures. Not only did he have the books of his adversaries burned in public but a number of heretics died at the stake, an atrocity remembered in Achèh many years afterwards.

Not that Nuruddin was averse to mysticism. Nor did he consider the *wujûdiyya* doctrine an uncommendable kind of mysticism, provided it was interpreted in such a way that the rights of orthodoxy were affirmed or, at least, the outward appearance of orthodoxy was maintained. It is not without its significance that this fierce opponent of Hamzah and Shamsuddin quoted with approval from the works of Ibn al-ᶜArabî and from those of his orthodox champion, ᶜAbd al-Razzâq al-Kâshânî, the commentator of the *Fuṣûṣ al-ḥikam*, nor that, in a somewhat later period, AbdurRauf, the Saint of Achèh, wrote an orthodox interpretation of Ibn al-ᶜArabî's famous lines (from the *Manâzil al-insâniyya*):

> We were lofty sounds (yet) unuttered,
> Held in abeyance on the highest peaks of the mountains.
> I was in Him, and we were you, and you were He,
> And all in Him was He; ask those who have attained.

The same lines are quoted in Hamzah's *Asrâr al-ᶜârifîn*, but AbdurRauf gives in his commentary (*Daqâᵓiq al-ḥurûf*) an orthodox explanation of the doctrine of the "Seven Grades" without even altering its terminology.

Orthodox guidance came also from the center of the Islamic world. When a number of Indonesian pilgrims in Medina applied for acceptance in the Shaṭṭâriyya fraternity, the venerable Shaikh Aḥmad Qushâshî aptly remarked that they wanted to be initiated into the deeper secrets of religion before they had mastered the elementary knowledge. This remark hits the nail on the head, for that was what the Indonesians had been doing from the very beginning. Aḥmad Qushâshî ordered his pupil and successor, Ibrâhîm al-Kûrânî, to write an orthodox commentary on a book of the Indian mystic, Faḍl Allâh of Burhanpur, because, as he said, it had come to his knowledge that many Indonesian readers of this work had by misinterpretation of the text strayed away from the path of truth.

With Ibrâhîm al-Kûrânî studied a number of Indonesian theologians who, in the latter part of the seventeenth century, stood in high repute in their country, such as, to mention only two of the best known among them, AbdurRauf, the national saint of Achèh, who introduced the Shaṭṭâriyya fraternity in Indonesia, and Shaikh Yusup, the national saint of southern Celebes. Shaikh Yusup was banished to the Cape by the Dutch East India Company and died there, but his mortal remains were brought back to his native country.

As appears from these facts, the Indonesians had established contacts with the holy cities in the first half of the seventeenth century. People not only from Sumatra but also from Java went there; the Court of Bantĕn—in the westernmost part of Java—repeatedly sent missions to Mecca in quest of information on religious matters or to ask for commentaries on difficult books, such as the *Insân al-kâmil*, the *Book of the Perfect Man*, written by ᶜAbd al-Karîm al-Jîlî.

The cause of orthodoxy was also furthered by pious Arabs who settled down for a while in Indonesia, a country where they could always be sure of meeting with respect, particularly when they claimed descent from the holy Prophet. Some sayyids attained political influence by entering into the service of native princes who wished to profit by their worldly wisdom. Others married into princely families and even became rulers and founders of dynasties, as was the case in a few petty principalities of eastern Sumatra and Borneo. In later years a regular emigration from Ḥaḍramaut set in, and a great number of Arabs from the lower classes of Ḥaḍramaut came to Indonesia in search of a living. As the Arab community increased in number, however, it gradually lost the esteem of the native population. But until recent times pious members of this community acted as schoolmasters and preachers and were held in high regard on account of their religious zeal.

Still, the principal thing was that the Indonesians had found their way to the holy country and that thereby a new channel had been opened by which religious knowledge could be obtained. Several Indonesians spent a considerable time in the centers of Islamic learning and studied with prominent scholars all over Arabia. After returning to their native country, they settled down as teachers of religion, or they were appointed to posts connected with public worship and religious jurisdiction. The local chiefs often requested them to write books on various subjects, and in this way the religious literature in Indonesian languages gradually acquired a more varied character. Moreover, as the Indonesians grew better acquainted with the religious literature of Islâm, the dividing line, not only between orthodoxy and heterodoxy but also between what was consistent with Islâm in Indonesian society and what was not, became clearer. By this time part of the religious law and custom had generally amalgamated into a single whole that to most Indonesians seemed perfectly workable, so that the equilibrium attained after the first centuries of Islamization could not be easily disturbed. Attempts to bring about a stricter observance of religious law and to remold Indonesian life into greater conformity with the standard pattern of orthodoxy, though not infrequent, did not as a rule meet with lasting success outside limited circles.

This curious laxity, however, did not prove incompatible with absolute loyalty to Islâm and a profound respect for Muslim learning and piety. In Sumatra, Minangkabau, the central part of the west coast of this island, and Achèh—both regions where customary law in many respects has not been outbalanced by the law of Islâm—have always been famous as centers of Islamic studies.

An eighteenth-century writer on Sumatra even put on record that the country of Minangkabau was regarded as the "supreme seat of civil and religious authority in this part of the East." This attachment to the study of religion, however, engendered in the long run the forces that tended to the disintegration of the established order, and the more so because, as things were, the number of theologians that could be suitably incorporated into the structure of Minangkabau society was very small. No wonder that it was from the class of independent theologians that the leaders arose who, about a hundred and thirty years ago, decided to make a clean sweep of everything in Minangkabau society that was a disgrace to truly Muslim life: the matrilineal social organization, the law of succession, and the indulgence in all kinds of illicit pleasures and pastimes. A long and bloody civil war—the Padĕri war—ensued, and peace could only be restored after the defending party had asked for and procured the armed intervention of the Dutch colonial government. The ancestral form of Minangkabau society was maintained, but, as the underlying causes of the conflict had not been removed, the country continued to be divided against itself. Ever since, controversies about issues that in themselves were rather unimportant have given rise from time to time to protracted quarrels.

In the latter half of the nineteenth century, for example, adherents of the Naqshibandiyya fraternity, which had penetrated from

Mecca into Minangkabau, raised the standard of orthodoxy. Within a few years the country was rife with the wranglings between the Naqshibandiyya group and the adepts of the old-fashioned Shaṭṭâriyya mysticism, which besides a popular dilution of the doctrine of the "Seven Grades" included a good deal of local magic and sorcery. An outsider, however, would have had some difficulty in grasping the case in point, as the main issues of these passionate arguments were the pronunciation of Arabic, the establishing of the *qibla*, and the beginning and the end of the Ramaḍân fasting period. Sometimes the conflict broke out in such violence that the parties absolutely refused to attend Friday service together, and one of them built a rival mosque, with all the consequences of such a step. A third party entered the lists as well. It consisted of more legal-minded orthodox believers who, while stigmatizing a number of Naqshibandiyya practices as objectionable innovations, equally condemned both fraternities.

Another subject that was always harped on by militant orthodox theologians was, of course, the Minangkabau family system and the law of succession. Some of these champions of orthodoxy even went so far as to proclaim all property inherited under that law plunder. Whoever was in possession of such property was guilty, according to them, of a major sin, as he was "consuming the property of orphans." Therefore, such people were to be considered as *fâsiq* and could not legally act as witnesses to marriages. The lawfulness of marriages contracted with their assistance was to be repudiated, all connections with them were to be severed, and they were to be denied a Muslim burial.

There is no question but that these quarrels would not have been so vehement if they had not provided an outlet for long-pent-up feelings of ill will that were not purely religious in origin.

In the first decades of this century important changes took place in the Minangkabau region of Sumatra. Stimulated by such governmental measures as the abolition of the compulsory cultivation of coffee, the introduction of taxes levied in cash, the repeal of the rice-export prohibition, the building of roads, and the promotion of education on Western lines, a period of increased activity set in, in the economic as well as in other fields. Money economy more and more superseded the old economic system and bred a spirit of enhanced individualism, so that the hereditary authorities lost a good deal of their former prestige.

The same obtained in the religious field. Here too the traditional authorities were brushed aside, the principle of *taqlîd* as it had developed in the Muslim community after about A.D. 1000 was discarded by many, and in ever larger circles the ideas of Egyptian reformism gained ground. Consequently, new differences of opinion and practice were added to the existing ones, but, curiously enough, public discussion centered chiefly around four minor points: (1) whether the intention (*niyya*) before the ritual prayer should be said inwardly or aloud, as has been the practice within the Shâfiᶜî *madhhab* since Nawawî (thirteenth century); (2) whether the religious fraternities went back to the time of the Prophet; (3) whether it was obligatory to rise from one's seat at the recitation of the chorus in the story of the Prophet's birth; (4) whether it was in accordance with the sunna to gather in a house of mourning to have a religious meal there on the day of a person's death and the next following days and to recite the Koran and litanies on that occasion.

It was not long before more serious problems, of a political character, instead of such futile questions, claimed universal attention. After the first World War Communist agitation had been launched against colonial territories, and the former Dutch East Indies got their full share.

As economic conditions about 1920 had rapidly deteriorated owing to the serious slump in trade of those years, Communist propaganda found a willing ear. This was especially the case in Minangkabau where, despite outward appearances, the social order had lost a good deal of its coherence and Communist propaganda had donned the garb of Islâm. Not a few of the Communist leaders were recruited from the former pupils of the numerous reformist schools—young men who on account of their excellent training were destined for leadership anyhow. Such teachings of Egyptian reformism as stress the necessity of restating the principles of Islamic ethics in terms of social values undoubtedly had not been lost upon them, and the colonial situation as well as the tendency to fanaticism peculiar to the Minangkabau character were accountable for the rest. The most prominent leaders of the reformist movement, however, were opposed to Communism. But their counteraction was doomed to peter out, as they were mistrusted by the conservatives and the government and, moreover, silenced by Communist terrorization.

Communist agitation eventually led to the Minangkabau riot of 1927, which, badly timed, poorly organized, and unsupported by the mass of the population as it was, was easily quelled by the government. As was to be expected, after these events a tendency to check the process of social disintegration by reinforcing the ᶜâda became manifest in conservative circles. On the other hand, reformist ranks were swelled with numerous malcontents and erstwhile partisans of disbanded extremist political groups. There can be little doubt that this development accelerated the evolution of Minangkabau reformism in an anti-imperialist, nationalist, and socialist sense—an evolution that had already set in before the Communist riot.

Political feeling ran high in the next years. A local branch of the all-Indonesian Muslim political party (*Partai Sarèkat Islam Indonésia*)—which in Java already had a stormy life behind it—was established and scored considerable success. Even the Minangkabau branches of Muḥammadiyya, a nonpolitical reformist organization with its headquarters at Jogjakarta (Java), could only with some difficulty be restrained from taking part in political activities by special delegates sent from the central committee.

Shortly afterwards, radical reformist elements founded a political party of their own, which because of its Minangkabau origin was still somewhat communalistic in outlook. A long life was not allotted to these political organizations. Before long the government prohibited their meetings, and a few years later they had no choice but to dissolve. It goes without saying that the tranquillity which ensued was only apparent.

About the same time the Western-educated intelligentsia had gradually grown in number. While in Java or abroad for the purpose of education the younger generation had absorbed any number of progressive ideas. The mainspring of their activities was no longer religion. Therefore, the problems which these young men and women raised for discussion were quite different from those which had claimed the attention of the Minangkabau reformists only a few years earlier. The Western-trained younger generation fought against backwardness in every domain of life; it rebelled against compulsory marriage and polygamy, and it advocated the emancipation of women, more rights for married women, alimony for divorced women, etc., etc.; in short, it was concerned with the same questions that are at issue throughout the Muslim world, arising from the impact of Western ideas. Malay literature was stirred to new life and produced a number of problem novels wherein some of the conflicts and entanglements in Indonesian society that originated from the clash of ideas were treated. Some of these novels were very widely read.

This Western-educated younger generation had by 1930 almost

universally abandoned Minangkabau or Sumatran patriotism and all that it stands for and had been won over to Indonesian nationalism. Local problems fell into the background, religious controversies, even religion itself, lost much of its interest in the face of the overwhelming attraction of the new political and social ideals, and for many of the younger generation the shrine of nationalism became the only place of worship. It is, however, beyond the scope of this paper to sketch the outlines of the history of Indonesian nationalism.

Sometimes the complaint is heard that the Dutch colonial administration was very partial to the champions of *ᶜâda* as against those who advocated a stricter application of Islamic law. The support lent to the *ᶜâda* party of Minangkabau in the Padĕri war is quoted as a stock example of that partiality. But then, even in the eyes of many law-abiding Muslims, the fanatical zealots of the Padĕri war stand condemned for the atrocities they committed. Moreover, far from being biased against the *sharîᶜa*, Dutch rule in the Muslim regions of Indonesia was involuntarily but undoubtedly conducive to the strengthening of Muslim influence. This was because of two important principles of Dutch colonial administration: freedom of religion and noninterference in matters of religion, which indirectly proved beneficial to the intensification of Muslim feeling. It is true that hereditary local chiefs, particularly in former times, did not refrain from dealing firmly with innovators who propagated "newfangled" ideas and tried to discredit the established order of society by religious argumentation. But, in the long run, more and more local chiefs became civil servants and, irrespective of their personal feelings, avoided interfering in religious matters. Moreover, the publicity that inevitably befell high-handed action tended to prevent arbitrary measures. Such cases as were reported in the press were not the rule; they were exceptions and, therefore, caused considerable fuss. Neither orthodox nor reformist religious propaganda suffered from official obstruction, but regulations of an administrative character sometimes aroused considerable opposition, and against the political elements of Muslim doctrine the government always took a firm stand. Still, in spite of alleged hindrances, religious periodicals circulated freely, and numerous religious schools were founded. These facts may be taken as proof that the official attitude toward the propagation of the Muslim faith can hardly be characterized as hostile. The opposition to excessive orthodox and reformist zeal arose from Indonesian society itself, which showed little inclination to do away with its age-old institutions or to change abruptly its inherited way of life.

Let us now pass on to Java and try to survey the situation of Islâm on this island. Of course we can only cast a few glances here and there, and it is out of the question that the few remarks that I can make here will do justice to the centuries-long history of Islâm in this part of the world.

The Javanese ascribe the first preaching of Islâm in this country to a number of saints, all of whom were adherents of a very pronounced mysticism.

Although the Islamization of Java must have been a complex series of events, Javanese tradition has compressed the long period of religious change into one single event of paramount importance, viz., the downfall of the Hindu-Javanese kingdom of Majapahit. This downfall is said to have been brought about by the armed intervention of "the nine saints" (*wali sanga*), whose residences are to be sought, according to Javanese tradition, in the coastal area of northeastern Java. This tradition is certainly not false in so far as at the beginning of the sixteenth century the political and economic hegemony shifted from Majapahit—situated in the interior of eastern Java—to the ports of the northeast coast.

The number of these saints, sometimes eight, sometimes nine, is rather curious. It is difficult to decide who belongs to this group and who does not, and it is impossible to ascertain the historical identity of most of them, however elaborate the way in which their family relations are recorded in the Javanese chronicles. Moreover, the tenets that Javanese tradition ascribes to each of them are as vague as their personalities.

One cannot deny that at least one or two of them seem to have been historical persons, but the stories that are told of the others are purely fictitious, as, for example, that of Siti Jĕnar, who was condemned to death for an utterance similar to the incriminating words spoken by al-Ḥallâj, a mystic and martyr who was crucified in Baghdad in A.D. 922.

Apparently the total of nine is not the result of addition; it seems rather that one must look for its origin in pre-Islamic thinking. In Hindu-Javanese cosmological mythology nine was a very important number, and it is possible that the nine *walis* occupy the places of the nine guardian-deities who presided over the points of the compass in the old cosmological system. Should this hypothesis be valid, it would help to explain why the Javanese ascribe the origin of things so decidedly un-Muslim as the shadow-play, the orchestra, the kris, etc., to Muslim saints. In doing so, they postulated the unity of culture and religion. The nine saints not only were the initiators of the new era but dominated the whole period that followed upon the Hindu-Javanese age and was named after them *jaman kuwalèn*, the "age of the saints." Not until later generations had been more thoroughly indoctrinated in the tenets of Islâm and had imbibed a more genuine Islamic spirit did they begin to take offense at these earlier attainments of Javanese civilization.

Javanese literature bears witness to the struggle between those who clung to the old views and the old way of living and the protagonists of stricter views and a more genuine Muslim life. The most important work in this connection is the *Sĕrat Chĕnṭini*, an encyclopedic poem of great length, perhaps composed about 1815 but in part probably of a somewhat earlier date. In the form of a travel story, the authors of this work portray scenes of life in the interior of Java as it must have been going on for at least two centuries at the date the work was composed. We follow the travelers on their way from one halting-place to another. Sometimes, they stay for a while in one place, preferably in a *pĕsantrèn* (religious school) or in a settlement headed by a *kyai*, an independent religious teacher. They make ample use of the opportunity of listening to the elaborate discourses of these holy men and discuss the most diverse subjects with their hosts. Profound and even abstruse topics of mystical speculation are treated abundantly, alternately with amusements of a very worldly and even scandalous character.

The authority of these spiritual leaders, however, was not unassailed, as at that time orthodoxy was asserting itself. But the authors of this long-winded "study of manners" were filled with the utmost respect for the religious teachers who headed these schools and settlements and did not side with orthodoxy. They scoff at the daily duties imposed by Islâm, and they have a low opinion of the official scribes who hold functions at the mosques. In this opinion the *Sĕrat Chĕnṭini* does not stand alone. Satirical works written in the same strain are by no means lacking in Javanese literature.

As already remarked, the *Sĕrat Chĕnṭini* gives a detailed description of life in the old religious schools. Of course these schools were not only halting-places for wandering students. Resident students sometimes stayed there for years. After they had completed their studies, they were authorized to teach in their turn and to act as spiritual guides to others. In this connection it may be remarked that *ngèlmu,* as the Javanese pronounce Arabic *ᶜilm* ("knowledge"), in particular denotes all kinds of secret knowledge. The ultimate goal of the quest for learning was initiation into esoteric doctrines, without which all religious knowledge is without taste or flavor, as the Javanese put it.

We are well acquainted with the teaching provided by these religious schools. As everywhere in Oriental countries, instruction took place by word of mouth, but the pupil wrote down what he considered important or copied fragments from manuscripts for his personal use. In this way a curious kind of religious vade-mecum came into existence. It is one of Snouck Hurgronje's many services to Islamology that he saw the paramount importance of these notebooks (in Javanese called *primbon*) for the study of Indonesian Islâm and started to collect them wherever he could. In these notebooks one may find the most heterogeneous matters. All the domains of religious learning are represented, but the majority of the contents nearly always pertains to mystical lore, in which orthodox mysticism stands side by side with outspoken monism.

Numerous expositions represent the relation between God and man in a dualistic way by comparing it to the relation between lord and servant (*gusti—kawula,* the Javanese equivalents of *rabb* and *ᶜabd*). This image was perfectly clear to a people who still thought in terms of feudalism and whose ethical code was based upon the firm conviction of the inequality of man.

Other expositions dwell on the meanings of favorite apophthegms of Indonesian mysticism, as, "To know one's self is to know one's Lord," the well-known *man ᶜarafa nafsahu faqad ᶜarafa rabbahu;* and "Man is My innermost secret and I am his secret" (*al-insân sirrî wa-anâ sirruhu*). These sayings, however, are interpreted as pertaining to the fundamental unity of microcosm and macrocosm; and a favorite means of demonstrating this unity is to arrange corresponding items in man and in the universe in groups of equal number. In this way the secrets of all that is are laid open. "All that is" may also be summarized in one word: *I* (*ingsun*). This doctrine concerning the all-embracing *I* is one of the cornerstones of Javanese metaphysical speculation.

Still other notes expatiate on the doctrine of the "Seven Grades" that we have already mentioned in connection with the Sumatran mystic, Hamzah Fansuri. In Java, too, this doctrine is very well known, and the same may be said of ᶜAbd al-Karîm al-Jîlî's *Book of the Perfect Man* (*al-Insân al-kâmil*). Citations from this work abound in the religious notebooks, and the Leiden library contains manuscript copies of it with an interlinear Javanese translation.

The religious fraternities have also left their traces in the *primbon*. Pupils who were authorized to instruct others always mention the spiritual genealogy of the teacher who initiated them into the fraternity. These genealogies enable us to trace the spread of these mystical orders back to their starting points. It appears, for example, that the Shaṭṭâriyya Order was introduced from Medina in the middle of the seventeenth century; it is the oldest among the fraternities, and in the long run it became the most degenerate. Thus it is no wonder that in the notebooks spells and incantations of indigenous origin are found mixed up with the customary *ṭarîqa*-matter of litanies, prayers, *dhikr*-formulas, etc.

Such formulas—along with indications for their use—were also transmitted in the religious schools, for spiritual exercises as practiced elsewhere in the meetings of mystical fraternities formed a rather important part of the curriculum of the *pĕsantrèn*. As appears from the *Sĕrat Chĕnṭini*, music, dancing, and singing as a means of inducing a state of individual or collective trance alternated with other performances with a religious background. Curiously enough, in these religious centers pre-Muslim dances were also performed, as well as very worldly exhibitions, juggling- and fakir-tricks. One may safely assume that the autohypnosis which is a *conditio sine qua non* for many of these performances provided the link between native and foreign practices of a kindred character. From the *pĕsantrèn* many of these semireligious amusements spread into the Javanese interior and have survived until the present day.

These few remarks may suffice to show that Javanese religious literature contains many other things besides the usual subject matter of elementary religious instruction. And there is little doubt that these other things were considered of major importance by the men who wrote them down. Actually I should not use the past tense here: these things have continued to be important to large circles of the population of Java.

Nevertheless, in Java, as elsewhere in Indonesia, orthodoxy has gained ground to a considerable extent, and so has reformism. Nothing, however, would be more dangerous than a hasty generalization. Java is a large island, and its population, although throughout agrarian in character, does not show the same religious sentiment everywhere. In the westernmost part of the island—the ancient sultanate of Bantěn—rigid orthodoxy is dominant. Among the Sundanese of western Java, who for the greater part are equally orthodox, a milder disposition generally prevails, and in certain circles reformism has been readily accepted. In Java proper, however, the religious situation is much more complex; every shade of religious feeling, ranging from old-fashioned Javanese Islâm with its antinomian and latitudinarian tendencies to the more enlightened ideas of modern reformism, may be found.

Reformist ideas were brought from Egypt by Indonesian students as well as propagated by a progressivist group among the Arab population of Indonesia. As its main theses are well known, I need not dwell on them here. In Indonesia the situation was as follows. The reform movement radiated mainly from two centers: Minangkabau and central Java. Most probably, however, it would never have spread so widely in so short a time if its propagation had remained the concern of individuals. As it happened, in Java this propagation was taken in hand by a religious association, Muḥammadiyya by name.

This association, which was rather inconspicuous at first, was founded at Jogjakarta in central Java in December, 1912, but its almost miraculous growth did not begin before 1923, after the decline of the Sarèkat Islam, a prenationalistic movement wherein Islâm was the bond of union. In this organization the political element very soon came to prevail over all others. As its ups and downs are described in detail in the *Encyclopaedia of Islâm,* I need not enter into its history here.

To return to Muḥammadiyya, from fifteen in 1923 the number of its local branches steadily increased to more than nine hundred in the period immediately before the war. Apparently the reformist conception of Islâm was just what a great number of middle-class people—merchants, tradesmen, landowners, small manufacturers, schoolteachers, clerks, etc.—had been looking for. Since the beginning of the twentieth century, Western education had increased considerably in volume and had called forth an intellectual awakening which brought about a higher evaluation of reason. This had resulted in a growing disapproval of prevalent religious views and practices, which to a large extent were considered devoid of all rationality. Moreover, the impressive attainments of Western civilization—where reason allegedly held sway—had prompted the opinion that reason was the fountainhead of all progress. Now reformism emphasized the rational character of Islâm. No wonder that it was successful with a class of people newly rationalist but still religious in outlook. In reformism they found the means to assert themselves as Muslims *and* rational beings, and it furnished them with the arms to repulse the attacks of Christian missionaries, whose activities had intensified after the first World War.

Nevertheless, the efforts of the Christian missions served as a model for the activities that Muḥammadiyya embarked upon. First and foremost came the propagation of the Muslim faith—here, as in India, called *tablîgh*—and the training of propagandists (*muballighs*). *Muballighs* acted as preachers and catechists; some of them were sent to different places all over the archipelago to promote the aims of the association and to help in the founding of local branches. Once founded, these became the centers of various activities, all organized in the orderly and methodical way that was characteristic of this association.

For the task which Muḥammadiyya had set itself was not limited to preaching, the promotion of religious instruction, and the publishing of religious books. Schools were founded, teachers were trained, and all kinds of social work were done. Muḥammadiyya set up orphanages and houses for destitute children, asylums for the blind and the poor, policlinics and hospitals—partly with money from public funds. Women were organized in a separate union, called Aishiah (after ᶜÂʾisha, the Prophet's wife), with a subsection for girls. In some towns special mosques for women and girls were opened, and regular courses for the religious instruction of the latter were established. Boys were incorporated in a boy scout movement, called Hizbul-Watan. At the two big festivals of Islâm, ᶜÎd al-Qurbân and ᶜÎd al-Fiṭr, mass gatherings in the open air were organized, which became a regular feature of public life. From all this it will be clear that the leaders of the movement strove to build up a religious organization of a very wide scope that was to encompass all social life. With one exception, however. Muḥammadiyya abstained as an organization from taking part in political life, though it did not object to its members doing so. This was not always the case, however, outside Java. As a matter of fact, in the outer provinces—especially in those regions where there were no political organizations—local branches of Muḥammadiyya often provided the only outlet for incipient political feeling. Again and again branches were founded at the instigation of progressive strangers with whom malcontents belonging to the resident population had joined hands. Therefore, it is no wonder that local authorities, both secular and religious, were on the alert and sometimes tried to curb the progress of the organization. They had little chance of success, however, as the antithesis between traditionalists and reformists was destined to become a common feature of Indonesian society throughout the archipelago.

During the war internal disputes fell into the background. They could not have been continued anyhow, because under the Japanese regime—at least in Java—associations were first dissolved and then forced into co-operation after having been allowed again by the military authorities.

As is well known, the Japanese followed the same tactics as their Nazi ally and tried to stifle the life of the subjugated peoples by means of all-embracing organizations controlled by their henchmen. In this way the *Mashumi*—abbreviation of *Majlis Shura Muslimin Indonésia,* "Consultative Assembly of Indonesian Muslims"—came into being. It stood, of course, under the close supervision of the Gunseikanbu Shumubu, the Bureau for Religious Affairs of the Japanese military administration, and its only purpose was to tighten the usurper's grip on the population and to strengthen the Japanese war effort.

As the Japanese were very well aware of the influential position still enjoyed by the *ᶜulamâᵓ* among the mass of the people, they endeavored to exploit this prestige in their own interest. As early as 1942 the Japanese head of the Shumubu made a tour through Java to lecture to the religious teachers and mosque officials. Everywhere they had received orders to be present when the colonel with his claptrap retinue of Japanese *hajis*—in Arab attire—arrived. Courses were established at Jakarta, where religious leaders who proved willing to co-operate with the military government got special training in anti-Western sentiments and Great-East-Asian ideology. In every district these puppets were charged with the task of indoctrinating the peasant population with the same spirit, first and foremost with the aim of insuring the delivery of the harvest to the Japanese authorities. Even a military Muslim corps called *Hizbullah,* "The Army of God," was trained by a Japanese *haji.* The Japanese, however, made one serious mistake with regard to Islâm. They should have remembered that a true Muslim bows down only to worship God, and should therefore have kept their cult of the "divine Emperor" to themselves and not have forced the people to do obeisance to the Japanese flag and to bow in the direction of the Imperial Throne—which by serious Muslims could only be considered as acts of idolatry.

The first Muslim political party that was founded after the war also bears the name of "Mashumi." To some extent, it may be called a continuation of the Mashumi of the Japanese period, because it drew largely upon the same groups that had been merged into the old assembly and profited by making use of what was left of its organization. It commands a large but indeterminate body of followers among the rural population, but its chief constituent elements are mostly such people as in Indonesia are considered middle-class. Nevertheless, progressive politicians are by no means lacking among its leaders.

The Mashumi is, numerically, without doubt the most powerful party in the country. Still, it is not unrivaled. A number of dissidents and political opportunists left its fold and constituted parties of their own, as, for instance, the more conservative *nahḍat al-ʿulamâʾ*—before the war an association of orthodox mosque personnel—and the *Partai Sarèkat Islam Indonésia.* The latter organization bears the name of the once famous Sarèkat Islam that about thirty-five years ago was the paramount power in Indonesian political life. It was founded by some of the epigones of the old party, allegedly out of discontent with the socialist sympathies of many of the younger Mashumi leaders.

Muḥammadiyya has been reinstated in its former position. From its headquarters at Jogjakarta it carries on its manifold activities in the domains of religion, education, and social improvement. At the end of 1951 its various subsections numbered about 160,000 members in all. It controlled more than 2,000 schools of different types with a personnel of more than 4,000 and a total of 230,000 pupils. The number of *muballighs* was about 8,000; about 3,000 buildings were in use. All this constitutes a very remarkable effort. No other Muslim organization in Indonesia can point to similar results.

In ancient Indonesia "to live religiously" meant to abstain from the affairs of this world, and the conversion to Islâm did not change this notion. It is to the credit of Muslim reformism that it has shorn religion of its extreme otherworldly character, and this is undoubtedly the reason that this new conception of Islâm has proved such a vital force in Indonesian society. Its adherents may lay claim to far greater merit than those partisans of extreme orthodoxy who—like the followers of the Darul-Islam in western and central Java—fight the Indonesian government, allegedly for the realization of a purer, but at all events utterly obsolete, conception of the Islamic state.

In this connection it may be remarked that the Darul-Islam movement is not the only postwar symptom of the desire for a Muslim state among the Indonesians. In two other regions—in Bantĕn and in Achèh—the religious leaders seized political power immediately after the Japanese defeat. These events did not come as a surprise to those who knew the real feelings of the population of those regions.

In Bantĕn the people had always put their trust much more in the independent religious teachers than in the civil and religious authorities appointed by the government. So it is no wonder that at the withdrawal of the Japanese army the Bantĕn population urged their religious leaders to step in and assume civil authority. It is true that this theocratic government nominally proclaimed allegiance to the Indonesian Republic, but at the same time it made it clear that it wanted to be left master in its own house without interference from the central government. The religious leaders, however, did not prove equal to the requirements of civil administration, and, as the difficulties increased, they became more and more disposed to leave their uncongenial task to the proper functionaries. So with the lapse of time the theocratic local government gave place without friction or disturbance of order to a secular one.

In Achèh events took a different course.

At the beginning of this century the Dutch colonial government had succeeded after long years of guerrilla warfare in putting an end to the unsettled conditions in this turbulent border region of the Netherlands Indies. It had abolished the sultanate and had subjugated the local chieftains and the religious leaders (*ᶜulamâ˒*) by force of arms. The former, with few exceptions, had accepted the *pax neerlandica* and had been integrated into the machinery of the colonial administration. The latter, however, had more difficulty in submitting to the "unbeliever." Although in the course of time the full edge of their implacability had somewhat worn off, they showed themselves to be inaccessible to modern ideas, and, in general, even the moderate reformism propagated by Muḥammadiyya did not appeal to them. On the contrary: the *Pusa* (abbr. of *Persatuan Ulama Seluruh Achèh,* "All Achèh Union of ᶜUlamâ˒"), an organization which, within a few years after its foundation in 1939, had covered a great part of the country with a network of local branches, youth clubs, and boy scout units, was frankly antireformist in character.

At first this organization, while still under the supervision of local chieftains, confined its activities to religion and sports. Before long, however, militant malcontents from other social classes joined hands with these fiercely orthodox *ᶜulamâ*ᵓ. Many of those who for whatever motive were dissatisfied with the existing order but who, owing to the complete absence of political organizations in Achèh, had hitherto not found a rallying point joined the Pusa youth clubs and semimilitary boy scout organizations.

The news of the Japanese victory in Malaya must have acted like strong wine on their imaginations, as the fulfilment of their long-cherished hopes seemed near at hand. So when a fifth column, organized at Penang in Malaya, penetrated Achèh, immediately followed by Japanese invasion troops, the Pusa, enticed by the promise of Muslim rule which the Japanese most likely had not hesitated to encourage, went over to the invaders lock, stock, and barrel.

But neither their primary goal—to get rid of the hated "kâfir" rule—nor the second—to square accounts with the ruling class and to replace the local chieftains by their own men—materialized during the war. It is true that the Japanese deliberately took various measures to lower the position of the local chieftains while gratifying the *ᶜulamâ*ᵓ party by making a number of concessions and by granting its adherents posts in civil administration and judicature, but they were far too clever not to play off one group against the other. They managed to keep both of them in check and to utilize the co-operation of both to strengthen their war effort. The "unbeliever" was gone, but the anti-Christ (*Dajjâl*) had come in his place, as a current Achehnese saying had it.

The astute Japanese policy could not prevent the relations between the two groups from growing more and more strained. In the vacuum produced by the withdrawal of the Japanese occupation army, the accumulated tension came to a violent discharge. In a bloody civil war which lasted from December, 1945, till February, 1946, the ruling families were swept away, and the Pusa became the paramount and only power in Achèh, one to be handled, moreover, only with the utmost care even by the Indonesian Republic in whose name these zealots had allegedly acted.

So far not much has been said about Indonesian modernism. I am afraid, however, that it is rather difficult, if not almost impossible, to say anything conclusive about it. If we take modernism in a broad sense, three groups might perhaps be distinguished.

The first group comprises all those who, under the influence of Western irreligious ideologies—in particular of Communist ideology—have completely broken away from religion. It is impossible to estimate the numerical strength of this group, because however imposing, for example, the growth of labor unions under Communist control may be, it would of course be absurd to presume that every member of these unions has done away with religion and has become a confirmed believer in dialectical materialism. Yet Communist propaganda is not without its effect. In this connection mention may be made of an extremely interesting Malay novel, written by an Indonesian from western Java. This novel, which is significantly entitled *Atheis* ("atheist"), may be taken as a case study. The author describes in a very convincing way the intellectual and moral evolution of a young man who in his early youth was greatly influenced by ascetic mysticism but who changes from a fervent Muslim into an atheist. One may suppose that this novel is mainly autobiographic; nevertheless, it does not represent a solitary case.

The second group consists of Western-educated people who apparently have lost all interest in their ancestral religion, either because they reject popular Islâm as it is practiced in Indonesia and are not satisfied with orthodoxy or with the somewhat shallow and obsolete rationalism of Egyptian reformism or because their attention is monopolized by other things, such as nationalism and the struggle for political power.

A third group, finally, is made up of all those intellectuals who by their sometimes vociferous criticism show that they have not lost all interest in religious matters. I must add, however, that—as yet—they are at their best when criticizing institutions deemed incompatible with modern views; on the doctrinal side their position is far less clearly defined. Iqbâl's famous book on the reconstruction of religious thought in Islâm—which at the date of its appearance passed completely unnoticed in Indonesia—has of late begun to attract some attention. But, of course, people who can read—and understand—Iqbâl are not very numerous.

DISCUSSION

Mr. von Grunebaum asks in what way the Javanese Muslims coped with the problem of non-Muslims in their midst.

Mr. Drewes answers that the problem of non-Muslim communities hardly exists in Java. Such communities are few in number and small in size. One of them is a very small backward group of mountaineers: the Badui of South Bantĕn (western Java), who strive to live in strict seclusion from their Muslim neighbors and from the government and who seem to have been influenced neither by Hinduism nor by Islâm. Another peculiar group is that of the Tĕnggĕrese of Mount Bromo (eastern Java), who have kept away from Islâm since the seventeenth century, when eastern Java at last became Muslim, but seem to be losing ground. Furthermore, there are a few groups of recent origin, as, for instance, the Saminists in the region of Blora, who claim to profess an "autochthonous" religion, as over against Islâm, which they style a "foreign" creed.

Such doctrines are apt to arise with a certain regularity. There exist also literary works, as, for instance, the *Sĕrat Dĕrmagandul,* in which the religious observances of Islâm are turned to ridicule and the religion itself is rejected as being foreign to the true Javanese character. The preachers of such doctrines touch strings that meet with a ready response in the hearts of quite a number of Javanese, for many among this people inwardly or openly harbor feelings of revolt against ritualistic Islâm as distinct from "true Islâm" (*Islam sĕjati*). By this name go any number of doctrines that are hardly reconcilable with Islâm; nevertheless, in professing them, people are not aware of this discrepancy and in general cling to the name of Muslim. One should never forget that survivals from the pre-Islamic past are very numerous in Javanese culture. A good deal of Hindu mythology, hardly influenced by centuries of Islâm, is still living on in Javanese literature and in the shadow-play (*wayang*). With the heroes of these plays every Javanese is familiar. In his conduct he is inspired by their example, and their actions and considerations furnish the material for the Javanese science of character and moral code. In this syncretist environment people do not care to draw with precision the dividing line between Muslim and non-Muslim; religious intolerance never has been characteristic of the Javanese. This does not alter the fact that in the last decades before the war in certain circles Muslim consciousness was far more lively than before, and that from time to time considerable commotion was caused whenever Islâm was slighted, especially when the person of Mohammed had been made the object of unfavorable comment. And the more so, when writings to that effect had flowed from the pens of Christian missionaries.

In Sumatra the situation was different. Here the Muslim population of the coastal areas detested the heathens of the interior, and mention is made of violent measures to exterminate them.

In the latter part of the nineteenth century, Christian missionary activity created a Christian stronghold in the Batak country, which in part is still heathen up till the present time. Although in certain regions of this country where Islâm had already acquired a firm footing the relations between the two religions used to be far from friendly, it seems that here too in the long run religious differences have lost much of their importance.

(Lately alarming news came from southern Celebes, where partisans of a rebellious faction led by Kahar Muzakkar committed atrocities against Christian Toraja and attempted to convert them to Islâm by violent means. Kahar Muzakkar is said to have come to a secret understanding with the Darul-Islam movement of Java.)

M. Le Tourneau would like to hear more about the existence of the Darul-Islam party in Indonesia and the part it plays.

Mr. Drewes answers that it is very difficult to get reliable information about this movement, apart from newspaper reports about its hostile incursions into neighboring districts. The leader of the Darul-Islam faction, Karto Suwiryo, is no stranger in the political arena. He was one of the minor leaders in the prewar Partai Sarékat Islam Indonésia, where he showed himself a convinced non-co-operator. Shortly before the war he founded a new Islamic party, as in his opinion the P.S.I.I.

—which in 1937 had cast out H. A. Salim and his followers for propagating the renunciation of non-co-operation—was not consistent enough in its maintenance of this declared principle of *hijra* towards the colonial government. So the conflict may be said to have already lain dormant during the Japanese occupation. It became acute when the Indonesian republic did not turn out to be a theocratic Muslim state and when conditions favoring an outburst had been created by the absence of a powerful central authority. But it is obvious that other motives too must be taken into account: revolutionary action is likely to attract all kinds of malcontents.

Mr. MINORSKY asks for the meaning of the word *kyai*.

Mr. DREWES replies that the word in Javanese denotes a venerated old man, and especially an independent religious teacher not belonging to the official scribes connected with the mosques. It often has the connotation of "teacher of mystical and secret doctrines."

M. BRUNSCHVIG would like to know more about the process of conversion to Islâm, as we can observe it today. Is it a collective phenomenon or the act of single individuals? Does the new convert feel that he has acquired a moral and social superiority over his old status?

Mr. DREWES replies that in Malay quasi-historical literature the collective conversion to Islâm of towns and regions is sometimes represented as having been brought about by the visit of a holy man from elsewhere in the Islamic world. This saintly person, however, has an easy task, as the king of the country has already been notified by a dream that an important event is about to happen. The holy man interprets this dream, and the king, his court, and his subjects become converted to Islâm. But, although here and there collective conversions may have occurred, this is nowadays certainly not the case. Conversion to Islâm in general is a step taken by a single individual, whereas the conversion of entire villages to Christianity is not so uncommon. After going over to either Islâm or Christianity the neophyte cannot but feel that he has acquired a moral and social superiority over his old status; why else should he embrace a foreign creed?

M. ABEL asks if there exist any investigations into the sources of the Indonesian mystical and sectarian tracts Mr. Drewes has mentioned. M. ABEL has learned that Islâm was brought to Indonesia by the merchants of southern India, and he suspects that in the circles they represented a particular philosophical and universalist mysticism was well known. The old basis of those doctrines is given by the *Rasâ᾽il Ikhwân al-Ṣafâ* (*ca.* 970), which we find still in use in certain parts of India. He would be very much interested to know if anybody has ever cared to compare this "encyclopedia" with the Indonesian tracts.

Mr. DREWES answers that we have very scanty knowledge of the beginnings of Islâm in Indonesia. As Islâm was brought by merchants and seafaring men, perhaps we should inquire into the popular traditions of South Indian Islâm rather than search for books. Literary sources begin to flow in the sixteenth century; the oldest specimens of Islamic literature in Malay, as, for instance, the romances of Amîr Ḥamza and Alexander the Great, clearly derive from Persian and Arabic sources. As to the philosophical position of the oldest mystical literature, here the influence of Ibn al-ᶜArabî and ᶜAbd al-Karîm al-Jîlî is unmistakable. A comparison with the writings of the Ikhwân al-Ṣafâ has never been undertaken.

Questioned by M. CAHEN and Mr. SCHACHT about the origin of these Indian merchants, Mr. DREWES replies that they were not of Arabic descent. They were Indians who knew Persian, as is proved by the Persian verses they inserted into their books. People who translated into Malay sometimes remarked at the beginning of the book that it was designed for those who did not understand Arabic and Persian, naming thus both languages on the same level.

Mr. SCHACHT remarks that, as Mr. Drewes has mentioned, Islâm came to Indonesia from the Indian coast. That explains its Shâfiᶜite character there. Handbooks and catechisms reveal this Shâfiᶜite tendency clearly. The Mâṭurîdî doctrine has from the beginning been associated with Ḥanafî tendencies. So it would be interesting to know the date of these little treatises with Mâṭurîdî dogmas, which have been mentioned.

Mr. DREWES cannot remember any explanation of the use of this Mâṭurîdî catechism. Today, however, the most popular is the Sanûsî creed, which may have been brought from Mecca.

TURKEY: WESTERNIZATION

BERNARD LEWIS

IN RECENT years Turkey has shown a striking contrast with the other Muslim countries of the Middle East. In foreign policy, most of these have treated the West with attitudes ranging from sullen but expectant neutrality to outright hostility. In internal affairs, most of them have gone through a religious and political reaction along broadly parallel lines: in Egypt, from Nahas via Faruq to Naguib; in Syria, from Quwwatli to Shishakli; in Persia, from Musaddeq via Kashani to an uncertain future. On all sides we have seen the decay and collapse of parliamentary government and the growth of dictatorship. At the same time, the nationalist phraseology of leaders has masked a decline in liberal constitutional nationalism associated with the ideas, derived from France, of *nation* and *patrie*, and an increase in the sentiment of religious, or rather communal, solidarity, expressed in words such as *umma* and—with its old Arabian connotation of the kin-group in arms—*qaum*.

And yet, while these things have been happening elsewhere, Turkey has become a member of the Council of Europe and then of the Atlantic Pact—and not a grudging member, but a willing, even an enthusiastic, one, far more so in fact than some other countries whose geographical location might, one would have thought, more readily have predisposed them to take part in an Atlantic organization.

Moreover, Turkish foreign policy has been paralleled—and perhaps made possible—by a similar internal development: a successful and continuing movement of Westernization, the growth and improvement of parliamentary government. This last found striking expression in the free and fair election of May, 1950.[1] But subsequent events were in a sense even more impressive. After the victory of the Democrats, there was a dangerous period when growing bickering and intolerance between the two main parties imperiled the effective functioning of parliamentary institutions, while the emergence of seditious organizations spreading racial and clerical ideas threatened the very existence of the Turkish Republic. In the face of this danger the two main parties suspended their differences and closed their ranks. Their action was a notable demonstration of the strength both of patriotism and of democracy in Turkey. I should perhaps add that as soon as this major threat seemed to be averted the party leaders gave another, equally convincing, display of their mastery of democratic procedure by at once resuming their conflicts.

Why did all this happen? One could no doubt make a case for the inclusion of Turkey in that historical and cultural entity we call Europe. For that matter, though the Atlantic does not flow into the Bosphorus, and even in our atomic age is unlikely to do so, it is easy enough to find reasons for Turkey's readiness to join a defensive alliance against the Soviet Union. Turkey's geographical position and historical experience make her more conscious of a possible Russian threat than are her southern neighbors; at the same time, her linguistic affinity with many of the Soviet peoples makes her more keenly aware of the actualities and potentialities of Soviet imperialism and therefore perhaps more tolerant of the Western variety. Yet all this amounts to no more than a partial and inadequate explanation. Turkey is, after all, a Middle Eastern and Muslim country, with centuries of experience shared with other Middle Eastern Muslim states, and countless ties of religion, culture, custom, law, and memory. Purely strategic and political considerations alone are insufficient to explain something that has become more than a difference of government policy, something that amounts to a change in the whole orientation of national life and civilization. The recent history of the other countries of the Middle East has made one thing abundantly clear: whatever the advantages to Turkey of a Western alignment, no government that was willing to grasp these advantages would have been able to survive unless there had been a deeper and more general predisposition toward the Western orientation—and in a deeper and more general sense than a simple political and military alliance.

Two points may be noted at this stage. One is that the Turks have the advantage of realism and practical sense, derived from the long exercise of sovereignty. Turkey is not a new state, fabricated in the committee room, nor yet an ex-colonial dependency, with its outlook still colored by the fight to achieve independence from foreign rule. The Turks have always been masters in their own house and thus have been able to develop a capacity for realistic assessment and resolve that is lacking elsewhere, together with a willingness to accept responsibility for their own decisions and the consequences that arise from them. My second point is that the movement of Westernization began earlier and went further in Turkey than elsewhere. The pro-

Western foreign policy of the Republic is but one aspect of a general reorientation. Among other signs of Westernization we may note: the relatively successful working party and parliamentary government; the growing individualism and self-reliance of the masses; the modern novel, the sustained effort of constructive narration—that most Western of literary forms, which in Turkey alone of the lands of Islâm has really struck root; the beginning of polyphonic music and perspective painting—still immature, but far in advance of anything to be found in other Islamic countries; the theater; Western mathematics and physics; team games—Egyptians may excel in sports of individual performance, such as table tennis and swimming, but only the Turks in the Middle East can field a really effective football eleven; sociological historiography; and a growing respect and understanding for abstract principles and impersonal institutions—more precisely, loyalty to the state rather than the sovereign, to the party and program rather than the leader, and so on.

During the nineteenth and early twentieth centuries the experience of Turkey in Westernization was in general shared with the former Arab provinces of the Ottoman Empire. Since 1918 there has been a complete divergence. In Turkey the stream has been broadened and deepened; elsewhere it has been deflected or turned back.

Turkey is, then, very different from other Islamic countries, even of the same region, in many important respects. These differences are complex and of multiple origin—rooted in geography, history, and that intangible thing we call "national character." A question that may concern us here is this: How far are these differences part of Turkish civilization and national identity—how far are they permanent and innate, how far just the result of recent circumstances and events? The question is of more than academic interest. As De Tocqueville observed of the French Revolution, when the revolutionary tide ebbs and the flood subsides, the traditional landmarks re-emerge, and the stream of history flows in much the same course as previously. In our own time this observation has been confirmed in Russia. If we would know what is happening in Turkey, it is important to understand how many of the growths we have seen are floating on the surface of the floodwaters, how many are rooted on the riverbed.

Clearly there is a difference in Turkey due to national culture and characteristics. No one would deny the differences between, say, English, French, and Italian cultures, nor that they all form part of the common civilization of Western Christendom. We may perhaps formulate our questions thus: (1) What are the non-Islamic elements which, combining with and acting upon Islâm, have given it its special quality in Turkey? (2) Has the divergence of Turkey from the rest of the Islamic world in our own time gone beyond that of national diversity within a common civilization and amounted to adherence to a different civilization? The questions are obviously interrelated, since any answer given to the second must be based on evidence considered for the first. It would be pretentious and even absurd for me to attempt to give a comprehensive answer to either of these questions, least of all to the second, which belongs to the realm of prophecy rather than of history. It may, however, be useful to enumerate and survey—in an admittedly schematic form—some of the factors involved.

The problem, in one form or another, has during the past century greatly exercised the Turks themselves, and it may therefore be useful to begin with a brief glance at their own views on the subject.[2]

Until the nineteenth century the Turks thought of themselves almost exclusively as Muslims. So completely had they identified themselves with Islâm that the very concept of a Turkish nationality was submerged—and this despite the fact that they had maintained their own language and statehood. They had not even retained to the same degree as the Arabs and Persians an awareness of identity as a separate group within Islâm. It may be noted in passing that the concept of Ottomanism was a nineteenth-century innovation under European influence. Previously "Ottoman" was understood not as a term of nationality but rather as a dynastic term, like Umayyad, Abbasid, or Seljuq. The idea of Turkishness in the modern sense appears only in the mid-nineteenth century and is derived from various sources. Among those which influenced its emergence and development we may mention the Hungarian and Polish exiles who came to Turkey after the unsuccessful revolutions of 1848, some of whom were converted to Islâm and played some part in introducing the nationalist ideologies of the time to the Turks; Turkish students in Europe, and especially in France; European Turkological research and the new knowledge which it brought of the ancient history and civilization of the Turkish peoples; the Russian Turks and Tartars, who encountered Russian pan-Slavism and reacted against it with a growing national consciousness of their own, nourished—by an odd paradox—by Russian Turkological discoveries; the influence of the subject peoples of the Ottoman Empire, who as Christians were more open to national ideas coming from the West and who in time helped to transmit the infection to their imperial masters.

At first these ideas were limited to a small circle of intellectuals, but gradually they spread far and wide, and victory was finally symbolized by the official adoption, for the first time, of the names "Turkey" and "Turk" for the country and people of the Republic. The growth of the sentiment of Turkish identity was connected with the growing movement away from Islamic practice and tradition, and toward Europe. This began with purely practical short-term measures of reform, intended to accomplish a limited purpose; it developed into a large-scale, deliberate attempt to take a whole nation across the frontier from one civilization to another. Here too the change found a striking symbol—the reform of the alphabet. Script has always been recognized as an outward sign of religious identification, and religion as the spiritual stamp of a civilization—I need only mention the divided destinies of the languages and peoples of Yugoslavia and India to make my point clear. In Islâm there was another outward token of religious and social classification—the headgear. That too was forcibly changed.

After the Turkist and Westernizing movements had established themselves, an interesting new development appeared: the assertion of identity with earlier, pre-existing local civilizations. This movement has its parallels in some other Islamic countries and is of course a consequence of the importation of the European idea of the secular and territorial fatherland and of a mystical and permanent relationship between the land and the people who inhabit it. In Turkey it gave rise to the so-called Anatolianist movement and to the Hittite and Trojan theories. It is interesting, we may note in passing, that, while the Turks claimed to be kinsmen and descendants of the ancient Anatolians, they made no such claim concerning the Byzantines, who had the threefold disadvantage, for this purpose, of being Greek, Christian, and, above all, extant. No doubt had the Jews disappeared like the other ancient Middle Eastern peoples, the Palestinian Arabs would have identified themselves as readily—and probably as rightly—with the Banû Isrâʾîl as their southern and northern neighbors do with the Pharaohs and the Phoenicians. The movement in Turkey is partly political, with the purpose of encouraging the Turks to identify themselves with the country they inhabit—and thus at the same time of discouraging dangerous pan-Turanian adventures. But, despite its politically inspired excesses and absurdities, the Anatolian theory of the Turkish historians contained, or rather brought to light, important elements of truth.

We may, then, distinguish three main streams of influence—or, if you prefer, lines of tradition—that have gone to make modern Turkey: the Islamic, the Turkish, and a third, composite one that for want of a better name we may call local. In this last we may include other elements besides the Anatolian.

LOCAL

By this term I wish to describe a complex and diverse pattern of tradition and culture. One strand is the Anatolian, the importance of which was stressed in the Turkish official thesis but which we should not disregard on that account. The Hittites have left the most striking remains and have been the subject of the most publicized theorizing, but the other ancient peoples of Anatolia have no doubt also left their mark. The Anatolian is, however, not the only strain. The Ottoman Empire from its first century was a Balkan as well as an Anatolian power, and Rumelia was for long the main center. Only in our own day has it lost its central position. And linking the two there is Byzantium-Constantinople-Istanbul—the imperial city, with its millennial traditions of state and civilization.

Any visitor to Turkey, especially one entering from the south or the east, must at once be struck by the vigorous survival of these local traditions within Turkish Islâm. Many things will bring them to his attention—the Anatolian village house and mosque, so different in style and structure from those of Syria and Iraq; the Balkan, almost European, tonalities of Turkish music of the kind called "popular," as against the "classical" music in the Perso-Arabic manner; the Byzantine-looking cupolas on the mosques and the Greek and southeast European decorative motifs in both formal design and peasant handicrafts.

The survival of Anatolian elements in modern Turkey is now beyond dispute. There is no need to assert that the Turks are Hittites or that the Hittites were Turks, but it is clear that there was a large measure of continuity. This becomes clearer with the parallel progress of archeological and anthropological work in Anatolia today. It is true that there was large-scale Turkish colonization in Anatolia—of this more in a few moments—but the indigenous population was neither exterminated nor entirely expelled. The Greek upper class and the Greek cultural layer were replaced, and in time the inhabitants were re-assimilated, this time to Islamic and Turkish patterns. They retained much of their own culture, especially in what pertains to agriculture and village life: the alternation of the seasons, sowing and reaping, birth, marriage, and death. With these things the newly imported Islamic culture, here as elsewhere essentially urban, had less concern.

The Rumelian influence, after the conquest, came from the top rather than from the bottom. Unlike Anatolia, most of Rumelia was never assimilated either to Islâm or to the Turkish language. The peasant masses remained Christian, alien in language and culture as well as in religion, outside the cultural horizon of the Turks. But the Balkan peoples had an enormous influence on the Ottoman ruling class. One of the most important channels was the *devshirme*, the levy of boys, by means of which countless Balkan Christians entered the political and military elites of the Empire. Nor was that all. Even the local Christian landed ruling class was not wholly destroyed, as was once thought, but survived to some extent on its lands and was incorporated in the Ottoman system. In the fifteenth century there were still Christian Timariots—military fief holders—in Albania.[3] Then and later, Rumelian Christian troops served in large numbers in the Ottoman forces, both as feudal cavalry and as common soldiers, while converted Rumelians were to be found holding fiefs and commands all over the Asiatic provinces of the Empire. The great role of the Albanians and Bosniaks in the Ottoman Empire is well known. Together with other Rumelians, they continued to play an important part in the *Tanẓîmât* and subsequent reforms.

The Byzantine heritage of Turkey was at one time much exaggerated. Some historians attributed almost everything in Ottoman state and society to one or another source in Byzantium and spoke of massive borrowings of Byzantine institutions and practices after the capture of Constantinople in 1453. Perhaps the most extreme formulation is that of Jorga, who speaks of Ottoman Istanbul as a third, Turanian Rome. In a well-known monograph, Fuad Köprülü has shown that much of this is erroneous and that, in fact, the Byzantine elements in Ottoman civilization are very much smaller than had previously been supposed.[4] Moreover, these elements date from before the conquest of Constantinople, in most cases, indeed, from before the establishment of the Ottoman state. Some borrowings can be traced back to the time of the Anatolian Seljuqs, others even to the caliphate, from which they came to Turkey as part of classical Islamic civilization itself. It was natural for the Seljuqs to borrow during their long cohabitation with Byzantium, at a time when that state had not yet dwindled into the pale shadow that the Ottomans encountered.

But if the Byzantine elements have been exaggerated and misdated, they are nevertheless there. Though perhaps fewer, they are at the same time older and more deeply rooted—and some are no doubt older than Byzantium itself. The survival of Byzantine motifs in architecture has already been mentioned. But something so central and so typical in a society as its religious architecture cannot be an isolated phenomenon. The Byzantine elements in the Turkish mosque—so universal and so persistent—must express some deeper social and cultural affinity, all the more so in a society like Islâm, where all is under the sign of religion. To suggest but one possible line of thought: perhaps we may associate the domed basilica type of mosque with the appearance—for the first time in Islâm, and under Turkish rule—of ecclesiastical hierarchy, with muftis presiding over territorial jurisdictions, under the supreme authority of the Shaikh al-Islâm, the chief mufti of the capital, whom we may describe, perhaps a little fancifully, as the archbishop-primate of the Ottoman Empire.

One other aspect of local influence may perhaps be considered here. Rumelia and Constantinople are part of Europe, and the Ottomans have from an early stage in their history been in contact with Europe—longer and closer than any other Islamic state, not excluding North Africa. The Empire included important European territories, in which it absorbed European peoples and institutions. It also maintained contact with the West through trade, diplomacy, war, and—not least—immigration. The late E. Jacobs, in a recently published article, drew attention to the interest of Mehmed the Conqueror in Greek and Western culture.[5] This was no isolated phenomenon. Not a little knowledge of the West was brought by the many renegades who sought a career in the Ottoman service. Before the nineteenth century, Ottoman borrowings from Europe were mainly of a material order and were restricted in both scope and effect. But today it is almost a truism that there can be no limited and insulated borrowing by one civilization of the practices of another but that each element introduced from outside brings a train of consequences. We should perhaps reconsider the significance and effects of early Ottoman importations from Europe such as cartography, navigation, shipbuilding, and artillery, followed in the eighteenth century by printing, military engineering, and the Italianate style in Turkish architecture, exemplified in the Nuruosmaniye mosque in Istanbul.

One example may illustrate how earlier reforms and importations prepared the ground for the large-scale attempts at Westernization from the time of Selim III onwards. Among Selim's most famous reforms were his military and naval cadet schools, with printing presses for textbooks and French as a compulsory language. They were much helped by the fact that printers were available, because Turkish had been printed in Istanbul since 1729 and other languages much earlier, and that European-style military schools with foreign instructors had functioned since 1734 at the latest.

TURKISH

We come now to the Turkish strand in our pattern. Our hypothetical visitor to Turkey will encounter at once the first and visible (or rather audible) sign of Turkishness—the Turkish language, which, despite long subjection to alien influences, survives triumphantly. Scholars have noted the remarkable capacity of Turkish to resist, displace, and even supplant other languages with which it has come in contact. With the Turkish language, as a sign of Turkish tradition, our visitor may perhaps associate the habit of authority and decision, and therefore of self-reliance, which the Turks have retained from their historic role in the Islamic world. And perhaps, with a little effort of imagination, he may sense a feeling of purpose and direction in the air, that sometimes jars but more often stimulates.

Language was indeed the main—or at any rate the most readily identifiable—contribution of the Turks to the diversified culture of the Ottoman Empire. As once the Arabic language and the Islamic faith, so now the Turkish language and the Sunnite Islamic faith were necessary qualifications for membership of the dominant social class. In Ottoman Turkish was created a rich and subtle means of expression, a worthy instrument of an imperial civilization. But there is no true parallel between the Ottoman ruling class and the Arab ruling class that had dominated the Islamic empire under the Patriarchal and Umayyad caliphs. The Ottomans had no racial arrogance or exclusiveness, no insistence on "pure" Turkish descent—nothing equivalent to the segregation on a lower level of the *mawâlî*, the non-Arab converts to Islâm, by the Arab masters of the early caliphate. Islâm and the Turkish language were the entry qualifications which opened the door both to real power and to social status to Albanian, Greek, and Slav as well as to Kurd and Arab. For a time the Turks showed little national consciousness—far less, for example, than the Arabs or Persians. The pre-Islamic Turks were after all no savages, but peoples of a certain level of civilization, with their own states, religions, and literatures. Yet, save for a few fragments, all was forgotten and obliterated in Islâm, until its partial recovery by European scholarship in the eighteenth and nineteenth centuries. There is no Turkish equivalent to Arab memories of the heroic days of the Jâhiliyya in old Arabia, to Persian pride in the bygone glories of the Kayânian and Pîshdâdian emperors of Iran, even to the vague Egyptian legends woven around the broken but massive monuments of the Pharaohs. Save for a few fragments of folk poetry and of genealogical legend, all the pre-Islamic Turkish past was forgotten, and even a newly Islamized Turkish dynasty like the Karakhânids in the tenth century forgot their Turkish antecedents and called themselves by a name from Persian legend, the "House of Afrâsiyâb." Even the very name "Turk" and the entity it connotes are, in a sense, Islamic. Though the word "Turk" occurs in pre-Islamic inscriptions, it refers only to one among the many related steppe peoples. Its generalized use to cover the whole group, and perhaps even the very notion of such a group, date from Islâm and even became identified with Islâm; and the historical Turkish nation and culture—even in a certain sense the language—in the forms in which they have existed in the last millennium, were all born in Islâm.[6]

But the real Turkish element in Ottoman society and culture, if unselfconscious and unarticulated, is nevertheless profoundly important. In the ruling class, non-Turkish elements were, as we have seen, present and at times even predominant: Rumelian and Byzantine in the administration, the army, economic life; Perso-Arabic in literary and religious culture. The Turkish element was revived in the late fourteenth century, when the Ottomans, expanding into eastern Anatolia, encountered larger groups of Turkish nomads, with their tribal organization and traditions intact and not yet scattered, disintegrated, and affected by local influences as in the western part of the peninsula. There are a number of signs of the rise of a kind of Turkish national consciousness, such as the assumption by the Ottoman sultan at this time of the old Turkish title of "Khan," and the adoption of the Oghuz legend, which linked the Ottoman ruling house with Turkish antiquity and became the official account of the origins of the dynasty.[7] With this movement we may associate the later literary tendencies described by Köprülü in his monograph on the first pioneers of Turkish national literature,[8] and also the brief vogue of Chaghatay Turkish language and literature among the Ottomans. This movement was limited and in many respects transitory, but it had an important effect in reaffirming the position of the Turkish language and thus of all that accompanies and is contained in language in the life of a people. It is significant too as the first major appearance, in the Ottoman state, of the nomadic Turkish element, which was now an important part of the Turkish population.

It is, as Wittek has pointed out, as an ethnic reservoir that the Turkish nomadic tribes are important in the Ottoman Empire.[9] They were not a ruling element as such but were rather treated with alternating mistrust and contempt by the state and the ruling class. They were, however, the reserve on which the ruling class drew. The movement of the tribesman into Ottoman society took place in several ways. One was the process of sedentarization, by which the nomads were settled on an increasing scale in different parts of Anatolia and became peasant cultivators. This was due partly to the operation of normal economic processes, partly to deliberate government policy. Ömer Lutfi Barkan, in a series of important studies, has drawn attention to the significance of deportation in Ottoman history: the transfer of populations from one place to another for settlement and colonization.[10] Sometimes these deportations were penal, sometimes they were intended to serve political, economic, and military ends. Thus, for example, transfers of populations were made to newly conquered provinces or to disaffected areas. In all these movements the nomadic population was largely drawn upon. Nomadic settlement was not limited to the countryside. Evidence in both documentary and literary sources shows that there were tribal quarters in many towns. Such a process was inevitable in view of the close economic connection between the town, on the one hand, and the peasants and tribes, on the other—the two latter, increasingly Turkish.

This seepage, if one may call it so, of Turks into the town and country population, and thus eventually into the governing elite, preserved and reinforced the Turkish character of Ottoman society, so that even the revolution of our time has been described with some justice as the emergence of a by now Turkish Anatolia, asserting itself against the cosmopolitan civilization of Constantinople and Rumelia—in other words, as a victory of Turks over Ottomans, typified by the transfer of the capital and the change of name of the country.

The conscious effort in modern Turkey to return to Turkism is important politically, as it affects the basis of polity and direction of policy of the state, but it is limited in its effects in other fields. The old Turkish civilizations were too thoroughly obliterated by Islâm for any real revival of ancient Turkish culture to be possible. There have of course been attempts, the most noteworthy and most discussed being the language reform. There have also been some rather self-conscious but sometimes quite effective adaptations of folk material, as, for example, the use of the syllabic beat in place of the quantitative Perso-Arabic prosody, and the employment of Turkish melodies in modern orchestral compositions. A good example is the Karagöz Suite, based on Anatolian melodies and at the same time strikingly reminiscent of Stravinsky's *Petrushka.* But modern Turkish literature and art owe far more to Europe than to any such deliberate experiments with old or popular material. The real importance of the Turkish strain in Turkey must be sought in uninterrupted survivals in deeper layers of society, and these layers are now coming to the surface, with results yet to be foreseen. As Wittek has remarked: "La Turquie se turquise."[11]

ISLÂM

We come now to the third factor—to Islâm, Turkish Islâm itself, which despite a period of eclipse has recently shown renewed vigor in Turkey and is still clearly a major, if not the major, element in the collective consciousness of a large proportion of the Turkish nation.

The Turks first encountered Islâm on the frontiers, and their faith has from then till now retained some of the peculiar quality of frontier Islâm, of the militant and uncomplicated religion of the frontiersmen.[12] The Turks were not forced into Islâm, as were so many other peoples, and their Islâm bears no marks of constraint or subjection. On the frontiers of the caliphate, in east and west, the march-warriors had still maintained the simplicity, militancy, and freedom of early Islâm, which elsewhere had been lost in the transformation of the old Islamic theocracy into an Oriental empire. From all over that empire, those who could not adapt themselves to the new order, those who for spiritual or material reasons felt the call of the frontier, joined the bands of the borderers and waged war against the infidel and the heathen for God, glory, and booty. In Central Asia, one of the two most important frontiers, the Turks, converted for the most part by wandering missionaries and mystics, joined in the struggle against their cousins who were still heathen and, as the military classes of the caliphate came to be more and more exclusively Turkish, began to play a predominant part in it. In the late tenth century the first great independent Turkish sovereign in Islâm, Maḥmûd of Ghazna, used his power to lead an army of Turks to a frontier war on the grand scale for the conquest of Hindu India. In the eleventh century the Seljuqs unleashed a new wave of Turkish invaders across southwest Asia, who wrested new territories for Islâm from the Byzantine Empire and infused into the Islamic Orient the martial and religious vigor which enabled it to withstand and eventually throw back the great European offensive of the Crusades.

The Islâm of the Turkish frontiersmen was thus of a different quality from that of the heartlands of Islâm. Unlike their brothers who had gone to Iraq or Egypt as Mamlûks and been brought up in the very different atmosphere of the old Islamic capitals, the free Turks were Islamized and educated in the borderlands, and their Islâm was from the first impregnated with the special characteristics of the frontier. Their teachers were dervishes, wandering monks, and mystics, usually Turkish, preaching a very different faith from that of the theologians and the seminaries of the cities. Not for them was the subtlety—or the laxness—of Abbasid Baghdad, the easy-going tolerance and diversity of a mixed urban civilization—or the meticulous and exclusive orthodoxy of the schools. Theirs was a militant faith, still full of the pristine fire and directness of the first Muslims—a religion of warriors, whose creed was a battle cry, whose dogma was a call to arms. This was the faith—and the preaching—which the first Turks brought to Anatolia. And then, as the *ghâzî*, the dervish, and the nomad conquered, converted, and colonized the peninsula, the old Islamic traditions of government and civilization established themselves in what became the cities of a new sultanate, and the frontiersmen and dervishes moved on to seek new adventures on the western fringes, by the Aegean and in Europe. As the *ghâzîs* marched westwards, their Anatolian conquests became a province of the Seljuq Empire and the traditional pattern of Islamic life was gradually impressed on the country. Muslim bureaucrats and literati, jurists and theologians, merchants and artisans, moved into the newly acquired territory, bringing with them the old, high, urban civilization of classical Islâm. So too the Aegean and Balkan acquisitions of the Ottoman borderers were in time transformed into a new Muslim empire. As once-conquered Sivas and Konya, so now first Bursa, then Edirne, finally Istanbul, became Muslim cities, centers of Muslim life and culture, decked with all the panoply of orthodox Islâm.

From its foundation until its fall the Ottoman Empire was a state dedicated to the advancement or defense of the power and faith of Islâm. For six centuries the Ottomans were almost constantly at war with the Christian West, first in the attempt—mainly successful—to impose Islamic rule on a large part of Europe, then in the long-drawn-out rear-guard action to halt or delay the relentless counter-attack of the West. This centuries-long struggle, with its origins in the very roots of Turkish Islâm, could not fail to affect the whole structure of Turkish society and institutions. For the Ottoman Turk, his Empire, containing all the heartlands of early Islâm, was Islâm itself. In the Ottoman chronicles the territories of the Empire are referred to as "the lands of Islâm," its sovereign as "the Pâdishâh of Islâm," its armies as "the soldiers of Islâm," its religious head as "the shaikh of Islâm"; its people thought of themselves first and foremost as Muslims. Both "Ottoman" and "Turk" are, as we have seen, terms of comparatively recent usage in their modern sense, and the Ottoman Turks had identified themselves with Islâm—submerged their identity in Islâm—to a greater extent than perhaps any other Islamic people. It is curious that while in Turkey the word "Turk" almost went out of use—except in one special and rather derogatory sense—in the West it came to be a synonym for "Muslim," and a Western convert to Islâm was said to have "turned Turk," even when the conversion took place in Fez or Isfahan.

A counterpart of this identification may be seen in the high seriousness of Turkish Islâm—the sense of devotion to duty and of mission, in the best days of the Empire, that is unparalleled in Islamic history, not excluding that of the caliphate. Which of the Abbasid caliphs, for example, can show anything to compare with the loyalty, the intensity of moral and religious purpose, that clearly impelled the early Ottoman sultans—the inexorable devotion to duty that made the aging and dying sultan, Sulaimân the Magnificent, face the hardships of yet another Hungarian campaign and go from the comforts of his capital to the rigors of the camp and a certain death?

It is perhaps in the realm of law that one can see most clearly the seriousness of the Ottoman endeavor to make Islâm the true basis of private and public life. As Schacht has recently reminded us,[13] the Ottoman sultans gave to the *sharîᶜa* a greater degree of real efficacy than it had had in any Muslim state of high material civilization since early times. The Ottoman *Qânûnnâme* is not an exception to this, for it is in no sense a legislative enactment but only a set of rules, drafted by officials for administrative convenience, and formulating existing law and practice. In a sense it may even be said that the Ottomans were the first who really tried to make the *sharîᶜa* the effective law of the state, to apply it throughout the land, and to give full recognition and authority to the courts and judiciary that administered it. The Abbasid *qâḍî* cuts a miserable figure beside his Ottoman colleague. Appointed by and answerable to the central authorities, he was compelled to abandon to them important fields of jurisdiction and was wholly dependent on their rather dubious cooperation for the execution and enforcement of his judgments. The Ottoman *qâḍî*, on the other hand, *was* the central authority in the area of his jurisdiction, which in the Ottoman system of provincial administration was known, significantly, as a *qaḍâ*—the area governed by a *qâḍî*, as a *vilâyet* was governed by a *vâlî*. Moreover, he was one of a proud and powerful hierarchy of juridical and theological authorities, ready to support him in any clash with the military and political institutions and presided over by the Shaikh al-Islâm and the two *qâḍî* *ᶜaskars* in the capital—so great and revered that the sultan himself rose to his feet to receive them when they came to offer him their greetings at the Bayram festival. So it is laid down in the *Qânûnnâme* of the House of Osman.[14] The Abbasid caliphs were theoretically subject to the holy law and could be deposed for violating it, but this rule was a dead letter in the absence of any authority or machinery for enforcing it. The Ottomans, however, recognized a supreme religious authority—the highest instance of the *sharîᶜa*—with power to authorize the deposition of the sultan. The actual role of this authority, the Shaikh al-Islâm, was of course determined in the main by the play of politics and personalities. The significant thing from our point of view is that such an authority, with such a jurisdiction, should have existed at all and have been recognized.

Another characteristic of Turkish Islâm, of a rather different kind but of similar significance, is the social segregation of the *dhimmîs*. The Ottoman Empire was tolerant of other religions, in accordance with Islamic law and tradition, and its Christian and Jewish subjects lived, on the whole, in peace and security. But they were strictly and completely segregated from the Muslims, in their own separate communities, with their own separate lives. Never were they able to mix freely in Muslim society, as they had once done in Baghdad and Cairo, or to make any contribution worth the mention to the intellectual life of the Ottomans. There are no Ottoman equivalents to the Christian poets and Jewish scientists of the Arabic golden age. If the convert was readily accepted and assimilated, the unconverted were extruded so thoroughly that even today, five hundred years after the conquest of Constantinople, neither the Greeks nor the Jews in the city have yet mastered the Turkish language, though neither people is lacking in linguistic versatility. One may speak of Christian Arabs, but a Christian Turk is an absurdity and a contradiction in terms.[15] Even after thirty years of the secular republic, a non-Muslim in Turkey may be called a Turkish citizen, but never a Turk.

The first characteristic of Turkish Islâm that we have noted is then—paradoxically—the extent to which the Turks have effaced themselves in Islâm. We may find others. It is natural to look first to the popular, mystical, and more or less heterodox forms of religion which in Turkey, as in most other Muslim countries, flourish alongside the formal, dogmatic religion of the theologians and correspond to a far greater degree to the real religious beliefs and practices of the people. The different orders, *ṭarîqas,* that between them have commanded and perhaps still command the allegiance of the great majority of Turkish Muslims certainly preserved much that is pre-Islamic in their beliefs and still more in their traditions and observances. Turkish scholars have drawn attention to the Central Asian survivals: the elements of shamanism, even of Buddhism and Manicheism, retained by the Central Asian Turks after their conversion to Islâm and brought by them in various disguises to the west. No less important are the many examples of Muslim-Christian —or, if you prefer, Turko-Greek—syncretism in popular religious life: the countless common saints and common holy places, common festivals, and common practices and beliefs.

This kind of survival on the popular level is almost universal in Islâm and has its parallels in the persistence of old Celtic, Germanic, and Slavonic customs in a Christianized form in Europe. Popular Islâm has always been looked upon with suspicion by the theologians and by the state, perhaps more so in Turkey than elsewhere, and it is significant that even today the government of the Turkish Republic, though according tolerance and even encouragement to a limited revival of orthodoxy, has so far severely repressed all manifestations of activity by the *ṭarîqas.*

It is not, however, on the popular, but on the formal, level that we encounter one of the most characteristic qualities of Islâm in the Ottoman Empire—the quality to which I have already alluded and to which I am tempted to give the name "architectonic." Here for the first time in Islamic history is created a real institutional structure—a graded hierarchy of professional men of religion, with recognized functions and powers, worthy of comparison with the Christian churches or the priesthoods of the ancient empires. The dictum that there is no priesthood in Islâm remains true in the theological sense in that there is no ordination, no sacrament, no priestly mediation between the believer and God, but it ceases to be true in the sociological and political sense. The origins of the great Ottoman religious institution can no doubt be traced back to the sultanate of the Great Seljuqs, when schools and schoolmen were organized to counter the threat of the Ismâʿîlî missionary and the Fâṭimid mission. But only in the Ottoman state did the religious institution reach maturity and fulfil its function as the guardian of the faith and the law.

All the Muslim successor states of the Ottoman Empire still bear the stamp of Ottoman Islâm and retain the Ottoman style of organized, institutional religion—all, that is, except one: Turkey. There, where the penetration of state and society by Islâm had gone farthest, the reaction against it was the most violent. The story of the secularist reforms of Kemal Atatürk is too well known to need retelling: the disestablishment of Islâm, the repeal of the *sharîʿa* and the modern codes derived from it, the destruction of the hierarchy, and the rest. During the last few years there has been a limited return to religion. I have discussed this at length elsewhere and will not revert to it now.[16] The new religious movement is of complex origin: partly it is just a reappearance of the old clerical elements, survivors of the Empire, taking advantage of the new liberty that reigns in Turkey; partly too it arises from real religious feeling, from the revolt of a profoundly religious people against the coldness and emptiness of the secularist creed, which, in the words of Adnan Adivar, had made Turkey into a "positivistic mausoleum." The problem—an enormous one—is how to reconcile a revival of Islamic faith with the social, political, and cultural reforms accomplished in the last century. Many people in Turkey nowadays talk of the need for a Turkish reformation and sigh for a Turkish, Muslim Luther. Personally I am very doubtful about this. The Turkish genius—like the Anglo-Saxon—is practical rather than theoretical. In my view, the Turks are unlikely to produce a Luther or a Calvin, but, on the other hand, it is just conceivable that they may succeed in producing a Muslim Turkish equivalent of the Anglican Church. And that would probably serve their purpose just as well.

We have now passed in review the three main trends in Turkish life and culture. In our own time we must add a fourth: Western civilization, which in Turkey as everywhere else in the world has struck with devastating impact against the existing order. At the beginning of this paper I offered some observations on the forms and effects of Western influence in Turkey, and, since Westernization forms the topic of another paper, I shall not add to them now. I should however like, in conclusion, to revert very briefly to the point with which I began—the differentness of Turkey from other Middle Eastern Muslim states—and to see if it is possible to get any further toward understanding or even defining it.

There are, I would suggest, two points—two concepts—in relation to which we may consider those features and characteristics which set modern Turkey apart from her Muslim neighbors and bring her nearer to both the merits and the faults of the Western world. One is the notion of process, the tendency to view a sequence of events not as a simple series but as a process in time or, in organic terms, as a development; the second, related to it, is the notion of organism, of organic structure—the ability to conceive a whole made up of interrelated and interacting parts, rather than a mere congeries of separate, disjunct entities. These qualities are, I suppose, central to the modern Western form of civilization. They are the prerequisites of our physical and natural sciences; they determine our vision of the individual and the group, of man and the universe, and thus shape our institutions and our thought, our government and our arts, our industry, our science, and—save the mark—our religion. They make—to name but a few examples—the difference between the Western novel and the Oriental tale, Western portraiture and Oriental miniature, Western biography and Oriental stereotype, Western government and Oriental rule—and perhaps between Western restlessness and Oriental repose.

For better or worse, these qualities have, in the course of the last century and a half, become more and more effective in Turkish public life—in the structure of state and law, in the formulation and direction of aspiration and policy, in the reorganization of social and even of private life. They are already discernible in certain manifestations of the arts and sciences, where these go beyond the purely imitative. In the present forms in which these qualities appear in Turkey they are certainly of Western and indeed recent provenance and seem at times to be of but precarious tenure. But we may try, however tentatively, to see if they can be brought into relation with qualities in Ottoman or Turkish civilization which created, shall we say, a predisposition to accept them. The capacity for analysis and synthesis of the modern historian and the feeling for the development of character and plot of the modern novelist may have their precedents in the Ottoman chroniclers and memoranda writers, with their discussion of causes and analysis of effects.[17] Even the modern constitutional republic is not entirely an importation. The Ottoman state, based on law and hierarchy, is some ways nearer to it than to the amorphous and shifting society of classical Islâm. The problem—which I have done no more than touch upon here—of the possible deeper affinities between Turkey and the West is of more than passing interest. In recent years the achievements and hopes of the whole reform movement have once again been brought into dispute and even, so it seemed for a while, into jeopardy. In the long run it will be the deeper rhythm of Turkish life, rather than the rapid surface movement of our time, which will determine the future relationship of Turkey with Islâm, with the West, and with herself.

DISCUSSION

Mr. Caskel adds out of his own personal experience with all classes of Turkish people (when he was an interpreter in the first World War) that he sees three main national characteristics which set Turkish people apart from their Muslim brothers.

There is a Turkish dynastic feeling which does not go back to the person of Mohammed. (Mr. Spuler would claim a similar dynastic sentiment for Persia.)

The character of the Turks seems to be impregnated with a certain solid sobriety. Mr. Caskel recalls the thoroughness of Turkish philologists, as compared with the Persian literary tradition. Their work, e.g., the *Qâmûs* of Fîrûzâbâdî (1329–1415), translated by ʿÂṣim (d. 1819), or the commentary on Ḥâfiẓ (d. 1389) by Sûdî (d. *ca.* 1597), not to speak of all their schoolbooks on Arabic grammar, metric, poetic, etc., is still very useful for the Western Orientalist.

Finally, Mr. Caskel calls attention to a certain trustful cordiality he sees in the Turkish national disposition. We find it reflected even in official writings, such as the Eszterházy corpus of Turkish documents in Hungary.

Mr. Minorsky agrees with Mr. Caskel and adds that the popular character of Turkish religion indicates a split in Turkish society: the intellectuals are incomprehensible to the great masses. In the common people the Ottoman Empire continues to live, as can be easily observed in a market place of a big town. There are also geographical differences: Istanbul is different from inner Turkey. The most striking trait in the Turkish character is the Turks' sincerity; they despise irreligious people.

M. Cahen goes into the details of the question of Byzantine influence upon the Ottoman Empire. So much inaccurate nonsense has been written about alleged influences that we experience today an excessive reaction against them. We have to distinguish between different fields of possible influence, such as the religious, the administrative, or the small particular trends of everyday life.

We are not surprised to find no religious influence; but very much in the same way all Byzantine administrative organization was eliminated in Seljuq Asia Minor. The Seljuq government continued rigorously the traditions of the Seljuqs of Iran without admitting any new Byzantine tendencies. On the other hand, if we descend to the level of everyday life, its economic organization, and its local setup, we find that it must have been quite out of the question to eliminate at once all the ways of the previous regime.

We observe that the Seljuqs and their agents despised deeply everything the word "Turk" stands for. Three years ago, for an article which has not appeared yet, M. Cahen studied a small book called *Seljûq-nâme,* written by an anonymous petty bourgeois of Konya at the end of the thirteenth century. This author—he represents not even the point of view of the Seljuq government but simply the voice of a middle-class man in Seljuq Asia Minor—uses the designation "Turk" exclusively for the "barbarous" and "unbearable" Turkoman frontier population. In the same period and even earlier than this source, the foreign travelers who pass through the country use "Turkey" to designate Asia Minor. The country is "Turkish" for them, although the indigenous population has remained there, because they are aware that it is completely integrated into the Turkish ethnopolitical framework. The same travelers do not remotely think of designating Syria or Egypt by a separate ethnical name; for them those countries also belong to the "Turkish" Near East.

M. Brunschvig mentions one particular problem he has not been able to solve, even by asking the help of several Turkologists. It has to do with the big periodical (not weekly) village fairs; they are called in Turkish *panayir,* which is obviously the Greek *panegyris.* We know of fairs in the Byzantine Empire from the twelfth century on, but they must have existed much earlier in the Hellenic and Hellenized territory. They were combined with religious pilgrimages and so took the name of *panegyris.* On the other hand, we have a tradition which seems of non-Hellenic, Anatolian, or Turkish Seljuq origin. There existed, as M. Brunschvig has learned from Mr. Osman Turan, professor at Ankara, periodical fairs in the thirteenth century—one of them especially important, in the heart of Anatolia, called *Yabanlu bazar,* which means "bazaar of the desert fair"—held under the open sky, according to a pattern known from the East and the Far East.

We find ourselves with a problem of origins which seems very complex; it has to do not with administrative or political practices but with that practically permanent substratum, so difficult to lay hold of, which is formed by the economic life of those populations in the Middle Ages.

Then M. Brunschvig, following a different line of thought, takes up the question of the present conference and its future. He would like it to become not *the* Conference on Islâm but the first International Conference on Muslim Civilization, and he has a few remarks to offer about its future possible organization.

He would like to avoid the situation of certain great international congresses where everyone reads his paper, which is listened to with more or less attention, and at the end nothing remains but the personal contacts that may be established. This can be avoided if the conference has one or more "centers of interest." Here it has had the opportunity of meeting for the first time upon a very large general theme. Mr. von Grunebaum was certainly right to give it this ample and flexible frame, within which opinions could be compared for the first time. For the future, perhaps a program should be established which could, if necessary, be extended over more than one conference, and perhaps the "centers of interest" might be as many as two or three each time, as is the case in the Société Jean Bodin.

We need in that case proposals of subjects for possible future conventions which would be elaborated by the future organizer of them. M. Brunschvig himself formulates the following subject he would like to see among the "centers of interest" of a future conference: Inquiry into the notion of decadence and stagnation as applied to Muslim history, and study of the reasons for the phenomenon.

Mr. VON GRUNEBAUM accepts the proposal gladly. He emphasizes the necessity of collaboration in Muslim studies, which is due to the enormous masses of material Islamists have to cope with. The topic suggested is very interesting and must be attacked co-operatively. The financial difficulties of the project, however, require serious consideration.

NOTES

1. On this election, see B. Lewis, "Recent Developments in Turkey," *International Affairs*, XXVII (1951), 320–31.

2. See, further, B. Lewis, "History-writing and National Revival in Turkey," *Middle Eastern Affairs*, IV (1953), 218–27.

3. See Halil Inalcik, "Timariotes chrétiens en Albanie au XVe siècle, d'après un régistre de timars ottoman," *Mitteilungen des Österreichischen Staatsarchivs*, IV (1952), 118–38.

4. Köprülüzade Mehmet Fuat, "Bizans Müesseselerinin Osmanlĭ Müesseselerine Teʾsiri hakkĭnda bâzĭ Mülâhazalar," *Türk Hukuk ve Iktisat Tarihi Mecmuasĭ*, I (1931), 165–313. Italian translation by the Centro di Studi Italiani (Istanbul) and the Istituto per l'Oriente (Rome), Rome, 1953.

5. E. Jacobs, "Mehemmed II, der Eroberer, seine Beziehungen zur Renaissance, und seine Büchersammlung," *Oriens*, II (1949), 6–30.

6. Thus, the term "Turk," since the spread of Islâm, is never applied to non-Muslims, even if they be of Turkish origin and language. Cf. P. Wittek, "Türkentum und Islam. I," *Archiv für Sozialwissenschaft und Sozialpolitik*, LIX (1928), 489–525.

7. P. Wittek, "Le Rôle des tribus turques dans l'empire ottoman," *Mélanges Georges Smets* (Brussels, 1952), pp. 665–76.

8. Köprülüzade Mehmet Fuat, *Milli Edebiyatĭn ilk Mübeşşirleri* (Istanbul, 1928).

9. "Le Rôle des tribus ...," *op. cit.*

10. The most recent is his "Les Déportations comme méthode de peuplement et de colonisation dans l'empire ottoman," *Revue de la Faculté des Sciences Économiques de l'Université d'Istanbul*, XI (1949–50), 67–131; Turkish section, pp. 524–69.

11. "Le Rôle des tribus ...," *op. cit.*, p. 676.

12. The significance of the frontier and of the frontier warrior (*ghāzī*) in the evolution of Turkish Islâm has been studied by Wittek in a series of notes, articles, and monographs beginning in 1925 (*Zeitschrift der deutschen morgenländischen Gesellschaft*, LXXIX, 288 ff.). For a general survey, see his *The Rise of the Ottoman Empire* (London, 1938), where references to earlier studies are given.

13. J. Schacht, *Esquisse d'une histoire du droit musulman* (Paris, 1952), p. 79.

14. Köprülü, "Bizans Müesseselerinin . . . Teʾsiri . . . ," p. 196.

15. The use of the expression "Christian Turk" to describe Christian populations of Turkish speech such as the Gagauz of the Dobrudja is of course restricted to scientific usage.

16. B. Lewis, "Islamic Revival in Turkey," *International Affairs*, XXVIII (1952), 38–48. For a somewhat different assessment, see L. V. Thomas, "Recent Developments in Turkish Islam," *Middle East Journal*, VI (1952), 22–40.

17. These qualities are of course to be found to some extent in the best Muslim chroniclers, especially the great Persian historians of the Mongol period. They do not, however, reach the degree of development of the later Ottoman historiographers.

PART V

THE CHALLENGE

WESTERN IMPACT AND ISLAMIC CIVILIZATION

WERNER CASKEL

Two conditions have to be met to make a civilization ready merely to receive cultural stimuli: first, a consciousness of being inferior; second, contact between the two cultures at more than one point and for some length of time. As an example let us look at the Ottoman Empire and Egypt as representatives of Islamic civilization—and Egypt may be considered a separate commonwealth in spite of its legal link to the Ottoman Empire. Here it can be seen that in both these countries the military-political and technical-economic superiority of Europe was recognized at the end of the eighteenth century. A more permanent contact was not established until later, around 1825; it consisted essentially in the appointment of European teachers, in sending pupils to Europe, and in the translation of textbooks and other books in specialized fields. It took another forty-five years or so until the framework of Islamic culture in these countries was shaken through the reforms that took place at the borders. In the beginning these reforms originated in the despotic will of Maḥmûd II (1808–39) and of Muḥammad ᶜAlî (1805–49). But the resisting forces had to be removed before this will could become effective. In the Ottoman Empire this took from 1814 to 1831 (fall of the Kölemen in Baghdad); in Egypt, six years (1811, annihilation of the Mamlûks). What is essential is that Muḥammad ᶜAlî soon after wiped out completely the agrarian system which had been started under the Mamlûks (in the Ottoman Empire this was never achieved), for in this way Muḥammad ᶜAlî made possible the flourishing of Egyptian agriculture, and his new land grants in the 1830's laid the groundwork for the distribution of the large estates today. The invitation of French specialists and the sending of pupils to France—about a hundred and ten young people were involved between 1826 and 1834[1]—served during the reign of Muḥammad ᶜAlî mainly military-technical purposes, if this concept is understood in its widest sense.

That the first translation from French belles-lettres was not published until 1859 is due to these practical objectives. This first attempt showed no effect whatsoever on the intellectual life of the country, which at that time was still based on the vernacular. The Arabic taught in the schools founded by Muḥammad ᶜAlî, and which, since it had been made the official language under Saᶜîd Pâshâ (1854–63), was used in all government offices, was stiff. And what was written at the Azhar can be termed scientific jargon rather than a literary language. The number of men who at the time of the khedive Ismâᶜîl (1863–79) were able to write a polished Arabic could be counted on one's fingers. Almost all of them were officials of the higher ranks; the immigration of Syrian literati and journalists had—with one exception[2]—not yet taken place.

It was in Syria, loosened up by the Egyptian occupation and by missionary schools, that the revival of classical Arabic and of Arabic philology made its beginning, thanks above all to the efforts of Nâṣîf al-Yâzijî (1800–1871) and Buṭrus al-Bustânî (1819–83). Though in the beginning only Christians supported this movement, an association founded in 1857 to further the task, al-Jamᶜiyya al-Sûriyya, was joined also by Muslims.[3]

The development in the Ottoman Empire resembles that in Egypt; there too military-technical matters formed the entering wedge, but, owing to resistance in the country, wars, and the interference of the powers, reforms were achieved much more slowly. In the improvement of schools the Ottoman Empire, even in Constantinople, lagged far behind Egypt. On the other hand, the Ottoman Empire was ahead in the reform of the judiciary, that is to say, in the fixation by laws[4] of governmental jurisdiction which up to then had been based on caprice and custom, and in the transfer of the administration of justice from corporations and officials to regular law courts (1864).

The first translations into Turkish from French belles-lettres also appeared in 1859. But these translations had an immediate effect on the intellectual life, for, though Ottoman Turkish showed foreign influences in its vocabulary and in certain sentence constructions, it was alive in a much wider circle than was literary Arabic in Egypt. And there existed in Turkish a literature which made slow but constant progress and which reached a fair level, both in prose and in poetry. Besides, apart from theology and mysticism, the Ottoman Turks had preserved and kept alive to the nineteenth century some of the treasures of the two older languages of the Islamic civilization (i.e., Arabic and Persian).[5] Among the people there was spread a strong dynastic feeling, among the educated a consciousness of history, though in a somewhat confused fashion, and everywhere was present the conviction that in the Ottoman Empire the religious community of Islâm had been realized.

THE STATE

It can indeed not be denied that the Ottoman Empire, with the sultan-caliph as "protector of Islâm"[6] at its head, continued, in spite of all historical distortions, the old Islamic concept of the state as a religious-political community under the Imâm-Amîr al-Muᵓminîn. This concept of the state was shaken around 1865 when the ideas of the French Revolution and French constitutionalism began to gain ground among the Young Turks. But this circle was too small, the time in which their spokesmen—Namık Kemal[7] in his political articles in *Tasviri efkâr* and ᶜAlî Suᶜâwî Efendi in his Ramazan lectures—could be effective, too short (to the middle of 1866), the pressure of the old too strong, for them to be able openly to advocate the new approach. Only after the return of the Young Turks from Europe (at the turn of the year 1871/72) did Namık Kemal through the words *vatan/patrie* and *millet/nation* set afire political passions among the educated.

What never became clear to him was that Ottoman patriotism separated from religion was an impossibility. Rather he thought that the new spirit could be reconciled to Islâm understood correctly, that is, primitive Islâm. On the other hand, his concept of history, nourished essentially from European sources, led him to believe that the superiority of Europe over Islâm began only in the sixteenth century. This unintegrated coexistence of thoughts can be inferred from his use of words: for instance, in the article "Istanbul fethi" ("The Conquest of Istanbul"), where the expressions *asakiri Osmaniye* ("the Ottoman soldiery"), *Islam ordusu* ("the army of Islâm"), and *orduyu hümayun* ("the Imperial army") are used interchangeably.[8] Side by side with this patriotic movement there existed a pan-Islamic movement in which was revived the claim of the religious-political community to unite all Muslims—a fantasy, derived from the past, with which to compensate for the present weakness of the Muslim countries. The Young Turks themselves were caught in this movement; it had been in existence for some time before the man who first gave eloquent expression to it, Jamâl al-Dîn al-Afghânî, appeared in Constantinople (1870).

In Egypt something like a public opinion began to come into existence around 1872, at the time when Jamâl al-Dîn arrived in Cairo. The circle which was politically active there was wider and reached higher than the one in Constantinople. The effect of a paper like *Abû Naḍḍâra Zarqâ* went farther than that of the *Tasviri efkâr* because it was written in the vernacular and because its cartoons appealed to all. But in his lectures Jamâl al-Dîn addressed himself to the social and intellectual elite; even the heir apparent, Taufîq, was among his supporters. He wanted to waken the Muslim peoples and states from their sleep; he warned them of the European powers, and most of all of England. Occasionally he talked in revolutionary terms. In a speech he gave in Alexandria occurred the sentence:[9] *anta, ayyuhâ 'l-fallâḥu 'l-miskîn, tashuqqu qalba 'l-arḍ . . . fa-limâdhâ lâ tashuqqu qalba ẓâlimi-ka? Li-mâdhâ lâ tashuqqu qalba 'lladhîna yaᵓkulûna thamarata atᶜâbi-ka?* ("You, poor fellah, you split the heart of the earth . . . why don't you split the heart of your oppressors? Why don't you split the heart of those who nourish themselves with the fruit of your labors?") This was directed partly against the khedive Ismâᶜîl and his mismanagement, partly against the European exploiters of this weakness. Since the national bankruptcy in 1876 the fellahs had suffered under an unbearable taxation. The misery was increased through the dismissal of civil servants and officers, and the fact that the British and French controlled financial policy and had given office to many Europeans incited the hatred of foreigners. This was the backdrop of the stage on which figures, set in motion on threads moved by the policies of the great powers and the Sublime Porte, performed that tragic spectacle, the revolt of ᶜUrâbî Pâshâ. A wave of patriotic enthusiasm and blind fanaticism that swept over the country brought servitude instead of the freedom of which men had dreamed.

In Syria Buṭrus Bustânî took *al-waṭaniyyatu min al-dîn* ("Patriotism is part of religion") as motto of his review, which he started in 1870. Before him Ibrâhîm al-Yâzijî (1847–1906) had pronounced Arab patriotism more clearly: *tanabbahû wa'stafîqû, ayyuhâ l-ᶜarabû* ("Awaken, O Arabs . . . !"). But the poem was spread only orally.[10] Yet a considerable period of time elapsed before the Syrian Muslims too were attracted to the national awakening.

I am unable to present here how, under pressure of events, Ottoman patriotism changed into Turkish nationalism and how this in turn activated Arab nationalism, and what results this had at the time of the first World War, nor can I recount its final consequences: the formal break of the government of Kemal Atatürk with the Muslim concept of the state and with the *sharîᶜa*. Orthodox quarters considered this a break with Islâm altogether. Among other reactions that of ᶜAlî ᶜAbd al-Râziq is interesting: *al-Islâm wa-uṣûl al-ḥukm*, in 1925. Neither in the Koran nor in the sunna is there a proof for the necessity, *wujûb*, of the caliphate. The principles of government rest on reason and experience. In other words, a justification of Kemal's state.

The new self-understanding of Islâm that came to the fore in the *Six Lectures on the Reconstruction of Religious Thought in Islâm*[11] of the Indian philosopher, poet, and lawyer, Muḥammad Iqbâl (d. 1938), also turned to the concept of the state: In Islâm it is the same reality which appears as church, looked at from one point of view, and state, from another. It is not true to say that church and state are two sides or facets of the same thing. Islâm is a single unanalyzed quality which is one or the other as one's point of view varies. Since Iqbâl is considered the spiritual father of Pakistan, these sentences are also of practical importance. Whether they can be made part of a modern constitution is very doubtful. As a matter of fact, Pakistan's constituent assembly has not yet achieved its aim.

The idea of pan-Islâm was taken up again in 1922 by the Syrian-Egyptian reformer, M. Rashîd Riḍâ, in *al-Khilâfa wa'l-imâma al-ᶜuẓmà*. It happened too late or too soon. For only now, through the founding of Pakistan, has it been brought closer to realization. Islâm is the only *raison d'être* for the existence of Pakistan. This is why from the beginning Pakistan has favored a pan-Islamic policy, or, to put it more cautiously, a policy of Muslim brotherhood, while neglecting its relationship to India, which to the outsider would seem much more important. This attitude, and especially Pakistan's championship of Muslim rights in Palestine, has met with gratitude in all Islamic countries with the exception of Turkey. The establishment of the state of Israel is felt to be the deepest wound inflicted on Islâm in a long time. It is true the defeat hurt Arab national pride in the first place. But the passion stirred up among the masses by the advance of Zionism, lasting to this day and not only in the Arab countries affected by it, shows that the national motive is imbedded in a religious, pan-Islamic context.

SOCIETY

The Koran, encompassing spiritual and worldly matters, provides the possibility of a Muslim society. This society owes its comparative uniformity to the sunna and the law. Strange as may seem to us some of the threads which *ḥadîth* and *fiqh* have woven around this society, a plausible interpretation can be found for them. Again I quote Iqbâl: "In the evolution of such a society even the immutability of socially harmless rules relating to eating and drinking, purity or impurity, has a life-value of its own, inasmuch as it tends to give such society a specific inwardness, and further secures that external and internal uniformity which counteracts the forces of heterogeneity always latent in a society of a composite character." To this must be added something else: into this fabric have been woven the social-ethical and the purely human values which are peculiar to Islâm. If this net is torn, there is danger that these values will be lost. We have to keep in mind that the possibility of secularizing these values, with the help of which Christian ethics were saved even for those outside a church, is barred to the Muslim.

It is hard to say when Muslim society began to assimilate to European society, if an arbitrary judgment is to be avoided—in Egypt, perhaps under the khedive Ismâᶜîl (1863–79), and in the Ottoman Empire under the sultan ᶜAbd al-ᶜAzîz (1861–76). If Muslim civilization in the French Maghrib and in India resisted assimilation longer than in the free countries, this is because—and here I refer back to the first sentence of this lecture—any existing inferiority was felt to be only external, that is, in terms of physical power, and not spiritual. Also assimilation in the other countries, too, ran a slow course. Even in Turkey, where assimilation was enforced by law, many survivals of the old societal forms are alive underneath the European cover. The greater speed of assimilation in the last decades can be attributed to contacts with things Western established by wider strata through films and through the radio.

A few words on the position of women. Its background seems more important to me than the truly accidental rules laid down by the Koran. On one hand, there is the naïveté of classical antiquity with which Islâm treats sexual matters; on the other, the taboo which is spread over women and which is symbolized by the veil.

This taboo has shown itself to be quite tenacious. The section "The Status of Women in Islam" in Sayyid Amîr ᶜAlî's *The Spirit of Islam* may perhaps be considered a first attempt at weakening this taboo, although the author, in accordance with his apologetic purpose, exalts rather than criticizes the position of women in Islâm. Generally speaking, I believe the influence of reformist pamphlets on the process of assimilation to be quite inconsiderable. Assimilation comes to pass through the upper classes imitating European customs and through the lower classes later imitating the upper classes; as to the entering of women into economic life, that is the consequence of economic difficulties. The same process in reverse could be observed in 1939 in the effect which the countermovement, originating in Wahhâbî Arabia, had upon the tribes of the Syrian desert: the womenfolk of the great shaikhs were not to be seen, while there was no restriction about talking to the wives and daughters of the other Bedouins.

ECONOMY

Everywhere the agrarian system of Islâm can be traced to the principle that the state makes over the yield of a certain territory to an individual—who may also be the representative of a community—in return for specified obligations. Thence the possibility, on the one hand, of a combination with tax farming and, on the other, the development of the hereditary holding of large estates. In all its forms the system was complicated through local customs as, for instance, the old *musâqât,* etc., and was burdened by abuses, bureaucratic and otherwise. It is true that everywhere there were reforms from time to time, but since reforms, at least in the Ottoman Empire, were never more than partially executed, the legality of titles to property became painfully uncertain. As a result production declined so that the Empire in this regard too lagged behind Europe at the beginning of the nineteenth century.

It was, on the other hand, just the yearning for technical innovations, the falling-off of exports as compared to imports, the naïve attitude toward financial obligations, and the ruthless exploitation of these weaknesses through European capitalists which led to the financial catastrophes of 1876 in Egypt and in the Ottoman Empire.[12] Then the political influence of the great powers caused a continuation of the building and the investments. When after the first World War—in Egypt even later—a reaction occurred, it was the state that endeavored to build up an independent economy. There was a complete lack of private initiative. During the first period of contact with the West up to the 1830's, the distrust of the state, based on the experiences of centuries, was so great that earnings in all classes of Muslim society were invested (apart from foundations) in gold and jewelry, later to be replaced by investments in land.

As a consequence the Muslim countries, with the exception of Turkey, are to this day economically and financially dependent on Europe and the United States. If in addition the lack of technical education, the lethargy of the population, due partly to the climate, and the great poverty caused by the flight from the farmlands are taken into consideration, it is not surprising that the pressure to overcome this backwardness is especially great. "To learn and to act," Iqbâl had already preached in his *mesnevi* (poem in couplets), *Pas chih bâyad kard ay aqwâm-i sharq* ("What Then Needs To Be Done, O People of the East"). And this call was intensified after the war. A short survey of the last volume of the *Islamic Review*[13] shows an abundance of articles that ask for economic and social reforms, the authors of which range from ᶜAllâl al-Fâsî, trained by the *ᶜulamâ*ᵓ of Qarawîyîn Mosque in Fez, to the left wing of the students of Iqbâl. These reforms are to be made to harmonize with the principles of Islâm. What exactly is meant by "principles of Islâm" either is left in the dark or is expressed in a more or less dilettantish form. Thus, for instance, the attempts to develop from the *sharîᶜa* a modern "Economic System of Islâm," to replace interest through the institution of *muḍâraba* or to reintroduce *zakât* for the purpose of social welfare work.[14] From this development it also becomes clear that the quietistic ethics of Ṣûfism are a thing of the past.[15]

RELIGION

We shall start with reformism, the form into which scientific and popular theology has been driven through the influence of Western thought and its rejection of it. The reformers encountered Western thought not in the shape of theology but in historical works that carried the stamp of rationalism or positivism, in textbooks of the same character,[16] in popular scientific presentations, and, furthermore, in the criticism meted out to Islâm both by scholars (E. Renan) and by missionaries.

Islâm faced all of this completely unprepared, for dogmatic theology was frozen in its last rationalistic stage. One need only consider the little and the big *ᶜaqîda* of Sanûsî (d. 1486) in the west or the *mawâqif* and *ᶜaqâ*ᵓ*id* of Îjî (d. 1335) in the east.

Nor does the last great compendium of medieval knowledge under a mystical aspect, the *Marifetname* of Hakki,[17] open a path to Europe, except perhaps via the chapter: "fewaidül teṣrih" ("The Usefulness of Anatomy").[18]

Thus a wholly new beginning needed to be made. It is well known that it was Muḥammad ᶜAbduh (d. 1905) who took the decisive step. In two respects his theology is influenced by Western thought: in his concept that the prophets' task was the gradual education of mankind, to be concluded by Mohammed, and in the ideal of the reconciliation between faith and knowledge. In his fight against abuses he reaches past Ibn Taimiyya (d. 1328) and Ibn Qayyim al-Jauziyya

(d. 1350) to the unadulterated teachings of primitive Islâm, which he idealizes into a system of ethics.[19]

His disciples lack the truly Muslim catholicity of the master and also his human breadth.[20] But two of them founded the Salafiyya, the only reformist movement that resulted in the formation of a community. They were Muṣṭafà Ṣâdiq al-Râfiʿî, who passionately battled for clear formulations, and M. Rashîd Riḍâ (d. 1935), a man with a more systematic mind.

While these Egyptian reformers "attempted to free Islâm from the crust into which it had hardened," their Indian counterparts meant to prove that "Western civilization is readily compatible with Islâm."[21] They too go back to primitive Islâm, reading into it the ideals of nineteenth-century liberalism and humanism. The same goes for the Egyptian modernists with their more literary orientation.

The distortion of history which is apparent in these notions is not an isolated phenomenon. It is ever again frightening to find that even the best minds completely lack comprehension of a certain historical situation, of a criticism attuned to the sources themselves.

Articles on these subjects in the already mentioned *Islamic Review* show the same modernistic views, for instance, in an idealized image of the Prophet. But there are two new tendencies: political intentions, revealing themselves everywhere, and the one-sided definition of Islâm as a community religion. The religious doubts of the individual are passed over.

The religious life itself will have to be treated briefly. Even before the war a revival of religiosity in Turkey was found to be taking place. Individual cases of a return to the cult, both during the war and after, are known to me. In this connection the order issued by Naguib's government which makes the united performance of the *ṣalât* compulsory for all civil servants and for all the employees of major enterprises is of importance. One more question: Is the eschatological consciousness, which after all was the point of departure for Islâm, still alive in the upper classes? Do Heaven and Hell begin to disappear here as happened in the nineteenth century in many circles, at least among Protestants?

Looking back once again, it can be seen, first, that there was a certain reaction to Westernization in the revival of pan-Islamic thought and in the use of the power of the state in favor of religion; second, that the attempt to combine technical and social reforms with the principles of Islâm remained pure theory. For this reason I should like to devote the end of my lecture to a movement which has tried to achieve a religious and social reform from the point of view of a "fundamentalist" reformism and to use for this purpose Western techniques and organizational methods. I am speaking of the Ikhwân al-Muslimûn, founded by Ḥasan al-Bannâ in Egypt.

Ḥasan al-Bannâ, born in 1906 in a small village in the province of Gharbia,came from a typical Muslim milieu. His father was a watchmaker and at the same time imam and *khaṭîb* of the village mosque; his evenings he spent studying the classical *ḥadîth* collections and the *musnad* works, and he himself wrote on these subjects. The boy grew up with the Koran, learned it by heart, while his imagination was kindled by the Egyptian folk tales. After going through a preparatory school (*iᶜdâdiyya*), he entered at fourteen years (1920) the teachers college in Damanhur and was accepted in 1923 in the Dâr al-ᶜUlûm in Cairo. In 1927 he passed, as always at the head of his class, the final exams. He then went to teach elementary school in Ismailia. In 1933 he was assigned to Cairo.

His home life had equipped Ḥasan al-Bannâ with three things for his career: with the social-ethical imperative of Islâm, *al-amr bil-maᶜrûf wa'l-nahy ᶜan-il-munkar*, "to command the good and to prohibit the bad"; a yearning for practical work—he liked to tinker in his father's trade; and a fair share of peasant shrewdness.

At the age of twelve, that is, at the age at which religious receptivity begins, he heard the *dhikr* of the Ḥaṣâfiyya. From then on his allegiance belonged to this fraternity until he received in 1923, in Damanhur—where its founder, Ḥasanain al-Ḥaṣâfî, is buried—the *ṭarîqa* from his son. Much of what he found there he had been looking for elsewhere and was to go on looking for, that is, a common effort in literary, religious, and welfare organizations. In such activities he developed his ability for organizing.

In the course of his study at the Dâr al-ᶜUlûm he went through a crisis: he felt himself split into a thinking self and into another self which trod the mystical path. In the end his inclination to pedagogy and to *irshâd*, the religious guidance of men, ended his doubts. In a paper assigned the students in the Dâr al-ᶜUlûm he had described, naïvely in form and tone yet clearly, the office to which he felt himself called: he would like to teach the children, but also the parents, through talks and conversations, through letters and books, while he moved from one place to another. For this aim he considered himself to be prepared through a knowledge of the good and the beautiful, through perseverance and a readiness for self-sacrifice, through a hardened body, and through association with like-minded friends.

What led him onto this path was the estrangement from the faith and the customs of Islâm and the ignorance of the masses which he encountered in Cairo; later, the religious barbarism of the workers in Ismailia. His concepts of reform had been shaped in the spiritual battle which in 1925 had begun between the conservatives and the reformists and which even in the beginning of the 1930's still agitated him.

In the fall of 1927 he came to Ismailia and first of all attained a certain social position by frequenting the houses of the *ᶜulamâ᾽*, the shaikhs, and the notables. Then he mixed with the people. He visited the big coffee-houses, crowded with workmen in the evenings, and there behaved like an Anglo-Saxon revivalist preacher; in a tumbledown *zâwiya* he taught them to perform the ablutions and the prayers. In March, 1928, he and six of his adherents founded the Ikhwân al-Muslimûn; by the time of his assignment to Cairo in 1933, ten other groups from Suez to Port Said had been founded. Each new group was expected to do something useful: to erect a mosque, a Koranic school, or a workshop. He himself founded a school for girls in Ismailia. In Cairo he continued this activity. In 1934 forty groups of the Ikhwân were operating. All this happened in so unspectacular a fashion that the Ministry of Education was for many years unaware of the fact that the teacher, Ḥasan al-Bannâ, was identical with the *murshid al-ᶜâmm* of the Ikhwân al-Muslimûn. From the time of Ismailia the core of the Ikhwân consisted of fellahs and workers, and this is still true today.

Ḥasan al-Bannâ did not provide a finished program when he founded the association; rather the *daᶜwa*, the "call," the teaching of the Ikhwân, was gradually developed until it came to a temporary conclusion in 1938. Ḥasan al-Bannâ himself has designated the concept *šumûl maᶜnâ al-qur᾽ân*, "the all-embracing character of the Koran," as its basic principle and has defined Islâm as follows: "Islâm is a creed and is service of God, fatherland and nation, religion and state, spirituality and action, book and sword."[22]

The kinship of his message (*daᶜwa*) with the Salafiyya becomes apparent in the following sentence of Bannâ: "The Ikhwân believe that many views and sciences which have been joined to Islâm and have taken on its coloring actually show the color of the ages in which they were created and of the peoples who lived in those ages . . . therefore we have to understand Islâm in the way in which our pious predecessors, the Companions and the Successors, understood it and we have to stop at those limits . . . without allowing ourselves to be chained by something other than what God has chained us with."[23] The Ikhwân's assessment of the civilization of the West becomes clear from these words: "We urgently need to enlist the assistance of its technique and sciences; every useful improvement which does not dissolve the personality is a new force which supports the structure of the community [*umma*]."[24]

In 1938 the program was considerably enlarged. The Ikhwân now represent "a doctrine of the predecessors, a way of following the prophet [a Sunnî *ṭarîqa*], a door to mystical reality [a Ṣûfî *ḥaqîqa*], a political body, a sport club, an association for the advancement of science and education, an economic corporation and a social ideal."[25]

This enlarging of the task of the Ikhwân is accompanied by a strengthening of its organization. Before, this organization had consisted only of a central office and the groups; now the groups were, according to a well-known pattern, divided into troops (*katîba*), cells (*khaliyya*), and so on, with the *maktab al-irshâd* with Ḥasan al-Bannâ at its head hovering over it all. A feeling of solidarity was strengthened by the obligation to recite the *Maʾthûrât* which the master had put together on the modernized model of the *Dalâʾil al-khairât*[26] and similar works. After the war the brotherhood grew further.[27] Scouts and semimilitary associations were added. The Ikhwân in Cairo pledged allegiance directly to the *murshid ʿâmm*, the other groups through their heads, and they were obliged to renew this pledge, *baiʿa*, on the occasion of their first personal meeting with the *murshid.*

At the same time the economic and social activity of the Ikhwân increased considerably. Let us mention here a spinning concern and a weaving establishment where the workers were invited to invest in shares, a company for commerce and construction with 3,400 shares in Alexandria, a newspaper publishing firm, a printing plant, and agricultural enterprises. Schools for boys and girls, evening courses, tutorial circles preparing for civil service exams—these last are very important in Egypt—trade schools, and hospitals, the largest in Tanta.

Owing to their being experienced in enterprises of this kind, the Ikhwân's proposals for social reform make good sense: progressive taxes, an inheritance tax, minimum wages, limited working hours, restrictions on the labor of women, ban on child labor, hospital and illness insurance, minimum holdings by the fellahs, and distribution of state lands among them.

Their educational program too betrays experience. The need for character education is being stressed; a harmonizing of the different types of schooling is proposed as well as the introduction of religious instruction at the universities.

By contrast their demand for a state permeated by religion is based on pure theory, as is their case for unification of the legal and judicial systems under the auspices of the *sharîᶜa;* the reason given for it is remarkable, though: "that man may know that he stands condemned by the law of God that has come down from heaven, not by the law that was set up by man."[28]

Their foreign-policy program was by far more intransigent than that of the wildest nationalists, and they justified the primacy assigned to the liberation of their own country with the *ḥadîth: al-aqrab aulà bil-maᶜrûf,* "The one nearest to you is most worthy of your action." What went beyond independence was formulated hazily though cautiously: a rapprochement among the Muslim countries in education, social order, and economy—pacts which were gradually to lead up to a brotherly Muslim federation and finally to a caliphate with the mission to offer Islâm to the world.

This program, both outside and inside the country, would have been of no consequence had there not been the driving power of Mahdism behind it. At a congress in 1938 Ḥasan al-Bannâ addressed the Ikhwân in the following terms: "When in times to come you will number three hundred bands, each of them equipped spiritually with faith and creed, intellectually with knowledge and education, physically with drill and sport, then come and ask me to wade with you through the waves of the seas, to reach with you for the clouds of the sky, and to war with you against stiff-necked tyrants, and I shall do it, if it be God's will."[29]

Even then, as one can see, Bannâ had to dampen the zeal of the hotspurs; after the war he found himself in the same situation, but, in view of the political tensions, expressed himself much more carefully.

In the beginning the government paid very little attention to the Ikhwân, but this changed as soon as the war broke out. In 1940, under the impact of the occupying power, a number of severe measures were taken against the brotherhood. In 1944 the government of Naḥḥâs Pasha took a more lenient attitude; besides, I believe it safe to assume that even before, in spite of the Ikhwân's demand for abolition of all parties, relations had been established between the Ikhwân and the Wafd and that these were continued until the ban of the Ikhwân. After the war all chains were removed. But their political demands and their demonstrations led in the fall of 1946 to new countermeasures. Nevertheless, after the outbreak of the Israeli-Arab war, the *katîbas* of the Ikhwân went into battle not as a part of the Egyptian army but as troops of the Arab League. They fought so well that after their return Nuqrâshî Pasha considered them so dangerous in view of the general excitement about the defeat that he made some acts of violence the excuse for dissolving and dispossessing the brotherhood (December 8, 1948). Three weeks later the prime minister was assassinated, certainly by a member of the Ikhwân, but hardly with the knowledge of Bannâ, who was too intelligent not to foresee the consequences. On February 12, 1949, Bannâ himself was shot to death. Nuqrâshî's successor, a member of the same party, possibly afraid of more assassinations, instituted a veritable persecution of the Ikhwân. Again, the Wafd, which took over the government at the end of January, 1950, partly lifted the reprisals. The Ikhwân now made Ḥasan Ismâᶜîl Bey al-Ḥudaibî, a former undersecretary of state, their *murshid ᶜâmm.*

In 1951, at the beginning of the unrest in the canal zone, the *katîbas* of the Ikhwân again came to the fore, this time with official backing. At the end of the year they were joined by an unprecedented number of students and members of the educated classes; it was not their program for reform, though, which brought them this increase, but their demand for a break with England. Then came the black day in January, 1952. One is driven to the conclusion that the leadership of the Ikhwân, like that of the Wafd, had lost control of the radical elements who were responsible for that witches' sabbath.

The government of General Naguib has fallen heir to the fruits of the twenty-five years of the *daᶜwa* of the Ikhwân. For this very reason I am inclined to think that the movement has passed its peak.[30] We shall have to admit that this movement, in spite of some regressive tendencies and in spite also of their unfortunate entanglements in politics, represents something unique in Westernized Islâm: the transformation of faith into action.

DISCUSSION

M. Le Tourneau: What comes out the most clearly, I believe, when the Muslim groups of today are examined as a whole is an impression of extreme uncertainty. On the one hand, we have noted several times (Mr. Lewis has done so again this morning) *a deep attachment to the traditional values of Islâm* and the *marked desire to restore them to their place in the world concert* and give them back their former strength. To arrive at this result, many think the best way is to return to institutions which have proved themselves, to resuscitate a past, although in principle the past is never resuscitated, and thus to re-establish the Muslim civilization in its effectiveness and, if not in its pre-eminence, at least in its eminence. Some even think the re-establishment of the caliphate would be one of the best ways to come to this result. On the other hand, we note an *imperious desire to shake off an inferiority complex* which the ascendancy of the West has brought forth in many Muslim groups, if not in all, for a century. Many Muslims who are aware of this inferiority complex think that the best way to get rid of it is to fight against the West with its own arms, that is, to use not only the techniques but also the ways of thinking and perhaps even the ideas that have been the leaven of Western civilization since the Renaissance. Some, it is clear, have clung to this course and have so fully incorporated a certain number of Western notions that they can hardly use them as means any more; the notions have truly become an integral part of them. Among these many Western concepts whose use and absorption by the Muslims can be noticed, that of "nation" is certainly one of the most efficacious. On the practical level can be noted in most of the present-day Muslim groups a tendency to *create a modern political and social tool*, to *adopt the political techniques and institutions of the West*, and there can even be found (which Mr. Caskel has truly remarked in connection with the Muslim "brotherhood") the need to act—and act effectively—which for centuries seemed to have forsaken Muslim minds. Up till now these tendencies, which can be considered as ideal and theoretical tendencies, have been rather poorly inserted into reality and remain to a very large degree divergent, if not contradictory. I will offer as proof, among a thousand examples, only the debates over the constitution of the state of Pakistan, which have already lasted several years. With regard to this constitution, it is clear that the partisans of tradition and those of modernism conflict seriously and that up till now—at least to my knowledge—they have not yet found common ground and effective and real results in their debates. I will offer as another proof, and limit myself to these, the periodical debates which seriously agitate the Arab League to the point even of at times threatening its existence. This confusion of the present Muslim groups seems to me to be carried to its peak in a certain number of countries which in the present vocabulary are called "dependent" and which, as a result of the daily and dominant presence of Europeans, are subjected in the highest degree to this sort of experience and accordingly react in a way which is perhaps a bit more clearly defined, a bit more marked, than in other cases. That is why I have thought I could set before you some signs of certain cultural, social, and political phenomena which can be observed at the present time in North Africa and which seem to me to be of a sufficiently general validity for the whole of the Muslim lands.

First let us note the dualism which I pointed out in beginning these few reflections. On the one hand, European culture—in fact, French culture (except in the Spanish zone of Morocco)—is developing on a very wide scale and at a pace very seriously accelerated in the last few years. Since the end of the war, for instance, the number of Moroccan Muslim students who attend the Western-type schools has passed from 35,000 in 1945 to more than 190,000 at the present time. Given the experience which you have of these problems, not only of the cultural problems but of the problems of educating teachers and the budgetary problems which this presupposes, you see the effort which has been made and the ongoing pace at which, I want to emphasize, things are proceeding at this moment. But it is not only in this quantitative sphere that development is taking place; it is also on the qualitative level. For the young people who receive either the rudiments of French culture or a more extended French culture in the secondary schools and then in the universities are now very seriously stamped with French culture. The phenomenon is visible even in Morocco, where the activity of the West is recent and goes back only about forty years. It is even clearer in a country like Algeria, where the traditional culture was poorly developed before 1830 and where, consequently, Western influence has been exerted more easily and for a much longer time: many Algerians have French as their normal medium of expression; they cannot speak French within their family, if they want to be understood by the old grandmother or the old aunt who has not been to school; but when they speak, not only with Europeans, but among themselves quite by themselves they use the French language and French ways of thinking. It is quite certain that a political man like Ferhat Abbas is very deeply stamped by the Western culture which he has received. M. Brunschvig was referring the other day to the infatuation of certain bourgeois families for the purely European institutions, where they do not fear to send their daughters. I believe this observation can be broadened, for in itself it does not have a very general validity; in fact, in Morocco the secondary institutions for Muslim girls are still only in their infancy, and it can be understood that several families are resigned to sending their daughters to European secondary institutions. But what is more significant is that where there is a choice, that is, in the case of boys, many Muslims even of Morocco prefer to send their sons to the French *lycée* where Arabic is taught only as a foreign language—that is, fairly superficially—rather than to the mixed Franco-Muslim *collèges*, where the Arabic culture is substantial, forms an integral part of the instruction, and cannot at all be considered an extra. Now a number of Muslims, and not only political friends of France who might desire to gain the approval of the authorities in this way but marked and listed opponents, send their sons to the French secondary institutions rather than to the Muslim *collèges*.

M. Brunschvig: There is the question of access to higher education later.

M. Le Tourneau: No, since in the Muslim *collèges* the preparation for the *baccalauréat* is satisfactorily assured.

M. Brunschvig: They have the feeling that the instruction given in the *lycées* prepares them better for later careers, liberal careers, which only higher education makes possible.

M. Le Tourneau: I shall answer M. Brunschvig by saying that through experience, since I have been in a Franco-Muslim *collège* of Fez for ten years, I can affirm that this feeling is mistaken, for the technical preparation in the Muslim *collèges*—I can say the general culture which is given there—is completely comparable to that which is given in a French institution. To the point that, when I was director of the Muslim *collège* of Fez a few years ago, I was not very well regarded by the European population, for it was claimed that I attracted to the Muslim *collège* the best French professors.

M. Brunschvig: I know that, but I do not think the indigenous Muslim population is convinced of the actuality of the very good quality of instruction which you yourself give in the Muslim institutions.

M. Le Tourneau: There, there are political complications upon which one cannot validly base oneself.

At the same time, then, as the Western culture is developing in the manner I have just described, both on the surface and in depth, there is to be observed also, and this is the second term of the contradiction, a marked rebirth of Arabic culture, or even of Islamic culture, in North Africa. The best example which can be given of this, I think, is the increase in numbers at the traditional university of Tunis, where at the present time are reckoned, including the provincial branches, almost 15,000 students, whereas in Morocco where matters are less advanced the Qarawîyîn University of Fez and its branches reckons only about 3,500 students. In any case this represents considerable numerical progress, since only thirty or forty years ago the traditional students of the mosques of Morocco were hardly more than a thousand. This development of Arabic culture is, moreover, facilitated, of course, by the entry of the eastern press, by the contacts now made easier, by the pilgrimage, now possible for quite a large number, and finally, perhaps above all, by listening to the radio broadcasts of Cairo or elsewhere.

We have, then, in the course of formation in the countries of North Africa, two sets of youth with extremely different methods, ideas, and also, of course, sentimental and aesthetic coloring, so that I greatly fear for the equilibrium of that country, in that more and more we will be witnessing very serious ideological conflicts within the Muslim societies of North Africa. In the political struggle at the present time, those who have been educated in the traditional ways and those who have been formed in the Western way join forces quite readily, but it is in a purely negative sense, and, if one day it should be a matter of constructing, I do not think the union would remain secure.

On the social level I shall point out two types of phenomena which seem to me particularly significant of the present situation: on the one hand, the birth and development of a veritable proletariat and, on the other hand, the evolution of family customs.

The birth of the Maghribî proletariat—I shall not speak of the others—is not a purely local phenomenon; you know that better than I. It is due to manifold causes, the first in order of importance being the considerable demographic growth which is to be observed in the Maghrib. It is estimated, for lack of a precise registry of vital statistics, that every year 300,000 persons more must be reckoned in the Maghrib—I mean in the Muslim community, the others not varying very greatly. On the other hand, it is quite clear that the introduction of European activities occasioned a call for labor to which the Maghribî countries at first had difficulty in responding; hence after the first World War the French colonists of Algeria made every effort to prevent the exodus of Algerians to France, fearing to lack labor for their own enterprises. The state of mind has quite changed at the present time. This Maghribî proletariat is distinguished, of course, by an extraordinary concentration. The typical city from this point of view is Casablanca, where, in place of the approximately 20,000 Muslims of the year 1912, there are reckoned at the present time at least 400,000, among whom are probably 250,000 who can be considered as proletarian. Casablanca is not the only city of the sort; quite a few others are to be found in Morocco and in Algeria, where Oran, Algiers, and Bône are the chief centers of attraction. In Tunisia, a less industrialized country where the mining activities are more dispersed, the phenomenon is less striking, but it exists. This relatively recent proletariat is at present the subject of important studies. A first but very provisional balance sheet has been published recently by Robert Montagne under the title "Naissance du prolétariat marocain" in the collection of the *Cahiers de l'Afrique et l'Asie*. It is the result of a very wide inquiry directed by Montagne and put into effect locally by administrators, teachers, physicians, social workers—in short, an inquiry as exact as possible. Up till now it has dealt especially with the coastal region, with Casablanca and Port Lyautey as centers. It is in progress elsewhere and notably in the region of Oudja. For Algeria a similar inquiry has been set on foot by Montagne, not only on the proletariat which exists in Algeria but also, and perhaps especially, on the Algerian proletariat which emigrates to France and presents there quite a large number of problems. I cannot therefore talk to you in a perfectly sure way of the proletarian phenomena, since the studies concerning them are still in their beginnings or in a provisional stage. This does not prevent us from already picking out certain common traits from what we do know. I shall mention to you also a recent Algerian novel by a writer called Mohammed Dib, entitled *La grande maison* (Paris, 1952). The action takes place in the proletarian milieu of a city, fairly traditional, however, since it is Tlemcen, and will give you some indications seen from within with regard to the poor and uprooted classes of North Africa. It is written in French—a sign of the cultural phenomenon I was speaking of just now.

The first observation that can be made with regard to these proletarians is that they are uprooted. All or most of them come from the countryside, or even from very distant countrysides. Thus at Casablanca are to be found fairly dense numbers of people from the confines of the Sahara, well beyond the Great Atlas. You can imagine how far people of this sort are removed from their own element when they find themselves suddenly plunged into an enormous city, living at a completely different pace from that which they have known in their original country. Furthermore, they no longer have, to protect them and serve them as guardian, the social armament to which they were accustomed—that of the family and that of the tribe; and thus, not only in the sphere of their material habits, but also and perhaps especially in the sphere of their moral life and their spiritual life they find themselves suddenly abandoned in the midst of an enormous human anthill. These city dwellers of very recent date are thus beginning to form a sort of new social stratum which did not exist at all in the Maghrib only fifty years ago, with altogether distinct characteristics—so distinct that at least in Algeria it serves as support for a unique political movement upon which I shall say a few words soon, the Movement for the Triumph of Democratic Liberties of Messali Hadj. This proletariat is in a very large degree cut off from traditional attachments; it has not, all the same, fully taken on a working-class consciousness, in spite of the considerable efforts which have been put out, especially in Tunisia by the Confédération Générale du Travail, to enrol the Tunisian workers. These latter have finally set up a special organization, the "Union Générale de Travailleurs Tunisiens" (U.G.T.T.), which, in addition, later became affiliated to the New Dastûr Party but which shows clearly that these workers, proletarian though they are, retain also, and perhaps above all, an ethnic, a racial, consciousness.

The industrial proletariat is not the only one to be born in the Maghrib. There is also a rural proletariat, especially in the regions of strong colonization as, for instance, the region of Bône or the plain of the Mitidja in Algeria, or the region of Meknès or of the Gharb in Morocco. But this rural proletariat has not at all the cohesion nor the class consciousness of the industrial proletariat: for one thing it is made up not of uprooted people but rather of people found locally, who consequently remain within their original framework and retain the social and moral defenses; further it is obviously more scattered than the urban proletariat. However, one must be aware of this rural proletariat, for it is possible that a few years from now it will in the end play its role, at least at certain points.

I now come to my third point: the evolution of family customs in certain cities, the largest, and also sometimes in certain rural regions, those where emigration is important, for example, Kabylia in Algeria. There we have to do with every degree of development, a whole range of varied individual cases which are not readily connected together. In the bourgeois classes can be found a marked tendency to monogamy in time and space. Here the European conception of family life has without any doubt considerably influenced the state of mind of the young. I have myself witnessed the following scene: certain advanced Moroccans took one of their comrades who had married a second wife sharply to task, reproaching him for this as a sort of treason, as a step backwards, and especially as a return to a situation of inferiority. What this implies is monogamy—and not only monogamy in space but at the same time the desire, when getting married, to keep the same wife as long as possible, perhaps even till death. I do not claim, naturally, that this involves a revolution in morals, for in many bourgeois families of Fez or Tunis monogamy, monogamy till death, was already an actual fact. Nevertheless, the phenomenon seems to me to have spread in a fairly important way, though I would not yet say it has become general. You will find indications of this moral and family evolution of the Maghribî bourgeoisie in several articles by a French monk settled in Tunisia, the Reverend Father Demeerseman, who published a whole series of studies on these questions in the course of the years 1951 and 1952 in the review *IBLA*, which is the organ of the White Fathers of Tunisia. Furthermore, these young people desire, since it is in their minds a matter of a stable union, to know before marriage the woman whom they are to marry; conversely, moreover, the girls, when they begin to be advanced, also want to know beforehand what man they are taking the risk of binding their whole lives to. I do not claim in this case either that the phenomenon is perfectly general and that engagements after the Western custom have completely entered into the way of life, but it is interesting to notice that there exist a fairly large number of examples of it. Furthermore, once married, the young couple tries to lead a family life of its own, that is, to live no longer in the large family house with the father and mother and married brothers, but to have its special lodging, to make itself more independent of the traditional family. That, not only through a desire, which is fairly frequent among the young people, to get loose from the family ties when they have reached adulthood, but also in order to be better able to live in their own way, that is, in a way which begins to resemble that of the West. A fairly large number of young Muslim couples can now be seen going together to the theater or to the cinema, walking arm in arm in the street, whereas only twenty years ago such a thing was inconceivable and unseemly in Morocco. These points are details, but it is certain that women are in the course of taking, as a result of this development, a much more important place in family life. For as a result of her husband's allowing her a great deal more freedom as regards the outside world she is taking on more important responsibilities and is beginning to participate, when she is advanced, not only in the growth of the little child, but also in bringing up the young man or the young woman. Accordingly she has a place in the family which is beginning to parallel fairly closely, in some cases, that of a Western woman. The extreme case of these advanced couples is that, more and more numerous now, of the Muslim who, usually in France, has married a non-Muslim woman. Many students and now many workers have married European women, many have naturally returned to the Maghrib with their wives and, with certain exceptions, do not expect to make them lead a purely traditional life. There can take place in this field some quite unhappy tragedies, but on the whole it can be thought that the mixed couples (which exist exclusively in this direction, or nearly so) produce social results (I am not even speaking of sentimental results) which are really quite encouraging.

In the proletarian classes also the family has evolved as a result of the uprooting of individuals, but up to the present it has not generally developed in the same direction as the bourgeois family. It has too often evolved, as the inquiries into the proletariat of Casablanca show, in the direction of an abuse of the liberty which was suddenly discovered—an abuse not only on the part of the men but also on the part of the single women working in factories, of whom a fairly great number are now to be found in the fish or vegetable canneries in Casablanca, Safi, and Agadir.

In general, there is to be found in the two extreme environments of the proletariat and the advanced bourgeoisie of the cities a gradual and still very cautious emancipation of the girl and of the woman, an emancipation which is due to the European example, it cannot be denied, and, further, to the development of education. For in this evolution girls' education is playing an ever more important role. Finally, in a number of cases the advancement of the woman is due to the action of a certain number of advanced and courageous young men who have preached by example and have been the first to practice these advanced ways by sending their daughters to school and giving more liberty to their wives. Examples of this are not yet very numerous, but this development might, in my opinion, proceed very rapidly, given the significant development of education in these last years.

All the remarks I have just made on the evolution of the Muslim family hold, I repeat, for limited circles, and hardly at all for the rural regions, with a few individual exceptions which do not reach far. It is interesting to observe that even some regions where, in fact, emigration is very important provide no example of a marked development in family life: for example, the region of the Moroccan Anti-Atlas (a mountainous massif between the Oued Sous and the Oued Draa) from which spring in very significant numbers merchants who maintain modern sugar-and-spice stores and actually command the sugar-and-spice market in Rabat, Casablanca, etc.; or Mzab in Algeria; or the island of Djerba in Tunisia. On the contrary, here we are in what I might call "sanctuaries of conservatism" in family life.

The confusion of the Muslim society of the Maghrib shows itself equally well in the political life of the country. Here I shall not enter into the details, for it would require much too much time, and, further, I should run the risk of impassioning the debate, but I shall try to confine myself to a certain number of general indications.

There is to be found in North Africa, except perhaps in Tunisia or, at least, in certain regions of Tunisia, a considerable mass of people for whom politics does not exist. This mass has conservative tendencies, but by inertia and not by conviction, and its attitude is shown in the Algerian elections, where even under the best conditions, for instance, those of the second French constituent assembly in the month of June, 1946, in which Ferhat Abbas and his party gained a considerable success, one finds on the average 50 per cent of abstentions among the registered voters. Now it cannot really be said that the administration had discouraged the voters at the time of this consultation. It is, then, a mass which is in general indifferent, conservative through inertia. But at certain moments this mass can suddenly catch fire and be carried off by a sort of sentimental impulse, as, for example, at the time of the serious riot of the Constantine district, principally around Sétif and Guelma, in 1945. In short, we have here a dense mass, in general without political importance but which, in certain particular circumstances, can suddenly have considerable weight in the destinies of the country. This formless, inorganic mass is of course worked over by a certain number of political forces which try, from without, to set it in motion and to draw it, each to his own side. These forces can, in my opinion, be reduced to four types.

One type is the conservatives—but conservatives by conviction, not by inertia. These conservatives are of course the people of position who consider that, after all, the regime is not bad. In 1953 these people of position won a clear victory in Morocco. The personalities of the Sharîf Kattânî and of the Pasha Glaoui can symbolize perfectly this conservative tendency. It exists also in Algeria in a number of very important instances. It is clearly less marked in Tunisia, where the development of men's minds has been more considerable and where, as I told you just now, at least in certain regions, there exists a popular political consciousness, for example in the Cape Bon and the Sahel, which does not allow of positions so marked as those of the Moroccan or Algerian conservatives.

Then as a second group are to be found the reactionaries, those who would like to return to the traditional Muslim state, at least as they imagine it, in the belief that the innovations introduced more or less recently into the administrative and political system of North Africa are bad and can only harm religion and deteriorate consciences, and that consequently it is needful to return to the past. These reactionaries are grouped in Algeria around the reformist *ᶜulamâᵓ* and in Tunisia around the Old Dastûr Party; in Morocco they have not found an independent political expression, at least up to the present. But within the Istiqlâl Party there exists a strong tendency in the direction I have just indicated to you, which could be suggested with the name of Sî ᶜAllâl al-Fâsi, who has a traditional education and has much more sympathy for a Muslim state of the traditional type than for any sort of constitutional monarchy of a Western type.

In contrast to these reactionaries, the third group is made up of progressives, determined advocates of a modern state. They consider that the Muslim countries cannot achieve a satisfactory international position if they do not adopt a certain number of Western political and administrative methods. Hence the formula of Ferhat Abbas, which is that of the Algerian Republic, a parliamentary republic in which distinctions of race and of religion should not appear. Hence the ideas, less clearly expressed but which nevertheless seem evident enough—I do not think I am misrepresenting them—of the Istiqlâl and of the New Dastûr, which seem to be oriented toward a constitutional and parliamentary monarchy of a European type. There are even to be found in Morocco, in certain elements of the Democratic Independence Party, of the Qaumî Party, and also in certain parties which in the last two years, in the midst of the troubled atmosphere of the Moroccan cities, have begun to multiply, a few professed republicans. I do not know if there exist in Tunisia tendencies of this kind.

The fourth political force which is trying to maneuver the mass of which I was just speaking is peculiar to Algeria. It is that of the proletarians of Messali Hadj. Here we find a formation which approaches the Ikhwân al-Muslimûn of which Mr. Caskel was just now talking. For we have to do with people whose class-consciousness is fairly strong and who try, at the same time, in a way intellectually not yet very elaborate, to attach themselves to the Muslim tradition. It is probable that some day a similar party will find expression and independence in Morocco, whereas in Tunisia, as a result of the relative absence of the proletariat, matters will probably be less precise. I mentioned to you that the U.G.T.T., which might have been able to serve as nucleus for this party, at once Muslim and proletarian, is in fact very closely attached to the New Dastûr.

Finally I shall mention, for the record, that a few individuals are to be found who have enrolled in various Western parties. The most numerous have obviously turned to the Algerian, Tunisian, and Moroccan Communist Parties; they have turned to these Communist Parties because these figure as opponents of the existing authority and uphold more or less firmly, according to the circumstances, the nationalist claims of the Muslims of the three North African countries. Certain Muslims are affiliated with the Socialist Party. There exist Muslims in the Radical Party. There exist such also in the late Ralliement du Peuple Français (R.P.F.) Party of General de Gaulle. There even exist such in the Mouvement Républicain Populaire, which all the same has a very clearly Catholic label. Before the war there existed Muslims, for that matter, in Oranie, who adhered to the Parti Populaire Français of Doriot.

I mention these facts because they show a real confusion in the Muslim political consciousness of North Africa under Western influence. Most of the tendencies which I have just indicated, except that of the conservatives, clearly have a point in common—their spirit of reaction against European political rule, sometimes even against the sheer presence of Europeans in North Africa. I hasten to add that these reactions against the presence of Europeans in North Africa are not very numerous, if they are sometimes a bit violent. But if many of these tendencies have a common feature on the level of opposition, on the level of building a future they obviously are not much of the same mind, and the spirit of revolt which they manifest seems so far almost exclusively negative. There have indeed been schemes of reform elaborated by Muslim elements; one of the most famous and the most significant is the plan for Moroccan reforms published in 1934, at a time when the Committee for Moroccan Action, the nationalist party, had been in existence scarcely four years. It is fairly curious to study, for in it are to be found all sorts of diverse tendencies and an obvious lack of political maturity. It is certain that a scheme elaborated in Morocco at the present time would be much more coherent and bear witness to much more maturity than that of 1934. I wonder, however, if it would succeed in uniting around itself the whole body of advanced Moroccans and, further on, the whole of the Moroccan intellectual youth.

This purely local picture of the reactions of certain Muslim groups to the massive influence of Europe seems to me capable of being applied nonetheless to a certain number of Muslim groups in the world—other than the Muslim groups of Europe, perhaps. I do not have the impression that the Yugoslav or Albanian Muslims are undergoing the same complex of circumstances and reacting in the same way as most of the other Muslims. Probably this is true also of the Muslims of China, about whom I must say I have practically no information. Finally there is a very important question mark—the Muslims who live in the Soviet Union. We do not have sufficient information about them either, at least on the points I am dealing with, for on many other points we have an abundant documentation furnished by the Soviet Union itself; on the problems of evolution, on the exact situation of Islâm in the

Muslim republics of the Soviet Union, we are only very partially informed. I shall point out nevertheless that the Documentation Française has already brought together, and is still bringing together, a fragmentary but abundant documentation in Russian or local languages on the Muslim questions of the Soviet Union.

To conclude, I think I can say that most of the Muslim countries have set off on the path of renewal under the direct or indirect impulse of the West. During a longer or shorter time their march was joyous or at least confident. I have personally lived through, not the beginnings of the Moroccan Protectorate, but a period which was not yet very far removed from the beginnings, when the confidence between French and Moroccans was on the whole fairly well established. Little by little the Muslims felt more or less confusedly that their own deep ideals were not always in accord with those which were brought to them from without. They also realized with experience that the conduct of their guardians was not always so disinterested as they thought at first and as they naturally wished. Finally, they believed that the final outcome which was made to gleam before them in declarations and discourses was actually very distant and that it was time to make full speed ahead. It is with this phase of their evolution that were born the unrest which we observe in most of the Muslim countries and the impatience of many advanced or intellectual persons. Some, as a result of this unrest, condemn forever that West which they consider has lied and forsworn the promises it had made or was supposed to have made. Others try to save appearances as much as they can, so as to get the greatest possible advantage of the techniques or the ideas with which the West furnishes them, when once these have been mastered and truly incorporated into the Muslim state. Others again feel a sort of amorous resentment, and here I am referring to a certain number of my Moroccan friends whom I saw not long ago and who, although disappointed from many points of view, still felt a great attachment for the Western ideals and methods. It would not have required a great deal, I think, to have brought them back into a path of quite close co-operation. Others, finally, but not very numerous in my opinion, try more realistically to master their feelings, to take things as they are, and to make the best of a bad situation: these are the philosophers. But the philosophers never constitute the majority of a society. Almost all desire the independence which they have more or less lost for a considerable time, but they disagree on the means to achieve it. How to achieve independence? It is at this point in the play that, if I may say so, the stage becomes dark and the actors no longer see very well where they are going.

So far the Muslim renewal presents itself in a primarily negative aspect. Many things are still in course of being turned down, but the positive projects, the plans for reconstruction, remain very vague, very contradictory, and their realizations still very slight.

On the scale of history, this uncertainty and this maturity not yet achieved have nothing surprising in them; if we look at other historical evolutions, there is no time lost. But when one is placed on the scale of a generation, it is understandable that impatience should grow as the years pass and as events and declarations accumulate, and one must admit that this impatience sometimes degenerates into a fit of fever.

After Mr. Caskel's paper, Mr. von Grunebaum tells of the experiences of an American colloquy to which several members of the Ikhwân were invited; the academic members of the reunion who came from Muslim countries became suddenly prudent on their arrival.

Mr. SCHACHT adds that in his times the activity of the Ikhwân did not center in students of the faculty of law as has been said here; those students were anti-Wafdists because they were generally rich and belonged to the higher classes. With regard to Mr. von Grunebaum's observation, the effect of the presence of observers belonging to the Ikhwân upon the discussions of a conference may be due to the fact that the most radical opinion always prevails in a kind of mutual outbidding of extremist formulas.

Mr. VON GRUNEBAUM answers that Mr. Schacht is right and that the most radical opinion prevails, but, he thinks, Western scholars would not so easily give themselves the lie when they came under the shadow of a radical opinion.

Mr. SPULER asks Mr. Caskel about the position of the Ikhwân with regard to the Copts.

Mr. CASKEL replies that the Ikhwân are clearly against them. There is no thought of tolerance, but the Egyptian concept of patriotism considers neutral people rather as friends than as enemies. However, in Egypt the anti-Christian prejudice is still alive; it has disappeared in Syria.

Mr. SPULER asks M. Le Tourneau further about the relations of the French *colon* who adheres to Communism and to the Algerian Communist Party.

M. LE TOURNEAU explains that a *colon,* by definition, will not be a Communist. He is a French farmer who has received from the French government on very good terms a more or less extensive portion of land. The expression *colon* has at the same time a more general sense which derives from the highly conservative outlook of this category of farmers. It is used to designate the widespread conservative colonialist mentality of Europeans settled in Algeria. M. LE TOURNEAU knows a good number of industrialists, officials, even members of the liberal professions who have the *colon* spirit; this does not necessarily mean that they own land.

Consequently no relations, except very bad ones, exist between the *colon* and the Communist Party. M. LE TOURNEAU then speaks of Communism in general; he says that there are, naturally, a certain number of French workers and intellectuals in North Africa who are Communists. They are often subject to inner difficulties and crises of conscience because of the fact that—exactly as the proletarian of the U.G.T.T. does feel himself proletarian but at the same time first of all Tunisian—the French feel themselves proletarian and at the same time, if not first of all, French. The Communist Party often has trouble with its European members because of its policy of unconditional support of the Arab claims. It has never entirely collapsed, but it operates under rather unstable conditions.

Asked by Mr. SPULER if the number of Communists in North Africa is not very considerable, M. LE TOURNEAU replies that the number of party members is quite small. One can judge from the elections. In these last years the Communist Party has not had too much success at the polls in what is called the first electoral college, i.e., the electoral roll which consists especially of Europeans. Today there is only one Communist delegate in the Algerian Assembly, and even this delegate (he was mayor of Sidi-Bel-Abbès) has been defeated in the local polling and will probably lose his mandate in the Assembly as well.

Asked about Morocco and Tunisia, M. LE TOURNEAU replies that it is difficult to make any comments, because there are no real elections, not even for the French. The voting for the Moroccan Council of Government has only corporative importance. Those elected constitute three groups: members elected by the Agricultural Chambers, members elected by the Chambers of Commerce, and those of the so-called Third College, i.e., members elected by all the other professional associations. Only in the Third College may the political orientation of a man play a certain part. In the Moroccan Third College there is no Communist; in the corresponding Tunisian Grand Council there is at most one Communist delegate. It is clear that in the present situation the Communist Party has very little power over the European population of North Africa. There are a few Communist militants, very clever and industrious people, who for the time being are not able to stage any mass movements at all.

As regards the versatility of Communist propaganda in areas of mixed population, Mr. Lewis mentions that a few years ago (1945–46) there appear to have been, in effect, two Communist Parties in Iraq, one of them Kurdish, the other Arab. They seem to have been connected with one another, yet pursued two contradictory policies on the question of Kurdish autonomy. This was revealed in the course of polemics between *Al-Qâʾida,* the organ of the Communist Party in Baghdad, and a Kurdish Communist newspaper, published in the north.

As an example of the transformations Western ideas in general undergo when exported to the Near East, Mr. Lewis mentions an article on patriotism published in the journal *Hürriyet* (London) in which the Turkish poet, Namık Kemal, tries to inculcate the Western ideas of patriotism in his compatriots. From this article and also from a number of poems on patriotic themes by Namık Kemal, it is clear that the *vaṭan* (fatherland) of which he speaks is the empire of Islâm and that he does not distinguish clearly among the land, the people, and the religious community.

The ideas expressed in French and English for foreigners have nothing to do with the real life of the country. When, on the other hand, popular feelings are directed against the unbelievers, as recently in the canal zone, there is a lively response, churches are burned, as lately a Coptic one, and so forth.

NOTES

1. A. B. Clot Bey, *Aperçu général sur l'Égypte* (Paris, 1840), II, 334–35.

2. Edîb Isḥâq; cf. C. Brockelmann, *Geschichte der arabischen Litteratur* (*GAL*), *Supplement* (Leiden, 1937–42), II, 759. Cf. also, for the preceding statements, Aḥmad Shafîq Pasha, *Mudhakkirâtî fî niṣf qarn* (Cairo, 1934), I, 41 ff.

3. G. Antonius, *The Arab Awakening* (London, 1938), chap. ii.

4. 1858: promulgation of a penal code; the preceding commercial code does not fall under this category because it does not directly touch upon the civilization of Islâm.

5. Cf., e.g., Ziyâ Pasha's *Kharâbât* (Istanbul, 1291–92/1874–75); E. G. Browne has used the Persian part of the book in his *A Literary History of Persia,* while as far as I know the Arabic part has never been examined.

6. So even in the Ottoman constitution of 1876.

7. Cf. Th. Menzel, *Encyclopaedia of Islâm* (*EI*), *s.v.* "Kemāl Meḥmed Nāmiḳ."

8. A. Fischer and A. Muhieddin, *Anthologie aus der neuzeitlichen türkischen Literatur* (Leipzig and Berlin, 1919), pp. 2 ff.

9. Aḥmad Shafîq Pasha, *op. cit.*, I, 107–11.

10. Antonius, *loc. cit.*

11. Delivered in 1928/29; published in Lahore (1930) and in Oxford (1934).

12. For the developments leading up to them, cf. [A. D. Mordtmann], *Stambul und das moderne Türkentum*, Neue Folge (Leipzig, 1878), pp. 181–239.

13. Published by that wing of the Aḥmadiyya that "gradually threw over all that distinguished them from the ordinary liberal Muslims, including their former prophet" (H. A. R. Gibb, *Modern Trends in Islam* [Chicago, 1947], p. 61).

14. *The Islamic Review*, XLI (Woking, April, 1953), 31–32; July, pp. 9–10, 28–32; August, pp. 7–13.

15. The pessimism of ᶜAbdallâh ᶜAlî al-Qaṣîmî in his *Hâdhî hiya al-aghlâl* ("These Are the Chains") (Cairo, 1946) goes definitely too far. Cf. G. E. von Grunebaum, "Attempts at Self-Interpretation in Contemporary Islam II," *Perspectives on a Troubled Decade, Proceedings of the Tenth Conference on Science, Philosophy, and Religion*, ed. Lyman Bryson *et al.* (New York, 1950), pp. 146 ff.

16. Note especially the review by G. Levi Della Vida of Gibb's *Modern Trends*, *Journal of the American Oriental Society*, LXVII (1947), 217–18.

17. Manuscript in the possession of the Max Freiherr von Oppenheim Foundation.

18. About the initial difficulties of dissection in Cairo, cf. Clot Bey, *op. cit.*, II, 411; about those of dissection in Istanbul, Charles White, *Three Years at Constantinople, or Domestic Manners of the Turks*, trans. A. Reumont (Berlin, 1844), I, 123–24.

19. Cf. J. Schacht, *EI*, *s.v.* "Muḥammad ᶜAbduh."

20. His pupil, ᶜAbd al-Majîd Salîm, Shaikh al-Azhar, reports the following saying of Muḥammad ᶜAbduh on the occasion of his return from Europe: "I went there and found Muslims in word and deed. I came back and found Muslims in word and not in deed."

21. R. Hartmann, *Die Religion des Islam* (Berlin, 1944), p. 147.

22. *Min Khuṭab Ḥasan al-Bannâ, al-ḥalqa al-ûlâ*, p. 9.

23. *Ibid.*, p. 12.

24. *Isḥâq Mûsâ*, p. 200.

25. *Min Khuṭab*, p. 14.

26. By Jazûlî (d. 1465); cf. *GAL*, II, 252; *Supplement*, II, 359.

27. Formulated in the lengthy *Qânûn al-niẓâm al-asâsî.*

28. *Isḥâq Mûsâ*, p. 78.

29. *Min Khuṭab*, p. 24.

30. The literature of the Ikhwân, consisting mostly of undated pamphlets, is hard to obtain. We may mention the following items: *Mudhakkirât Ḥasan al-Bannâ, Min Khuṭab Ḥasan al-Bannâ, Rasâʾil Ḥasan al-Bannâ*. Dr. Isḥâq Mûsà al-Ḥusainî has attempted a fair appreciation of the movement in his *al-Ikhwân al-Muslimûn* (Beirut, 1952). The polemic of Muḥammad Ḥasan Aḥmad in *al-Ikhwân al-Muslimûn fî 'l-mîzân* (Cairo: Maṭbaᶜat al-ikhâʾ, n.d.) is lacking in objectivity. It was answered by the Ikhwân in the pamphlet *al-Ikhwân al-Muslimûn fî mîzân al-ḥaqq*. I have not reported on groups of Ikhwân in other countries, such as Syria, as the data do not seem reliable to me.

APPENDIX

APPENDIX

NOTES FROM THE LIÉGE LIBRARY ON VICTOR CHAUVIN AND ON IBN BUṬLÂN

The contribution of the University Library of Liége to the success of the Conference on Islâm was a double one.

a) An exhibition dedicated to the memory of the great Orientalist of Liége, Victor Chauvin (1844–1913), was organized in the reading room of the library. It contained (1) personal souvenirs of the deceased; (2) a rich selection from the works of his library, which he had willed to the University of Liége; and (3) selection from the notes and manuscripts assembled by Chauvin during his long career, the whole of which fills not less than 427 filing cases. They include, among other things, the material for Volumes XIII to XXII of his *Bibliographie Arabe*, the publication of which was prevented by the scholar's death.

b) A paper by Dr. Jeanne Gobeaux-Thoret (head librarian of the University of Liége and former student of Professor A. Bricteux) was offered to the Conference. It dealt with an unpublished manuscript of the *Tacuinum sanitatis* of Ibn Buṭlân (d. after 1068) (Bibliothèque de l'Université de Liége, MS 1041).

Abû-l-Ḥasan Ibn Buṭlân, the famous Christian physician and philosopher, lived in Baghdad in the first part of the eleventh century. He is the author of many works, one of them being an important treatise on pharmacopeia arranged in synoptic tables.

Julius von Schlosser, Léopold Delisle, E. Berti-Toesca, Otto Pächt, Ernest Wickersheimer, and G. Carbonelli have all emphasized the value of the illustrated copies of the renowned *Tacuinum sanitatis* (Bibliothèque Nationale de Paris, Casanatense di Roma, Wiener Staatsbibliothek, Biblioteca Nazionale di Firenze, Bibliothèque de la Ville de Rouen).

The communication was meant to show the importance of the Liége copy of the book and to investigate its place within the group of similar manuscripts.

The book offers a sequence of 169 drawings, retouched slightly with tempera and of a very original composition. The artist, who probably worked in northern Italy in the early fifteenth century, possessed an exceptional gift for drawing and was able to delineate his figures in very lively attitudes, contrasting favorably with the heavy poses and static scenes of the other manuscripts, which, however, are richer in color. The copy looks like a notebook for use in the workshop rather than a fully executed elegant copy. The manuscript is connected with those of Vienna, Rome, and Paris through its writing, its identical representation of certain painted scenes, such as the seasonal and hunting scenes, its text, and its selection of subjects for illustration, At the end it gives pictures of the juniper tree and of the clover, which are of Oriental origin and found only in the Liége copy.

The folklorist and the philologist will take as much interest in this manuscript as the art historian because of its selection of certain technical terms and certain graphic and grammatical peculiarities, which may help to establish the origin and localization of the manuscript.

Finally, the Orientalist will not remain indifferent to a monument which may help us to understand better the impact and function of the Orient in the life of the medieval West.

These reasons have persuaded Dr. Gobeaux-Thoret to prepare a complete edition of the manuscript with an adequate commentary. She would be glad to receive any suggestions which might help toward the solution of the many problems raised by this book, which represents in a way a whole encyclopedia of Italian life at the end of the fourteenth and in the early fifteenth century.

INDEX

INDEX

[This Index does not include certain overly common terms like "Muslim," "Christian," "Western," "Arabic," "Persian," and "Egyptian."]

PRINTED IN U.S.A.